Billy Wilder,
Movie-Maker

Billy Wilder, Movie-Maker

Critical Essays on the Films

Edited by KAREN MCNALLY

145 ↗
p. 103
15 minutes - 111

122 -
costin - Similar IT HOT

McFarland & Company, Inc., Publishers

Jefferson, North Carolina, and London

A version of "*Sabrina*, Hollywood and Postwar Internationalism," by Dina Smith, was first published as "Global Cinderella: *Sabrina* (1954), Hollywood, and Postwar Internationalism" in *Cinema Journal*, vol. 41, no. 4, pp. 27–51; copyright © 2002 by the University of Texas Press.

LIBRARY OF CONGRESS CATALOGUING-IN-PUBLICATION DATA

Billy Wilder, movie-maker : critical essays on the films / edited by Karen McNally.
    p.   cm.
    Includes bibliographical references and index.

    ISBN 978-0-7864-4211-9
    softcover : 50# alkaline paper ∞

    1. Wilder, Billy, 1906–2002 — Criticism and interpretation.
I. McNally, Karen, 1964–
PN1998.3.W56B53   2011
791.4302'33092 — dc22   2010044507

British Library cataloguing data are available

On the cover: Director Billy Wilder, circa 1970 (Photofest)

Manufactured in the United States of America

McFarland & Company, Inc., Publishers
  Box 611, Jefferson, North Carolina 28640
  www.mcfarlandpub.com

To Lena and Eddie McNally

Acknowledgments

I would like to express my appreciation to each of the contributors to this collection for their enthusiasm for the project, stimulating work and patience with the editing process.

Table of Contents

Part Three: Production
and Reception

Part Four: Europe,
America and Beyond

Introduction

Karen McNally

"I don't do cinema. I make movies." — Billy Wilder, American Film
Institute, 1986

Billy Wilder's lack of pretension as a filmmaker remains central to his
allure. His ability to create films aiming for a popular appeal, while barely
veiling biting social commentary in narratives that combine crime, moral
degeneracy and lightly pitched comedy, continues to inspire the warm appreciation of audiences. Critics, however, have often been less approving of
Wilder's work. Through his insistence that he makes entertaining films for a
wide audience, rather than for a select group of "cinema gourmets," Wilder has
intentionally distanced himself from notions of high art or avant-garde filmmaking. For his critics, this lack of affectation remains his weakness. Wilder's
populist approach has therefore been at the root of much of the critical debate
that circulates around him.

Andrew Sarris' infamous relegation of Wilder to the minor leagues of
directorial excellence exemplifies the ways in which Wilder has frequently been
defined. The cult of authorship, initiated by the French writers of *Cahiers du
Cinéma* and transported to the United States by Sarris, set about differentiating
the auteur, whose work exhibits a personal vision, from the merely proficient
director. Sarris' particular brand of auteur theory identified a "pantheon" of
directors, whose work purportedly exhibits "interior meaning" through the
tension created between the director's material and "personality," or "certain
recurring characteristics of style which serve as his signature."[1] Placing Wilder
in his "Less Than Meets the Eye" category, Sarris argued that his work displayed
"visual and structural deficiencies," and, further, that the director was "too cynical to believe even his own cynicism."[2] Wilder has frequently been accused of
lacking the kind of stylistic flourish that would distinguish his body of work.
Equally, an unrelenting cynicism ultimately diluted by happy endings, or the

1

"cancellation principle," as Sarris terms it, has been a consistent theme of critiques, resulting in the charge of a lack of conviction in Wilder's films. The extended implication has frequently been that the combination of cynicism and romanticism in the films' narratives and tonal quality is driven by a self-serving eye for the box office. John Simon, in his incessant swipe at Wilder, for example, argued: "Mr. Wilder tells us we are all fools and rogues. That is cynical. He sugarcoats this with laughs and miraculous conversions in which he himself does not believe. That is more cynical yet."[3] Amongst a raft of misjudged readings of Wilder's films, Simon manages to reduce *The Apartment*'s (1960) Fran Kubelik to "a ludicrous girl who allows a callow adulterer to lead her by the nose,"[4] suggesting a general lack of affinity for the kinds of characters and narratives Wilder is drawn to create. He has, however, not been alone in his scathing judgments. The famed critic Pauline Kael, in her review of the 1961 comedy of East/West relations, *One, Two, Three*, raised the specter of taste, another favorite issue among critics of Wilder, accusing the film of being "overwrought, tasteless, and offensive — a comedy that pulls out laughs the way that a catheter draws urine."[5] Her response was again prompted by her perception of a commercial imperative, with the added charge of a contemptuous attitude evident in his characterizations. Kael suggests: "His eye is on the dollar, or rather on success, on the entertainment values that bring in dollars. But he has never before, except perhaps in a different way in *Ace in the Hole*, exhibited such a brazen contempt for people."[6]

These critiques are easy to contest, perhaps Sarris' change of heart illustrating this most directly. In 1991 he was moved to elevate Wilder to his "pantheon," acknowledging that his fixation on visual style meant that "Wilder's remarkable flair for dialogue and the American idiom was downgraded," and that the complexity of Wilder's work was obscured by the fact that Sarris "never had to work very hard to enjoy his movies."[7] Sarris' reappraisal of Wilder suggests at the very least the arbitrary nature of his artistic rankings. More importantly, the kinds of misinterpretations to which Wilder has been subjected necessitate correction, prompting the exploration of a filmmaker who has increasingly been recognized as an influential writer-director and an insightful commentator on mid–twentieth-century American values. Wilder's significance might be approached from a number of industrial, national and thematic perspectives, which coalesce to illustrate his irrefutable place in film history.

The distinction Wilder makes between cinema and movies articulates his firm positioning within popular film. Initiated into mainstream filmmaking as a writer at Berlin's famous UFA studios before arriving in Hollywood, Wilder established roots in popular film that illuminate the basic elements of his approach. Wilder's ability to combine cultural commentary and entertainment in an unflinching manner frequently surprises and is at the heart of his individual brand of filmmaking. Equally, Wilder's various Hollywood roles as writer, director and, latterly, producer make him a key player in the studio system, while at the same time illustrating the levels of creative self-protection required of those working in Hollywood in the studio era. Wilder's career move from writer to writer-director in Hollywood was prompted by the desire for control of his scripts, just as his producer role indicates industry shifts away from studio to individual independent productions from the 1950s onwards. Wilder's career profile similarly highlights the transnational movements embedded in the film history of the twentieth century. Wilder's introduction to filmmaking in Berlin, his brief sojourn in Paris and arrival in Hollywood represents the path taken by numerous émigré filmmakers, who escaped the political climate in Europe and made an irreplaceable contribution to American film in the studio era and beyond.

In addition to his industrial positioning, Wilder's place within both popular film and transnational film history crucially informs his work. His Hollywood films are fundamentally those of an observing outsider in an American context, who at the same time finds himself returning to Europe, illustrating his indefinite national status and sensibility. Wilder's eye for contemporary urban American culture and his ear for the nation's vernacular reveal a core ambivalence. As infidelity enabler C.C. Baxter (Jack Lemmon) takes the use of postwar corporate language to its extreme in *The Apartment*—"that's the way it crumbles, cookie-wise"— and Phyllis Dietrichson (Barbara Stanwyck) and Walter Neff (Fred MacMurray) plot murder among the shelves of Jerry's Market in *Double Indemnity* (1944), they reveal a writer and director absorbed by American modernity, while he simultaneously draws attention to the dangers of conformity and consumerism and the cold reality of their consequences. In the same way, when Wilder transports his Americans to Vienna in *The Emperor Waltz* (1948) or to Berlin in *A Foreign Affair* (1948), he encourages his audience to contemplate the conflicting cultures of the old and new worlds, idealizing neither and uncovering layers within both.

Wilder's cultural ambivalence is the key to the characters he constructs and the narratives in which he places them. The films represent fluid ideas of cultural, political and individual identity that are drawn through characters and the stories they develop. Wilder's tales depict candidly the depths of human behavior but refrain from moral judgments. Instead, they reveal the complete moral compass individuals might allow themselves, examining the choices they make in the context of the expectations and possibilities of contemporary cultures. Wilder's approach is therefore one less of cynicism than realism about the human condition. Whether his characters cross boundaries of sexual morality or criminality, or transgress wider moral codes, Wilder resists condemnation. This reluctance is in part driven by both an admiration for the creativity of individualism, and a recognition of the cultural ethos that encourages the paths these characters take and consequently limits their culpability. Stephen Farber explains: "Wilder is always drawn to the hard-boiled, brash, vulgar quality of his Americans as long as they have the requisite energy and style."[8] *Ace in the*

Hole's (1951) Chuck Tatum (Kirk Douglas) spins out a news story of ex–G.I. Leo Minosa trapped by a cave-in, in order to resurrect his failing journalistic career, resulting in the man's unnecessary death. To Wilder, however, Tatum's guile and classic American ambition to achieve are less worthy of censure than is the heartless conformity and opportunism of the salesmen, politicians and "Mr. and Mrs. America" who descend to feed off the journalist's imaginative scheme and watch his victim's slow death.

Wilder additionally allows his flawed characters to alter their moral self-definition. Neil Sinyard and Adrian Turner clarify the approach to character development:

> A Wilder hero *never* degenerates.... A fundamental element in Wilder's structures is the possibility of redemption, a maturing of the hero towards a more humane outlook.... In every case, the hero has to choose *between* money and happiness, or peace of mind: he is always put to the acid test of sacrificing material for moral good.[9]

Tatum's eventual attempts to direct efforts to save his victim and subsequently confess his part in Leo's death are therefore representative of the light and shade in which Wilder paints his characters' moral identities. Their moral transformations, however, produce far more ambiguity than the cynical romanticism of which Wilder is frequently accused. The murders of Tatum by Leo's wife Lorraine (Jan Sterling), Walter Neff by Phyllis Dietrichson, and Joe Gillis (William Holden) by Norma Desmond (Gloria Swanson, *Sunset Boulevard,* 1950) see the characters' moral conversions go unrewarded. Equally, supposed happy endings more accurately reflect the lack of moral certainties which defines Wilder's work and disallows easy narrative closure. While C.C. Baxter travels through *The Apartment* from a point of self-interested denial to become what the film's moral conscience, his neighbor Dr. Dreyfuss, terms "a mensch — a human being," Baxter's resulting relationship with Fran Kubelik is sealed by her matter-of-fact closing line: "Shut up and deal." Wilder may unite his romantic losers, but cannot resist inserting his realistic take on the future of their relationship.

This lack of closure is only reinforced by Wilder's readiness to obliquely revisit some of his imperfect characters. The director's penchant for cinematic referencing stretches across his work, from Tom Ewell's *From Here to Eternity* (1953) fantasy in *The Seven Year Itch* (1955), to the multitude of screen citations, including *The Public Enemy* (1931) and *Scarface* (1932), that abound in *Some Like It Hot* (1959). By indirectly returning to his own characters, using stars to articulate the connections with earlier films, Wilder presses his audience to consider both these earlier incarnations and subsequent character and narrative paths. Jack Lemmon's Wendell Armbruster, Jr., in *Avanti* (1972) therefore reads easily as a thinly disguised version of C.C. Baxter. An uptight American businessman in Italy to collect his late father's body, the corporate concerns and passionless marriage of this upper-middle-class husband and father are made all the more conspicuous by their setting in the leisurely, amorous and carefree atmosphere of an Italian island. Baxter's moral conversion is therefore cast into doubt in an anti-climactic image of conformity and emotional numbness that again needs to be transformed. In the same way, William Holden reprises his Hollywood role for Wilder in *Fedora* (1978). From the duplicity of screenwriter Joe Gillis and the psychological disturbance of Norma Desmond, to the desperation of independent producer Barry Detweiler and the cold determination of famed actress Fedora, *Sunset Boulevard*'s death and madness have effected not the conclusion but the continuance of extreme behavior among the inhabitants of the film industry.

These aspects of narrative and character are central to Wilder's body of work and form a starting point for analysis of his films and his significance as a writer and director. Numerous other areas are there to be explored: the visual style so often dismissed as perfunctory but which produces memorable shots, like the image of Joe Gillis face down in Norma Desmond's swimming pool before several policemen gently remove him with a couple of pruning hooks; the key theme of disguise that provides a means of realigning gender identity in *Some Like It Hot* or carrying out a murder plot in *Double Indemnity*; and Wilder's persistent readiness to test the accepted boundaries of censorship and taste, undaunted by the dismay caused to Production Code censors or critics. While such issues of style, theme and industry importance have been identified — some approached through alternative lenses in this collection — there remains a paucity of scholarship on Wilder. In comparison with directors such as Alfred Hitchcock, Howard Hawks and John Ford, on whom the status of auteur has been bestowed without dispute, Wilder continues to be undervalued by omission. Individual films have received close attention, in particular in relation to notions of genre and gender, but these analyses have rarely extended to an acknowledgement of the films' location in the writer-director's thematic or stylistic trends. The books which have explored Wilder's work in some depth are therefore worthy of note. *The Hollywood Professionals, Vol. 7: Wilder & McCarey* by Leland Poague, *Journey Down Sunset Boulevard* by Neil Sinyard and Adrian Turner and, more recently, *Billy Wilder, American Film Realist* by Richard Armstrong and *A Foreign Affair: Billy Wilder's American Films* by Gerd Gemünden, each interrogate Wilder's significance, considering some core issues of theme, industry and cultural identity through in-depth analyses of his films. This collection aims to further correct the lack of scholarship on Wilder, revisiting some familiar topics through new approaches, and uncovering neglected areas of interest that will extend investigation of his work and re-emphasize Wilder's importance in the framework of transnational film history and American and European cultural commentary.

The anthology is divided into four parts: Matters of Genre; Representation, Image and Identity; Production and Reception; and Europe, America and Beyond. These sections identify some of the ways in which Wilder has been critically debated and analysed. They are not meant either to suggest an exhaustive study of Wilder, or to limit discussion to these areas. Rather, they point to key fields that open up space for the exploration of Wilder in fresh and innovative ways.

The approach taken to individual films in Wilder's body of work has frequently been through genre. In Part One: Matters of Genre, the contributions recognize these traditions, reinvigorating Wilder's association with film noir, and drawing attention to other, less conspicuous interventions in genre. In the opening essay, Lance Duerfahrd considers *Ace in the Hole* as an alternative film noir. Positioning the film in opposition to the classic noir with its urban setting and distinctive visual shading, Duerfahrd examines *Ace in the Hole*'s uncharacteristic visual style, considering how Wilder employs its desert location, lighting, and narrative and visual framing to articulate exposure rather than concealment. This alternative style, he argues, ultimately forces the audience to confront both the characters' motivations and its response. Dale M. Pollock and Katherine Arens focus on films that are often overlooked in discussions of Wilder's work, and yet which demonstrate well his hybrid approach to genre and the ways in which genre combines with Wilder's consistent themes and styles. *Five Graves to Cairo* (1943), Pollock argues, represents an original take on the World War II film, shifting through style, narrative and tone between comedy, war film and film noir. Rather than being limited by its genre, the film instead introduces such themes as moral ambiguity and masking that become key Wilder tropes and assume heightened significance in a war setting. Katherine Arens explores perhaps the most sidelined genre in Wilder's work, films she terms "comedies with music." *The Emperor Waltz* (1948) and *Irma la Douce* (1963) represent challenges to genre boundaries, reforming notions of the Hollywood musical through the influence of contemporary and traditional European culture and Wilder's Old and New World identities. The films' cultural internationalism, as well as their thinly concealed social commentary, make them ripe for rediscovery. Mark Jancovich returns the section to film noir, examining critical responses to a number of Wilder's films retrospectively categorized in the noir canon. Reviews of films such as the cycle-defining *Double Indemnity* and *The Lost Weekend* (1945) reveal the extent to which the films were received by critics as examples of the horror genre and located, in particular, within an identified trend of social realism. As Jancovich argues, Wilder's "horror-thrillers" become crucial in challenging accepted notions of horror's alignment with fantasy, and revisiting contemporary and historical genre definitions.

Part Two addresses Representation, Image and Identity, examining neglected characters, taking novel approaches to Wilder's mode of character construction, and exploring star image as an essential focus of his work. Wilder is frequently considered to be a director concerned with male characterization. Alison R. Hoffman contests this notion, exploring one of Wilder's most skillfully crafted female characters, *The Apartment*'s Fran Kubelik. Hoffman examines the ways in which the film frames its unconventional images of gender and sexuality around ideas of shame, positioning Fran and Baxter outside postwar patriarchal norms. Fran's active sexual desire and Baxter's feminizing vulnerability, argues Hoffman, act as a determined rejection of sexual shame, anticipating both the significance of Shirley MacLaine's screen image of sexualized single girl femininity and the decade's shifting sexual and gender conventions. My own chapter explores stardom and star imagery as one of Wilder's central thematic concerns and narrative strategies. Wilder's explicit referencing of star images moves beyond a simplistic fascination with the charismatic value of the Hollywood star. His exploitation of the images of Dean Martin and James Cagney instead becomes a means through which Wilder addresses key themes of innocence and disguise, interrogates notions of character, image and reality, and illustrates his cultural duality and ambivalence. An examination of the Hollywood narratives of *Sunset Boulevard* (1950) and *Fedora* (1978) reveals a heightened industry context for Wilder's narrative concerns, giving stars center stage and constructing image as the ultimate reality. In the final chapter of Part Two, Phillip Sipiora takes an alternative approach to Wilder, considering his characters and the relationships between them through the philosophical approach of phenomenology. Closely examining *Double Indemnity*, and through reference to Wilder's trope of masking and disguise, the essay examines the ways in which the characters represent ethical values. The characters' evolution, their discovery of their ethical values and consequent behavior, Sipiora argues, are ultimately bound up in their relationships and encounters with each other.

The collection moves on to Part Three, which considers Wilder in relation to issues of Production and Reception. Paul Kerr examines *Some Like It Hot* as the product of an emerging package-unit system formed through the collaboration of independent producers and talent agencies. Both the creative personnel and narrative style of the film, he argues, are fundamentally a result of the alternative strategies on which this system is based, making the Mirisch Company a co-author of *Some Like It Hot* alongside Wilder. The film's significance, the essay suggests, is to be found in the extent to which it acts to promote Mirisch and its package-unit system of production, and represents a departure from the products of the studio system. Ken Feil examines the 1964 sex comedy *Kiss Me, Stupid*, positioning the film in the context of taste debates and attempts by film censorship bodies to maintain their declining influence. The chapter explores opposing critical responses to the film, as middlebrow commentators resist the overt sexuality of an American popular film, limiting such transgressions to European art cinema, and others consider its lack of taste a high art commentary on American values. The debates surrounding the film illustrate the ways in which critiques of Wilder's work become bound up in notions of art, morality, taste and the desire for box-office success. Daniel Biltereyst returns to the topic of censorship, considering Wilder's dealings with the Production Code Administration, and extending his discussion beyond the United States to explore the response of European censors to Wilder's films. Wilder's negotiation of the Hollywood censorship process entails skillful strategies, acquiescing to some restrictions in order to divert attention from material which substantially exceeds the boundaries of censorship. European censors and pressure groups prove more problematic, the chapter suggests, as the offense taken at depictions of crime and sex in films including *Double Indemnity* and *Some Like It Hot* frequently results in cuts or bans that appear severe in comparison. Biltereyst argues for Wilder's authorship to be viewed in the context of his development of creative narrative strategies to counter censorship of his work, and his consistent readiness to challenge limitations in relation to representations of sex, gender and morality.

The final section of the book explores Wilder in relation to Europe, America and the world beyond, considering Wilder's varied cultural influences and the international reach of his films. Leila Wimmer's essay examines the often ignored product of Wilder's brief period in Paris prior to his arrival in Hollywood. *Mauvaise graine* (1934), she argues, represents an essential piece of transnational filmmaking, signifying the influence of German émigré filmmakers on the French film industry of the 1930s, and illustrating Hollywood's already mythological status for European writers and directors. Wilder's heightened state of imminence is suggested by the film's narrative of transit and migration, its road movie elements, and its avant-garde and realist styles inspired by European filmmaking. At the same time, *Mauvaise graine* crucially points the way to Wilder's Hollywood catalog, introducing themes of the insider/outsider and disguise, and combining crime and light comedy in a tale of urban modernity. Nancy Steffen-Fluhr also visits Wilder's position of exile, considering his work through the notion of a palimpsest. Films such as *Five Graves to Cairo* and *The Lost Weekend*, the essay explains, exist as layered texts, revealing beneath the surface an imprint of homelessness and death drawn from Wilder's émigré status and his personal and filmed experience of the Holocaust. The living dead men who haunt Wilder's mid-century films, and the metaphorical props that surround them, find their ultimate expression in *Ace in the Hole*'s symbolic representation of survivor's guilt and postwar grief, uncovering, contends Steffen-Fluhr, the director's emblematic layering beneath a surface of realism. The cultural and economic exchanges evident in America's postwar international relations are the focus of Dina Smith's consideration of Wilder. Her essay examines *Sabrina* (1954) in the context of the United States' interventionist foreign policy, as the film poses questions around American protectionism and European cultural influence or submission. With *Sabrina*'s gender relations playing out negotiations between the Old and New Orders, both succumb to remodelling, the essay suggests, as the characters' representative cultural trading makes a feminine Europe secure and tempers the United States' masculine capitalist detachment. In the final chapter of the collection, Sunny Singh moves beyond the familiar America/Europe framework of discussion, considering adaptations of Wilder's films in Indian cinema. The loose remakes of *Some Like It Hot*, *Sabrina* and *The Apartment*, she argues, rework Wilder's classics for the cultural ethos and socio-political concerns of their context, relating narrative and theme to India's post-colonial reimagining of modernization and urbanization. The outsider status of Wilder's characters and his urban focus, then, provide ample inspiration for the films, as the originals are transformed to address shifting debates around class, gender and social mobility in post-independence India.

The variety of topics considered through these essays and the originality of the approaches taken illustrate the extent to which the films of Billy Wilder provide a ripe ground for discussion and analysis. Wilder's work deftly blends shrewd social commentary with unashamed entertainment values and an innate cultural and moral ambivalence, lending the films a rare quality worthy of celebration. This anthology sets out to both mark this distinctive body of work and encourage its continued exploration.

Notes

1. Sarris, "Notes on the *Auteur* Theory in 1962," 1–8.
2. Sarris, *The American Cinema*, 166.
3. Simon, "Belt and Suspenders," 73.
4. Ibid., 71.
5. Kael, "Review of One, Two, Three," 63.
6. Ibid., 64.
7. Sarris, "Why Billy Wilder Belongs in the Pantheon," 10.
8. Farber, "The Films of Billy Wilder," 11.
9. Sinyard and Turner, *Journey Down Sunset Boulevard*, vi.

Part One: Matters of Genre

1. *What Exposure Is the World?*
The Desert Noir of *Ace in the Hole*

LANCE DUERFAHRD

> Lang sort of walked around, always, with the same look on his face: squinting, filled with thought, as if he were looking at the world, not just the movie, and thinking, "What kind of exposure is this? What exposure is the *world*?"—Billy Wilder on Charles Lang, cinematographer for *Ace in the Hole*

Ace in the Hole (1951) is one of the most strangely luminous film noirs ever made. Rejecting the genre's underexposed alleys and nocturnal urban settings, the film shreds the assumption that corruption is hidden and lurking in the shadows. *Ace in the Hole* transpires in the deserts of New Mexico, at perpetually high noon, a shadowless hour more suitable to a western than a noir. Light gathers with such intensity on all surfaces in the film that the platinum blonde hair of the femme fatale loses the phosphorescent quality of Barbara Stanwyck's in the dim interiors of *Double Indemnity* (1944) and blends in with the bright mineral backdrop of the rock cliffs. Seen in the desert daylight, Lorraine Minosa's hair seems less like a dangerous beacon than simply an index of her ambition to *look* like platinum blondes (Stanwyck, Monroe) whose images radiated in the darkened theater.

John Alton, cinematographer for such noir classics as *The Big Combo* (1955) and *T Men* (1947), once expressed the ambition to illuminate an entire scene with light only from a radio dial.[1] This light source, incidental and curiosity-provoking in Alton's scenario, becomes incandescent and incendiary in *Ace in the Hole*. Media consumption and production do not go on in the privacy of dramatic shadows, but publicly and as fuel to the spectacle. In exploring the obscene visibility of the media process, Wilder shatters the traditional noir aesthetic. The light that floods the screen of the film is not a *natural* light to be contrasted with the artificial and stylized illumination of earlier noir. In unfolding the lead character's ambition to find tabloid material in the desert, a mirage that can be circulated for profit, Wilder's film explores the unremitting light of publicity, the process by which the world becomes headline.

In the squint of his cameraman, Wilder says he detects something more than a technical concern about light meters and film stocks. How is exposure a transitional space between thinking about film and thinking about the world? How does this film precipitate this exposure-thinking?

Part of the tragedy of *Ace in the Hole* is the obscurity into which it was cast following its total failure upon release. The studio tried to make it more upbeat by renaming it *The Big Carnival*, and the film had neither video nor DVD release until 2007. Audiences must have had a difficult time adjusting their eyes to the strange light of the film after the funereal ornament of *Sunset Boulevard* (1950). The earlier film provides a more digestible critique of Hollywood. As case study or exposé that lifts the veil on the delusions of celebrity and on Hollywood production (the film famously overlaps at many points with actual film history), *Sunset* endows its revelations with a past-tense and nostalgic quality. Norma Desmond clinically insists on her autonomy from the media image that made her. Going further, she says she's relatively larger than the industry. When Joe Gillis says, "You're Norma Desmond. You used to be big," Norma replies with the quotable, "I AM big. It's the pictures that got small." *Ace in the Hole*, by contrast, defines the filmic subject not as big or small but in its openness to the media, its light-sensitivity, its spectacular potential. Exposure is about the skin of the subject being grafted onto the skin of the film. In *Ace*, the "I am" is never synonymous with the celebrity moment. Whereas celebrity and ontology merge in *Sunset Boulevard*, they only meet in destruction in the later film. In exploring the exposure process rather than being an exposé of journalistic practices, *Ace* implicates us in the creation of its own image.

The merciless quality that makes *Ace in the Hole* less commercially successful than *Sunset Boulevard* accounts for its singular power. In the place of a golden age of Hollywood after which it yearns, *Ace in the Hole* presents history as an endless layering of violence. Stealing from an Indian burial site as old as the settlement of America, Leo believes the Indian dead have trapped him. These fears are both assuaged and replicated by Tatum, who steals Leo's story for his own purposes and ensures Leo's doom. The journalist retains the archaic authority of the Fates. Our belated astonishment that no gun is ever drawn in the film clashes with its atmosphere oozing with threat and coercion. No space in the film exists outside the jurisdiction of profit and the dictates of power. For example, when the contractor explains that he thinks saving Leo would best be done by shoring up the walls (rather than drilling through the mountain, which is what Tatum wants), the Sheriff says, "There you are, thinking again. A few years ago you were a truck driver. Now that I'm sheriff you're a contractor. Do you want to be a truck driver again?" The autonomy of thought (the legacy of the film noir detective) is dispelled here in a world in which every choice sounds like an ultimatum.

Tabloid Thinking

Charles Tatum makes the ruthlessness of instrumental thinking appealing. The film does more than ask us to adopt a certain point of view; it asks us to collaborate with Tatum's ambition. Tatum spectacularly conjugates—in the negative—all aspects of New York City which he is missing in his small town exile: "No Lindy's, no Madison Square Garden, no Yogi Berra. No beautiful roar from eight million ants, cursing, fighting, loving. No shows. No *South Pacific*. No chic little dames across a crowded bar.... No 80th floor to jump from when you feel like it." Wilder strategically locates the beginning of the film at the very edge of film noir. The metropolis appears in *Ace in the Hole* only as conjured in the ambition of its main character. Though critics often locate the death of noir in later films such as *Touch of Evil* (1956) and *Kiss Me Deadly* (1955), *Ace in the Hole* already gives us noir in retrospect: its living cues have degenerated into a set of fetish items, homesickness for a genre in which there was no home. Instead of a memory flashback, we get a collection of souvenirs. The sense of displacement that characterizes the genre is here escalated in a figure that *seems to be in the wrong film*. The nostalgia is also ours, as we are surprised by the absence of the visual idiom Wilder instituted with *Double Indemnity*. The opening image, a static frame of dirt, bluntly articulates this film's distance from *Sunset Boulevard*. That film begins with a shot of a curb inscribed "Sunset Boulevard," which then tracks close to the pavement of the road before "picking up" the police who are on the way to the crime scene. In *Ace in the Hole* we have no title, just ground. Instead of a trajectory, we are given a static section of earth whose scale is as difficult to determine as its value. This dull heap of dirt resembles the contents of a prospector's pan before it has been shaken out. *Sunset Boulevard* begins by asking us to follow a story to the scene of a crime; in giving us a resistant surface over which the light plays with varying intensity, *Ace in the Hole* begins with a challenge to mine the image.

In her review of the film Penelope Houston describes the formidable allure of such a misanthropic figure as Chuck Tatum. She writes, "Kirk Douglas' brilliant performance, a more mature and harsh variation on the part played in *Champion*, establishes Tatum's driving force, his immense energy, his concentration."[2] Tatum's concentration is different from the concentration of a philosopher or a chess master. The way Tatum concentrates his homesickness into a series of absences invites a rhetorical understanding of Houston's term. Tatum's speech combines the tropes of synecdoche (part for whole) and hyperbole (exaggeration), charging each detail with a sensational energy. "Tabloid" derives from the nineteenth century process of compressing medicines into digestible tablet form. This reduction-into-pill form later described popular newspapers that condensed news into sensational headlines. Tatum's elegy for New York City is triggered by the news that chicken tacos have replaced his usual fare (chopped chicken liver) because nobody other than Tatum orders these items. Tatum says, "When the history of this sun-baked Siberia is written, these shameful words will live in infamy: no chopped chicken liver. No garlic pickles. No Lindys." The violation of Tatum's diet is a grave blow to his desire and his inalienable right to urban cuisine. His diatribe literally sounds like a *raison d'état*, borrowing from Franklin Delano Roosevelt's address to Congress after Japan attacked Pearl Harbor.[3] His citation allows him to read the missing synecdochal details of the city as if they were the names of the dead, and as if the culinary restrictions constituted a national wound.

Tatum not only speaks but listens as if he were writing his column. His ambition works like an ear implant that allows him to hear more ruthlessly. Having announced that he wants the "big scoop" (appropriately, an excavational instrument) that will help him get back to the city, Tatum demonstrates the attentiveness of an Indian in an old "B" western with his ear to the ground. Instead of listening for the movement of people in the distance, he's listening for the news before it happens. His ear is a mechanism of exposure. He makes a telltale exclamation to his colleagues: "What do you use for noise around here?" Noise does not happen incidentally and without outcome, but rather is a substance to be manufactured and instrumentalized. So when Tatum says "I like the sound of it," when told that Leo is trapped in "The Mountain of the Seven Vultures," we gauge that this is not a sign of his musical sensibility, but an estimate about how effectively the phrase will boom when recirculated. Tatum listens as if he were himself a transmitter, a hollow space in which the world reports itself (the word "report" refers originally to sound). Tatum receives every act of speech as a broadcast, as already mediated by the news apparatus in his ear. Its value is measured by how it will sound upon repetition. Though it is tempting to compare Tatum to the vultures after which the mountain is named, the journalist does not devour his pray once and for all. Like the mythic vultures feasting on Prometheus anew each morning after his body magically regenerates each night, the tabloid journalist seeks to endlessly skin his pray through repeatable transmission and consumption.

The Physiognomy of Ambition

The singular power of *Ace in the Hole* is the way in which it commits our ears to Tatum's project to tabloidize the world. Here we have to imagine an auditory equivalent to the traditional "point of view" with which audiences supposedly sympathize. The radical procedure taken by the film is to show how listening is a type of work, of writing, and how we, the audience, unwittingly perform that work as we engage the screen.

Wilder constructs a little theater of listening in the cave in which Tatum discovers Leo trapped under fallen rocks. Tatum talks to Leo through an opening not much bigger than his head. The conditions of the conversation forbid the traditional shot/counter shot structure that assigns the roles of active speaker and passive listener. This editing method is abandoned in favor of a more sustained focus on Tatum and his evolving states of reflective listening. The camera stays glued to him long after he asks his question. As Leo's replies cascade over the image of Tatum in close-up, Wilder endows Tatum's listening with an extraordinary sense of agency: the so-called "reaction shots" border on their opposite and become sites of action.

The close-up of the listening face is one of Wilder's recurring visual tropes. In *Double Indemnity*, for example, Phyllis Dietrichson beeps her car horn to signal that the coast is clear to her co-conspirator Walter Neff. We hear sounds of a struggle as Neff strangles Mr. Dietrichson, just out of frame. Instead of seeing the murder, we listen and study Phyllis in close-up as her iron stare is gradually offset by an archaic smile. About this moment William Rothman writes: "The scene of murder is at once real and a projection of this woman's imagination (and ours). This scene arouses her, turns her on (as it arouses us, turns us on)."[4] The scene from *Ace in the Hole* bears interesting similarities here. It is no less a scene of murder. As Tatum listens, he is already *writing his victim to death*, postponing the rescue so that he can metamorphose Leo into a week of story. Critic Nino Frank observes that one of the constant characteristics of film noir is "the dynamism of violent death."[5] Having protracted this dynamism into a two-hour bleeding confession in *Double Indemnity*, Wilder here slows it further (Leo will die of a more gradual asphyxiation: pneumonia) and supplies other instruments (the pen, the newspaper, the hungry readership). Tatum is a kind of serial murderer, aiming to bleed Leo into multiple editions. To become the face through which Leo's story is transmitted, Tatum must maintain Leo in his off-screen limbo. Leo's condition is so obscured by the prestige Tatum gathers from it that Boot wonders, "Is there a Leo really down there?"

Rothman's other observation that the off-screen event becomes a projection also applies. In *Ace*, the off-screen source of sound is projected in time as well as in space. We process Leo's words as they pass through the small disturbances in Tatum's face. His face acts like a weathervane for sound: at times, he rolls his eyes towards Leo, telling him, "Go on, Leo, that's worthwhile knowing." (To whom? we wonder.) At other times, he looks askance, as if he were using Leo's words to look inward. We gather that Tatum is projecting the future of Leo's story as news. Significantly, it is we, the audience, who project the future of its circulation: perhaps unwittingly, we begin to listen to the sound of what Leo is saying. Schooled in the semiotics of Tatum's ambition, we start to work for it: like criminals abetting a crime, we are "in on the job." Internally, but in response to Tatum's silent but animated visage, we read Leo as the means of Tatum's escape. Through this remarkably simple scenario, we do something other than empathize with a morally ambiguous character.[6] Empathy seems superficial compared to the collaboration we undertake with Tatum as we precipitate the arduous process by which Leo's story becomes Tatum's.

How do we listen to Leo in order to expose him, rather than to console or free him? Leo confesses many things to Tatum in the cave: that he is afraid and believes the Indian dead have trapped him for robbing their graves. As Leo's contemplation moves inward, we persistently drag his words out into the open. The film makes us prone to selling his fear out, as we make him into a scapegoat for all the larger historical thefts and genocide performed by the colonists on the Native Americans. Working in the name of Tatum's machination, we don't listen to Leo's words of despair and helplessness; instead we divine them for their exchange value, and reconstruct their sense as Tatum's opportunity. Leo says, "In the army I was plenty scared too. Like when my outfit landed in Italy. Only in the army it's different. Everyone is scared. The barge is going to land and you know you're going to die." We know that Tatum's implicit wish is to make everything into something that resembles a war — with the same duration, the same festival of consumption. As Tatum tells Boot over the phone from Escuadero, "Unless war is declared tonight, here is your front page feature." These words simmer in our ears as we listen to Leo's meditation on death. Leo's story is the replacement story for war. This comparison is sustained by the very production process of the film. To give a radioscopy of contemporary media, Wilder makes a film as if he were conducting war. The stampede of consumption within the movie required, in essence, a battlefield, and Paramount's public relations team claimed that the film featured "the largest noncombat set ever constructed."[7] The statement only draws attention to the way in which *Ace in the Hole* simulates a combat film. *Ace* is one of the most interesting and subterranean postwar movies because it deals not with returning veterans but with the returning rhetoric of war. Since we listen to Leo's confession with the hearing aid of Tatum's presence, which amplifies certain blind spots, certain potential areas for sensational reportage, we can strangely foresee the ways that Tatum will magnetize attention around Leo's dying as a continuation of the exposed condition of the soldier. Leo's death will become part of the public debt.

This foresight usurps the place of the flashback that structures many of Wilder's films from the period. In *Double Indemnity, Sunset Boulevard*, and, less emphatically, *Witness for the Prosecution* (1957), flashbacks submit the images to a double temporality, imbuing them with the pastness of a crime scene, yet pointing towards the future wound with which the film opens and from which the voiceover emanates. Wilder's flashbacks suggest the twining of fate and fatality that characterize the narrative structure of such noirs as Tourneur's *Out of the Past* (1947).[8] In *Ace in the Hole* the flash now goes forward.

The projective dimension Rothman discerns in the scene of Dietrichson's murder in *Double Indemnity* appears in *Ace in the Hole* in the way we project (literally, throw or pitch) Leo forward into a headline, and look for an angle into his words that would disclose their value as news. The dislocation in time that characterizes film noir narratives here happens within the spectator. Adopting Tatum's art of listening, we take up Leo's superstitions, fear, and grimy face, not as objects of intrinsic interest, but as commodities we envision into circulation. We will recall that the only two objects to fit through the opening to Leo's enclosure are the flashbulb of Herbie's camera and the long stick with which the priest marks Leo's brow as he reads him his last rites. The reporter's light and the extended inscriptive tool, the instruments of our comprehension, are also the equipment of Leo's exposure unto death. The flashforward retains the fatal gravity of its counterpart, the flashback, insofar as it refunctions the spectator's anticipation as the precipitation and elaboration of Leo's catastrophe. To anticipate in this film means to break the news and to begin scripting tomorrow's headline. Wilder never provides us with a glimpse of any of Tatum's actual prose in the *Sun Bulletin*. Our ears are already writing that column. "Far from realizing philosophy," Guy Debord writes, "the spectacle philosophizes reality, and turns the material life of everyone into a universe of speculation."[9] Watching *Ace in the Hole*, we cease being spectators and become speculators furthering the immaterialization of Leo's life into a media event.

Implication and Extrication

We are never neutral spectators to Wilder's films. About *Ace in the Hole* Stephen Farber writes: "Our own mixed response — fascination at the game, yet horror at the player's casualness about the stakes involved — proves that Wilder has been successful in conducting his most effective critique of the only way of life he admires. The film *implicates* us."[10] I am suggesting that the revolutionary quality of Wilder's film is the way it implicates us, not as the ambivalent and leisurely spectators of sport, but through our interpretive labor. The film sets the spectator up on the side of the production of the story, not its consumption. The difference between these two spectatorial positions is evident in the different responses inspired by *Ace in the Hole* and Wilder's *The Front Page* (1974). Recreating the atmosphere of the pre-noir news era, the later film displays the production of a newspaper without, however, enfolding us in this process. We marvel at the actual layout and printing of the front page, the newsroom banter recalling the velocity of the early talkie, and the overlapping sentences of men fighting for the best headline. Whereas *The Front Page* theatricalizes journalism, *Ace* demands that we think journalistically. Wilder achieves this through a deceptively simple visual structure. This style has long been the target of critics like Andrew Sarris, who claim it offers "less than meets the eye." Sarris writes:

"All of Wilder's films decline in retrospect because of visual and structural deficiencies."[11] In Wilder's film, the visual deficiency is also its power. The more it lacks (the less Tatum's face *does*), the more we fall into it (the more we *do*). Before his silent but agitated face, we spend a lot of the film *completing Tatum's thinking for him*: but at that point, whose thinking is it really? The film is all about the deception, the trap-nature, of the accident. The entrapment Wilder constructs for our ear should be taken in its full legal sense. Wilder has set up a situation that only seems objective, and has done so in order to have us commit ourselves, to act, to transgress, like the felon exposed by approaching an undercover officer.

Even Tatum's "turn," bringing a priest to give Leo his last rites, obeys the same visual logic. As Leo utters "Bless me, Father, for I have sinned" and "I'm sorry," Wilder immediately cuts to a shot of Tatum's face. Once again, we see Tatum listening as Leo's words cascade over his visage. As in the earlier scenes in the cave, this structure forces us essentially to understand Leo's words through Tatum's face. The film's visual structure detours the moment through the audience, so that we not only administer the confession but utter it on Tatum's behalf. We meditatively supply the depths to Tatum's memory and remorse. Critics point to this scene as a "powerful revelation of Tatum's self-recrimination."[12] This observation ignores the way in which the only thing revealed is Tatum's face, the silence of which compels us to articulate what Tatum grieves, whether it be Leo or the opportunity Leo offered.

Wilder makes our extrication, like Tatum's repentance, our own work. How deeply we've committed ourselves to Tatum and internalized his ambition becomes apparent at those moments when we hasten to disentangle ourselves. Sinyard and Turner write that "The film begins to react on *us*; we have been encouraged to identify with this force of irresponsible energy only for it to turn against us."[13] We can restate this by observing that we begin to react *to* ourselves and turn *against* our own investment in the character. Our ears signal this shift and start to listen differently. One of these instances occurs as Tatum expresses his disbelief at the doctor's diagnosis that Leo is going to die from pneumonia. "Nobody dies from pneumonia these days," Tatum says. Tatum's world is so defined by the headlines that he exemplifies a new solipsism for our era: *he can't accept the existence of anything that isn't (in the) news.* Tatum's statement has a peculiar ring, as if he were phrasing the untimeliness of death as unfashionability. It enjoins us to resist by asking, what is it that people die from? What *should* they die from? We reach for these questions as an emergency break.[14]

Wilder is unfairly categorized as a thoroughly cynical director.[15] Yet this dark film never allows the cool luxury of cynicism to enter into our response. The film repeatedly proposes images that resist the forced unity of media spectacles and instead break apart with their own antagonisms. Instead of a critique through montage à la Eisenstein (whom Wilder revered), Wilder stages actions within the same space so as to collapse the stability of the frame. As Tatum first enters the cave, for example, Wilder gives us a two shot of Lorraine lighting a cigarette and Mr. Minosa making the sign of the cross. *Double Indemnity* divides the single act of smoking into two supplementary gestures, revealing the mutual dependency between Neff and Keyes: it takes two men to smoke one cigarette. In *Ace* the smoking act is interrupted and offset by a co-present gesture that inserts a wholly incompatible value into the image. Film critic André Bazin praises the realism of *The Circus* (1928) in which "Chaplin is truly in the lion's cage and both are enclosed within the framework of the screen."[16] Smoking and the sign of the cross incarnate different codes, histories, and relations to time and the infinite that are just as incompatible as Charlie and the lion. It is impossible to keep our eyes straight as each gesture works independently from (and at odds with) the other. The screen of *Ace in the Hole* is repeatedly ruptured by antagonizing copresences: a pan showing a band charitably singing for Leo's cause, then someone selling the sheet music; Herbie telling Leo's mother, "We'd like to buy some gas" over her fervent but indecipherable prayer. Through this montage within the frame Wilder calls our attention to an unintegrated residue of exchange, an unpleasant aftertaste to the work of capital. Here Wilder's response to Andrew Sarris' negative review of his work is telling: "One has to live with Andrew Sarris," i.e., he and I occupy the same frame.[17] The strength of *Ace in the Hole* comes from the way in which it refuses such reconciliations between opposing forces.

Wilder enables the symbiosis between Tatum and his audience by cutting back on montage. *Ace in the Hole* even allegorizes the limitations of editing's capacity to cinematically articulate Tatum's ambition. This occurs in Tatum's four minute diatribe about returning to New York. Shot in a continuous take, it is interrupted with a reaction shot of surprise from Boot. Then we see a close-up of a shot glass and a liquor bottle, empty but partially concealed behind the papers on Tatum's desk. As Boot approaches Tatum to present him with the evidence of drinking, he angrily says, "I told you no liquor in the office! You broke your promise!" As he lifts up the bottle as "proof," however, Boot suddenly realizes (along with us) that Tatum has been constructing a ship in the bottle. The careful structure of the interruption resembles Kuleshov's experiment.[18] The sequence Tatum-Bottle-Tatum fills Boot with the sudden conviction that he now "knows the source" of Tatum's wild spiel. Tatum's diatribe is "evidently" the rant of a drunk. The question, of course, is what "object" could Kuleshov juxtapose to Tatum's face in order to signify ambition? Wilder's film shows how complex a desire ambition is, as it simultaneously promotes and destroys the world, the way Tatum, for example, wants to instrumentalize objects rather than merely "respond" to them, or consume them like a bowl of soup. In the course of the film, Tatum's face will indeed be juxtaposed with the "grieving widow" (Lorraine Minosa), but Wilder's editing never makes us attribute sadness to him.[19] We see, instead, how that image becomes valuable to him only as an image for his column, and only as it speaks to his opportunism. Boot mistakes Tatum's ambition for inebriation. Wilder explored the affinities between these states in

The Lost Weekend (1945). Ambition might be called inebriation for the sober. Wilder shows how Boot is "under the influence" of montage. Boot can't see the bottle for what it contains: a suspended and intricate structure, perpetually on view but out of reach. In short, a model for what will happen to Leo.

The Audience Within the Film

One of the challenges of films about the media is their representation of the audience. Contemporary films, such as Barry Levinson's *Wag the Dog* (1997) (about a media-engineered war in Albania which is designed to distract the public from presidential scandal), almost forego showing the consumers of these masterfully manipulative images. In purporting to level a critique at the media, these films only demonstrate the docility of the masses. This docility shows itself in ever new and celebratory ways. In *Wag the Dog* scores of shoes hanging from telephone wires signal the absent public's enthusiasm for a war hero named Old Shoe. The media-fabricated hero, a convict in fact, becomes the subject of a patriotic song performed by Willie Nelson. Nelson's song "Old Shoe" plays over the image of the shoes. In *Network* (1976) we hear the sound of countless but unseen fans screaming out the window, on cue from the charismatic host of the show they are watching, "I'm mad as hell and I'm not going to take it anymore." Spike Lee's *Bamboozled* (2000) features the return of a minstrel show and racist spectacle to network television. Yet there is a disturbing absence of reception that raises the question of who enjoys the *Mantan* show, and how it is consumed. There is, in fact, but one shot of someone actually watching *Mantan*: we see documentary footage of Bill Clinton laughing and clapping at the show, digitally superimposed over his television screen by Lee.

In aiming to demonstrate the media's ubiquity and power, these films swerve around the audience encounter. They give us vouchers for the audience which inevitably indicate the homogenized enthusiasm of the mass. Borrowing the measure for success that comes from the industry it is supposedly critiquing, *Network* references the Nielsen ratings to signify the extent to which the manipulation of the public is actually working. Wilder takes a different route. For him, the crowd is never a statistic, Nielsen-rated, but a visible density, traffic, a dynamic entity with effect. The film provides images of this: the Minosa restaurant going from empty to over-populated; a wave of people shooting like gunfire off the train that has stopped (the Leo event is the station in the desert); the new and uncanny emptiness of the desert after the crowd has departed, and the price of admission to the cave dwelling sign escalating from free to fifty cents to a dollar (this sign of mounting profit is the clock for this film). The production of the film bears witness to these crowds: faced with a limited budget, Wilder tells Paramount that they "didn't need to recruit all the extras they needed because gawkers would turn up on their own."[20]

The critical literature on *Ace* shares a judgmental attitude towards this inner audience. It inevitably characterizes the crowd in animal terms: "lemminglike," "a docile insectlike herd of average Americans," "seven thousand vultures who come to gorge off ... Leo's misfortune" and "stampeding morons."[21] Stephen Farber insists that these scenes demonstrate how Wilder's hatred for the masses exceeds his hatred for Tatum, since the crowd, "completely torpid and stupid, merely *feeds* impassively, ravenously on disaster, while Tatum, monster that he is, *creates* the disaster."[22] Yet Wilder's film seems to demonstrate the productive nature of consumption (including our own, as I have detailed above). As in the spreading of a rumor, the distinctions between a producer and a consumer of a news event are difficult to delineate. The crowd images address us so as to make us rethink the supposed passivity of spectatorship and intercept our lazy impulse to judge the crowd. Wilder achieves this by destroying the distinction between actor and extra. Introducing the Federbers, the first arrivals at the scene after reading about it in the paper, Wilder inserts them into every image of the crowd. Are these images of anonymous onlookers, or a family narrative phrased as the purchasing of sheet music, rides on the Ferris wheel, and Indian souvenirs? Adjusting to the scale of the crowd, our eye is frequently caught and forced to refocus by our recognition of their faces. This is the extent of our intimacy with the spectacle: a flash of involuntary recognition within the vast crowd, closer to a déjà vu than a knowing (like suddenly seeing a family member in the bleachers at a televised ball game). The surprise at locating the Federbers takes the place of incriminating what they represent. By making the anonymity of the crowd imperfect, Wilder obstructs our impulse to view them as nameless, animal-like, or as mere examples of easily manipulated consumers.[23]

Where Spike Lee gives us the President ("even him," we remark) as the single example of someone watching *Mantan* on television, Wilder chooses the first extra to embody the spectator. No less than Tatum, they are aspirant figures. The Federbers are extras keen on insisting on their status as actors on the media stage. Mr. Federber protests to the radio interviewer that he was the first on the scene and "wouldn't lie about a thing like that." They are the extras after whom all the others are superfluous, serial, extraneous. His strange pride in being the first consumer resonates as the last outpost of singularity in our mediated universe. The first to register the spectacular nature of the world, its consumability, undertakes an act of discovery, a new heroism. The spectacle is an ever-renewing continent, which perhaps is the reason Federber makes it sound like he's the first to reach the North Pole.

Tatum's Return/Wilder's Return

As suggested in my introduction, Wilder tackles issues explored in *Sunset Boulevard*, made immediately before *Ace in the Hole*. Yet the differences are more revealing than the similarities. *Sunset* examines the effects of the film industry, but through its highest denizen, the celebrity. The tragedy of the film comes from the industry turning its back on Norma. Leo's tragedy is that it didn't. The audience in *Ace in the Hole* is not Leo's delusion (Norma's butler writes Norma's ego-sustaining fan mail), but his agony. The real point of correspondence for Leo isn't with any of the fictional characters in *Sunset Boulevard*, but with the suspended body of actor William Holden as he performed the opening scene of the movie: Holden had to float for hours in the cold water, playing dead, above a mirror at the bottom of a pool, just so that the image of the journalists covering the story could come into view. That irony, the trick of the mirror (the shot looks as though it's viewed from the bottom of the pool), mixed with the pain of the actor's body, describes the miserable apotheosis of Leo into an image. It is the *making* of *Sunset Boulevard* that most accurately reflects the fictional story of *Ace in the Hole*.

To amplify the stakes of *Sunset's* media critique, Wilder excavates the earlier success of *Double Indemnity*. The later film strategically references the name of Walter Neff's insurance agency: Mr. Federber tells a radio broadcaster that he works for Pacific All Risk and that he hopes Leo has a good accident policy. Why does Wilder push the issue of insurance to the edges of *Ace in the Hole* and give Neff's calling card to an extra? Exposure to media, mimicking an exposure to the natural elements, introduces a new concept of mortality and a new incalculability of accident. When Tatum announces at the end of the film that "Leo Minosa didn't die; he was murdered," he is announcing a new type of murder, not by knife or gun but by exposure: death is defined here as a letting die, and "murder" is a correction to "dying."[24]

Wilder's heroes both go back to their jobs ... after committing their crime. Wilder's trenchant critique of the modern work ethic takes the form of a maxim: when you are bleeding and dying, go back to the office. What do the differences between these returns tell us? With Neff's return we see the insurance agency at night, where unheralded figures vacuum and clean up the trash of the work day. This is the work Neff is going to do for Keyes: he's going to leave him the story as it happened, its dirty work, whose agents Keyes overlooked. Neff's office memo to Keyes is simultaneously corrective, confession and love letter. *Ace in the Hole* implodes the genre of the confession. When Tatum announces to his editor that, "Other writers got the story. But it was the wrong story. Leo Minosa didn't die. He was murdered," it is impossible to say whether Tatum is publicly confessing his sins or merely proposing a juicier headline.

If Neff returns to the office to "sum up" what has happened, Tatum returns for a harsher reckoning with his boss and to offer a zero sum. Mirroring the first scene in which Tatum tells his future boss that he could make himself fifty dollars a day, the final image features Tatum making a more exorbitant offer: "Mr. Boot how would you like to make yourself a thousand dollars? I'm a thousand dollar a day newspaper man. You can have me for nothing." Tatum falls dead towards the camera. The terms of this final offer are both more profitable and more absurd. This is what makes the gesture so incisive, both a sabotage and support of the entire profit-over-the-dead-body operation of the film. The corpse is worth nothing, yet it produces, raising the incredible question of what work, what employment the corpse can endure. Tatum sends his corpse back to work. The final gesture is both an indictment of and an opportunity for profit. One wonders whether Boot will take up Tatum's implicit offer and write the story. There seems to be no rewind on the greed principle: its predicament is stated in the last gesture.

Death of the Face

Sunset Boulevard concludes with Norma declaring that she is ready for her close-up. *Ace* concludes with one for which we (and Tatum) are not ready. Tatum does not technically approach the camera, but falls in front of it. He falls accidentally, but not accidentally at all: the moment features the convergence of chance and contrivance explored in the film. So different from Norma's dramatic waltz towards the lens, this falling face continues to impress its weight upon us, even after repeated viewings. In its tumultuous trajectory through the film, Douglas' visage and its famously dented chin are where our anticipation pools. The film shows us how a face dies, not just through loss of blood but (for us) through loss of ambition.

The original script of *Ace* begins at a busy train station with a coffin being wheeled down the platform. Tatum utters in voiceover, "I always wanted to go back. Only I never figured on the baggage car."[25] In place of this flashback irony of the posthumous narrator (à la Joe Gillis) and the conversion of corpse into baggage, *Ace* ensnares us through Tatum's indomitable ambition to break the news, before finally depositing this corpse into our vision. The film benefits from these subtractions, and the concluding image is unremitting in the way it has no uptake, no deflection, no reverse shot. We are both stymied and riveted by how unattributable this face is: it suddenly freezes the work we've been doing in the course of the movie, and thereby makes it difficult for us to know when precisely we should get out of our seats. If this film provides any retrospect, we take it up on our own time: the image of Tatum's face issues us the receipt for his ambition.

Uninflected by ambition and deprived of prospect, this fallen face is the first image we view in the present tense. The shadow covering Tatum's face indicates how radically the film displaces the core element of the noir aesthetic. In this image, Wilder inaugurates a post-noir shadow, one without mystery or the hint, in Chandler's words, that it holds "something more than night." If Norma's final close-up meshes mug shot, head shot, and spirit photograph in one haunting confusion, Tatum's is impenetrable yet without ambiguity. Wilder has effectively exhausted the shadow. The film achieves this through an investigation, not of shadow but of the light by which people become public images, and by which these images circulate. It is difficult to motivate the shadow into which Tatum has fallen: what is its source? Fittingly, it seems that Tatum's face falls in the shadow of the camera itself, as if the camera had stopped exposing him. In this film, death is signaled by this stopping of exposure. Resting implacably on the screen, Tatum's face resembles ash and looks extinguished, as if the camera has taken his light rather than his picture.

Notes

1. Alton, *Painting with Light*, 56.

2. Houston, "Ace in the Hole," 45.

3. Roosevelt's speech begins, "Yesterday, December 7, 1941—a date which will live in infamy—the United States of America was suddenly and deliberately attacked...."

4. Rothman, *The "I" of the Camera*, 180.

5. Quoted in Borde and Chaumeton, "Towards a Definition of Film Noir," 19.

6. "Wilder's antiheroes are never *just* heels; he understands their human frailty too well to deny them the potential for self–examination." Lally, *Wilder Times*, 212.

7. The set was over 235 feet high, 1,200 feet across, and 1,600 feet deep, and included the cliff, roadside stands, a parking lot for 500 cars, and over a thousand extras. Sikov, *On Sunset Boulevard*, 317.

8. Fate is the element behind Wilder's claim that "*Oedipus* is a play *noir*." Porfirio, "Interview with Billy Wilder," 103.

9. Debord, *Society of the Spectacle*, 17.

10. Farber, "Billy Wilder," 378.

11. Sarris, *The American Cinema*, 166.

12. Sikov, 324. See also Sinyard and Turner's claim that "Leo's death is, for Tatum, a personal tragedy more than a professional one." *Journey Down Sunset Boulevard*, 133. Yet it's not clear that Tatum can experience his own privacy as anything other than professional tragedy. He tells the Sheriff that a dead man "does not make for a good story."

13. Ibid., 131

14. Another index to our immersion in the film: our double take at Herbie's suggestion to include a photo of a medicine man in full garb, "exorcizing the evil spirits." We bristle at the opportunism Herbie proudly brandishes in front of Tatum. The moment debunks the supposed neutrality of photographs.

15. "Too cynical to believe his own cynicism," says Sarris, 166.

16. Bazin, *What Is Cinema?*, 52.

17. Porfirio, 113.

18. Kuleshov demonstrates that an actor's neutral face acquires significance according to the images that precede and follow it. After editing the footage next to an image of a coffin, soup, or an erotic scene, Kuleshov discovered that the audience attributed sorrow, hunger, or physical desire to the face. See Kuleshov, "The Origins of Montage," 70.

19. After Lorraine makes a sexual overture to Tatum, he slaps her in the face and says: "Your husband's stuck under a mountain. You're worried sick. That's how the story goes."

20. Sikov, 317.

21. Quotations from Sikov, 323; Farber, 370; Sinyard and Turner, 130. Sikov, 324.

22. Farber, 370. Differentiating animal groupings (flock, murder, pride, gaggle), zoologists have been better readers of animals than critics have been of the crowd in *Ace*. What new species term is deserved by this crowd assembled in the desert for a media event?

23. Wilder says, "An audience is never wrong. An individual member of it may be an imbecile, but a thousand imbeciles together in the dark — that is critical genius" (*Billy Wilder Speaks*, 2006). Wilder's comment underscores how a crowd becomes a "critical" mass, different from the sum of its parts.

24. The dénouement of *Witness for the Prosecution* rests on the separation of like terms. After Christine stabs Leonard, the nurse cries, "She's killed him." "No, she has executed him," responds Sir Wilfrid, realizing his client's guilt. The film opens up a cinematic inquiry into the distinction between killing and execution, in the same way *Ace* investigates the more elusive distinction between death and murder.

25. Sikov, 314.

2. An Unconventional War Film
Death, Disguise and Deception in *Five Graves to Cairo*

DALE M. POLLOCK

Five Graves to Cairo (1943) is the one Billy Wilder film that has been largely overlooked and critically dismissed by all but a few Wilder scholars.[1] Occasional references usually concentrate on the startling bellicosity of Erich von Stroheim's performance as Field Marshal Erwin Rommel, recast from the feared Hun of World War I melodramas to the Nazi everyone loved to hate in the Second World War. But *Five Graves to Cairo* is much more than just von Stroheim's strutting egomaniac: it is a subversive contemporaneous war, espionage and suspense film without any significant combat sequences; a visually sophisticated and coherent creation that adapted the Paramount "look" to the demands of the World War II patriotic film genre; a layered and unexpectedly witty comedy of reluctant heroism thrust upon those who seem least prepared for it; a foundational cornerstone for Wilder's preoccupation with disguise, deception and masquerade throughout his oeuvre; and a dry run for the anticipation and impact of death on a film's central characters that would flower in Wilder's subsequent production, *Double Indemnity* (1944).

Wilder and his writing partner and producer Charles Brackett mixed standard war and suspense narrative devices with a distinctly non–American set of characters and perspectives in the way they structured the plot of *Five Graves to Cairo*. They went the dangerous route of introducing political, romantic and broad physical comedy into a war story whose outcome was still uncertain while the film was in production. This upset many critics and audiences at the time, reflected in *New York Times* film critic Bosley Crowther's contemporaneous review, in which he concluded: "Probably the most conglomerate war film to date. It has a little something for all tastes, provided you don't give a darn."[2] On the technical level of achieving this unusual aesthetic, Wilder's first collaboration with cinematographer John Seitz, and his continuing creative relationships with art director Hans Dreier and costume designer Edith Head, significantly challenged the traditional studio look for a war picture, and acted again as a template for even greater experimentation in mixing a realist documentary approach with stylized German Expressionist lighting, set design and camera framing. In short, *Five Graves to Cairo* is far different than the run-of-the-mill World War II film, characterized by Thomas Doherty as "disposable as art, dubious as history."[3] The confluence of unusual visuals, philosophical themes and character development in *Five Graves to Cairo* makes the film worthy of closer study. This is especially true of Wilder's frequent use of disguise, concealment and outright falsehood in depicting the true nature of some of his leading characters. "There are few life or death scenarios that prompt masquerade — but *Five Graves to Cairo* is one of them. In all of Wilder's work, some sense of survival depends on disguise," notes Gerd Gemünden.[4] He elaborates on that point by observing that in Wilder's wartime-set films, impersonation is amplified because of the larger setting for "deception, espionage or counter-intelligence."[5]

Five Graves to Cairo is the sole combat film Wilder directed, at least of the traditional wartime variety. (Several of Wilder's domestic comedy-dramas, including *Some Like It Hot* [1959], *The Seven Year Itch* [1955], *The Fortune Cookie* [1966] and *The Apartment* [1960] showcase moments of potent social combat.) Unlike many other contemporary war films, *Five Graves* is less about the actual war than it is about what accompanies it: the scheming, planning, boasting and spying that occupy the largest part of the film's ninety-six minutes. As Neil Sinyard and Adrian Turner have observed, "Wilder is [Ernst] Lubitsch after the bombs have fallen."[6] Co-written by Wilder and Brackett in 1942 with a "ripped from the headlines" urgency,[7] *Five Graves* served the twin purposes of the majority of Hollywood's wartime cinematic output: making money while helping the war effort. Paramount was the last of the studios to close its German distribution facilities, doing so only when the Nazi government shut them down in September 1940, and its propaganda efforts were more restrained than those of other studios, such as Warner Bros.[8]

The unpredictable effects of bad timing had to be fresh in Wilder's mind after the negative critical and commercial reception accorded Lubitsch's *To Be or Not to Be* (1942), which dared to portray Nazis in a humorous and satirical light.[9] For Wilder and Brackett, the predicted outcome of the war they would be filming was by no means assured either. The pair were officially assigned to adapt Lajos Biro's well-traveled play on August 10, 1942.[10] Paramount had long owned the rights to Biro's Romanian novel and World War I drama, which was filmed twice before, in 1927 by director Mauritz Stiller and in 1939 by Robert Florey. The more recent version, *Hotel Imperial*, starred Ray Milland, and had been released three years earlier to disastrous results. The stink of its failure was still in the air at Paramount.[11] With the suggestion from playwright Biro to update the story to the contemporary North African campaign, Wilder and Brackett saw their way into the material. They changed the lead character from female to male, put him in a heightened state of conflict, and used a variety of genre approaches to make the totally mythical story immediate and compelling. Few screenwriters have had to write a battle story while the battle was still in progress, as Brackett and Wilder did as they worked on the screenplay through the fall of 1942. The battle for El Alamein inspired the imaginary Sidi Halfaya that Wilder and Brackett were creating in their office on the Paramount lot.[12] Paramount executives must have been nervous as they followed the progress of the war in North Africa, particularly the growing dominance and invulnerability of Rommel (nicknamed by American and British headline writers "The Desert Fox") and his Afrika Korps. It was almost like watching a movie.

There was a first act of glorious British victories in late 1940 and early 1941, capped by the capture of Tobruk, as the Italians collapsed and retreated. Then came the long second act, which saw the triumph of early British victories reversed by Rommel's first offensive in the spring of 1941 that put Tobruk under siege. By the summer of 1942, Rommel was supreme: he was rolling right over the British Eighth Army, headed straight for Alexandria and then Cairo where he could control both the Suez Canal and the distribution of Middle Eastern oil. The stage was set for the third and decisive act of this critical part of the war.

This implicit three-act structure, which did not always resolve with an American or Allied victory in the final reel, was familiar to domestic film audiences in the early 1940s through sheer on-screen repetition. Among the popular war films such as *Desperate Journey* (Raoul Walsh, 1942), *Action in the North Atlantic* (Lloyd Bacon, 1943) and *So Proudly We Hail* (Mark Sandrich, 1943), few of them showed the Allies actually winning. Two films bear particular comparison to *Five Graves*: *Sahara* (Zoltan Korda, 1942) and *Wake Island* (John Farrow, 1942). The former occupies the same landscape and battle zone as *Five Graves*, and the latter was made by Paramount and dwelt on the supreme sacrifice American soldiers were making in the Pacific war effort. Wilder's film is the antithesis of both of these typical studio, movie star-studded propaganda efforts, making a different and more subversive appeal to wartime audiences through comedic misidentification and outlandish characters, as Wilder had done similarly in *The Major and the Minor* (1942).

Designing a War Film That Wasn't a War Film

The beginning of 1943 was a good time to be making a film about a battlefront that led off every wartime newsreel, was in the headlines every day, and featured an adversary who had won grudging praise from both Winston

Churchill and Dwight D. Eisenhower. Brackett and Wilder didn't waste the opportunity. After the film's opening credits comes this title card:

> In June 1942 things looked black indeed for the British Eighth Army. It was broken, scattered and in flight. Tobruk had fallen. The victorious Rommel and his Afrika Korps were pounding the British back and back toward Cairo and the Suez Canal.

This information was very familiar to American audiences. They did not need to be told Rommel's rank or first name, or be given a world map to show them where Tobruk was. They accepted the reality of the war as depicted on the screen, as they were conditioned to do by hundreds of hours of newsreels and other combat movies.

The plot of *Five Graves to Cairo* is deceptively complex, particularly for a World War II drama ostensibly about stopping Rommel's drive through North Africa. As the British Army retreats towards Cairo, Corporal John J. Bramble (Franchot Tone) is stranded in the Sahara, the lone survivor of a British tank crew. In shock and suffering from sunstroke, Bramble deliriously staggers across the desert searching for the nearest outpost. What he finds is the Empress of Britain Hotel in the Libyan border town of Sidi Halfaya. The village has been deserted and destroyed; no one remains but the hotel's owner, Farid (Akim Tamiroff), and the French chambermaid, Mouche (Anne Baxter). To the woman's chagrin, Farid conceals the English soldier as the Germans commandeer his hotel for the lodging of Field Marshall Erwin Rommel.

Mouche is unsympathetic toward the plight of any Englishman. She feels the British abandoned the French Army at Dunkirk, where one of her brothers was killed and another was captured. She has remained in Sidi Halfaya only to wait for the German Army and to bargain for her sibling's freedom, not to help the British. Despite Mouche's protests, Bramble assumes the identity of the hotel's club-footed deceased waiter, Davos, who was buried in debris during an air raid. Surprisingly, the disguise affords Bramble immediate access to Rommel. Davos was, in fact, a top-secret Nazi spy. This revelation inspires Bramble to remain at the Empress. It becomes his mission to steal the crucial secret of the five supply depots the Germans have buried from Tobruk to Cairo—which gave them a fighting advantage—and possibly turn the war in Britain's favor. Meanwhile, after being rejected by the misogynistic General, Mouche is desperately reduced to "entertaining" Rommel's deceitful Lieutenant Schwegler (Peter Van Eyck) in order to help her imprisoned brother. She and Bramble inevitably grow closer as they each struggle to save what is dear to them. When the body of the real Davos is uncovered in the rubble in the Empress' basement, Bramble must kill Schwegler and rely on Mouche to preserve his true identity. She makes the supreme sacrifice, and pays for it with her life, as Bramble discovers when he returns for her after the defeat of Rommel.

Unlike any other contemporary war film of its time, *Five Graves to Cairo* is unsettling from its first frame. The audience is greeted by the image of a lone tank determinedly trundling along in the midst of all that sand, like a ghost ship, the Flying Dutchman of the Libyan Desert. All of the tank's crew but one is grotesquely dead, murdered in Wilder's initial irony, not by the Germans but by the tank and its exhaust system. This is Wilder's first, but not last comment on the stupidity and futility of war, along with its ability to cause death with a perversity that seems simultaneously random and intentional. Like the war itself, the tank lurches on, carrying its cargo of death. It stops for nothing in its pursuit of its mindless goal, driverless, programmed to continually advance. Bramble, the lone survivor, has tumbled out of the tank's rather roomy interior in a weakened and dazed state. Unlike the audience, he can't keep up with the progress of the war. Fades and dissolves are used by Seitz from the outset to create a hallucinatory feeling to Bramble's ghastly experience in the North African desert.

Wilder has cleverly delayed revealing the protagonist of *Five Graves to Cairo* for as long as possible, but when it finally happens, the introduction is dramatic. The camera startlingly moves in and onto his identification tag, an extraordinary shot (cinematographer Seitz puts his lens less than ten inches from Tone's chest to achieve the zoom effect) that reveals Bramble's name and serial number.[13] Bramble seems so confused and weakened that we're not even sure he will survive. He is the embodiment of the unsuitable protagonist, a soldier who seems out on his feet, and not up to any serious assignment, let alone one that could decide the fate of World War II. Thus we see Wilder establish in *Five Graves* one of his enduring male types: the individual in a situation beyond his seeming comprehension or control, who nevertheless carves out an identity and a purpose that defies logic or even commonsense.

In a stunning shot the camera follows Bramble and his solitary footprints winding across the rippling, endless sand dunes. When a sun-stricken Bramble finally stumbles into nondescript Sidi Halfaya — or all that remains of it post-mortar attacks from both sides— the dowdy Empress of Britain hotel with its classic Arabic brick arch entrance seems like an apparition, an imaginary oasis of the British empire that would be particularly comforting to a British corporal. The proprietor, Farid, is on a ladder when Mouche enters with the laundry, and they watch in wonder as Bramble raves on. It slowly becomes clear that Bramble's seeming gibberish is actually supplying his backstory. In one of the film's rare concessions to sentimentality — de rigueur in early 1940s war cinema as a salute to heroism and service — there is a poignant reference to Bramble's missing comrades with his confused request for five extra blankets. Bramble lists the names of his dead comrades in honor, yet can't resist the sardonic remark that he last saw them "driving themselves to a funeral." All Bramble remembers about Tobruk is that it was "hotter than a blister on the Devil's heel," a vivid Wilderian image that is tremendously evocative in establishing the unnaturally hot environment visualized in Seitz's hallucinatory camerawork. As the German High Command arrives right on cue, Farid is forced to shelter

Bramble or repudiate Allah's most "miraculous of miracles," which for religious and plot reasons he cannot do. Farid possesses a conscience, another rarity in Hollywood war films and this particular war-torn environment. He has no such trouble disavowing his Egyptian heritage; he is Egyptian "only because my parents are Egyptian," as he reluctantly admits to Lt. Schwegler (Peter Van Eyck). Shirley MacLaine might have offered a similar line in *The Apartment*, explaining her blue-collar family background.

To survive, Bramble must impersonate the conveniently dead Davos. (Sinyard and Turner note that Bramble's willingness to put on Davos' clothes and built-up shoe is a curious portent of the crippled man's disguise Walter Neff will assume in *Double Indemnity*.)[14] Like the Wilder-created heroes in *A Foreign Affair* (1948) or *Hold Back the Dawn* (Mitchell Leisen, 1941), Bramble is never daunted by issues of nationality. He concludes, illogically, that he can successfully pass himself off as a dead, crippled Alsatian because "I'm Alsatian and he was my age." (Tone, a minor Paramount star who was usually cast as the wealthy gadabout, was believably neither. But he brings something vaguely subversive to the role; his shiftiness works for Bramble, who must be many things to many people.) When we do finally glimpse the real Davos' body in the rubble, he does not look at all to be Bramble's age, but twenty years older. It matters not. Bramble's risky impersonation survives even the piercing scrutiny of Rommel himself.

It is only after assuming this false identity that Bramble discovers who Davos really was: another imposter, playing an Alsatian waiter, but actually a German advance spy, in Rommel's employ. Now Bramble must maintain the Davos identity for his own protection, while simultaneously trying to discover the secret desert location of Rommel's supply depots.

The most dramatic "reveal" in *Five Graves* comes in von Stroheim's entrance as the imperious Rommel: head shaved and uniform immaculate, Rommel struts about like a proud peacock during this first appearance. Wilder subtly places the audience in the power position, looking down on Rommel from the hotel balcony, reducing him in size and seeing him for the popinjay he is. (It meant little that von Stroheim bore no physical resemblance whatsoever to the actual Rommel, who was tall, thin and mustachioed.)[15] Rommel finishes his opening monologue in German, with no subtitles, and then, with theatrical throat clearings, he gives the same message in English "to save the trouble of translation when they intercept this message." This also provides a means for Rommel to demonstrate his English-speaking skills, and makes plausible the English dialogue that dominates the film. Gemünden has written insightfully about the transcultural dimension to Wilder's work, his prolonged status of living inbetween the European world of his childhood and young adulthood, and his new identity as an American citizen and Hollywood success story. "Wilder's films often revolve around experiences of non-belonging and loss, frequently told from the perspective of an outsider," Gemünden notes.[16] This long-standing dichotomy allowed a filmmaker whose family would perish in German concentration camps to portray a Nazi general still with humor and complexity unseen in other Hollywood war movies of the period. He performs the same trick with Otto Preminger's portrayal of Commandant Von Scherbach in *Stalag 17* (1953) and with Marlene Dietrich's unrepentant Nazi mistress in *A Foreign Affair.*

Not only Germans received the Wilder treatment. The Nazis' buffoonish Italian allies are presented in the form of an off-screen aria that, as it becomes clear, is a live performance by General Sebastiano (Fortunio Bonanova, an actor Wilder was so fond of that he cast him in *Double Indemnity* too). The only seeming function for Bonanova's character, other than the historical representation of six Italian brigades in North Africa, is to offer periodic verbal jabs at the Germans. The most notable of these comes when Sebastiano bemoans Italy's fate in "getting the short end of the stick that stinks, as they say in Milano." The line was the subject of a dispute between Wilder and Brackett and Production Code chief Joseph Breen — its presence indicates who won.[17] Mussolini's army didn't generally fare well in Hollywood war films. Doherty describes Fascist Italians in all of the combat films in the early 1940s as "hapless understudies who possessed none of the threatening elan and menacing aptitude of the Teutonic Nazis."[18] This stereotype is reinforced in films like *Sahara*, in which an abandoned Italian soldier metamorphoses from a cowardly enemy into a brave ally. At least Wilder and Brackett confined their stereotypes to Italian opera.

The Unsuitability of Heroism

A further complication is introduced with the appearance of the captive British officers who knew the real Davos. Wilder is merciless in adding one story complication after another, ever ratcheting up the pressure on the hapless Bramble's capabilities and adding to the suspense of the plot's final outcome. In this sequence, Wilder echoes the establishing shot of Bramble by again dramatically zooming in on the soldier's dogtag, this time signalling his true identity to the British officers. Unable to resist a third reference to the same prop, Brackett and Wilder then use the dogtag-draped bottle of scotch as the object of General Sebastiano's veneration as the true "Bramble." The British major confirms what Bramble already knows: he has "a bigger job," being a spy, rather than the easier, if more final task of offering himself as a martyred assassin. Bramble now understands that his mission is not suicidal: he cannot simply murder Rommel and sacrifice his own life. He must solve the mystery of the supply depots, and somehow get that information to Allied headquarters in Cairo. It turns out the martyr role has already been assigned to Mouche by Brackett and Wilder. For Bramble, there are no heroics ahead, just orders to be followed.

It is typical of Wilder's perverse sense of humor to force Bramble to play not one, but two versions of Davos: waiter Davos and German secret agent Davos. In eliminating Rommel, he also faces two contradictory assignments: one for the Germans in Cairo, and one for the British in Sidi Halfaya. Sometimes it seems as if Rommel is trying to make Bramble's job easier; he gladly offers up his ostensible secrets, like a magician offering up his sleeve for inspection. He cannot help boasting to his captive audience about the very nature of his scheme, that rather than relying on the military tradition of supply lines reaching the troops, Rommel will have his men reach the supplies he has hidden "right under your very noses," as he taunts the British officers. "Where? That is Question 21," he adds, displaying his knowledge of contemporary American radio programming.

Ironically, Bramble seems to get looser and looser as the gravity of his situation grows, emphasizing his unsuitability for the role of spy or hero. He can even confide a Wilderian fantasy to Mouche: "If the circumstances in which we found ourselves weren't so peculiar, I might turn you over my knee and spank you, with abandon." Mouche, who at first seems the clichéd saucy French maid played with an execrable accent, will be forced to shift her position constantly by the story machinations of Wilder and Brackett. Not only did Baxter have to control her wobbly French phrasing, but she had to keep changing moods to suit the plot points. At first, she just seems irritated by Bramble's very presence, a living reminder of the English soldiers who deserted her brother and the rest of the French army at Dunkirk. But, in a way, Bramble uses Mouche just like his competition, Lt. Schwegler, wants to use Mouche. Schwegler's motive is the common wartime urge for available women who can be emotionally manipulated in exchange for sex. Bramble asks more of Mouche; he demands actual sacrifice. One of Wilder's darkest ironies in *Five Graves to Cairo* is that if Mouche had just slept with Schwegler, she would not have died.

Wilder and Brackett are unwilling to stop twisting their plot, and in the final turn, the body of the real Davos appears thanks to a second round of shelling, albeit beginning to smell and with dirty fingernails from trying to claw his way out of the rubble. Bramble can't handle much more of this. All he can come up with is the line, "Davos could have been more considerate and died further away." Standard war-movie suspense devices are employed routinely by Wilder throughout the film, such as having the air raid siren sound at the exact moment that Bramble is copying Rommel's map, along with the irony of having Royal Air Force bombers trying to kill the British hero who has in his possession the knowledge that can defeat Rommel.

By the end of the film, Mouche is teary-eyed about the British, and open in her revulsion and loathing of the Nazis, particularly after learning of Schwegler's deceptive telegrams purporting to inquire about her brother's fate. Even though she dies to save Bramble at the film's conclusion, Mouche represents for Wilder survival in wartime, in which only self-interest rules. Wilder is forced by genre conventions and the politics of the time to make Mouche sacrifice herself for the greater cause, but we sense he admires her for her very personal reasons for hating war, as opposed to every other character who acts out of patriotism, ego or fear. This is the same realization Bramble reaches. He must become personally involved in gaining and passing information, but he must do it as someone else. The absence of actual family ties, the trauma of losing a tankful of crewmates, and the lack of competing alternatives allows Bramble to commit himself fully to the war, even at the risk of his own death.

Deviating From the Hollywood Norm

Five Graves to Cairo differs from most major Hollywood war films in its focus and style. In comparison with the enormously popular Paramount release Wake Island in late 1942, Wilder's film seems almost anti-patriotic. Director John Farrow's film opened with the Marine Corps symbol and theme song, and audiences were immediately told that the story they were about to see would be told "as accurately and factually as possible." As opposed to the realism evoked by Seitz's cinematography and Wilder's carefully chosen desert locations utilized in Five Graves to Cairo, films such as Wake Island made ample use of process photography and obvious sets, or relied on Army-supplied war documentary footage. It was the kind of World War II film that showed tearful children waving goodbye to their daddies going off to war.

Wilder disdained the buddy comedy model employed by Wake Island, The Story of G.I. Joe (William Wellman, 1945) and even the more restrained Sahara, and instead tried to show characters such as Bramble on their own, at their wits' end, and confronting a very personalized death, as opposed to the random bullet or shell that rapidly eliminates characters in the traditional combat film. Wellman does a masterful job in The Story of G.I. Joe of playing the death of one G.I. solely off the reactions of his comrades, stressing the group ethic of communal survival over the life of a single careless or unlucky soldier. Wilder and Brackett go in the opposite direction, and demonstrate how the survival and success of Bramble can change the actual outcome of the war. In films such as G.I. Joe, the Germans are never personalized into identifiable individuals. There is only one scene of a German taken prisoner, and he remains stolid and impassive throughout. In Sahara, a captured German officer is stereotypically perfidious and evil from the moment of his introduction, and ends up killing his reluctant Italian ally. There is personal sacrifice called for in Sahara, but it comes from African-American actor Rex Ingram, who in typical Hollywood fashion must sacrifice his black character for the survival of the white squadron, and dies in a superhuman effort to choke the traitorous Nazi before he can betray the rest of the tank crew. Wake Island, Sahara and The Story of G.I. Joe all use familiar tropes, such as the crying puppy dog whose guardian soldier has just been killed, or the melodrama of seeing one crewmember after another picked off. Wilder avoids this sentimentality by focusing on Bramble's lone struggle. The only other comrades he encounters are either dead (at the film's inception) or prisoners more powerless than he is (the British officers whom Rommel loves to taunt).

By casting the unassuming Tone, Brackett and Wilder also avoided the star vehicle that *Sahara* was clearly designed to be, showcasing Humphrey Bogart as the ultimate tough American fighting machine who could not be intimidated or discouraged. *Five Graves to Cairo* may be about one man matching his wits with the smartest Nazi general around, but Bramble cannot succeed by himself. He must have the co-operation and support of Farid and Mouche, characters whom Wilder spends great care in setting up and in fine-tuning their emotional resilience. Characters from the anti-war resistance had a great popular appeal to American audiences, because they were just "regular folks" who suddenly found themselves under the heel of the Germans, and were mad enough to do something about it.[19] By using characters such as Mouche and Farid in critical ways to ensure Bramble's safety and ultimate success, Wilder offered wartime audiences a change from the usual Allies-hero/Axis-villain dynamic.

John Ford, when questioned about the propaganda aspects of *The Battle of Midway* in 1942 by editor Robert Parrish, told him: "Don't you ever let me hear you use that word again in my presence as long as you're under my command."[20] Wilder evinced a similar attitude with *Five Graves*: the point of the film is not just to drum up anti–German and pro–Allies sentiment (which *Five Graves* certainly does in its final montage of General Montgomery's successful offensive with the British Eighth Army), but to explore the role of the individual caught up in circumstances that demand more than simply what is required to do the job. This focus on one person, rather than the group structure of the squad or platoon, distinguishes *Five Graves to Cairo* from its contemporaries.

Wilder did share a common "colonial propensity for Anglophilia," as Doherty puts it,[21] and thus we see Bramble as the embodiment of the stiff upper-lipped and admirably resolute British characters who populated some of Hollywood's best films during the early years of the war. But by casting an American actor to play a Brit, Wilder once again undercut the easy Hollywood assumption that all a successful war movie needed to be was inspirational, to rally the faithful and embolden the fearful. Instead, Wilder relies on satirizing Rommel's egotism to put the Nazi in his place. Bernard Dick calls Rommel "too civilized for caricature, too tragic for vilification,"[22] but Wilder and Seitz, in the way they present and shoot von Stroheim in the role, put him in his place as a martinet on steroids. Yet even Rommel's reputation was resuscitated after the war — in *The Desert Fox* (Henry Hathaway, 1951), Rommel became a tragic figure embodied by the dour James Mason rather than the Napoleon-esque character von Stroheim took such pleasure in creating in *Five Graves to Cairo*.

Establishing a Visual Style in the Comedy-Drama

Collaborating closely with black and white cinematography master Seitz, art directors Hans Dreier and Ernst Fegte, and costume designer Edith Head, Wilder shot *Five Graves* in a close-in style that would become a trademark of mixed dramatic-comedic filmmaking. The contribution of in-house studio departments such as production design and costume creation is often undervalued in the critical analysis of a film's visual impact. This influence was especially pronounced at Paramount, where Dreier and Head were department heads and studio veterans, wielding great creative power within the confines of the studio system.[23] Wilder had already worked with Dreier and Head on his debut directorial effort, *The Major and the Minor*, and he made far greater demands on their talents in *Five Graves*. The careful use of detail in settings like the slightly decrepit interior of the Empress Britain hotel and the accompanying wardrobe, such as von Stroheim's dazzling white dress uniform, enriches the film's visual style greatly. Since Wilder and Seitz are dealing with a stage play as source material, they must rely primarily on two- and three-person grouped medium shots. There's not much for Seitz to do with the camera, since ninety per cent of the action takes place in the hotel's confined rooms, which were designed as four-wall, rather than three-wall sets. To compensate for these physical limitations, Seitz made the most of his contrast lighting within the interiors, minimizing his key lighting and using screens and grids for almost every shot. Sikov says of the cinematography in *Five Graves*: "The look is gorgeous but understated, combining the bold visual play of Sternberg's *Morocco* with Hawks's self-effacing restraint."[24] Wilder would work again with Seitz in his other black and white visual masterpieces, *Double Indemnity* and *Sunset Boulevard* (1950).

Less obvious are the vital contributions made by Dreier, Fegte and Head. The Paramount Art Department presented Wilder with a wonderful recreation of a war-demolished village and hotel exterior, even if they were used only sparingly for the arrival of Bramble and the comings and goings of the Germans. The subtlest element of the film's visual design is the use of light from both a cinematographic and design perspective in the hotel interiors. Light is always streaming in through rattan-shuttered windows, creating light and dark backgrounds in almost every scene. There are moments when *Five Graves* even resembles *Casablanca* (Michael Curtiz, 1942), made a year earlier with the more elegant North-African setting of Rick's American Café. Fegte, a Hungarian-born artist who began working in film in 1919, was considered the finest draftsman in the Paramount Art Department, and was assigned to the film by Dreier, who was himself an art director of some of the German Expressionist classics made at Paramount's UFA-EFA studio in Berlin, where Wilder too had worked.[25] All of the backgrounds in *Five Graves* have surprising visual depth, often two or three levels deep. The distressed architecture of the hotel, from whitewashed brick to dark wooden beams and idle overhead fans, is used to maximum visual impact by Seitz's roving camera, unusually mobile for this period of largely fixed camera technology. Wilder employs Seitz's elegantly active camera to move the film's point of view around constantly, never staying with just Bramble's perspective, even though the film is constantly concerned with his actions and motives.

Seitz's most impressive cinematographic work takes place on the film's few exteriors, where he makes magnificent use of the bleak desert landscape (Yuma, Arizona doubling for Libya), the overarching cloudy sky, the harsh shadows made by oppressive desert sunlight. It was virtually unheard of for a war film to be shot on a distant location rather than a studio backlot or wilderness ranch.[26] But Wilder insisted on duplicating as closely as possible an actual desert location, and the realism of the setting has an enormous impact on the realism of the story. Seitz used reflectors, black velvet and natural lighting to achieve the sense of penetrating heat that Wilder wanted to communicate. Because Seitz had shot only ninety feet of film when the tank used for principal photography broke down, Wilder ended up shooting the entire sand dunes sequence in just two days.[27] Seitz practiced shooting in the Arizona desert night to see how far he could push the Kodak film stock, and in one test the footage came out almost completely black.[28] He also used the great cloudy sky above the desert for maximum atmospheric effect. These stark images gave Seitz his second of seven Academy Award nominations for best cinematography.

Wilder and Seitz's other great success in *Five Graves to Cairo* is their use of layered action within the frame. The filmmakers take full advantage of the different visual planes in the hotel, the movement in the frame keeping the film dynamic and engaging. The sequence of Bramble hiding behind the slatted reception desk simultaneously heightens the suspense, gives insight into the characters of both Mouche and Schwegler, and is visually stunning. Characters are constantly ascending and descending, as their moral choices broaden and narrow with the change in dramatic circumstances. When Bramble is bent on accomplishing his goals, he almost always is climbing up, or looking at the Nazis below him, beneath him morally as well as physically. This technique mirrors Wilder's layered approach to storytelling: this is a war movie, but also a comedy, no matter how high the stakes. Seitz's visual approach consistently informs character. Mouche, who has an agenda from the start, is literally blocked from Bramble in much of the early staging of their relationship. She comes into Seitz's camera range only when Farid appeals to her for help, and we discover how much she hates the British for leaving her brothers to die at Dunkirk. She has a personal reason to hate the randomness of war, as opposed to every other character in the film, whose motives stem from patriotism (the desire to win at war) or survival.

Seitz's camera also provides interesting transitions from day to night and exterior to interior, virtually unseen in the newsreel-style visual approach of most studio World War II films. This is exemplified by the beautiful moving camera tracking shot that plays over General Sebastiano's opera aria and follows Bramble as he carries out Rommel's order to stop the music. It feels like a fluid master shot, even though there are two subtle edits as Bramble passes Mouche in the hallway. The shot visually reinforces Bramble/Davos moving from one world to another in his disguise and deception. Every scene with strong emotional impact is dramatically lit by Seitz, especially those involving Mouche and Bramble and the unspoken sexual and emotional tension between them. Wilder steals from *It Happened One Night* (Frank Capra, 1934) for his own "Walls of Jericho" scene, but it does give Anne Baxter her one movie-star moment in the film, a gorgeously lit close-up of her as she lies on her back in her bed, her eyes glistening and almost tearing up. This is contrasted with the harsh lighting on Franchot Tone's lean and determined face. The visual elements are not arbitrary; the entire sequence leads up to an important plot point as to who will answer the buzzer to respond to Rommel in Room Five, a beat accentuated by Wilder's cut to the number 5 on Rommel's door. Rommel's room evokes the Paramount white set look that defined their romantic and domestic comedies of the 1930s: von Stroheim wears white pajamas (Head was an expert designer of sleepwear) and is positioned against white brick walls and fixtures. There is also an effective use of a white beaded curtain behind von Stroheim's sitting position that allows for passing shadows and a vertical contrast to the horizontal line of the men sitting at Rommel's table. Rommel's room seems enormous, but the small-sized von Stroheim always stands out in the frame, his white shirtsleeves echoed by the glaring sun on the white bricks of the walls. Arches and doorways are everywhere, distracting the audience from the reality that almost every scene is set within a confined room.

The services of a costume designer on a standard World War II film seem unnecessary; in *Five Graves* there are primarily German uniforms and British uniforms, although Bramble sheds his quickly. Within this limited palette, Head does minor wonders. Nothing exceeds von Stroheim's extravagant white uniform, accompanied by a riding crop with a white feather duster at its end, which he also uses as a fly swatter. The uniform becomes an unconscious precursor of Max Mayerling's chauffeur's uniform in *Sunset Boulevard*, which will be worn again in a Head design with equal aplomb by von Stroheim. Head uses contrasting black and white wardrobe throughout *Five Graves*, although the symbolism is rarely clear — the protagonist and antagonist both wear white, for example. But Mouche is almost always dressed by Head in variations on black, while Bramble in his Davos disguise is the only character other than Rommel to wear bright white, in Davos' immaculate white shirt set against his dark vest. In her unfinished autobiography, Head discusses her use of black and white to create a sharp contrast in the clothes Barbara Stanwyck wore in *The Lady Eve* (Preston Sturges, 1941). The black on white, all black, all white wardrobe helped "to make her appear a tad coarse," Head revealed,[29] and the same approach seems to have been taken with Baxter's Mouche, who has conflicting motives throughout the film, both positive and negative. The final confrontation between Bramble and Mouche has Bramble in white, Mouche in dark black skirts and a white lace shawl, and a swinging white shaded lamp defining the visual space between them. While Mouche and Bramble negotiate literally who will live and who will die, the wardrobe subtly changes. When Bramble finally departs, he is in all black, and Mouche's white shawl is accented in all of her shots. Wilder also effectively uses Rommel's black riding crop contrasted with the white tassel whipping Mouche's pale, frightened face. The final note in this white/black leitmotif is Bramble's victorious return to the Empress Britain with a white parasol for the now-sainted Mouche, who sacrificed her life for Bramble's successful escape. And Bramble sports a white ascot in his otherwise drab desert British uniform. The film ends with a field of white graves, a white parasol left on Mouche's final resting place. Even in a black and white movie, special attention is being paid to the use of black and white to define setting, character and visual emphasis.

Disguise, Deception and Death

By bestowing on Bramble the identity of a dead man, Wilder brings disguise and deception to full circle with the death and rebirth of Davos. Sinyard and Turner see the entire film structured around cultural tensions largely resolved through disguises and deceptions, but by having Bramble first survive almost-certain death, then avoid it again and again at the hands of his French collaborators and German employers, we see that death plays a resolving role for the first time in a Wilder film. Everyone in *Five Graves to Cairo* pretends to be what they're not. Even Rommel poses as an archaeologist to plant his stashes of fuel and ammunition. This kind of dark masquerade was first explored by Wilder in *The Major and the Minor*, but the stakes were much lower, perhaps. In both films, according to Bernard Dick, "Wilder started with a ruse and worked outward, lightening it for comedy, darkening it for melodrama."[30]

This theme would occur again and again in Wilder's work. Imposture and disguise would be explored in *The Apartment, Witness for the Prosecution* (1957), *The Private Life of Sherlock Holmes* (1970) and *Kiss Me, Stupid* (1964), but rarely would the result be the potential death of almost every significant character. By placing these particularly high stakes into an unconventional war movie, Wilder and Brackett explored the shifting relationship between men and women, between so-called allies and so-called enemies, and between Teutonic superiority and British cleverness. They were working out themes that would preoccupy their partnership, and would continue through Wilder's later collaborations with I.A.L. Diamond.

Five Graves to Cairo thus can be seen as a groundbreaking, fully-developed instance of thematic and character exploration by a filmmaker still finding his auteurial voice. It clearly established ideas and motifs that Wilder would return to frequently in his work that dealt with deception, disguise, the unsuitability of the protagonist for the task at hand, and how death becomes a constant threat to the character driving the film's action. Although dealt with seriously by only a few Wilder scholars, *Five Graves to Cairo* shows itself open to further interpretation and study as a foundational work in Wilder's oeuvre, and one that can yield rich insights into Wilder's philosophical priorities and filmmaking style.

Notes

1. Sinyard and Turner, *Journey Down Sunset Boulevard*, 65–75.
2. Crowther, "Five Graves to Cairo."
3. Doherty, *Projections of War*, 3.
4. Gemünden, *A Foreign Affair*, 105.
5. Ibid., 105.
6. Sinyard and Turner, 7.
7. Sikov, *On Sunset Boulevard*, 182.
8. Dick, *The Star Spangled Screen*, 67.
9. Doherty, 126–27.
10. Lally, *Wilder Times*, 119.
11. Sikov, 182.
12. Ibid., 183.
13. Ibid., 190.
14. Sinyard and Turner, 69.
15. Madsen, *Billy Wilder*, 65.
16. Gemünden, 3.
17. Sikov, 185.
18. Doherty, 143.
19. Dick, 146–47.
20. Doherty, 26.
21. Ibid., 40.
22. Dick, 195.
23. Heisner, *Hollywood Art*, 166.
24. Sikov, 187.
25. Heisner, 179.
26. Head, *Edith Head's Hollywood*, 72.
27. Sikov, 187.
28. Lally, 124.
29. Head and Ardmore, *The Dress Doctor*, 43.
30. Dick, 39.

3. *Syncope, Syncopation*

Musical *Hommages* to Europe

KATHERINE ARENS

Two entries in Billy Wilder's œuvre as director-screenwriter have been particularly difficult for critics, in no small part because they are light screen comedies with music filmed by a master most known for black comedy and drama: *The Emperor Waltz* (1948) and *Irma la Douce* (1963). *Emperor Waltz* is generally dismissed as Habsburg nostalgia, Wilder's tribute to the lost Austro-Hungarian Empire of his birth, undertaken as a favor to a producer needing a new property for Bing Crosby. *Irma la Douce* is also considered a stopgap, Wilder's attempt to find a vehicle for Marilyn Monroe and Jack Lemmon.

These received views, however, are creations of Hollywood history, misdirections about the nature of filmmaking and the film industry in its first century, encouraged by Wilder's own copious interviews purportedly giving "just the facts" about his work. These two Wilder orphans were notable commercial successes: their scripts earned Writers Guild of America nominations, as well as sundry Oscar nominations. The disparity suggests that, just as Louise Brooks did for silent screen Hollywood, Wilder was instrumental in writing film history through interviews, taking his screen legacy into his own hands. Scholars have accepted his self-fashioning as an American film master in an era when Hollywood was, in fact, anything *but* American. The accepted but dismissive "histories" of *The Emperor Waltz* and *Irma la Douce* bear witness to scholars' insistence that the film industry came into its own in the United States—a syncope, a persistent blind spot in film historiography, given the flood of talent from Hitler's Europe.

These two Wilder films show us a lost era of *international* film production and a European popular culture industry that could be not only commercial, but also socially challenging and artistically relevant. They reveal Wilder as a film artist refusing to be an *auteur*, working within studio constraints to transform the everyday, traditional, and conventional into his own inventions. Wilder was the director who took on *Double Indemnity* (1944) because it was considered unfilmable under the new code restrictions, managing here as elsewhere to open a space in Hollywood for a critique of society through mass culture.

The Emperor Waltz and *Irma la Douce, hommages* to European theater, need to be considered not failures or incidental pieces, but rather experiments designed to challenge the audience to expect more of the film, constructed by a master with broad command not just of screenwriting and filmmaking, but also of theater literature, performance conventions, and contemporaneous experiments in genre and social commentary. They document Wilder's multi-layered negotiation between his contemporaneous American audiences and the European traditions in which he learned his craft. Recontextualizing how each film challenged, Wilder reveals how he syncopated a legacy from Europe for new audiences.

Like many of Hollywood's World War II era emigrants, Wilder saw film as a relevant social medium and re-cast Europe's traditions for the Americas. These two films challenge traditional film history to consider how an international medium was naturalized into precise national contexts, and how national film industries responded to the planning and goals of those producers, writers, and directors.

The New Hollywood Operetta?

The Emperor Waltz disconcerts those who favor Wilder's contemporary films and his *film noir* palette — a big-budget, Technicolor extravaganza starring Bing Crosby and Joan Fontaine, not quite the typical 1930s operetta or musical comedy film. It is dismissed as "a weird film for Wilder to make" and "one of Wilder's weakest films," if not his worst[1]:

> *The Emperor Waltz* is Wilder and Brackett's first taste of defeat. The lavish production is only moderately and spasmodically amusing, and despite a hard-sell campaign by Paramount, the film fails. It does contain Wilder's first piece of dashing *mise en scène*: an opening ballroom sequence which is a bang-up piece of burlesque of Viennese romance, combining splendor, lightness and smart movie-making.[2]

Co-writer Charles Brackett called the picture a "stinker."[3] Wilder purportedly had an attack of megalomania when he got a big budget and Technicolor.[4] Ed Sikov summarizes "*Emperor Waltz* was a clinker."[5] Kevin Lally considers the film "a throwback to Wilder's earliest Hollywood screenwriting days, when he was pigeonholed into the Bavarian ghetto of innocuous, Mittel European musicals like *Music in the Air* and *Champagne Waltz*."[6]

Such assessments obscure more concrete indices of public and industry success: after the film's world premieres in April 1948, Bing Crosby garnered good reviews; Brackett and Wilder got a Writers Guild of America nomination for best script for a musical, and the film was nominated for Oscars for its costumes and score. Overall, it was an acceptable commercial success.

Wilder's oft-repeated account of the film's origin seems authoritative, including a self-deprecating final assessment that "No good deed goes unpunished." In the tale's most elaborate version, told to Cameron Crowe, he stresses that he took up the film on his fortieth birthday as a favor for Paramount, emphasizing circumstance rather than calculation:

> *The Emperor Waltz* came out of a bravado gesture that I made in a meeting at the front office. They did not have a good picture for Bing Crosby. And I just said, "Why don't we just make a musical?" But it was not really a musical, because a musical is a thing where people, instead of talking, they sing to each other. The songs are plot scenes, and they sing. And I started kind of fumbling around there for a plot, and that was kind of, well, the dog — ... The dog, and it was just kind of *ach* ... (*Struggles to find a positive, but gives up.*) We had nothing. I was just kind of improvising there. The less time you consume in analyzing *The Emperor Waltz*, you know, the better. There's nothing to explain, there's nothing to read into *that thing.*[7]

Contradicting other accounts, Wilder also claims a good working relationship with Crosby. His charming tales thus may fall well shy of the truth, gauged to remind the public that he controlled the studio's hottest properties: Crosby at the height of his visibility and Joan Fontaine, who purportedly took this film to audition for Max Ophüls' *Letter from an Unknown Woman* (1948) — a film by another Austro-Hungarian refugee.

Wilder and Brackett were, as they began the film, elevated into Hollywood's highest studio circles. Ed Sikov cites a 1946 interview with Louella Parsons that confirms this status, as she asks what would come after their *The Lost Weekend* (1945) hit (and its eventual Oscars):

> Charlie answered first. "This time we're just having fun," Brackett said. "It's an operetta called *The Emperor Waltz*."
> "And instead of the bat and mouse," Billy chimed in, "we're having Bing Crosby and Joan Fontaine."[8]

The "bat and mouse" refer to the most famous of Viennese operettas, Johann Strauss II's *Die Fledermaus* (*The Bat*, 1874). They would, therefore, follow up a serious film about a drunk with a comedy based on an operetta about one. The quip was designed for the publicity machine, but it also contains potential barbs about his leads: there is no mouse in the operetta, except for the German word for bat, "flying mouse." The operetta's eponymous bat was an inebriate in a costume, the target of an elaborate revenge joke, perpetrated with the aid of a chambermaid who wanted her break as a stage singer.

Given this clear provenance, why does Wilder insist in retrospect that there is "nothing to read into" the film? Personal tragedy may have played a role.

Ernst Lubitsch died on 30 November 1947, between the film's 1946 shooting and its 1948 release. After seeing some rushes—in a genre that Lubitsch had himself pioneered—the elder director had charged Wilder with stealing the dog conceit from him.[9] That may have taken the wind out of the joke for Wilder. Still, at the time, Brackett and Wilder understood their project. Their screenplay's opening page sported a warning situating their work quite consciously, as "not a fantasy," "not an operetta," and

> not set in Graustark, Flausenthurm, or any other mythical kingdom. It is set in Vienna, 1901. It should be anchored to that time and place with good strong chains of reality.... Just because it plays in Vienna, don't let's have everyone talk like Herman Bing. And just because it's in Technicolor, don't let's have the Emperor wear canary-yellow jaegers and a purple jock strap.
>   And now, soldiers of Paramount: on to new glory.[10]

Although critics like Sikov believe that Wilder "hated operettas" since his 1930s plethora of screenplays in Europe,[11] this notice takes particular aim at the Hollywood film operetta, rather than its Viennese stage cousin.

Associated with names like Fred Astaire, Eleanor Powell, Ginger Rogers, Ruby Keeler, and Dick Powell, early Hollywood musical films often sported the thinnest of plots to showcase randomly inserted musical and dance performers. But film operettas had a more distinct pedigree, reaching back to King Vidor's *La Bohème* (1926, with Lillian Gish) and transformed in the hands of directors like Ernst Lubitsch. His milestone *The Merry Widow* (1934), based on Franz Lehár's 1905 hit,[12] starred Maurice Chevalier and Jeanette MacDonald in what is now considered a cinematic masterpiece (cited in Wilder's opening montage). The genre had even already been parodied with historical accuracy, in 1938's *Sweethearts* (dir. W. S. Van Dyke), which shows how a Broadway operetta duo fared when only one of them got a contract for the film version.

Scholars attribute Wilder's willingness to take up the genre to his discovery that his Austrian-Jewish family had been decimated in the Holocaust, leading to his producing "a lavish, high-budget effort to come to terms with himself and his doubled-edged identity."[13] In consequence, scholars take the film's central conceits as Wilder's commentary about anti–Semitism, Nazis, and racial stereotypes: "a Viennese-Tyrolean reverie in glorious Technicolor" becomes "the tale of two dogs and how they rut" and "a film about genocide."[14]

That assessment does accommodate the film's most memorable subplot about a doggy "mixed marriage." Scheherazade, a black poodle belonging to the Duchess Johanna Franziska von Stoltzenberg-Stoltzenberg (the name means "proud mountain," and its doubling suggests the oldest of families), has been selected as the mate for the Emperor's pure-bred poodle. Scheherazade, however, meets the mutt Buttons, a double for the RCA Victor dog-mascot belonging to the traveling phonograph salesman Virgil Smith. The salesman falls in love with the Duchess, as their dogs consummate the relationship and have mixed-breed puppies. The prime minister who tries to drown them, "Semmelgries," is named to underscore the action: the Viennese physician Ignaz Semmelweis introduced sterile procedure into the Viennese maternity hospital. Smith defends and saves the little beasts, winning the Duchess, as well.

Having filmed the death camps for the U.S. Army, Wilder did not need to comment on World War II. Instead, the material presented Wilder with one of his favorite challenges, script battles with Joseph Breen and the Code office.[15] Wilder and Brackett had to expurgate dog sex and excretion references from their original script, including the canine-appropriate word *bitch*, but they managed to salvage *crap* and *poop*.[16] Not unimportantly, the material was also rich in the Hollywood resonances that Wilder loved. The dog mixed marriage has analogues in the famous canine marriage of Asta and Mrs. Asta from the enormously popular *Thin Man* series (starting in 1934). The Astas consummate a lusty relationship much more overtly than their owners, the perpetually inebriated Nick and Nora Charles, themselves engaged in an amusing but mismatched marriage between a socialite and an ex-gumshoe with a revolving cast of low-life friends.

Wilder had looked at several other highly visible commercial Broadway and Hollywood properties before settling on *Emperor*, including a possible *Count of Luxembourg* for Danny Kaye (another stage operetta) and an adaptation of a play by Hungary's most famous playwright, Ferenc Molnár.[17] These options speak to Wilder's ambitions in Hollywood. Molnár's play *The Guardsman* had played on Broadway in a David Belasco production before it was adopted as a replacement script for a film starring Nelson Eddy and Risë Stevens, based on Oscar Strauss' operetta *The Chocolate Soldier* (*Der tapfere Soldat*, 1908, filmed in 1941). George Bernard Shaw had refused permission to use the original source for the operetta, his *Arms and the Man* (premiered 1894). Molnár's *Liliom* (1909) had been filmed in French by Fritz Lang in 1934, with Charles Boyer, and it was re-adapted into the Rodgers and Hammerstein musical *Carousel*, premiering in a 1945 New York production directed by Rouben Mamoulian.

The studio was willing to fund Wilder's film competitively, on the strength of his *Lost Weekend* Oscar. *Emperor* was one of Wilder's few location productions, shot at Jasper National Park in Canada, and his first foray into color.[18] Wilder had three million dollars, but overran his budget by a million, purportedly using the money to repair real or imagined deficits in the landscape. He built a castle and an artificial island in the lake; he repainted roads that photographed the wrong color; he did the same to a field of flowers, brought in and planted as white, then judged too bright and turned blue.[19] The production was also bedeviled by Crosby's imperious behavior: he brought his own dialogue and gag writer who reworked the director's script.[20]

Wilder was clearly displeased with the whole situation, despite the large budget (matched later in his career only by *Sabrina* in 1954). Hellmuth Karasek, in German-language interviews with Wilder, notes that critics believe that the director Wilder rose up to become the extravagant emperor-director and willful sole dictator of the film: Wilder as Cecil B. de Mille, or even as a precursor of Cimino? ... What the critics who shake their heads have misunderstood — it was not about the megalomania of a director, but rather about Wilder's war with color.[21]

Karasek instead stresses Wilder's war with Technicolor. Working with Edith Head for costumes and Natalie Kalmus for the color did not go well.[22] In retrospect, Wilder claimed definite trouble with adapting: "Even the dialogue sounded wrong in color."[23]

Scholars take this war as an indication of the film's failure, noting that "Wilder did not trust his material the way Lubitsch did."[24] When they comment on issues like Wilder's use of yellow "as the perfect color for capturing the sunset of the Austro-Hungarian Empire,"[25] they see it as an attempt to rewrite the Kalmus color palette. They thus miss second references, like a possible visual joke by one of the twentieth century's soon-to-be leading art collectors: the Habsburg dynastic flag was *schwarzgelb*, yellow and black. In another context, Wilder commented: "[*Double Indemnity*] was in black and white, which is much more difficult to shoot than color. Black and white is a very difficult medium because you have to create your own values and shadings, whereas in color it's much easier."[26]

The gaps between these accounts point not to nostalgia, an "improvisation," or "a favor," but to very ambitious and strategic planning. Not only did the production use all the resources of the studio system, it also tried to integrate U.S. and European references and genre conventions. In its final form, *The Emperor Waltz* (like *Irma la Douce*) is *neither* a musical *nor* an operetta, as Wilder and Brackett knew: it is a film with music, structured to move beyond the traditional genres, convinced that art and commerce could come together for the audience.

Wilder's Cultural Capital

A new generation of German and Austrian film scholars has begun to re-evaluate how Wilder came to his distinctive filmmaking. Andreas Hutter and Klaus Kamolz (1998) tell us the detailed story of how the young Wilder, "roving reporter" and sardonic columnist in the Viennese press, consorted with the Tiller Girls and followed the Paul Whiteman orchestra to Berlin as their publicist in 1926.[27] This protégé of Europe's great journalist-columnists (*feuilletonists*) like Egon Erwin Kisch (the original "roving reporter/*rasender Reporter*") hob-nobbed with the intelligentsia of Europe at Berlin's *Romanisches Café* and *Café Kranzler*, took a job as taxi dancer to pay the bills (making a reporter's monthly salary in ten days' tips[28]), and turned that experience into a Weimar reportage of note (with the encouragement of another legendary writer, Klabund). On the side, he was a sports reporter and an advice columnist in literary drag, writing as a woman.[29]

By 1933, Wilder had made it: he had a car, the beginnings of an art collection, literary pseudonyms, and access to Vienna's and Berlin's vanguard because of his writing talent. As he began in the late 1920s to work with and for directors like Robert Siodmak and to garner top fees for scripts, he continued to write for the papers. When the *Reichstag* burned, Wilder realized that he needed to leave Germany. He and a rich female friend left Berlin on a train to Paris, carrying his Austrian passport and some art posters, the root of his collection.[30] As he went through his money, he went behind the camera for the first time, and then one of his scripts was optioned by Columbia, garnering him a job offer by January 1934[31]: "Der Rest ist Filmgeschichte."[32]

This continuity is critical for understanding Wilder's own film aesthetic, starting with his own first feature, the legendary *Menschen am Sonntag* (1930), set in a Berlin park. After sound filmmaking spread through the Berlin studios in 1930, Wilder's ability to write pithy vignettes and personal profiles translated well into scriptwriting. He established himself with UFA, working with their first-tier talent, including actors like Willi Forst, Willy Fritsch, and Paul Hörbiger, and writers like Erich Kästner, whose *Emil und die Detektive* he adapted in 1931.[33]

Operetta films—a genre Lubitsch had essentially created on film —were legitimate artistic contributions in this studio, in that composers like Franz Lehár had already contributed original music to the medium (the iconic song "Dein ist mein ganzes Herz/Thine Is My Heart Alone"[34]). Wilder's most successful foray into the genre was 1931's *Ihre Hoheit befiehlt/Her Grace Commands* (1931), eventually remade in Hollywood as *Adorable* (dir. William Dieterle, 1933). UFA music films were, however, not necessarily traditional. Hutter and Kamolz explain that UFA had already begun to transform the class structure commonly represented in the musical film, instead making "Volksstück[e] mit Musik/critical comedies with music,"[35] familiar from the European stage. Significant innovation lay behind these seemingly harmless films:

> a plea for filmic verismo, an analog to the then-current trend of New Objectivity, which stressed representation of unmediated experience, reproductions true to nature, a concentration on the every-day and often banal, and, beyond that, a mild protest against the falseness of the commercial (US and UFA) "dream factory."[36]

Wilder thus had more than the Hollywood studio system as reference points for *The Emperor Waltz*. Clearly, he saw his opportunity to innovate on the Hollywood genre, using not Fred Astaire and his tailcoats, but the resolutely bourgeois Bing Crosby — a significant class difference. His new "operetta" sought to bring a new social and historical awareness into the entertainment film.

Overall, Wilder seemed to be working toward a cultural fusion. *The Emperor Waltz* actually rewrites another "clash of cultures" property from U.S. literary history: Mark Twain's 1889 *A Connecticut Yankee in King Arthur's Court*, which had recently been adapted into commercially successful stage and screen properties. A non-musical version of *A Connecticut Yankee* had been filmed in 1931 with *Ziegfeld Follies* star Will Rogers as "Sir Boss," the Yankee inventor. A 1927 Richard Rodgers and Lorenz Hart musical (book by Herbert Fields) had run for 421 performances and then was revived for an additional 135 performances in 1943/44. *Emperor Waltz* precedes by a year the film of the musical *A Connecticut Yankee in King Arthur's Court*, also starring Crosby as a traveling salesman (1949, with Rhonda Fleming). Scholars thus take *Emperor Waltz* as Bing Crosby's "audition" for that film, violating chronology and failing to consider it as Wilder's own attempt to get the property. After all, the material might well have appealed to Wilder: the Broadway musical had made precisely the shift that the UFA films with music had. In *South Pacific, Oklahoma!* and *Carousel*, social criticism and class struggle had come onto the Broadway stage, and *Connecticut Yankee*'s stage revival had shown equivalent potential.

The original casting for the Emperor Franz Josef reflects Wilder's embrace of this class-reversing aesthetic (and his proclivity for employing Austrian émigrés). His first choice for the key role was an Austrian operetta and comedy star who had starred in *Fledermaus* and other Strauss operettas in Berlin. Oskar Karlweis had also been a great film star since 1930, when he, Willy Fritsch, and Heinz Rühmann starred in what is now considered a landmark German musical film: *Die Drei von der Tankstelle* (*Three Guys from the Gas Station*, 1930). Thwarting Wilder's attempt at casting across cultures and against type,[37] Karlweis did not end up doing the role of the Emperor in Wilder's film, purportedly because of a salary dispute.[38] He was replaced by Richard Haydn.

In this sense, the production was from the beginning more than "red, white and blue,"[39] even though many critics see it as "the first Wilder-directed film to touch on what would become a recurring personal theme: the clash between European sophistication and all–American directness."[40] Such assessments miss another cross-reference: Bing Crosby sings "I Kiss Your Hand, Madam," a song famous from a 1929 Marlene Dietrich film of that name (dir. Richard Land), looped there by legendary tenor Richard Tauber.

Closer viewers catch part of these intertexts. Karasek considers it "Wilder's most personal film" but also "his only foray into the beautiful idiocy of the operetta," "an educational novel, or better said, an educational operetta. In it, America educated Europe, freeing it from the darkness of class consciousness."[41] Karasek's Wilder, upper-class Viennese in origin, knows his operettas, as he moves beyond them in full knowledge of their history and potential:

> Wilder heightens the musical numbers until Austrian *Gemütlichkeit* (sociability) turns into a grotesque — suddenly one has the feeling that the film's baptismal sponsor is more Ödön von Horváth than Franz Lehár. Or perhaps better Ernst Lubitsch, who gave wings to many a scene through irony.[42]

Nonetheless, Karasek fails to expand on this additional historical intertext when he cites Horváth. That playwright was known until his death in Parisian exile for modernizing the language of the traditional Austrian *Volksstück* and bringing it to new social relevance, as he did in the most famous of his pieces, the prize-winning *Geschichten aus dem Wienerwald* (*Tales from the Vienna Woods*, 1931), with its critique of fascism and classism.

Karasek was perhaps misled by Wilder himself, who pushes literary analogues into territory of another sort altogether. The filmmaker remarks that he keeps up his German by reading *Josephine Mutzenbacher*, a turn-of-the-century anonymous Austrian *Story of O*, about a cheerful prostitute.[43] Karasek summarizes simply that "Wilder does his film an injustice":

> At least in the scenes with the Emperor, who appears distracted, pessimistic, and stooped under his mantle of power, it is clear how far Wilder deepens the operetta in the [film's] dialogues and conflicts: he discusses the narrow-mindedness, immobility, and arrogance of a world conscious of its weaknesses but unable to change them. Wilder diagnoses the ailments of Austria.[44]

Karasek's assessment still ignores the Duchess' marriage to the future millionaire as a calculated social critique. Such clues about how Wilder worked, tying film and literary aesthetics, pop up repeatedly in these German interviews, as they do in English-language ones. Thus Karasek will note that the later UFA musical films handled the relation of song and spectator differently than did their Hollywood equivalents.[45] Wilder then adds a distinctive literary comment about connection with the audience: "I don't believe in 'epic' breaks like Brecht, I want to keep hold of the audience that I have won over to the illusion of the film."[46]

Maintaining such an audience connection while preserving the verisimilitude of the film narrative becomes critical in Wilder's comedy world. In the *American Masters* tribute to Wilder, even Jack Lemmon falls into the trap of underestimating Wilder's connection to the stage. In *Some Like It Hot*, Lemmon reports, Wilder made him use a memorable and seemingly unmotivated set of maracas to punctuate the dialogue. Lemmon failed to see the point until he watched the film in the theater: the maracas served to factor a "laugh pause" into the film, so that comic dialogue was not swallowed up by the audience's reaction. These are the issues of timing and tempo that recur in Wilder's interviews.[47]

Wilder was thus in *The Emperor Waltz* not just *citing* two theater and film histories, he was making the film *literate* about its own history and about the related arts. Not a conventional operetta in tailcoats, his "operetta" enacts a transition: the countess accepts Virgil Smith, and then notes laconically that her ex was six foot two and one of the most handsome men of the monarchy. She's had the "waltz dream" of the monarchy, and now will instead choose the physically unprepossessing Smith and the money he will make — a nice twist on all those patrician East-Coast American heiresses who married into the European nobility in the early twentieth century. And the film's "education" of the audience *out* of the operetta dream occurs on several levels, as it will in most Wilder scripts. The film's title is, after all, *The EMPEROR Waltz*, an allusion to Johann Strauss II's *Kaiserwalzer* (Op. 437), dedicated to a meeting of the Austrian and German Emperors in 1889 that commemorated a concert hall opening. Its original title was "Hand in Hand," and so Wilder's choice represents an inevitable political reference from a Viennese-born director who would have known this most famous of Waltzes (second only to *On the Beautiful Blue Danube*).

Wilder, literate in larger cultural networks, clearly had identified a parallel transformation in UFA music films and Broadway musicals and tried to enact a parallel in his own work. Schooled to careful audience calculation, Wilder produced in *The Emperor Waltz* a popular success that remains a failure only to scholars and critics who take it as derivative rather than as an *hommage* to the best in contemporary culture and popular art on two continents.

Re-Adapting Europe

In over a decade between *The Emperor Waltz* and *Irma la Douce*, Wilder's other film with music, the director would repeatedly craft rapprochements between European and U.S. cultures, most notably in *A Foreign Affair* (1948) and *One, Two, Three* (1961). Yet repeatedly, scholars take them as political reactions to the Cold War rather than as signs of Wilder's more active aesthetic program. If *The Emperor Waltz* was an exercise in evolving a film/stage genre, then *Irma la Douce* can be seen as a more full-scale attempt to bring other forms of European sensibility to a broader U.S. public increasingly removed from politics and from European cinematic art traditions. Predictably, however, scholars like Gene D. Phillips acknowledge *Irma*'s "commercial success" but critique the plot as "far-fetched and lacking in true comic invention."[48] Nonetheless, *Cahiers du Cinéma* liked it, no matter that others dismissed it as "a one-tracked and over-long exercise in Feydeau naughtiness."[49]

Wilder's own narrative again helps to deflect scholars from what was overall a successful film, covering up its European roots. *Irma la Douce* started its life as a French stage musical, with book and lyrics by Alexandre Breffort, and music by Marguerite Monnot. It opened in London's West End in July 1958, where it ran for 1512 performances, and then moved to Broadway in 1960 with the same (1961 Tony-winning) lead actress (Elizabeth Seal) for an additional 524 performances (and additional music by John Kander, important for *Cabaret*, a subsequent Broadway prostitute musical). I. A. L. Diamond noted that he and Wilder had seen the show in Paris and liked its premise, although not necessarily its execution.[50] That account underplays some additional facts about the source: Alexandre Breffort had since 1934 been editor of Paris' most important intellectual satire magazine, *Le Canard enchaîné*; Monnot was Edith Piaf's composer. No wonder, then, that Wilder was drawn to the project.

Underplaying the international breadth of his project's concept, Wilder tells Crowe that

[*Irma la Douce*] was a little bit of a period picture, the twenties or so. Again, it was a sort of mezzo-musical. But I missed. It was too broad in certain scenes. It didn't work. There is always something wrong about people not speaking the language of the foreign country where the picture takes place. And you could not stand a Lemmon or a MacLaine speaking English with an accent, either. It's false. It just does not work.[51]

This is a perfectionist looking backward. Wilder had first thought of making it in black and white but ultimately shot it in color.[52] Wilder later quipped: "If I had my way, I'd reshoot ninety-five percent of that thing."[53] At the time, Wilder relished the challenge of the blue material, "the story of a man who is jealous of himself": "We are doing it with taste and feeling. It will strike a happy balance between Tennessee Williams and Walt Disney."[54]

Yet the later Wilder would repeatedly elide his own probable motivations. In an interview, for example, he comments that he didn't like making films based on plays,

but I kind of hope that the three versions I did were improvements on the originals: *Sabrina Fair, Stalag 17, Witness for the Prosecution* ... to give an Academy Award to a man who directs a play is like giving the removalists who took Michaelangelo's *Pietà* from the Vatican to the New York's World's Fair a first award in sculpture.[55]

Yet he also understood the difficulties: "When the original author says, 'hey, that's a good job,' or 'that's the way I visualized it,' or 'you did it even better than what I had in mind when I wrote it,'" that was a sign of success in adaptation.[56] Such statements stem from a man instrumental in forming the Screenwriters Guild, one who became a director because he "wanted to protect the script. It's that simple."[57]

Wilder had acquired the property in 1960 for $330,000, being careful to retain the film rights, which enabled him eventually to negotiate profit-sharing for himself, MacLaine, and Lemmon.[58] Yet before he took it up, he made *One, Two, Three* and entertained the possibility of a Marx Brothers movie.[59] He had intended Charles Laughton to play Moustache, the bartender-narrator, but the actor ultimately was too ill to do more than run lines with Wilder. Wilder purportedly considered the film for Marilyn Monroe, although he also mentioned Liz Taylor and even Brigitte Bardot to journalists[60] and may, I believe, have even orchestrated Monroe's exit from the project, dropping remarks in an Art Buchwald interview that alienated Monroe.[61] The perhaps convenient delays led to the casting of Shirley MacLaine.

As Wilder refashioned the stage musical, he "first removed the sixteen musical numbers,"[62] although André Previn's Oscar-winning score retained motifs from the original show's hit "Dis Donc" in Irma's dance number. What

Wilder's choices meant may not even have been evident to Diamond, who commented only "musicals as such are not our forte."[63]

Critics like Lally comment that "it may no longer be a musical, but it still feels like one."[64] Such remarks do factor in the prior decade's innovations in Hollywood musicals, since John Houston's *Moulin Rouge* (1952) and the artificial Technicolor glory of Vincente Minnelli and Arthur Freed's *An American in Paris* (1951). And indeed, *Irma la Douce* shows a Wilder interested in this tradition. For instance, its early washing scene may be a tribute to Rouben Mamoulian's *Love Me Tonight* (1932, with Maurice Chevalier and Jeanette MacDonald), and to its innovation of taking the songs out onto the street and blending street noise into the music. Wilder's meat market scene references *An American in Paris* and Kelly's performance of "I Got Rhythm" to a group of street children. Other Hollywood references pervade the film, including a character who "lost his manhood when the bridge on the River Kwai fell on him," an unsubtle reference to the film's sweep of the Oscars for 1957. Wilder renamed the ancillary prostitutes Suzette Wong (after the popular *World of Suzie Wong* [1960]) and Lolita (released as a film in 1962).

Seen from an international perspective, however, Wilder's intertexts appear even more compelling, in an era when not only new forms of music films appeared, but also *auteur* cinema about prostitutes unmasking the pretenses of the bourgeoisie proliferated. *The Umbrellas of Cherbourg* (dir. Jacques Demy, 1964) was already in production with Catherine Deneuve, a completely sung love story taking artificiality to new heights. The French New Wave would soon offer films like *Belle de jour* (dir. Luis Buñuel, 1967, based on a 1928 novel). In Italy, Federico Fellini offered the era's most iconic prostitute film in *Nights of Cabiria* (*Le notti di Cabiria*, 1957), with a Nino Rota score. It starred his wife, Giulietta Masina, as Cabiria Ceccarelli, a prostitute in a bad Roman neighborhood. Like Wilder's *Irma*, Cabiria keeps looking for love, but is taken advantage of, even in a demeaning offer of marriage. *Irma la Douce* retold such stories in an ironic happy end variant, still critical of the bourgeoisie.

Again, Wilder may have been trying to push the Hollywood musical film in new directions:

> The most important part of the process is to find something that appeals to the theatergoer. The idea is to find something popular into which you can inject humor and life at the highest level. Never force it, but be popular.[65]

He challenged his audience not as the idiosyncratic *auteur* of the New Wave, but by using the best of established formulae from two continents to create something beyond both. International *auteur* film had decided it was time to critique the bourgeoisie, and Hollywood understood stylized musicals. In critics' assessments, *Irma la Douce* did not manage to synthesize these two appeals to the audience, but its U.S. box office success, together with the lasting image it gave MacLaine,[66] argue that he may indeed have managed to inject a new kind of life into this film by combining traditions.

Wilder the Internationalist

Wilder's myth has always proclaimed him the most Americanized of émigré directors: "I made myself very unpopular with a group of German and Austrian refugees, because I surrounded myself only with the Americans. I wanted to learn the language."[67] The language that Wilder learned, however, was more than American vernacular English: it was a second language of genres and formulae, the building blocks for films. He explained his overall process in general terms:

> There are two ways of writing and directing a picture. You take a very complex, gothic, curled idea, and you try to uncurl it to show them what it is. Or you take a very simple idea and curl it yourself.[68]

The familiar description of the famous "Lubitsch touch" has him "curling" an idea this way: "Lubitsch would just say, 'Here is two and there is two, and let the audience add it up.' That is the trick."[69] And that trick Wilder adapted as his own, necessarily moving beyond Lubitsch because the audience had. As Wilder noted with respect to *Double Indemnity*:

> The audience is so far ahead of you. Nowadays even further because their eyes and their ears have been so sharpened by all the television they see.... You have to stimulate their minds and you have to make them work with you and once you do that, that's fine.... And if you're not smart enough to make them participate in the game that is going on, you lose.[70]

This echoes the European aesthetic that Wilder learned at the start of his career, yet with a distinct add-on from the contemporary scene: he seeks to engage the audience, not gratify his own ego, and to achieve "the popular and successful picture."[71]

Anglo-American critics see in Billy Wilder a wit and a cynic with "a sardonic view of the world. His was a European outlook without the underlying American optimism that colored so many of the films of his friends and colleagues in Hollywood."[72] During an American Film Institute tribute, Walter Matthau quoted Wilder as saying "The situation is hopeless but not serious." What he seems not to have known is that this is a very old joke about how an Austrian general would report on a battle (a German would say the opposite). The Wilder who made *The Emperor Waltz* and *Irma la Douce* absolutely knew that filmmaking was *always* hopeless. His generation of émigré directors, producers, and screenwriters relied more on pragmatics than optimism. They knew the limits of their audiences, and the tools that could be applied to engage them, and so any number of them are remembered as the most flexible directors in Hollywood (e.g., Curtiz, Lubitsch, and Preminger).

Billy Wilder added to this mastery of craft a profound sense of a cultural moment on an international stage — his distinct contemporary voice. But because film scholars prefer to pursue directors as *auteurs* or members of the studio system, they have undervalued what these two films with music set as their challenge. The Wilder reclaimed through his "musicals" joined European and U.S. film trends within the mechanisms of the commercial cinema and studio systems (including publicity, screenwriting, and casting). He did so to take his audience beyond the conventional and asked it to question its own prejudices, as he asked Hollywood to work outside of its traditional comfort zone. Film scholars must be asked now to recover Wilder as working broadly within international culture, not just in the studio.

Notes

1. Sikov, *On Sunset Boulevard*, 260, 268.
2. Madsen, *Billy Wilder*, 74.
3. Sikov, 267.
4. Karasek, *Billy Wilder*, 13.
5. Sikov, 255.
6. Lally, *Wilder Times*, 167.
7. Crowe, *Conversations*, 276–77.
8. Sikov, 259.
9. Ibid., 267; Lally, 171.
10. Sikov, 260.
11. Ibid.; Zolotow estimates about 200 scripts or scenarios as a ghostwriter (41).
12. Poague, *Hollywood Professionals*, offers a standard account of thematic parallels between Wilder and Lubitsch.
13. Sikov, 261.
14. Ibid., 262, 269.
15. Ibid., 263.
16. Ibid., 264.
17. Lally, 166.
18. Dick, *Billy Wilder*, 124.
19. Sikov, 266.
20. Ibid., 265.
21. Karasek, 339; all translations mine.
22. Colpart, *Billy Wilder*, 57.
23. Lally, 169.
24. Dick, 125.
25. Ibid., 124.
26. Allyn, "Interview," 93.
27. Hutter and Kamolz, *Billie Wilder*, 71, 86.
28. Ibid., 103.
29. Ibid., 111, 117.
30. Ibid., 203.
31. Ibid., 226.
32. Ibid., 228.
33. Ibid., 161.
34. Ibid., 171.
35. Ibid., 175.
36. Ibid., 131.

37. Wilder's *Sunset Boulevard* (1950) used other survivors of bygone eras. His silent film director is named Max von Mayerling, another Austrian allusion to where crown prince Rudolf committed suicide, and to a series of films made by Anatole Litvak, most notably 1936's *Mayerling*.

38. Sikov, 263.

39. Dick, 127.

40. Lally, 170.

41. Karasek, 336–37, 338, and 336, respectively.

42. Ibid., 339.

43. Ibid., 332.

44. Ibid., 338.

45. Ibid., 80.

46. Ibid., 81.

47. Ibid., 82–83, 296.

48. Phillips, "Billy Wilder," 204.

49. Madsen, 132.

50. Lally, 328.

51. Crowe, 87.

52. Sikov, 468–69.

53. Ibid., 477.

54. Ibid., 471, 270.

55. Higham and Greenberg, *Celluloid Muse*, 251.

56. Allyn, 95.

57. Hunter, "Dialogue," 73.

58. Sikov, 445, 468.

59. Lally, 310.

60. Sikov, 446–47.

61. Lally, 310.

62. Madsen, 127,

63. Lally, 328. Note that Diamond was described by Audrey Wilder as "the most famous collaborator since Quisling" (Stevens, ed., "Billy Wilder," 302), perhaps indicating tensions not generally acknowledged.

64. Lally, 330.

65. Hunter, 74.

66. This film would be the basis for the American musical and movie *Sweet Charity* (1966; music by Cy Coleman, lyrics by Dorothy Fields and book by Neil Simon). The original Broadway cast starred the choreographer Bob Fosse's wife, Gwen Verdon, but the 1969 film starred Shirley MacLaine, reprising a role very like Irma.

67. Hunter, 73.

68. Ibid., 75.

69. Ibid., 75.

70. Allyn, 92.

71. Stevens, ed., 332.

72. Ibid., 304.

4. Realistic Horror
Film Noir and the 1940s Horror Cycle
MARK JANCOVICH

In his discussion of Billy Wilder's *Double Indemnity*, James Naremore refers to the film as "a definitive film noir and one of the most influential movies in Hollywood history,"[1] a film that is central to Wilder's reputation as one of the key directors of film noir. However, if Wilder is closely associated with noir today, he was understood very differently in the 1940s, the period that gave rise to his key classics of film noir. The point here is not simply that, as Naremore and others have pointed out, the films identified as film noir today were not categorized as such at the time of their original release, but also that most of the films later seen as noir classics, including those made by Wilder, were originally identified as horror films in the 1940s.[2] While the thriller and the horror film are commonly seen as quite separate categories today, they were virtually indistinguishable terms in the 1940s, and films were described as thrillers on the grounds that they provided "thrills and chills." Hence the term "thriller" was often indistinguishable from that of the "chiller," and was used for films that were supposed to appeal to the "thrill seeker," films that were "terrifying," "hair-raising," "spine-tingling" and shocking"; that would make one's "flesh creep," one's "blood curdle" or give one "goose-bumps."

Another sign of the relationship between the thriller and the horror film was the association with German directors such as Wilder.[3] In 1944–45, four films were released that have come to represent the consolidation of film noir proper. Not only were all four films directed by German émigré directors— *Double Indemnity* (dir. Billy Wilder, 1944), *Laura* (dir. Otto Preminger, 1944), *Phantom Lady* (dir. Robert Siodmak, 1944) and *Woman in the Window* (dir. Fritz Lang, 1945)—but they were also associated with horror on their original release in the United States. For example, in its review of *Phantom Lady*, the

New York Times saw the film as one that was clearly tailored to its director, Robert Siodmak, "a former director of German horror films."[4]

This association between German directors and horror may explain why German directors such as Wilder, Lang and Siodmak were quickly put to work on horror productions as the 1940s horror cycle began to pick up momentum after the success of *Cat People* (1942), even though many of the German directors who became associated with film noir had little or no association with expressionism prior to their arrival in America. As Koepnick points out, "when considering the ways in which exiled film workers may have imported Weimar sensibilities to Hollywood, acts of performative repetition and unforeseen redress clearly outnumbered instances of direct transfer."[5] For example, despite the perception that Siodmak was a "former director of German horror films," Koepnick claims that "his directorship prior to Hollywood had showed no expressionist predilections whatsoever."[6] Indeed, as Greco points out, in Europe he had been "on his way to becoming a successor to René Clair until the Nazis came and [he] was forced to flee."[7] The expressionist qualities of many of these German directors' Hollywood productions were not necessarily due to their preoccupations prior to their arrival in America, but rather due to the ways in which they were required to fulfil the industry's perceptions of them as Germans. Even many non–German Europeans were associated with horror, so that figures such as René Clair found themselves involved in films such as *And Then There Were None* (1945), an adaptation of an Agatha Christie mystery, which was clearly identified as a horror film by its studio, exhibitors and critics.[8]

In other words, there was a sense of confusion between expressionism and German cinema on the one hand,[9] and between German and European cinema on the other. Germany had been one of the most commercially and critically successful of European cinemas, and it shaped much of Hollywood's understanding of Europe. Furthermore, expressionism was a clearly identifiable style to which other European cinemas sometimes alluded in bids for commercial or critical success.[10]

The association between the thriller and the horror film was also marked in the gendered address of many films. If many of the films defined as film noir today were often identified as horror in the period, they were not seen as a self-contained group of films, but as part of a larger production trend that included those films that are known today as examples of the Gothic (or paranoid) woman's film.[11] As a result, while critics currently tend to present film noir as a masculine genre, particularly through an association with the figure of the hardboiled detective, many of the films commonly cited as early examples of film noir were actually woman's films. For example, *Phantom Lady*, like many other thrillers of the period, features a central female character that takes on the role of lead investigator[12] and is menaced by a psychologically disturbed male killer. Like many women in the so-called Gothic (or paranoid) woman's film of the period, she is therefore required to investigate the mystery of male psychology in order to survive.[13]

If the female investigator has often been ignored as a figure, critics of the 1940s were acutely aware of her presence, certainly when compared to the so-called "femme fatale," a figure of rather dubious significance in the 1940s.[14] Not only is the femme fatale far less common than is usually implied, but the term conflates quite different figures of femininity under a very questionable communality. In addition, while a cycle of "female monster" pictures did emerge in the early 1940s,[15] these were usually identified as horror films, and when, in the mid to late 1940s, these female monsters began to acquire a less fantastic shape, the figures that emerged were discussed in terms that have little relation to the figure of the femme fatale as she is understood today. Most significantly, these female monsters were not part of an attempt to demonize the independent woman of the war years, but were associated with the wartime push for women to take on roles outside the home. Consequently, the women often identified today with the femme fatale were associated with wartime condemnations of the "slacker," a figure whose association with the domestic was presented as greedy, lazy and selfish.

The emergence of these figures takes place alongside an even more fundamental transition. In the mid 1940s there was a shift in critical tastes that is often associated with the release of Rossellini's *Rome, Open City* (1945), but that can actually be detected earlier in the critical reception of Wilder's *The Lost Weekend* (1945). Reviews of *The Lost Weekend* identified it not only as a horror film but as a brave and "realistic" film that was willing to handle the difficult and controversial subject of alcoholism. The topic of alcoholism was also related to a shift in the critical evaluation of psychological materials. While the "psychological" was largely associated with horror and fantasy in the early 1940s, so that the *New York Times* could talk of "German horror films" and "German psychologicals" as though these were interchangeable terms,[16] by the mid–1940s psychological materials became associated with realism through an association between the psychological film and the social problem film.

As a result, there was a shift in critical tastes from Gothic fantasy to social realism, from historical to contemporary subjects, and an overt preference for "social commentary" rather than "escapism." This shift also resulted in a concern with film censorship, in which censorship was accused of preventing films from handling serious, adult subject matter, and a simultaneous celebration of the unvarnished and unglamorous as a sign of significance.

The following essay will therefore examine the critical reception of Billy Wilder's career during the 1940s and the ways in which his films were associated with horror. It will therefore consider his changing reputation from a figure associated with light comedy to one who was increasingly seen as a filmmaker able to circumvent the Production Code Administration and offer "realism." At this time, realism was often seen as requiring a rejection of censorship and a handling of subject matter that was often seen as taboo. However, Wilder was not seen simply as a filmmaker who plumbed the seedy and sordid, but as one who was able to justify his transgressions with a sense of delicacy, taste and social responsibility. This essay will therefore start out with a focus on his early circumvention of the Production Code with *The Major and the Minor* (1942) and the supposedly horrific aspects of *Five Graves to Cairo* (1943), before analysing the critical significance of *Double Indemnity*, a film that was seen as a model of the new horror film and one that had skillfully evaded censorship. The next section then moves on to investigate the pivotal role of Wilder's *The Lost Weekend* in debates over realism, a film whose largely rapturous reception predated the film often identified as the standard bearer of the "new realism," *Open City*. Finally, the last section explores Wilder's shift from "realistic horror" with *The Emperor Waltz* (1948) and *A Foreign Affair* (1948) before his triumphant return with *Sunset Boulevard* (1950), another film that was strongly associated with horror and was claimed to have cleverly evaded censorship.

"Fun in a Haunted House": Censorship, Comedy and Horror

Like Siodmak, Billy Wilder had no real background in German expressionism, and might seem an unlikely director of horror-thrillers. Even once he arrived in Hollywood, he was better known for witty comic scripts, and his first directing role was clearly in that vein. Nonetheless, while this first directorial effort, *The Major and the Minor*, was described as "a charming comedy romance,"[17] there were also some hints of what would follow. As a result, while its central idea of a grown woman posing as "a little girl" gives the film "a cute twist on the mistaken-identity gag," the writing partnership of Wilder and Brackett was seen as providing a very specific flavor to the film: "it takes more than a twist to make a picture, and that's where the Messrs. Wilder and Brackett have come in — by writing a script which effervesces with neat situations and bright lines." However, while the film is praised for its light tone in which the story is played "with spirit and taste" and there is no "suggestion of a leer," the script is also described as making for a "delightful" but also a "cunning" film. If Wilder and Brackett were "two fast boys with a script," it is also claimed that: "Sly boys they are, too. You'd never dream the Hays office would permit a scene of rather intimate proximity between Miss Rogers and Ray Milland in a Pullman car." In other words, the script is supposed to be a "cunning" evasion of the Production Code Administration, in which the writers "have managed to put by a deliciously risqué contretemps."

If this film suggests the talent for evading censorship restrictions that would prove essential to the "realism" of both *Double Indemnity* and *The Lost Weekend*, Wilder's next film, *Five Graves to Cairo*, gave some indication of his talent as a horror director. Although the film is clearly identified as "an incredible comedy-melodrama — yes, comedy is what we said,"[18] the repetition was necessary because this aspect of the film was "completely out of key with the performance of Mr. von Stroheim," who appears as Field Marshall Rommel within the film. While the film is a "comedy melodrama," von Stroheim's presence is very much associated with both horror and "realism." He is not only "a shade on the terrifying side" so that he "gives you the creeps and the shivers," but it is the "realism" of his performance "that chills the bones." Despite the strange presence of this horrific and realistic performance within "this fanciful story," the film is seen not as a failure but rather another clever piece of trickery from "Charles Brackett and Billy Wilder, a couple of old-hand Paramount wags, [who] have dressed it up with shenanigans which have the flavor of fun in a haunted house." In other words, the writing team have found a perfect way of blending the comedy and the horrific to provide quality entertainment.

Unlikely as it might sound, these projects (along with Wilder's German background) were therefore seen as qualifying him for the "new horror cycle" that was gathering momentum by 1943, and he was given the job of filming James M. Cain's notorious novel, *Double Indemnity*, a novel regarded as virtually unfilmable due to the restrictions of the PCA. Furthermore, while it is often seen as a tough, male-oriented narrative, it is Miss Thelda Victor, a female secretary at Paramount, who is often claimed to have brought the property to the attention of producer Joe Sistrom. After enthusiastically devouring the novel in "the ladies lounge," it is suggested, she was so enraptured by the story that she declared it to be "simply sensational" and "a natural for Billy Wilder."[19]

This "natural" was clearly identified as a horror film on its initial release in the U.S. Reviews asserted that the film provided "sheer horror" that "will put all those who see the picture ... under a nightmarish spell for days."[20] It was not only a "tale of murder," that was "shocking and almost breathlessly exciting,"[21] but "a spine-chilling film" with "a brooding, terrifying atmosphere." While some stressed that it shared "the very quality that has lost so much sleep for readers who indiscreetly picked up the book too close to bedtime,"[22] others maintained that it "achieved the curious cinematic power" that Hitchcock had been able to achieve only on "occasions." It was even claimed that *Double Indemnity* was matched only by a "foreign picture called 'M,'"[23] Lang's study of a compulsive child-killer which was seen by critics in the 1940s, and even today, as one of the classics of the horror film. Furthermore, *M* was so strongly identified with horror that its star, Peter Lorre, felt unable to escape an association with horror for the rest of his career.[24] As a result, the response of critics is probably best summed up by the *New York Daily News*, which referred to *Double Indemnity* as "the most terrifying study of crime ... that has ever reached the screen," and one that was "not for the kiddies, nor for adults with faint hearts or weak stomachs."[25]

This designation of *Double Indemnity* as an "adult film"[26] highlights one of the key features in the reception of the film, the critics' focus on its "realism." If the 1940s horror cycle had largely been associated with Gothic fantasy prior to 1944, *Double Indemnity* marked a transformation in the cycle, in which its materials increasingly became associated with the values of "realism." This would really come to a head with Wilder's next horror thriller, *The Lost Weekend*, but critics clearly used *Double Indemnity* to champion "realism" and oppose it to censorship. For example, writing on the attraction between its lead characters, Walter and Phyllis, an attraction that provides part of the motivation for their murder of Phyllis' husband within the film, the *New York Post* wrote: "The passion is not cloaked in the beauty of love. It's just a little raw, though effected in a smoothly realistic manner."[27] The reviewer therefore saw the film as an antidote to anyone "who has ever complained that the movies emphasize taffy-pull aspects of living." When critics discussed realism at this time, they defined it as a frank, unvarnished and incisive depiction of life that was opposed to the supposedly romanticized, glamorized and consoling presentations that were not only evident in the majority of Hollywood's output but were also defined as a product of censorship by the Production Code Administration. As a result, while the film was claimed to feature "the Cain characters with the full load of loathsomeness that the author saddled upon them,"[28] and to be preoccupied with the "seamier side of life,"[29] it was not condemned by critics but rather praised as "a landmark in the art of cinema."[30] Wilder was said to have "consistently avoided the sensational mannerisms" that would normally have been associated with this kind of material, and to have done so due to an admirable "singleness of realistic purpose." If it was a "grim" portrait of life, it was not a seedy film but rather "as grim a tale of human frailty as any since Eric Von Stroheim [sic] shot the works on the masterpiece, 'Greed'"— high praise indeed.

In contrast to these extraordinarily positive responses, the *New York Times* maintained that "the very toughness of the picture is also the weakness at its core,"[31] and suggested that the film was cold and lifeless. Like the other reviewers, it associated the film with the horror genre through the claim that it was "designed to freeze the marrow in an audience's bones," but it also proposed that "the sole question in this picture is whether Barbara Stanwyck and Fred MacMurray can kill a man with such cool and artistic deception that no one will place the blame on them." It is therefore a story only for such "folks as delight in murder stories for their academic elegance alone," and ends up a film of "monotonous pace," whose characters "lack the attractiveness to render their fates of emotional consequence." If the film has "a realism reminiscent of the bite of past French films," this allusion is not meant as a compliment, and Wilder is even accused of a psychological malevolence reminiscent of the disturbed villains of the period:

> He had detailed the stalking of their victim with the frigid thoroughness of a coroner's report, and he had pictured their psychological crack-up as a sadist

would pluck out the spider's legs. No objection to the temper of the picture: it is as hard and inflexible as steel.

In this way, the film is damned through its art-house associations with "French poetic realism," with the terms "artistic" and "academic" being synonymous with the "frigid" and "sadistic," a denial of everything that is vital and human, so that Edward G. Robinson's insurance investigator is "the only one you care two hoots for in the film."

Furthermore, although Barbara Stanwyck's character, Phyllis Dietrichson, is today seen as one of the iconic examples of the femme fatale, the reviews actually made little of this character and simply referred to her as "a destructively lurid female."[32] Stanwyck is praised for her performance, but there is little sense that Phyllis represents a particularly new or distinctive figure of femininity. Despite the common claim that the femme fatale was a reaction against the independent woman war worker,[33] Phyllis is hardly seen as representing the new feminine independence of the war years but rather its opposite, the selfish slacker. She is described as "a homicidal wife,"[34] a "girl who married a man for what financial security he can offer [but] is bored with her bargain."[35]

Nonetheless, *Double Indemnity* was to prove vital to the development of the "horror-thriller," and it marks a shift toward realism in both the 1940s horror cycle and its critical reception. As the *New York Times* claimed about the growing number of tough crime dramas being made by the studios:

> The apparent trend towards such materials, previously shunned for fear of censorship, is traced by observers to Paramount's successful treatment of the James M. Cain novel, "Double Indemnity," which was described by some producers as an emancipation for Hollywood writing.[36]

"Frank and Uncompromising": The Lost Weekend and the Realistic Horror Film

This shift to realism in the "horror-thrillers" was even more emphatic in the critical reception of Wilder's next film, *The Lost Weekend*. As we have seen, although many film histories see *Open City* as marking a shift in critical taste,[37] the critical celebration of realism can clearly be seen in reviews of Wilder's film, despite the fact that these reviews appeared a year before those for *Open City*. For these critics, realism was not primarily a matter of verisimilitude, but of social commentary, and it required a "frank and uncompromising" investigation of that which lay hidden, repressed or censored.[38]

Many critics saw *The Lost Weekend* as "a naturalistic horror picture,"[39] or even as "a realistic horror picture,"[40] a film that was generically identified as part of the 1940s horror cycle but was also seen as possessing a realism that enabled it to transcend the cycle. As a result, it was supposed to have "more shudders than any horror thriller,"[41] but also to feature "an almost nightmarish intensity"[42] that it was suggested made the film "terrifyingly real."[43] It is therefore hardly surprising that Kracauer lists it as one of the key examples of "Hollywood's Terror Films,"[44] and its capacity to terrify is commented on frequently in reviews: one scene is described as "unnervingly terrifying,"[45] while another reviewer referred to the same scene as one of "sheer, maniacal terror."[46] Furthermore, the film not only featured a "shocking and magnificent climax,"[47] but was also associated with horror through references to the "phantoms [that] pursue" its protagonist,[48] "the horrors of [his] five-day drunk,"[49] and the "horrors of [his] night in the psychopathic ward."[50]

Thus, while many reviews noted that the film "cannot be placed in the category of pleasant,"[51] they also presented the film's unpleasantness as its key virtue. Moreover, if many earlier examples of the 1940s horror cycle had been seen as examples of the woman's film,[52] many critics sought to distinguish *The Lost Weekend* from the feminine. They stressed that it "isn't a pretty picture"[53] and, while it might rank high amongst the best films of the year, it "certainly isn't the prettiest."[54] However, while the film was described as "horrible"[55] and even "sordid,"[56] it was also described as a "fascinating"[57] film that "is the most daring film that ever came out of Hollywood."[58] While the rest "of Hollywood merely took fright at any suggestion of putting this story of sordid drunkenness on the screen,"[59] the filmmakers are praised for producing "a picture of rare power and integrity"[60] that doesn't flinch from presenting its topic with "tremendous realism."[61] As a result, while it was praised for not being a tasteful, feminine film, it was also suggested that its distasteful elements made it "thoroughly adult."[62]

As a result, this "realism" was not restricted to the "wholly authentic" settings within which the story is located, but rather it was associated with the ways in which the film tackled "a real problem": the "plight of the dipsomaniac."[63] Furthermore, its depiction provides not only a description of the problem but an "almost clinical analysis"[64] that operates as "a study of the surface symptoms,"[65] but also at least tries to give some sense of the "inner motivations."[66] However, while some had reservations about its success in explaining these "inner motivations," or complained that there "is no opportunity to measure this complete portrait of the dipsomaniac in action against the man he once was,"[67] there was a strong sense that the film was not just a gripping "shocker," but that it was a brave and serious attempt to tackle a pressing social problem. Nor was praise for the film modest. For example, the *New York Herald Tribune* described it as "a milestone in movie-making" and "every inch a cinematic masterpiece,"[68] while the *New York World-Telegram* described it as "a miracle of inspired film craftsmanship."[69]

Similarly, the *New York Times* championed the film as "an over-whelming drama which every adult movie-goer should see,"[70] although it also had some reservations about the film. Again, it stressed the relation to horror and described the film as a "stark and terrifying study of a dipsomaniac" that "puts all recent 'horror' films to shame." In addition, it depicts "the gruesome details of five days in the life of a chronic lush" in ways that are "blood-chillingly real." As a result, while "this picture is not a gay evening on the town," it is an "adult" film that treats a serious topic with "honesty." Instead of "the usual phantasmagoric tricks" associated with psychological films, *The Lost Weekend* is praised for its "sharp, photographic comprehension," which results in "a shatteringly realistic and morbidly fascinating film." While the film is described as "a straight objective report, unvarnished with editorial comment," its "objectivity" is not simply a matter of describing or replicating the surfaces of social life. On the contrary, the *New York Times* terms the film "objective" to distance it from "temperance morality," but there is still a strong sense that "the ills of alcoholism and the pathos of its sufferers are most forcefully exposed and deeply pitied," while Ray Milland's performance "catches all the ugly nature of a 'drunk,' yet reveals the inner torment and degradation of a respectable man who knows his weakness and his shame."

Nonetheless, if the film "ranks with the best and most disturbing character studies ever put on the screen," the *New York Times* was also critical of one aspect of the film — "the reason for the 'dipso's' gnawing mania is not fully or convincingly explained" — and this absence is due to the film's omission of the novel's explanation: "an unconscious indecision in his own masculine libido." As a result, the film is seen as a brave exposure of social problems that is let down by its one concession to censorship, and rather than being condemned as pretentious for its psychological themes, its strengths are associated with its psychological realism, while its weakness is that it does not go deep enough psychologically.

Vienna, Berlin and Hollywood: Fantasy, Realism and the Return to Horror

Ed Sikov has noted the oddness of Wilder's choices as a director during the 1940s, with the oddest being *The Emperor Waltz*, "a light-hearted, musical farce-romance" that he selected as his follow-up to the Oscar-winning realism of *The Lost Weekend*.[71] However, if Wilder was attempting to distance himself from horror with this film and its follow-up, *A Foreign Affair*, he would return to the horror film at the end of the decade, with *Sunset Boulevard*. *The Emperor Waltz* was described as "a fanciful bubble" of a picture, and one that was distinguished by its sumptuous visual spectacle: "Picture it all in Technicolor, with the courtiers in flashing uniforms, the ladies in elegant dresses and Bing [Crosby] in an old straw hat, and you have a fair comprehension of the atmosphere." However, while "there's nothing staggering in the way of music or plot in this spoof," the scriptwriters "Brackett and Wilder have made up with casualness and charm — with a great deal of clever sight-humor — for the meagreness of the idea." Crosby is also seen as an asset so that, while nothing "he says is likely to be mistaken for deep philosophy," it was predicted that the film would do well and "should turn the blue Danube to tinkling gold."

Wilder's next film, a comic musical romance set in the troubled conditions of postwar Germany, is another strange creature, which features the odd juxtapositions of *Five Graves to Cairo*. Again, it was claimed that the skill of Wilder and Brackett as scriptwriters, and Wilder as a director, succeeded in blending these apparently incompatible materials. As the *New York Times* review of *A Foreign Affair* put it: "Maybe you think there's nothing funny about the current situation of American troops in the ticklish area of Berlin. And it's serious enough, heaven knows, what with the Russians pushing and shoving and the natives putting on their own type of squeeze."[72] However, the review also reassured its readers that the film was "a dandy entertainment," even if it did have "some shrewd and realistic things to say." In other words, while it was seen as an entertaining romance, it was not seen as a "fanciful bubble" but as a serious social commentary on "how human beings behave when confronted by other human beings." Rather than simply applying idealistic standards to the complex moral issues of the black market and "fraternization" with foreigners, Wilder and his associate "have looked realistically upon the obvious temptations and reactions of healthy soldiers far from home."

However, while "this sort of traffic with big stuff in the current events department might be offensive to reason and taste" in a romantic comedy, if it had been given a "less clever presentation," it is argued that the director and his co-writer have the "wit, worldliness and charm" to achieve a perfect blend of elements rather than a distasteful clash. They have therefore "made these observations in a spirit of fun and romance," although "there is bite, nonetheless, in the comment which the whole picture has to make upon the irony of big state restrictions." Indeed, the realism, commentary and humor all come together precisely through the sense that these filmmakers are opposed to restrictions and censorship:

> For the Messrs. Brackett and Wilder, who are not the sort to call a spade a trowel, as was eminently proved by their honest and hard-hitting "The Lost Weekend," are here making light of regulations and the gravity of officialdom in a smoothly sophisticated and slyly sardonic way.

If the film "has serious implications," the filmmakers "have been happily disinclined to wax morose about the problems presented by the population," and achieve a "sophisticated" tone through a "sardonic" and "cynical" attitude. To put it another way, their social criticism is accomplished precisely through the humorous rejection of pomposity. Certainly, this attitude could be criticized as a classic liberal refusal of position, but it depends on creating the sense of blend and balance in which extremes are ridiculed and rejected, an attitude position that fits perfectly with the climate of postwar culture, particularly in the war-torn city of Berlin.

However, while these films saw a move away from horror, even if *A Foreign Affair* was still seen as closely allied to the realism of *Double Indemnity* and *The Lost Weekend*, Wilder returned to horror in 1950 with *Sunset Boulevard*. Indeed, the association with horror was clear in the reviews, which referred to this "frank, caustic drama"[73] as a "great motion picture"[74] that was both "eerie"[75] and "macabre."[76] Not only did it feature a "shock effect" that "is at least as high as that of such earlier Brackett & Wilder productions as the alcoholic *Lost Weekend*,"[77] but it was also claimed to have "the mood of a good ghost story: a pet chimpanzee is solemnly buried by candlelight; the wind sighs through a pipe organ; rats scurry across the bottom of an empty pool."[78] Even the film's main setting is described as "a mausoleum-like Hollywood mansion" that has been preserved down "to the last monstrous detail." While Norma Desmond, the aging movie star around whom the story revolves, is often referred as a classic femme fatale today, she was clearly related to the psychologically disturbed killers of the horror cycle of the mid–1940s. She is "a faded, aging silent screen star,"[79] who seduces "a penniless cynical young script writer," Joe Gillis, with "easy comforts,"[80] before finally murdering him in a homicidal rage at the end of the film. However, the murder is not simply a crime of passion, and she is described as a psychologically deranged figure: "a hopeless egomaniac" and a "psychopathic star."

Moreover, if the femme fatale is often claimed to be a backlash against the independent woman of the war years, Norma is hardly a figure of independence. On the contrary, she is a "wealthy, egotistical relic," who is entirely obsessed with her own image and dependent on the illusion of the adoration of her fans: "the millions of people who have never forgiven me for deserting the screen." In other words, she is not only "desperately yearning to hear again the plaudits of the crowd," but exists in a fantasy world that others are required to maintain for her, particularly the character played by Erich von Stroheim who is described as "the dedicated guardian of her self-centred dream."[81] This dependence and denial is also a feature of her passive-aggressive relationship with Gillis: when "an attachment with a girl his own age jolts him out of his abyss," she "holds him down with lavish gifts and an attempted suicide." Norma's rival operates in overt opposition to the aging star: she is not only young but an independent woman, "a studio reader, with writing ambitions." While the femme fatale is commonly seen as a figure of seductive sexuality, Gillis is seduced instead by Norma's money. Indeed, he is the one who uses his sexuality to seduce her, or at least he "does nothing strenuous to thwart her unsubtle romantic blandishments," and is therefore referred to as "a kept man" and a "gigolo."

Reviewers did have one significant complaint about the film, suggesting it was marred by the fact that "the authors permit Joe Gillis to take us into the story of his life after his bullet-ridden body is lifted out of Norma Desmond's swimming pool."[82] Although this is often praised today as an audacious device, it was referred to as "completely unworthy of Brackett and Wilder." One of the reasons for this may have been precisely that it was too reminiscent of the kinds of trickery often associated with radio horror at the time, a form that was seen as vulgar and sensationalist. However, despite this supposed lapse, critics tended to praise the film as a "frank, caustic drama,"[83] which was once again celebrated for its "realism," and for the cleverness with which its authors had prevented "an essentially tawdry romance from becoming distasteful and embarrassing." As a result, reviewers suggested that the film not only "quickly casts a spell over its audience" but also "holds it enthralled to a shattering climax."

Conclusion

As we have seen, then, despite perceptions of Wilder today as a director of film noir and/or comedy, during the 1940s he was understood as one of the horror genre's key directors, and as a figure crucial to its transformation from Gothic fantasy to contemporary realism. Furthermore, his ability to circumvent the restrictions of the Production Code Administration was seen as central to not only establishing a model for other horror films, but also for a more general "emancipation" of Hollywood filmmaking.

The critical reception of Billy Wilder's films also demonstrates that, while horror is strongly associated with fantasy today, the genre was actually central to discourses of cinematic realism during the 1940s. While later periods would associate horror with Gothic fantasy and the thriller with contemporary realism, the 1940s was a period not only in which such distinctions had not yet come into being, but in which horror was actually essential to debates about realism and understood as a genre crucially concerned with the attempt to plumb social and psychological taboos.

Notes

1. Naremore, *More than Night*, 81.
2. See Jancovich, "Thrills and Chills," 157–71.
3. Of course, Wilder was actually Austrian, but it is hardly surprising that Hollywood failed to appreciate such a distinction, particularly given that he had worked for UFA.
4. Crowther, "'Phantom Lady,'" 15.
5. Koepnick, "Doubling the Double," 85. See also Koepnick, *The Dark Mirror*.
6. Koepnick, 85.
7. Greco, *The File on Robert Siodmak in Hollywood*, 4.
8. See Jancovich, "'Two Ways of Looking.'"
9. As Elsaesser points out, expressionist films made up only a small part of German film production during the Weimar period, despite the fact that it has come to be seen as representative of German output within the period. Elsaesser, *Weimar and After*.
10. One example of this is Hitchcock's *The Lodger* (1927), a story of Jack the Ripper in which he drew heavily on expressionism.

11. Jancovich, "Thrills and Chills."
12. Biesen, *Blackout*; Hanson, *Hollywood Heroines*.
13. Jancovich, "Bluebeard's Wives" and "Crack-Up."
14. Jancovich, "Phantom Ladies."
15. Jancovich, "'Female Monsters.'"
16. Crowther, "'Phantom Lady,'" 15.
17. Crowther, "The Screen: 'The Major and the Minor,'" 21.
18. Crowther, "'Five Graves to Cairo,'" 21.
19. See Shearer, "Crime Certainly Pays on the Screen," 77. See also Sikov, *On Sunset Boulevard*.
20. Cameron, "'Double Indemnity,'" 253.
21. Creelman, "'Double Indemnity,'" 254.
22. Cook, "Double Indemnity Excels," 253.
23. Barnes, "Double Indemnity," 253.
24. Youngkin, *The Lost One*.
25. Cameron, "'Double Indemnity,'" 254.
26. See Klinger on the "adult film" in the late 1940s and the 1950s in *Melodrama and Meaning*.
27. Winsten, "Warning to Insurance Fakers," 253.
28. Cook, "Double Indemnity Excels," 253.
29. Winsten, "Warning to Insurance Fakers," 253.
30. Cook, "Double Indemnity Excels," 253.
31. Crowther, "Double Indemnity," 21.
32. Ibid., 21.
33. Cook, "Duplicity in Mildred Pierce."
34. Barnes, "Double Indemnity," 253.
35. Cook, "Double Indemnity Excels," 253.
36. Stanley, "Hollywood Crime and Romance," X1.
37. See, for example, Staiger, *Interpreting Films*.
38. Crowther, "'The Lost Week-End,'" 28.
39. "The New Pictures" (December 3, 1945).
40. Cameron, "'Lost Weekend,'" 90.
41. Creelman, "'Lost Weekend,'" 93.
42. Pelswick, "'Weekend,'" 92.
43. Barnes, "'Lost Weekend,'" 90.
44. Kracauer, "Hollywood's Terror Films."
45. Pelswick, "'Weekend,'" 92.
46. Cook, "'Lost Weekend,'" 91.
47. Barnes, "'Lost Weekend,'" 90.
48. Cook, "'Lost Weekend,'" 91.
49. Pelswick, 92.
50. Creelman, "'Lost Weekend,'" 93.
51. Winsten, "Calling All Drunks," 91.
52. Jancovich, "Bluebeard's Wives."
53. Pelswick, 92.
54. McManus, "Ray Milland KO's Kid Booze," 92.
55. Cameron, "'Lost Weekend,'" 90.
56. Barnes, "'Lost Weekend,'" 90.
57. Cameron, "'Lost Weekend,'" 90.
58. Ibid., 90.
59. Cook, "'Lost Weekend,'" 91.

60. Winsten, "Calling All Drunks," 91.
61. Pelswick, 92.
62. Creelman, 93.
63. Pelswick, 92.
64. Creelman, 93.
65. McManus, 92.
66. Ibid., 92.
67. Winsten, "Calling All Drunks," 91.
68. Barnes, "'Lost Weekend,'" 90.
69. Cook, "'Lost Weekend,'" 91.
70. Crowther, "'The Lost Week-End,'" 28.
71. Crowther, "Bing Crosby Rambles," 19.
72. Crowther, "Jean Arthur, Marlene Dietrich and John Land a Triangle," 19.
73. T.M.P., "Gloria Swanson Returns to the Movies," 15.
74. Ibid.
75. "The New Pictures" (August 14, 1950).
76. Clurman, "Movies: Very Clever," 22.
77. "The New Pictures" (August 14, 1950).
78. Ibid.
79. T.M.P., "Gloria Swanson Returns to the Movies," 15.
80. Ibid.
81. "The New Pictures" (August 14, 1950).
82. T.M.P., "Gloria Swanson Returns to the Movies," 15.
83. Ibid.

Part Two: Representation, Image and Identity

5. *Shame and the Single Girl*
Reviving Fran and Falling for Baxter in *The Apartment*

ALISON R. HOFFMAN

Premiering the same weekend in June of 1960, both Billy Wilder's *The Apartment* and Alfred Hitchcock's *Psycho* thrust the subjects of illicit sex and gender trouble onto American movie screens, the latter using horror to shock audiences into a sexualized frenzy, and the former fusing romantic comedy with dramatic melancholy. Like *Psycho*, *The Apartment* conflates the sexuality of its working-class "single girl" with pain and death, suggestively drawing audiences up-close to her morally ambiguous sexual desire, and then, in an abusive gesture, punishing her for that desire. However, unlike *Psycho*'s Marion Crane, *The Apartment*'s leading single girl, Fran Kubelik (Shirley MacLaine), makes it out of her film's narrative world alive, though just barely. Caught between the neo–Victorianism of the 1950s and the coming sexual revolution of the late 1960s, Fran is mired in her simultaneous, contradictory sexual and socio-economic desires. Her job as an elevator operator in a New York City skyscraper housing a large insurance corporation, Consolidated Life, affords her social engagement and (limited) economic mobility in the public sphere, just as it — as the company's name suggests — restricts her in a space of constant sexual harassment and gender discrimination. She sleeps with Consolidated's Director of Personnel, her older, married boss, Jeff Sheldrake (Fred MacMurray), while she longs for a safe, "stable" marriage of her own; she enjoys the freedoms of living single, yet appears starved for domestic companionship. Unraveled by her desires and their mistreatment and abuse by Sheldrake, who literally treats her as a commodity by attempting to pay for the sexual relationship he has had with her over several months, Fran becomes flooded with shame. On Christmas Eve, her shame becomes so overwhelming, she attempts suicide by overdosing on sleeping pills in the apartment that, like her body, is rented out to Consolidated's executives for their extra-marital trysts. The young man who "rents" out this apartment and discovers Fran's nearly lifeless body, C.C. "Bud" Baxter (Jack Lemmon), already has a painful crush on her. Baxter is a lonely and single underling at Consolidated who similarly suffers, but also benefits, from the company's executives' power abuses. In exchange for loaning out his bachelor apartment to his philandering bosses, Baxter receives promotions at work, climbing the corporate ladder vis-à-vis his complicity in its hierarchical status quo: the gendered and sexualized system of power and dominance that privileges and maintains a lying and cheating white capitalist patriarchy.

Yet Fran's attempted suicide — the hard truth of her punished body and the stakes of its survival — throw a wrench into that system. After a lengthy and rather brutal section at the film's mid-point when Baxter and his neighbor, Dr. Dreyfuss (Jack Kruschen), revive Fran through a series of various "shocks" to her body (i.e., induced vomiting, multiple cups of hot coffee, hard slaps to her face, forced marching throughout the night), a small revolution, sexual and gender-wise, begins to foment in the apartment, transforming the space and its inhabitants from white capitalist patriarchy's conformists to its misfits. As Baxter, happily embracing his role as nurturer and caregiver, nurses Fran back to health over the course of a few days, the two radically open up to one another, confessing and sharing their individual shame: accepting, mirroring, and, ultimately, embracing her sexual "immorality" and his failure to master (or even his failure to completely *desire to master*) phallic masculinity. By New Year's Eve, both Fran and Baxter have decidedly rejected the patriarchal system that has compartmentalized and abused them, tossing off its rules and initiating their own set of ethics grounded in interdependence and a subtly queer, gender-bending tenderness. Quite explicitly, the film posits white capitalist patriarchy and its rigid performance of phallic masculinity as unethical, empty, and ultimately, undesirable.

While many critics interpreted *The Apartment* as being "preoccupied with sex,"[1] and, indeed, its overt sexual themes were bold for a Hollywood product circulating in the cinematic marketplace in the early 1960s, nonetheless, I see and *experience it*, more accurately and tellingly, as being preoccupied with shame. Existing "equally strongly in men and women,"[2] shame is "the affect of indignity, of transgression and alienation."[3] Since shame is an affect, it works and appears physiologically, yet it is produced through experience, and when it is witnessed, it most often transfers like a "quickly spreading and flooding" contagion to the person(s) looking on.[4] Hence, shame is produced within and through discourse, yet it manifests itself — as a physiological affect — at the site of and through the body. Drawing from recent theories on shame by various scholars and psychologists, along with cultural histories of both the sixties' "single girl" and postwar non-phallic masculinities, I hope to brush against and illuminate *The Apartment*'s anticipatory modeling of new kinds of misfit, sexually revolutionary gendered subjectivities vis-à-vis its productive use of shame and, hence, its idiosyncratic mode of *counter-shaming*. While I have no interest in recovering *The Apartment* as a proto-feminist or queer film, especially considering its very conventional aestheticization of the victimized and punished single girl's body, I am interested in how, through form and content, it uses shame *productively* to first acknowledge, then accept, and even slightly promote, active female sexuality and desire, and alternative, more vulnerable, feminine forms of white masculinity.

The Apartment, a decidedly American shame text of the mid-century, lays bare and even wallows in the shame experienced by those partially incorporated, but ultimately outside of, white capitalist patriarchy — those troubling and weakening its ideological and economic power through resistant performances of semi-promiscuous female sexuality, and feminine male vulnerability. Importantly, through its use of comedy and empathic interaffectivity expressed through mise en scène and editing, Wilder's film comes to lovingly embrace its characters' shame, encouraging audiences to simultaneously situate themselves within its affective space and imagine more progressive possibilities that lie elsewhere, ahead in time. In this way, I believe, *The Apartment* anticipated and helped clear a path towards the coming sexual and gender revolution. While perhaps "the political agenda of the 1960s did not produce the utopia it promised, the sexual revolution resulted in an irrevocable reconfiguration of identity."[5]

Shame Theories

"You say that shame cannot make a revolution. I answer that shame is itself already a revolution."[6] — Karl Marx

Quite appropriately, shame as a subject and distinct psycho-somatic phenomenon itself remained hidden until the years marked by the sexual revolution, a time when both counter-cultural movements and then popular culture encouraged everybody to "let it all hang out." Beginning in the early 1970s, psychologists finally outed shame through an outpouring of literature "redressing a long-standing neglect of the subject."[7] Shame theorist Helen Block Lewis argues that a key reason for the closeting of shame can be attributed to "a prevailing sexist attitude in science, which pays less attention to nurturance than to aggression"; however, once the literature on shame began to flow, it became "apparent that, although it is easily ignored, shame is ubiquitous."[8] Later on, from the 1980s to the new millennium, an increased interest in shame marked the fields of psychology and the humanities, "most notably in the work of affect and shame theorists like Tomkins, Lewis, and Donald Nathanson."[9]

Nathanson's seminal text on the subject, *Shame and Pride: Affect, Sex, and the Birth of the Self* (1992), elaborates on Tomkins' hypothesis that shame is a biological affect occurring "whenever desire outruns fulfillment."[10] Shame engulfs us when we must withdraw from positive affect, so "we cannot feel shame where there is nothing to lose." Alas, "whoever feels shame the most is the most desirous of positive affect; whoever feels shame the least has renounced most successfully the goal of positive affect."[11] In Nathanson's formulation, those experiencing the deepest shame are also those experiencing the deepest yearnings—yearning for recognition and connection with another person, yearning for something that exceeds the typical boundaries of social acceptability and normativity. When that yearning hits up against negative affect, shame spreads over the body, remarkably shifting one's comportment: withdrawal sets in, the shoulders sink down and slump, the skin blushes, and the eyes avert, desperately attempting to avoid contact with other faces and, especially, other eyes. Shame, indeed, is the affect most closely integrated with sight.[12]

So strong is shame's affective potency that simply bearing witness to another person's shame causes it to spread; in other words, "seeing shame itself provokes a shame response."[13] Queer theorist Eve Kosofsky Sedgwick, in her brilliant study of shame in literature, considers this contagious quality of the shame affect:

> One of the strangest features of shame—but perhaps also the one that offers the most conceptual leverage for projects like ours—is the way bad treatment of someone else, bad treatment by someone else, someone else's embarrassment, stigma, debility, bad smell, or strange behavior, seemingly have nothing to do with me, can so readily flood me—assuming I'm a shame-prone person—with this sensation whose very suffusiveness seems to delineate my precise, individual outlines in the most isolating way imaginable.[14]

Shame's power to infect and flood those who witness it cannot be overlooked, and this contagious quality of shame raises important questions related to visuality in general, and cinematic spectatorship, in particular. Certainly, as film theorist Liza Johnson argues, "cinema is flooded and flooding with affect; its absorptions move the viewing subject to tears or laughter or fear or sadness, and shame is no exception."[15] Much later in this piece, I want to return to the space—or the encounter—where shame's contagion and cinematic spectatorship collide, and how *The Apartment* carefully negotiates this collision, managing to keep its audience's eyes glued to the screen, despite its many dense spectacles of shame.

Before shifting the discussion there, though, the discursive elements of shame must first be fleshed out. Expanding on Tomkins' formulation of shame as a bio-physiological affect, Nathanson's work takes it a crucial step further, situating shame within the realm of discourse. Nathanson finds that affects, though working on and through our bodies, emanate from the social world and an historical space and time: affects, he finds, are conditioned by context. The affect of shame, especially, is both encultured and individuated, social and bio-logical. Nathanson writes:

> Each individual will form, for shame as well as for other affects, a lexicon of ideoaffective complexes based on the interplay of nature and experience.... Our lifetime of shame experiences will form our archive of shame and thereby influence for each of us the development of the self.[16]

So the affect of shame is differentiated for every individual based on their "archive" of experiences, and that archive is conditioned by the social world and its cultural codes. Shame, according to Nathanson, functions like a feedback loop: it both reflects and produces the social and cultural, forming and regulating identities. In fact, "shame becomes the most social of the negative affects because it modulates, regulates, impedes, contains, the interest and enjoyment that power all sociality."[17] The power of shame, Nathanson believes, is so strong that it constitutes a "primary force in social and political evolution," and "our reaction to it and our avoidance of it ... becomes the emotion of politics and conformity."[18]

Nathanson's implications about shame's social power here are massive and, I believe, extraordinarily useful when thinking through the radically shifting politics of culture and bodies in the U.S. between the post–World War II years and the Vietnam War era, periods signifying, respectively, conformity and non-conformity to the ideals, regulations, and phobias of a distinctly American brand of white capitalist patriarchy. Writing specifically about sexuality, Nathanson locates the cultural revolution of the sixties as a *counter-shaming* movement that worked to undo the "shame associated with everything about sex in the 1950s"—an "era of change [when] sex itself moved from the shadows onto its own stage."[19] In this respect, *The Apartment*, in its loving recognition and display of sexual and gender-related shame, helped clear the air for the initiation of the sexual revolution's counter-shaming project. By centering his narrative on and encouraging audiences to easily identify with a sexually active single girl and a non-phallic man who, quite overwhelmingly, display the bodily symptoms or *comportments of shame* due to their inability to fully incorporate themselves into the world of white capitalist patriarchy (and then, in a counter-shaming move, they reject that world altogether), Wilder constructed, in my view, a deceptively potent argument in praise of non-normative, misfit sexualities and genders. That he managed to do this through persuasive doses of comedy is especially meaningful, since, not surprisingly, "laughter is the best defense against shame."[20]

Shame on Fran

> "Suitably and unwittingly, the task of clearing the air and loosening public inhibitions fell to Shirley MacLaine. In *The Apartment* ... she makes kookiness sad, not elegant; promiscuity human, not trashy."[21]—
> Marjorie Rosen

If ever there existed an actress perfectly poised, in 1960, to play *The Apartment*'s role of the shame-laden single girl, Fran Kubelik, it was Shirley MacLaine. As Rosen's words suggest, one of the most enabling aspects of MacLaine's stardom throughout the 1960s, and particularly in *The Apartment*, was "clearing the air" and "loosening public inhibitions" when it came to sex. Rosen conjectures that MacLaine's "elfin soulful innocence ... shielded her from public outrage."[22] The fact that MacLaine's sexually promiscuous roles of the sixties all manage to perfectly balance "feminine virtue with unconventionality" also provides compelling reasons as to why her star shone so brightly during that decade, despite it being tarnished by countless overtly sexual scenes.[23] As film historian Hillary Radner, writing about women in American cinema of the 1960s, suggests, representations of the single girl in Hollywood films of that decade "present a utopian fantasy of a woman free from the social and sexual constraints that appeared to limit her mother. Her girlishness also responds to and contains the anxieties that a woman no longer under the yoke of patriarchy (yet is still subject to the whims of capital) might evoke."[24] MacLaine's own career echoes this duplicitous position of the single girl — at once independent from and dependent on patriarchal structures, simultaneously working for and victimized by male dominance in the public sphere. In a revealing memoir about her work in Hollywood, *My Lucky Stars*, MacLaine precisely recognizes this double bind, coming to consciousness that she "had carved a career out of playing victims," and particularly, victims of the sexualized, single girl variety.[25]

Adding to Rosen's points and MacLaine's sharp insights about her own on-screen roles of the decade, I am struck by the thickness of shame MacLaine inhabits and exudes in nearly every one of her parts throughout the sixties, and how so many of these films metonymically link single girl sexuality with death. For example, in William Wyler's *The Children's Hour* (1961), MacLaine's character, Martha, becomes so overwhelmed and shamed by her lesbian desire for her friend Karen (Audrey Hepburn) that she hangs herself. In Robert Wise's *Two for the Seesaw* (1962), MacLaine is cast as a beatnik dancer pining for the affections of an older man who ultimately leaves her to return to his wife. Over the course of that film, MacLaine's single girl character, Gittel, becomes pregnant and nearly dies from an illegal abortion. *Woman Times Seven* (1967) features MacLaine playing seven different sexually obsessed women in seven short films about adultery. In one of these short films, simply entitled *Suicides*, MacLaine's character makes a suicide pact with her lover. Finally, at the end of the decade, MacLaine was typecast yet again in Bob Fosse's musical *Sweet Charity* (1969), playing a sex worker with a heart of gold who nearly drowns after being pushed off a bridge by her boyfriend. While the sameness of these parts speaks to Hollywood's ubiquitous lack of imagination and diversity when constructing women's characters, and its perverse mode of continually punishing those characters, MacLaine's roles and performances of the 1960s particularly register the dense anxiety hovering around single girl sexuality. Indeed, *The*

Apartment largely contributed to establishing these trends for MacLaine, and the sixties-era celluloid single girl in general. Yet at the same time, Wilder's film, unlike the others mentioned above, never trivializes its single girl's excessive desire (and, hence, shame), opting instead to take it seriously, and encouraging audiences to (perhaps contagiously) empathize.

Reviewing the film before its premiere, the *Hollywood Reporter*'s movie critic James Powers wrote of his empathy with her character. Powers perceptively describes Fran's shame-prone contagiousness and how it promoted his own empathy and, most likely, similar reactions in other audience members. Powers notes that MacLaine's performance of Fran produces "acute identification, so strong it hurts."[26] Scanning the film's numerous displays of shame, I find that one of the most "acute" ways it works to establish this painfully strong identification with Fran is through its many close-ups of her shame-comported body, especially her face: her slumped shoulders, withdrawn posture, downcast eyes glazed over in withdrawal, and often her abundant tears and sobs. In the three scenes that couple Fran with Sheldrake, the affective flood of shame takes over her body, and after her Christmas Eve encounter with him, Fran enacts the ultimate gesture of shame, attempted suicide. During these scenes, Wilder centers the frame on Fran's face, allowing the dramatic and affective weight of the moment to build slowly and steadily through the gradual shift in her comportment from relative ease to withdrawal to total shame. The "acute identification" that Powers locates in the film resonates during these intense, painful moments. Their intensity is amplified by Sheldrake's complete lack of empathy with Fran and, certainly, an equally complete lack of his own personal shame or even ethical self-awareness.

MacMurray's Sheldrake, described as "detestable" by Powers, demonstrates an affective indifference to Fran's desire and shame. One particularly colorful review describes Sheldrake as embodying a "sleazy nastiness," a "horrible symposium of all the treachery and wet-lipped lechery of the middle-aged man determined on an extra-marital sex life."[27] Sheldrake, entitled and certainly "sleazy," interacts with Fran as if she is just another object of exchange, a female body existing solely for his pleasure. His empty or total lack of identification with Fran works to heighten and increase ours as spectators. Slyly, *The Apartment* nudges viewers to disidentify with an embodiment of white capitalist patriarchy by representing Sheldrake's emotional register as one of falseness and cruel indifference. Without a doubt, throughout the film our empathy is disciplined towards the shame-laden single girl.

The film also encourages spectatorial identification with Fran by way of two key shame-laden objects: her shattered compact mirror, and the one hundred dollar bill given to her by Sheldrake. Fran's compact mirror makes its first appearance at the moment when she and Sheldrake meet at their usual public-yet-semi-private space, Rickshaw, an underground, dimly-lit Chinese restaurant. At this moment in the film, as Fran sits across from Sheldrake in their slightly hidden booth, sipping a frozen daiquiri, she offers a soliloquy to him about the loneliness of her single girl life: the repetitive nature of their illicit relationship, the typicality of married men's "summer flings" with the "elevator girl" or the "manicurist," and the "ugly" nature of her own rationalizations for participating in such a relationship in the first place. Her comportment is one of shame, of course, her eyes soon become watery. As Sheldrake attempts to reassure her, promising that he is in the midst of planning a divorce from his wife, Fran pulls out her compact mirror and attempts to fix herself up. The next day, when Sheldrake comes to visit Baxter in his newly acquired "junior executive" office, Fran's compact reappears. Baxter pulls it from his pocket and hands it to Sheldrake, telling him that he found it on his couch, and that the mirror "was broken when I found it." Sheldrake responds with a laugh and a smile: "Yeah, she threw it at me. You know how it is. Sooner or later they always give you a bad time. You see a girl a couple of times a week and right away they assume you're going to divorce your wife. Now I ask you, is that fair?" Here, Sheldrake's reaction to the mirror exposes both the level of his deceit with Fran, and his extreme narcissism. The third and final moment when Fran's compact mirror appears is a pivotal one, as it reveals to Baxter that Fran is, indeed, Sheldrake's girl on the side, not the "nice, respectable girl" he perceived her to be. Baxter's realization about Fran and Sheldrake's affair devastates his own romantic hopes, just as it further rattles his faith in Consolidated's corporate ethics. This scene also makes explicit the severity of the deep shame that Fran embodies as a result of her affair with Sheldrake. During the office Christmas party, again in Baxter's office, Fran hands Baxter the mirror to check out how he looks in his new "junior executive" bowler hat. Instantly, Baxter recognizes the broken mirror, handing it back to Fran with shattered resignation. Fran grabs it, pronouncing that she likes the broken mirror the way it is, stating, "It makes me look the way I feel." At this point, Fran displays her shame both self-reflexively and to Baxter, albeit somewhat unknowingly. For the first time in the film, Baxter's cheery perception of Fran shifts, and immediately he becomes a witness to her shame, becoming a bit flooded by it himself.

If the broken compact mirror symbolizes Fran's fractured sense of self-worth, then *The Apartment*'s second shame object, the one hundred dollar bill from Sheldrake, functions as a final shattering blow to that fracture. The money that Sheldrake hastily gives Fran — straight from his money clip, no less — as a last-minute "Christmas gift" during their Christmas Eve rendezvous in Baxter's apartment, sets her shame over the edge, nearly breaking her to death. Fran refuses to actually take the money from Sheldrake's hand, so he places it in her purse himself. She then stands up and proceeds to undress, vacantly presenting her body to Sheldrake since, as she puts it, it has "already been paid for." After Sheldrake leaves to catch the train home to his suburban, picture-perfect family, Fran wanders around Baxter's apartment, sobbing uncontrollably. She later tries to pull herself together, but then finds the one hundred dollar bill in her purse. She stares at it, stares at herself in the mirror, and then, with resolve, overdoses on sleeping pills. When Baxter finds her that evening, he notices an envelope on the night table next to Fran's body; the envelope is scrawled with Sheldrake's name. Opening the envelope with Fran's consent, after she's been revived, several scenes later, Baxter finds the one hundred dollar bill. In a symbolic move, Fran insists that Baxter return this shameful, "pay off" money to its owner. With this return, Fran begins to assert her refusal to any longer be Sheldrake's salable sex object. Through this bold refusal of his money, Fran slowly begins her systematic rejection of white capitalist patriarchy and her attachments to those representative of it. Returning Sheldrake's money, and in such dramatic fashion no less, Fran says "no" to power, and takes a step towards a different, more equitable kind of cultural economy.

Shame on Baxter

> "What does it mean to turn away from the phallus, to refuse to cathect to its dictates, to turn away from it and reject shame?"[28]— Sally Munt

While the phallus looms large in my perception and interpretation of *The Apartment*'s configuration of mid-century masculinity, most scholarship on the film situates its male characters within the parameters of various fifties-era pop-sociologists' accounts of the "organization man."[29] Male intellectuals and writers such as William Whyte, David Riesman, and C. Wright Mills penned popular, critically-praised sociological studies of "what they perceived as a dangerous and growing conformity in the United States," the loss of individuality and moxie in the (typically white) American male due to his "other-directed-ness," a desire to please and fall in step with both his superiors and peers.[30] Similarly, novelists John Cheever and Sloan Wilson, particularly in the latter's best-selling *The Man in the Gray Flannel Suit* (1955), warned readers against the societal dangers that arise when white men align themselves too closely to the logic of the American corporation and its enervating, stultifying demands of "success" at all costs. A central fear and shameful image lay at the heart of these pop-psychologists' and novelists' analyzes: a "new feminized man who had lost his traditional manhood."[31] Though *The Apartment* weaves in threads inspired by the "organization man's" pressure to conform at the workplace, and certainly the film presents a pessimistic view of the corporation altogether, Wilder's vision, significantly, does not encode any fears of male feminization. In fact, it does quite the opposite. The film posits that, indeed, corruption and ethics of domination rule the landscape and politics of the American corporation. Yet, unlike the pop-psychologists and novelists Wilder may have drawn inspiration from, he instead envisions traditional masculinity *as the problem*, not the answer. With *The Apartment*, Wilder locates the corporation's politics of corruption and domination as symptoms of a larger disease: "traditional manhood," as it is idealized by white capitalist patriarchy. Refreshingly forward-thinking and non-nostalgic for a "lost" or buried masculinity, *The Apartment* anticipates new kinds of masculinity, relishing in the spirit of Felix Guattari's much later assertion that "if a man breaks away from the phallic rat race inherent in all power formations, he will become involved in ... feminine becoming."[32] And that's a good thing, human-wise.

Becoming a "human being," or, as Dr. Dreyfuss puts it, "a mensch," requires Baxter to first become more feminine and, later, to embrace that femininity — not to be ashamed of it. Yet, as the film establishes Baxter's character through both his relationship to his bosses at Consolidated, especially Sheldrake, and his location within the mise en scène, it becomes apparent that Baxter's gender identity and its bodily expression fuses the feminine with the masculine. If Sheldrake's comportment typifies phallic masculinity and patriarchal entitlement — tall, upright, controlled, confident, big, self-interested, indifferent to others — then Baxter's represents its opposite. Baxter's failure to fully master Consolidated's executives' style of masculinity makes him a "schnook" in their eyes, and, often, they refer to him as such. Baxter's "schnooky" body, compared to Sheldrake's, appears small and insubstantial, hunched over, submissive, and weak with illness. Obsessively concerned with his appearance, and, specifically, whether or not he is getting his performance of the "junior executive" right, Baxter exhibits an extraordinary amount of self-consciousness throughout the film, so much so that he frequently loses control of himself, bodily and verbally. In his heightened self-consciousness, Baxter finds himself constantly slipping, spilling, and saying things he shouldn't be saying. Try as he might, Baxter just cannot contain himself, and in the mid-century, white capitalist patriarchal economy that he attempts to fit into, that's a problem. Within Western patriarchal culture, in general, that's a problem, and, more specifically, a *feminine* problem. Shame theorist Sally Munt elaborates on this problem, sketching out how "within Western traditions of psychology and psychoanalysis a healthy person is one that knows how to manage and contain 'their' emotions within the individual self. This masculine bounded self has become ubiquitously aspirational, its reverse is found in the feminine."[33] Baxter, indeed, lacks those boundaries required for a successful performance of a tightly "bound" masculinity; physically and emotionally he is unfurled and shame-prone. Lemmon's frenetically embodied performance as Baxter, as it is contextualized through the film's mise en scène and editing, revels in this unbounded-ness, and, hence, femininity. That Lemmon played a "temporary transvestite" in Wilder's *Some Like It Hot* just one year before the release of *The Apartment* also heightens the femininity of his body and persona.[34] Perhaps in its most radical move, *The Apartment* ultimately privileges Baxter's non-phallic, feminine maleness over conventional phallic displays of patriarchal masculinity. In this regard, Wilder's film, by its conclusion, shifts away from the phallus, and refuses "to cathect to its dictates," powerfully turning from it and repudiating shame.[35]

Baxter's body functions as that which enables such a rejection. Throughout the course of the film, it represents just about everything else but a phallic symbol, and, as such, his character offers a compelling example of postwar "deviant" masculinity, a type of masculinity "whose defining desires and identifications are 'perverse' with respect not so much to a moral as to a phallic standard."[36] Even though the penis is not the phallus, but simply "the object in which notions of power are grounded" in a patriarchal society, Baxter never seems to be concerned with his.[37] While all of Consolidated's executives obsessively worry about when and for how long they will get the chance to use their penises to have sex with their mistresses in Baxter's apartment, once Baxter actually gets *the girl they all want* alone in his bed, his desires seem far more emotional than prurient. He's much more interested in caring for Fran, rather than fucking her (or, for that matter, fucking her over). In fact, early on in the film when Baxter's neighbor, Dr. Dreyfuss, mistakenly assumes that he's doing an excessive amount of fucking and asks if he will donate his body to science once he dies, Baxter responds with a shrug and a laugh: "My body? I'm afraid you guys would be disappointed." Quite simply, his penis (and penetrating women with it) just doesn't concern him much.

Situated within his apartment, a domestic space in which he takes pride, Baxter also turns away from phallic masculinity, taking pleasure in the feminine. Home alone, eating his frozen dinner while watching television, his popular cultural tastes reveal his overwhelming preference for the feminine over the absurdly phallic: uninterested in excessive displays of violent masculinity found on Western-themed programs that occupy the televisual space of almost all the channels on his TV, Baxter much prefers to tune into *Grand Hotel*, a melodrama starring Greta Garbo and Joan Crawford from 1932. At home and in the workplace, Baxter situates himself into more feminine activities and performances of gender. During various points in the film, he takes on the typically feminine roles of maid (cleaning up after his bosses), secretary (diligently scheduling "appointments" for them while working in a "typing pool" that includes women and minorities), nurse (looking after Fran), and cook (happily preparing a lovely dinner for two, purchasing new linen napkins and all).

In each of these roles, Baxter maintains an openness to the needs of those he assists, especially when caring for Fran. This non-phallic openness he displays with her, personally speaking, keeps me falling for him screening after screening of this film. Indeed, *The Apartment*'s most moving and resonant moments, as I experience them, occur at its mid-point, when Baxter becomes flooded with the contagion of Fran's shame as he works through the night with Dr. Dreyfuss in an attempt to keep her alive. Here, Baxter feels Fran's pain as if it were his own, embracing her shame, and eventually loving both her and himself all the more for it.

The Stakes of Shame

"I, too, overflow; my desires have invented new desires, my body knows unheard of songs. Time and again, I, too, have felt so full of luminous torrents that I could burst.... And I, too, said nothing, showed nothing; I didn't open my mouth, I didn't repaint my half of the world. I was ashamed. I was afraid, and I swallowed my shame and fear."[38] — Hélène Cixous

If shame cannot be felt when there is nothing to lose, then there must be much at stake in *The Apartment*. While dense moments of shame take over the screen throughout the film, its middle portion — or perhaps, more appropriately, the *body* of the film — presents beat after beat of shame displays for over thirty minutes. From the point in the film when Baxter discovers Fran's body in his room on Christmas Eve, up until their spaghetti dinner on Christmas Day, every scene explores the density of shame and its contagion, allowing it to overflow. With the film's, indeed, "luminous" releasing of sexual and gender-related shame, and through its project of counter-shaming, it begins the difficult, exciting work of "repainting" and re-writing mid-century America's phallic codes of power and dominance.

Shame's visceral charge resonates with particular strength during the moments when Baxter and Dr. Dreyfuss revive Fran through various bodily "shocks" to her system. Once Dreyfuss arrives at the apartment and inspects Fran, he and Baxter immediately carry her into the bathroom. With a medical pump in hand, resolved to "clear that stuff out of her stomach if it isn't too late," Dreyfuss begins the brutal work of keeping Fran alive. Baxter runs to the kitchen to make coffee and then returns to the bedroom, quickly peeking in at Fran and Dreyfuss, witnessing this heavy shame spectacle. With the activities in the bathroom remaining off-screen, but their unsparing sounds clearly audible, Wilder's camera steadily follows Baxter as he, and the audience, register the gravity of the situation. While listening to the sounds of Fran throwing up, the comportment of shame washes over Baxter's body; he becomes flushed and perspired, his shoulders hunching. Later on, Dreyfuss attempts to awaken Fran by repeatedly slapping her face and holding smelling salts to her nose. The sounds of this scene, again, reverberate with a synaesthetic, corporeal brutality: this is what it must sound like to be slapped back into consciousness, these are the moans of a shamed woman coming back to life. At the beginning of this scene, Wilder cuts back and forth between medium shots of Fran's pained, semi-conscious body being awakened by the doctor, and Baxter's reaction to this spectacle. Then he cuts to a wide-shot just of Baxter, who, at this point, comports himself into an all-out shame stance: eyes closed in painful empathy, hand to the back of his neck, he slouches and leans on the wall just to keep from falling down. As if his body is feeling the physical and emotional pain that

Fran's is experiencing at that moment, Baxter is overwhelmed by shame's contagion. Her shame, from then on, becomes his, too.

The multi-sensory corporeality of this moment continues for another minute or so, as Dreyfuss then forces Fran to drink multiple boiling hot cups of coffee, the sounds of her gasping and choking filling the soundtrack. The several times I've seen *The Apartment* with a large audience, both in theaters and in my classroom with students, these moments of Fran's coming back to consciousness never fail to keep viewers uneasily shifting in their seats and/or emitting groans, gasps, and other verbal exclamations. This scene, a synaesthetic spectacle of affect that invariably models the contagiousness of shame, I believe, resonates particularly strongly for shame-prone viewers, those open to seeing and feeling shame and its "desires and attachments ... with a kind of singularity that demands neither identification nor repulsion." And as film theorist Liza Johnson articulates, these kinds of desires and attachments "function, perhaps, more like empathy."[39]

Arriving just after this empathy is catharsis. Shame can function as a "catalyst that has the potential for catharsis," if first it is confronted and attended to with tenderness. Then, perhaps, it can be transgressed and healed in a "reparative gesture."[40] "Collectivity," it is argued, serves as a "major possible route to healing."[41] Sharing shame through confession helps enable this collectivity and cathartic release. After these visceral scenes of Fran's revival and Baxter's dramatic empathy with her pained body and spirit, the two begin this work of healing through "talk therapy" with each other. On Christmas Day, the two play cards in bed and share a meal, all the while confessing their most shameful secrets. She talks of her several failed relationships with men, and he describes his own botched suicide attempt over a woman married to his best friend. A care and tenderness develops between Fran and Baxter, and by the time Fran leaves his apartment, their shared bond runs deep.

Though both temporarily return to serving Sheldrake and the white capitalist patriarchy that he and Consolidated represent, on New Year's Eve each garners up their strength and ethical imperative drive by dramatically ending their relationship with him. Baxter throws the symbol of Consolidated's access to phallic power, the key to the executive washroom, at Sheldrake and onto his desk, resolutely saying "no" to the system that has abused him and Fran for so long and without consequence. He walks proudly out of the office, out of a job, and absolutely self-assured.

Fran's relinquishing of Sheldrake, often intertextually quoted in many contemporary romantic films, finds her fleeing their usual booth at Rickshaw just before midnight. Wilder cuts from her vacant chair across from a celebratory, and suddenly alone Sheldrake, to Fran running quickly down the sidewalk, shoulders held high and smiling from ear to ear, to Baxter's apartment. Her comportment is one of pure pleasure and intention, the wind sweeping through her short, boyish hair. Released from her shame, she runs toward both acceptance and a new object of desire: a tender, non-phallic, feminine man who simply adores her. Talk about *transcendent catharsis*; this scene is it. Fran's run through the night towards Baxter on New Year's Eve, in its embrace of misfit difference and rejection of patriarchal normativity, helps to bring the changes of the coming sexual revolution ever closer, clearing the air, indeed, for new kinds of gender and sexual subjectivities to make themselves visible without (or at least with much less) shame.

When Those That Get Took Get Rebellious

"Humiliation always happens in a tyranny. And that foments revolution."[42]— Shirley MacLaine

At one point during Fran's recovery at Baxter's apartment, fully aware and critical of the fact that Baxter has also been exploited by Consolidated's specific brand of white capitalist patriarchy, Fran aligns her abuse with his, articulating a distinction between those who "take" and those who "get took." Sheldrake and his executive cronies, of course, are the "takers," while Fran and Baxter constitute those who have been "took," and thus left shamed and vulnerable. This moment in the film, both pivotal and resonant, works reflexively too. Always while encountering this scene in the film, I am both "taken" by its affective charge and "taken in" by Fran and Baxter, empathizing with them and also finding solace in the cinematic space of this apartment, a space where the humiliation of tyranny is recognized and examined, and a minor revolution begins to stir. This particular moment coaxes me, as a spectator, to also "take up" or contemplate the ways in which we have all been "took" by the mythologies of white capitalist patriarchy, and how to continue the work of demythologizing such a massive, stubborn ideological project.

Screening and considering *The Apartment* today, nearly fifty years since its premiere, I find it both comforting and prescient, a film reminding me that a culture of shame might only be exploded or revolutionized when the source of that shame and the shame itself are acknowledged and deeply felt by and within the mainstream and through popular culture. Importantly, just two years after the film's release, Helen Gurley Brown's proto-feminist, shameless celebration of young women's economic and sexual independence, *Sex and the Single Girl* (1962), became a national bestseller, and, of course, the following year, Betty Friedan's deconstruction of the "pleasures" of female domesticity, *The Feminine Mystique* (1963), set in motion the second wave feminist movement. According to feminist film historian Marjorie Rosen, writing in the early 1970s, *The Apartment* exemplified the "ambiguities of both Hollywood's and the country's attitudes toward illicit sex," and represented, without a doubt, an "overt breakthrough" in commodity cinema's often conservative moral codes.[43] *The Apartment*'s economic and critical success attest to its mass appeal; the film more than doubled its $3 million cost at the domestic box office alone and won five Academy Awards, including Best Picture, Best Director, and Best Original Screenplay (Wilder co-wrote the script with I.A.L. Diamond).[44] I like to imagine that the film's wide-reaching success signals that its audiences were ripe and wanting for its gendered, sexualized subject and themes, poised to take on and move beyond the modes of shame it images and critiques. Critical of patriarchal ideologies and the way in which they constrain and shame both women and men within Western capitalist culture, *The Apartment* allowed for audiences to breathe a cathartic sigh of relief, and to start imagining new horizons of possibility already becoming visible and being felt empathically.

Notes

1. Scheuer, "Wilder Touch Brightens Sly Sex at High Altitude," 11.
2. Lewis, *The Role of Shame*, 31.
3. Tomkins quoted in Nathanson, *Shame and Pride*, 146.
4. Wurmser, *The Mask of Shame*, 55.
5. Radner, "Queering the Girl," 3.
6. Quoted in Ruhle, *Karl Marx*, 52.
7. Lewis, xi.
8. Ibid.
9. Bouson, *Quiet As It's Kept*, 9.
10. Nathanson, 138.
11. Ibid., 251.
12. Munt, *Queer Attachments*, 224.
13. Johnson, "Perverse Angle," 1381.
14. Sedgwick, "Shame and Performativity," 212.
15. Johnson, 1381.
16. Nathanson, 250.
17. Ibid., 251.
18. Ibid., 16.
19. Ibid., 258–59.
20. Ibid., 16.
21. Rosen, *Popcorn Venus*, 306.
22. Ibid., 307.
23. Ibid., 307.
24. Radner, 3.
25. MacLaine, *My Lucky Stars*, 353.
26. Powers, "The Apartment."
27. Monsey, "Talent-Wise, Seductive-Wise."
28. Munt, 177.
29. See Daniel J. Leab's "A Walk on the Wilder Side: *The Apartment as Social Commentary*" for an especially strong analysis of Baxter as a failed "organization man."
30. Leab, 12.
31. Breines, *Young, White, and Miserable*, 28.
32. Guattari, "Becoming a Woman," 234.

33. Ibid., 13.
34. Straayer, *Deviant Eyes, Deviant Bodies*, 61.
35. Ibid.
36. Silverman, *Male Subjectivity at the Margins*, 1.
37. Kibby and Costello, "Displaying the Phallus," 224.
38. Cixous, "The Laugh of the Medusa," 245.
39. Johnson, 1383.
40. Giffney, "After Shame," x.
41. Munt, 26.
42. Quoted in Fuller, "An Undervalued American Classic," 26.
43. Rosen, 307.
44. Fuller, 26.

6. *"Have They Forgotten What a Star Looks Like?"*
Image and Theme with Dino, Cagney and Fedora

KAREN MCNALLY

There is nobody with whom I'm dying to work. There is just nobody around. Audrey Hepburn was the last one, and she is gone now. If you think of all the people who died — all the way down from Gary Cooper, Clark Gable, Spencer Tracy, blah blah blah blah — and the women too. Now they talk about Harrison Ford like he was a great star. He would have been one of the crowd. Sitting on the bench, in the dugout, were people like Claude Rains, George Raft, Charles Laughton.... Some great actors — there will never be another Claude Rains or another Charles Laughton. — Billy Wilder, 1994

Billy Wilder's comments given during an interview in 1994 bear witness to the director's fascination with stardom.[1] Couched in terms of acting ability and the possibilities for a productive working relationship, Wilder's definition of Audrey Hepburn as the last in an infinite list of stars from Hollywood's golden era, with an additional second rung of stellar names "in the dugout," nevertheless betrays his attachment to stardom, just as his disappointment with what passes for the contemporary equivalent, exemplified by Harrison Ford's uninspiring persona, locates the star in its true form in the studio era. Wilder's referencing of star images is evident across his work, from a cheeky Maurice Chevalier impression in *Mauvaise graine* (1934), to Robert Strauss' Betty Grable obsession in *Stalag 17* (1953), and from Tony Curtis' memorable Cary Grant impersonation in *Some Like It Hot* (1959), to Tyrone Power's trip to see a Jesse James movie in *Witness for the Prosecution* (1957). Wilder's interest, however, goes beyond the playful. McBride and Wilmington acknowledge that "Wilder is a quintessential fan," but at the same time "exhibits a sort of *saftig* Pirandellianism" in his movie star quotations.[2] By name-checking Marilyn Monroe in *The Seven Year Itch* (1955), or recalling her *Playboy* shoot via "The Girl's" "artistic" photos for *U.S. Camera*, Wilder raises questions around image, character and reality that become a feature of his films.[3] The explicit use of star images becomes a strategy that highlights some of Wilder's key themes, including innocence and disguise, and illustrates an essential cultural and political ambivalence towards both America and the émigré's Europe. The Hollywood narratives of *Sunset Boulevard* (1950) and *Fedora* (1978) further extend this appropriation of star images, providing a concentrated narrative context for Wilder's enthralment and the exploration of his thematic concerns.

Swapping Character for Image with Dino

By explicitly drawing on some of Hollywood's potent star images and privileging those images over individual characterization, Wilder insists upon their heightened significance in relation to the identity on screen. In his 1964 critically mauled comedy *Kiss Me, Stupid*, Wilder discards the notion of character, presenting instead Dean Martin in what *Time* referred to as "an orgy of self-parody."[4] Martin's performance in the film as "Dino" unambiguously displaces character in favor of a star image in the context of a nevertheless fictional narrative. In addition, Martin's active engagement with image-making further challenges prevailing ideas of the ways in which image and character interact.

Martin appears in *Kiss Me, Stupid* as the swingin' Las Vegas performer who needs a woman in his bed every night because "if I skip one night, I wake up next morning with such a headache." Wilder significantly chooses Martin's stage name "Dino"—conversely his birth name—to establish links to the star's Rat Pack persona. Martin's Americanized name was largely discarded during the late 1950s and early 1960s in stage and television appearances which featured the singer/actor/television host alongside Frank Sinatra, Sammy Davis, Jr., Peter Lawford and Joey Bishop, an excessively famous grouping dubbed by the press the Rat Pack. In constantly referring to Martin as Dino, this group of performers, led by Sinatra who pointedly retained his Italian surname, seemed intent on both emphasizing their recognition of and attachment to the "real" person, and distancing him from the associations of an earlier star persona. As the handsome and romantic Italian troubadour to Jerry Lewis' childlike Jewish comic in the highly successful double act, Martin and Lewis, established across nightclub, television and film performances, the star was complicit in the creation of the character of "Dean Martin," a safe version of the more ethnically-challenging Dino Crocetti. By unofficially reverting to his Italian name, Martin suggested a return to the authentic self in opposition to the character created with

Lewis, with which Martin had become increasingly frustrated. "Dino" was the amiable, hard-drinking, woman-loving, prat-falling member of the Rat Pack, an image tempered by commentary pitching Martin as a home-loving husband and father of a growing brood of children. By constructing an image in stage performances, on television and in films such as *Ocean's Eleven* (1960) and *Robin and the Seven Hoods* (1964), Martin ostensibly created a further character, a notion only reinforced by the suggestion of an alternative reality.[5]

Wilder's use of Martin in the film as "Dino" indicates his recognition of the character-styling of Martin's star image and the specific traits of that early 1960s characterization. The placement of this image in a fictional narrative enables Wilder to play with his recurring theme of stardom while more fundamentally questioning the basis of both image and character, as Wilder's "character" of Dino draws wholly on Martin's image which, in itself, functions through characterization. The overt complexity of this unusual mix continues to confuse observers. While *Time* acknowledged its self-parodying elements, the *New York Times* reviewer suggested Wilder was unsuccessfully attempting "a masquerade that is hardly a disguise," and William Schoell in his biography of Martin describes the figure in the film as "a popular Las Vegas entertainer named Dino (no last name), very, *very* much like Dean Martin."[6] Nevertheless, the film's opening scenes immediately articulate the key elements of the Martin image around which Dino is based. Opening outside The Sands in Las Vegas, the film references the Rat Pack's close association with the hotel where Sinatra and Martin were both shareholders and the stars performed individually but most famously together during the filming of *Ocean's Eleven*. A sign announcing "Jack Entratter presents DINO" alongside a caricature of the star is being taken down, establishing the realness of the situation — Martin performing at The Sands under its famous manager, Entratter — and the Vegas-based image of Martin on which Wilder's Dino draws. Martin's closing night is a mix of alcohol and sexual innuendo as he performs on stage, glass in hand, surrounded by showgirls. Continuously interrupting his rendition of Gershwin's "S'wonderful," he cracks staple Rat Pack jokes. "Is this a bit of terrific?" he asks, gesturing towards one of the showgirls. "Last night she was banging on my door for 45 minutes. But I wouldn't let her out." Following a reference to an upcoming movie with Sinatra and company, a comic fall at the end of the song cites the familiar comedic aspect of Martin's Rat Pack persona that dilutes the hard-drinking swinger image. Having fended off the advances of various showgirls requesting "one for the road," Dino then departs Vegas and runs into a police roadblock. Alluding to the botched kidnapping of Frank Sinatra, Jr., who was taken from a Lake Tahoe hotel room in December 1963, he enquires: "What's the matter? That Sinatra kid missing again?"

As the enforced diversion directs Dino towards the outrageously named fictional town of Climax, Nevada, Wilder has therefore fully established his "character" in relation to Martin's image as the hard-living but affable star of the Rat Pack. Dino then works within the narrative to display Wilder's simultaneous affection and compassion for stars and their self-obsessions, and his more substantial disdain for the considerably less appealing characters who surround them. Dino's intention to breeze through Climax, stopping only for gas and a restroom break, is thwarted by two budding songwriters who conspire to keep the star in town by sabotaging his car. Garage owner Barney (Cliff Osmond) and piano teacher Orville (Ray Walston) concoct a scheme whereby Dino will unwittingly become familiarized with the aspiring team's songs, decide to perform them and give the songwriters their big break. Dino's openly stated need for female company provides them with their plan of action. Once aware he is to be stranded in town for the night, Dino questions Orville about the "action," asking "What's with the broads around here?" Orville, with Barney's encouragement, decides to set Dino up with his wife while he surreptitiously performs his songs in the background. Sending his unsuspecting spouse Zelda (Felicia Farr) to her mother's, Orville hires local prostitute Polly "the Pistol" (Kim Novak) to assume her identity. This unpleasant and duplicitous little scheme unravels when Zelda returns to find another woman in her home, departs to Polly's habitat, the Belly Button club, and spends the night with her teenage heartthrob, Dino, in Polly's caravan.

Dino initially takes center stage in this comedy narrative, the sexual directness of which was the major concern of most critics. The *Time* reviewer suggested the film "seems to have scraped its blue-black humor off the floor of a honky-tonk nightclub."[7] As the interloper in this small town, Dino's frankness about his sexual needs and his casualness in appropriating the woman he believes to be Orville's wife, attempting to seduce Polly while Orville plays one of his songs on the piano, suggest a star's ego and sense of entitlement at which the characters take offense. Despite having engineered the situation, and as a result of having himself developed feelings for Polly, Orville launches a tirade against Dino's behavior:

> Him and his Rat Pack. They think they own the earth. Riding around in their white chariots, raping and looting and wearing cuffs on their sleeves.... To them, we're just a bunch of squares, straightmen, civilians. Any time they want to move in, we're supposed to run up a white flag, hand over our homes, and our wives, and our liquor.

This dose of envious frustration echoes various responses to the Rat Pack's apparently limitless powers. *Playboy*'s unstinting admiration for The Rat Pack, whom they termed "the innest in-group in the world,"[8] came under fire from some readers who objected to the magazine's "reverential and admiring tone" and the performers' "high school outhouse humor."[9] Similarly, the stars' close association with John F. Kennedy during and following his election campaign led to concern such as that expressed by a journalist for the right-wing *New York World Telegram and Sun* that "this unpredictable group of Hollywood characters may be presumptuous enough to assume they can have the run of the White House for the next four years."[10]

Orville's outburst points to a powerless public forced to yield to the whims of Dino and his Rat Pack associates. Wilder's wider narrative, however, argues for alternative interpretations of dominance, morality and culpability. Each of the "civilians" in the film plays a part in the scenario of deceit in which Dino unwittingly finds himself. While Sinyard and Turner suggest Orville is merely swept along by Barney's scheming,[11] both men actively structure what occurs, making Polly and Zelda accomplices in their ruse. The moral deception that results from the various adulterous flings is compounded by its basis in assumed identities, Orville with Polly as his "wife," and Zelda as "Polly," who sleeps with the idol of her youth to avenge her husband's presumed infidelity, nevertheless convincing Dino of the merits of her husband's song along the way. The film's characters are split into, as *The Apartment*'s (1960) Fran Kubelik (Shirley Maclaine) tells it, those who "take" and those who "get took," articulating Wilder's dual appreciation for his schemers and innocents. Stephen Farber explains:

> Wilder's faith is in dishonesty; he believes in the exuberance to be found in choosing your role and playing it to perfection. His heroes are his liars, his cheats, but he has a rueful, nostalgic affection for the foolish innocents who do not yet know the way of the world.[12]

The active individualists who drive Wilder's stories—Walter Neff (Fred MacMurray) in *Double Indemnity* (1944), Chuck Tatum (Kirk Douglas) in *Ace in the Hole* (1951), Joe/Josephine (Tony Curtis) in *Some Like It Hot*—inspire his admiration, but it is the naivety and vulnerability expressed by dupes like *The Apartment*'s C.C. Baxter and *Some Like It Hot*'s Jerry/Daphne (each played by Jack Lemmon) that Wilder finds most captivating.

Farber defines Wilder's innocents in obvious ways through Audrey Hepburn's eternal romantic in *Love in the Afternoon* (1957) or Jean Arthur's naïve patriot in *A Foreign Affair* (1948). Yet Wilder's depiction of innocence carries as much tone as is drawn through his morally questionable characters. In *Kiss Me, Stupid*, Wilder allows the unfortunate Polly to assume the middle ground between blame and innocence, indulging her fantasy of married life via the night she spends with Orville as his "Mrs. Spooner," as flawed as the film represents that fantasy to be. By providing the Belly Button escort with a concluding escape route, enabling her to depart Climax in her caravan with the $500 given to Zelda (as Polly) by Dino as payment for services rendered, Wilder rids her of both her real-life and assumed identities, suggesting the inadequacy of both and the possibility of renewal. Nevertheless, this becomes an additional factor in his portrayal of the star as the hero of this tale. While Polly makes her way out of town with her caravan, the songwriting team see their careers in the ascendant as Dino performs their chart-topping hit "Sophia" on his television show. Dino's candid revelation of his sexual voracity and his pursuit of Zelda/Polly in open view of his host appear, on the one hand, as indicators of a star's willful decadence and self-indulgence. However, whether his initial enforced encampment in Climax, or the seduction of/by Polly/Zelda concocted by Orville and Barney, or Zelda's play for him in disguise as Polly, Dino is drawn unknowingly into the games played by the inhabitants of small-town America, who exploit the star in their midst as a sexual or financial commodity. In contrast, Dino's lack of guile and simple sexual motivations make him Wilder's innocent victim. Wilder's familiar lack of moralizing refuses to condemn Dino for his appetites, and instead the Hollywood and Vegas star, and the notion of star imagery emphasized by the disappearance of characterization, represent the innocent and the real in opposition to the manipulative and the artificial.

Between America and Europe with Dietrich and Cagney

The movie star as a captivating innocent prone to manipulation in a duplicitous world, and the dominance of star imaging in relation to characterization underlie Wilder's engagement with stars and their images. Extending these approaches further, Wilder draws on his stars' images in the articulation of some of the broader themes of his work. As an émigré filmmaker alongside directors such as Fritz Lang, Otto Preminger and Douglas Sirk, Wilder exhibited through his films a sense of ambivalence towards both Europe and America and the cultural influence of both, something termed by Gerd Gemünden "a decidedly transcultural dimension ... a status of being in-between nations."[13] Much has been written about the impact of the émigrés in Hollywood throughout the 1940s and 1950s, in particular in relation to the retrospectively labelled film noir cycle, whose visual style owes much to German Expressionism, and whose narratives tend to examine the darker aspects of American society — *Double Indemnity* being a key example. Wilder's films demonstrate this ambivalence and in-between status through morally ambiguous narratives and characterizations, a fascination with and critique of American culture, and an equally dichotomous relationship to Europe. Films depicting the American abroad in an alien European landscape most prominently highlight Wilder's identity ambiguity, as his stars become tools to express thematic ambivalence towards the Old and New Worlds.

The ambiguities central to Wilder's representation of the Europe/America dynamic find an obvious means of expression through Marlene Dietrich's star image. Dietrich's early screen roles as well as her extra-cinematic wartime image become the basis for characterization in her films with Wilder, lending an extra component to their themes and narrative perspectives. Both *A Foreign Affair* (1948) and *Witness for the Prosecution* (1957) allow for the insertion of Dietrich's image through narratives which deal either essentially or more peripherally with World War II and postwar Europe. Casting Dietrich in both as a nightclub performer, the films emphasize the central positioning of her screen persona, drawing on similar roles from her defining performance in *The Blue Angel* (1930) to *Morocco* (1930) and *Blonde Venus* (1932), to name but a few. In *Witness for the Prosecution*, Dietrich appears on the stage of a Hamburg nightclub performing for over-enthusiastic American servicemen during World War II in trademark androgynous style, here a sailor's uniform, before her character, Christine, is rescued and brought to England by G.I. Leonard Vole (Tyrone Power). Leonard's subsequent trial for the murder of a wealthy widow casts Dietrich as the cold, calculating and unfaithful wife of an American hero caught up in a potential miscarriage of justice. Wilder's narrative conclusion, however, reverses these contrasting national identities, revealing Leonard's scheming, his guilt, and his betrayal with another woman, providing the moral context for Christine to exact revenge by stabbing her husband to death, and for Vole's defense lawyer, Sir Wilfred Robarts (Charles Laughton), to claim that rather than murder him, "she executed him."

More prominently, Wilder's explicit use of Dietrich's image in *A Foreign Affair* illuminates further for the narrative the slippery borders between morality and survival and between American and European imperatives. Dietrich's nightclub performer Erika von Schlütow, the ex-mistress of a high-ranking Nazi officer, now conducts an affair with Captain John Pringle (John Lund), part of postwar Berlin's occupying American force. Erika's apparently cynical self-interest is nevertheless duplicated by Pringle's black market deals and disinterest in increasing evidence of her Nazi sympathies. America's assumed moral and political authority is provided by Jean Arthur's upright Iowa Congresswoman Phoebe Frost, whose U.S. Congress fact-finding mission, intended to save servicemen from the possibility of "moral malaria," is exposed as flawed in its naivety when she witnesses American flags attached to prams pushed by fräuleins, and watches enthusiastic servicemen greeting Erika's erotically charged performances.

Dietrich's star image forms an intervening backdrop to these ambiguities, most obviously through Erika's performances, but most interestingly through the star's frontline propaganda efforts for the United States during World War II, which were a well reported aspect of her star image. As Wilder later noted, Dietrich had only recently returned from USO duties when production on *A Foreign Affair* began,[14] and she was additionally the first woman to be honored with the United States government's Medal of Freedom. Further, as Gerd Gemünden notes, by wearing one of her USO dresses in the film, Dietrich accentuates the connections between her screen role(s) and extra-cinematic image.[15] This aspect of her star image, which made the U.S. citizen a problematic figure in Germany just as it enhanced her image in the United States, increases her character's ambiguous status. In narrative terms, then, Erika's final exit to a labor camp becomes a humorous containment of both her activities and her fate, as an ever-increasing number of military policemen are assigned to escort her and prevent each other from succumbing to her charms. While Wilder allows the Americans the ultimately laudable intention of postwar reconstruction behind their day-to-day impropriety through the tiring efforts of Colonel Plummer, Dietrich's image works as a corrective to an American monopoly on political superiority, and equally counteracts the characterization of an untrustworthy and politically unreformed Germany. As a star identity, Dietrich personalizes Wilder's tale of postwar foreign relations, highlighting the complexities that mitigate against complacent definitions of national character and morality.

The central positioning of James Cagney's screen persona in Wilder's 1961 film *One, Two, Three* exemplifies, in alternative ways, Wilder's interjection of star image into theme. Cagney plays Coca-Cola executive C. R. MacNamara ("Mac"), who represents the firm's corporate forces in the western sector of Berlin's postwar divided city while aiming to reassert himself on the corporate ladder following his exile in various company postings. Mac's opening voiceover immediately draws the character as a corporate arch-capitalist, and at the same time highlights Wilder's cynical ambivalence, as Mac compares the "shifty" East Berliners' obsession with marching to the "peaceful, prosperous" Western sector where the inhabitants enjoy "all the blessings of democracy," pointedly illustrated by a shot of a Coca-Cola advertising hoarding. Mac aims to do both himself and Coca-Cola a favor by making a deal with some East German politicians to introduce the iconic American drink into Russia. His plans are disrupted when he and his wife Phyllis (Arlene Francis) are charged with taking care of his boss' seventeen-year-old "hot-blooded" and willful Texan daughter Scarlett (Pamela Tiffin), who swiftly proceeds to marry East German Communist activist Otto (Horst Buchholz). Mac's energies are subsequently spent in trying to save his Coca-Cola deal with the Communists and making Scarlett's pregnancy and Communist husband appear palatable before the arrival of his unsuspecting boss.

Mac acts as one of Wilder's individualists whose moral ambiguities are partly forgiven in appreciation of the creativity of his misdemeanors. As he reminds Phyllis when, tired of his philandering and their nomadic lifestyle, she threatens to leave him and return to the United States: "You knew the kind of a guy I was when you married me. I'm not one of those suburban jokers—nine to five in the office, home on the commuter train, cut the grass every weekend." Set on the stage of East-West postwar relations, this individualism becomes the American trait that counters a European predilection for deference and conformity. Telling the East German police that Otto is an American spy, or having his male assistant, Schlemmer, dress up as his secretary, Fräulein Ingeborg—ruses to alternately get rid of and rescue the Communist Party apparatchik—therefore distinguishes Mac from his submissive German staff, who stand to attention when he enters the room, and from Otto who, despite his protestations, moves from loyal Party follower to Coca-Cola corporate employee-in-the-making.

Wilder's preference is for his scheming American individualist, whose ambition and methods are borne in a patriotic corporate ethos. Mac is a capitalist in its most morally ambiguous form, accentuated by Wilder's direct insertion of Cagney's screen image into the text. The persistent rendition of "Yankee Doodle Dandy" from the cuckoo clock in Mac's office introduces this ambiguity, referencing Cagney's role as songwriter George M. Cohan in the 1942 biopic. The composer of the World War I favorite "Over There," as well as the film's title song, represents the kind of flag-waving entrepreneurship superficially characterized in Cagney's performance in *One, Two, Three*. This imagery is fundamentally complicated, however, by Cagney's indelible association with Hollywood's early gangster movies. Cagney's machine-gun–like delivery of dialogue, and a narrative progressing at high speed through car chases, double-dealing and supreme ambition, make this film as much an updated gangster flick as comedy fare. Gene D. Phillips notes, in fact, the script's foreword which directs: "This piece must be played *multo furioso*—at a rapid-fire, breakneck speed: 100 miles an hour on the curves, 140 miles on the straightway."[16] The thematic shift which accompanies this genre hybridity is highlighted, therefore, by the direct intervention of Cagney's screen image. A military policeman's familiar Cagney impersonations, Mac's threat to hit Otto with a grapefruit, recalling Cagney's famous scene with Mae Clarke in *The Public Enemy* (1931), and his loose repetition of Edward G. Robinson's *Little Caesar* (1931) line, "Mother of Mercy, is this the end of *Little* Rico?," all work to insert the Hollywood gangster and Cagney's specific association with this archetype into the characterization and narrative theme. Hollywood's representation of crime as "merely a left-handed form of endeavor," as *The Asphalt Jungle* (1950) describes it, which Robert Warshow identified in his insightful 1948 essay "The gangster as tragic hero," is emphasized in these films as a key trope of the generic representation of the gangster.[17] Through the direct insertion of Cagney's screen image in *One, Two, Three*, Wilder suggests an inverse alignment of the capitalist with its criminal counterpart. The corporate American, then, becomes the contemporary representation of the gangster's objectives, methods and morality, transporting his economic and political motivations overseas, and retaining a sense of the "tragic hero." As politically bankrupt Communists forego loyalty to the State when presented with a young secretary, and Otto appropriates Mac's coveted job in London, Wilder leaves his audience sympathizing with his gangster capitalist, while implicating both America and Europe, East and West, in political redundancy.

The Faces of Norma and Fedora

Wilder's fascination with stars has naturally led him towards narratives through which he has considered their positioning within the film industry.

These films heighten the sense of innocence around stardom, locating the characters as victims of Hollywood's obsession with youth and beauty, and provide an obvious framework for Wilder's central thematic device of role-playing and the masking of identity to interrogate ideas of image and reality. In *Sunset Boulevard*, the story of the decline of silent movie star Norma Desmond (Gloria Swanson) is narrated by the corpse of failed screenwriter Joe Gillis (William Holden), floating in a swimming pool after having been shot by the star in the grounds of her mansion. Feminist critics have traditionally argued that the male narrator, particularly in the film noir cycle, is necessarily established as the audience's point of identification, resulting in viewers being forced to accede to a patriarchal and frequently negative representation of female identity. In this way, as Lucy Fischer argues, Gillis' voiceover acts to privilege his description of events and, more specifically, his perspective on Norma. Gillis, indeed, suggests he is offering "the whole truth" in relation to the events that have occurred, "before you hear it all distorted and blown out of proportion." The audience is therefore predisposed to share his derision of the symbolic worn shabbiness of the mansion Wilder likens to Miss Havisham's abode in *Great Expectations*, his disdain for Norma's bridge group of silent era stars he refers to as "the waxworks," and his disgust at Norma's naivety and misplaced vanity as she prepares herself with "an army of beauty experts" for what she believes to be her return to the screen.

Fischer argues, consequently, that the representation of Norma as a Hollywood star is as "a particularly vicious character, a literal *femme fatale*," going so far as to label her "monstrous" and a "vampire ... waiting to ensnare her next unsuspecting victim."[18] By investing the narrator with such authority, however, this approach fails to acknowledge film noir's frequent characterization of the narrator as unreliable and culpable, whose subjective description of events is therefore tainted. The male voiceovers in films such as *Laura* (1944), *Detour* (1945) and *Gilda* (1946), for example, are destabilized as the evolving narratives reveal the characters' ambiguous or accountable positions. More significantly, Wilder makes plain his narrator's untrustworthy and self-serving nature throughout the film.[19] Gillis enters Norma's world by chance while attempting to give his creditors the slip, and stumbles upon a situation which he is eager to use as a means of resolving his financial difficulties. Indeed, he admits: "I dropped the hook, and she snapped at it." Having witnessed Norma's bizarre funeral for her pet monkey, and read the "wild hallucinations" in the *Salome* script she is preparing to revive her career, Gillis senses less sympathy than opportunity. Despite his damning judgment of her script, he accepts her invitation to edit the work, just as his professed discomfort as she purchases for him a camel's hair coat and tuxedo and engineers a New Year's Eve party for two fail to interrupt his role as gigolo to Norma's financial benefactor. Gillis' bout of conscience comes only when Betty Schaefer, the budding screenwriter with whom he has been developing both a film script and a romantic relationship, becomes embroiled in the saga, and his attempt to leave Norma results in his murder.

Joe's subjective narration, meant to serve his self-image as the victim of a deluded star's controlling self-obsession, is therefore disrupted by Wilder's clear characterization of his unprincipled motivations and behavior. At the same time, the director's contrasting depiction of Norma represents the star as the honest dupe in Gillis' deception, and the innocent victim of Hollywood's intentional construction and dismissal of the star. When Norma visits Cecil B. DeMille on the set of *Samson and Delilah*, mistakenly believing he is interested in her script, and the director momentarily humors her before dispatching her back to her decaying wilderness, Wilder gives her a literal return to the spotlight. When Hawkeye directs the light onto her, provoking warm recognition from the old-time extras who swarm around her, Wilder expresses his undoubted preference for the heightened stardom Norma represents. He gives space to Buster Keaton and Erich von Stroheim — as Norma's butler, ex-husband and director Max von Mayerling — not as "waxworks" but as further reminders of an exceptionalism Hollywood has dismissed and now misses. Joe and Betty represent the unadventurous young pretenders who include psychoanalysis in a script because, as Joe suggests, "psychopaths sell like hot cakes," and for whom the old stars are just "crazy movie people," whose pre–Method acting styles are the subject of mockery.

In contrast, Wilder displays Norma's lifestyle, behavior and ambitions as a glorious contrast to the bland business of contemporary Hollywood, where Paramount producer Sheldrake spends his days hunting for a vehicle for Betty Hutton or Alan Ladd. Norma gives voice to Wilder's disenchantment, mirroring the director's later comments on the shortcomings of Harrison Ford: "Look at them in the front offices. The masterminds. They took the idols and smashed them. The Fairbanks, the Gilberts, the Valentinos, and who have we got now? Some nobody." Wilder lets the audience see, in Norma's words, "what a star looks like," through the added charismatic value of Gloria Swanson. The Mack Sennett and Charlie Chaplin routines that reference Swanson's early films, and Swanson's 1929 film with von Stroheim, *Queen Kelly*, which Norma screens for Joe as one of her silent movies, blur the lines between the "real" star and character, intensifying the notion of stardom.[20] In the same way, the film's final scenes are given over to Norma as Wilder's star, enabling her to escape into madness rather than forcing her to accept the reality of her lost identity. Wilder's ultimate judgment is to punish Joe's exploitation of a star whose worth he failed to realize, and to resurrect Norma's stardom in the only way the narrative can allow. Using the television news cameras to gently direct Norma's exit in the company of the waiting police, Max becomes Wilder's on-screen collaborator in the promotion of stardom. Descending the staircase into the camera's close-up, Desmond and Swanson provide a fitting image for Wilder's celebration of and affection for the star.

Wilder's penultimate film saw the director fittingly return to a narrative based around stardom. Adopting his central trope of role-playing and masking in *Fedora*, Wilder continues to examine the deleterious effects which the film industry's fixation on youth and beauty has on, in particular, the female star. The narrative threads of deception and disguise which run through his work are combined here in an updated Hollywood tale, which emphasizes the essential construct of image in relation to stardom and questions the placement of reality. The physical masking of identity is a featured narrative device in Wilder's films, from Christine's disguise as a menacing cockney in *Witness for the Prosecution*, which convinces the jury of her infidelity and Leonard's innocence, to *Double Indemnity*'s Walter Neff, who boards a train disguised as the husband of Phyllis Dietrichson (Barbara Stanwyck), setting up the series of events for their murderous insurance scam. Role-playing and masking are taken further in *The Major and the Minor* (1942) and *Some Like It Hot*, where they become the central narrative focus as Ginger Rogers fakes a schoolgirl identity in order to take a train journey on a child's fare, and witnessing the St. Valentine's Day Massacre pushes Joe and Jerry into cross-dressing.

In an early considered analysis of Wilder's films in the October 1969 issue of the British journal *Cinema*, Robert Mundy identified the key theme of disguise, exploring this in relation to Erving Goffman's theories on role-playing and performed identity. Mundy suggests that "the process of Wilder's films is one of role disenchantment, a movement from Goffman's first pole of role acceptance to the second pole of role rejection.... Disguises are metaphors for roles in Wilder's films, and his protagonists change disguises."[21] This role-playing, therefore, frequently becomes part of a character's narrative transformation, adopting a disguise in a framework of deceit and immorality, and subsequently revealing their identity in an act of moral integrity. Mundy's pointed suggestion that the heroes "change disguises," however, indicates continuity in the individual's performance if not in the performed role. Equally, Wilder's admiration for the ingenious deception and the recurrence of the masking theme point to a fundamental assertion of the primacy of role-playing and image.

Tony Curtis' Cary Grant impersonation underlying Joe's assumed identity as oil magnate Junior in *Some Like It Hot* hints at the theme's obvious connections to stardom. As the ultimate role players, stars represent a heightened level of performance, and Wilder's explicit use of star images works to articulate the dominance of constructed identity to the exclusion of the "real." *Fedora* explores the notion of image in its native locale, driving the theme of role-playing and masking to its distant extreme with the literal displacement of a star by an image. The film's disturbing narrative concerns Hollywood star Fedora (Hildegard Knef), who retires from the screen after one of her regular bouts of plastic surgery leaves her face permanently scarred and confines her to a wheelchair after a resulting stroke. Retreating to seclusion in the Greek Islands on the pretense of an early retirement, Fedora finds her stardom resurrected when the

Academy of Motion Picture Arts and Sciences bestows on her a special Oscar, delivered in person by the Academy's president, Henry Fonda, to Fedora's daughter, Antonia (Marthe Keller), superficially disguised as her mother. In order to take advantage of the movie offers that follow, Antonia is required to permanently assume Fedora's identity, undergoing a physical transformation and taking on the role of actress and star, while her mother "becomes" her lover's deceased mother, Countess Sobryanski. When Antonia is eventually confronted by the realization that she can never regain her own identity, she commits suicide, jumping into the path of an incoming train.

The story is framed around two flashbacks, the first narrated by independent film producer Barry "Dutch" Detweiler (William Holden), and the second by Fedora/Countess Sobryanski. Holden's casting makes clear reference to Wilder's earlier Hollywood fable, signalling both the director's readiness to contextualize his star's behavior, and the unreliability of his protagonist's narration. As he observes the fans, journalists and cameramen attending Fedora's lying-in-state, so carefully stage managed by the Countess that he likens it to a film premiere, Detweiler recalls what he believes to be a true version of his experiences of the past two weeks. His voyage to Corfu has been an attempt to secure Fedora's services for a remake of *Anna Karenina* he is producing entitled *The Snows of Yesteryear*, aiming to trade on their one-night affair many years before when he was an assistant director on one of her Hollywood films. The illusory quality of his encounters with Fedora and the Countess is revealed, however, when the Countess unmasks herself as Fedora and relates the story of her disfigurement, her self-imposed exile from the screen, and the reconstruction of the image and identity of "Fedora" through her daughter.

Wilder's admiration for the creative scam and his belief in the star as a vulnerable victim are most tested in *Fedora*. The Countess' scheme is on a grand scale and, while extinguishing her daughter's identity and, ultimately, her life, achieves its goal of maintaining Fedora's star status, even enhancing her image through the construction of an improbably youthful version of her "real" self. Wilder provides a rationale for her behavior through the film industry's obsession with youth and a star's visual appeal, which accounts for the star's initial cosmetic procedures and for her willingness to transform her daughter in her own image. When her aide, Miss Balfour, complains that Antonia failed to match her mother as an actress, the Countess responds: "Aaah, acting. That's for the Old Vic, but every so often a face comes along the camera falls in love with. You're born with that." While Norma Desmond might properly claim, "We had faces," the obvious irony in the Countess' comment is that Antonia achieves stardom via Fedora's face, one she was not born with. Fedora's flourishing career and the audience and press response to her death validate the Countess' assumptions about the industry's approach to stardom, as the crowds flock for a last glance at the face in the coffin, unaware of the extent to which this face (reconstructed, in any case, following her suicide) is a mere image.

From Detweiler's perspective, Hollywood has developed into a film industry controlled by "tax shelter guys" who hold the key to movie financing, and the "kids with beards" who represent the current directing flavor, updating *Sunset's* "idiot producers" and "message kids." His reference to lost stars like Gable, Tracy and Crawford, and the Countess' receipt of a letter of condolence from Marlene — "a real fighter" — also express Wilder's yearning for Hollywood movie stardom, at the same time as Henry Fonda's appearance as himself (a further image) serves as a sidebar suggesting the more realistic expectations of youth and beauty placed on a male star. These reminders of the movie star ideal form a legitimating background to the Countess' strategy, expressed in her own words: "People were tired of what passes for entertainment these days. Cinéma vérité, the naked truth, the uglier the better. They wanted glamor again, and who was I to disappoint them?"

Star image becomes the ultimate disguise requiring the performance of a role and the eclipsing of identity. The moral realization and consequent character transformation normally required of Wilder's role-players is absent here. Instead, *Fedora* establishes identities continuously subsumed by roles, and image as the only reality. While the Countess has unmasked herself to Detweiler as Fedora, like Norma Desmond she retains her role and maintains the image of Fedora for public consumption. The film's conclusion leaves an adoring audience worshipping a "false" Fedora while the "real" Fedora takes the place of a deceased Countess and, as Detweiler reveals, passes away in this guise six weeks after her daughter's funeral. Yet the image of Fedora remains, refuting notions of the false and the real, and advocating the primacy of image. The Countess' fond memories of "Dutch," and her rapid demise following the death of her daughter, reveal a further mask of "cement and stainless steel" required for the maintenance of stardom, and convey Wilder's underlying affection for his stars. The lasting image is that of Fedora. As the Countess tells Detweiler, in the style of Norma Desmond: "Endings are very important. That's what people remember — the last exit, the final close-up."

Conclusion

Wilder seems intent on giving stardom its "final close-up," distinguishing stars from the unremarkable in an increasingly commonplace Hollywood. His industry stories emphasize the sense of the extraordinary crucial to stardom, bringing into play his admiration for the distinct individual, whatever the self-obsessions and moral ambiguities. At the same time, his stars frequently represent his innocents, more schemed against than scheming, highlighting the ways in which stardom and star imagery becomes a key means through which Wilder articulates a number of recurring themes. Disguise, role-playing and Wilder's ambivalent sensibility in relation to American and European culture are each drawn out through his engagement with stars. Ultimately, though, Wilder's explicit referencing of star images, and the position stardom takes as a central narrative concern, provoke questions around the nature of image and the real. Character becomes image, and image becomes identity in Wilder's films. After all, that's what people remember.

Notes

1. Kirkham, "Saul Bass and Billy Wilder in Conversation," 179.
2. McBride and Wilmington, "The Private Life of Billy Wilder," 4.
3. The term "Pirandellian" refers to the work of Italian playwright and novelist Luigi Pirandello, whose major concerns Eric Bentley describes as "the relativity of truth, multiple personality, and the different levels of reality." Bentley, *The Pirandello Commentaries*, 3.
4. "Hipster's Harlot," 69.
5. Aspects of this image are also apparent in less obvious ways in Martin's non–Rat Pack films, including *The Young Lions* (1958), *Some Came Running* (1958) and *Rio Bravo* (1959).
6. Weiler, "Kiss Me, Stupid," 22; Schoell, *Martini Man*, 204.
7. "Hipster's Harlot," 69.
8. Legare, "Meeting at the Summit," 43.
9. Shaw, *Sinatra*, 268.
10. Brownstein, *The Power and the Glitter*, 160–61.
11. Sinyard and Turner, *Journey Down Sunset Boulevard*, 247.
12. Farber, "The Films of Billy Wilder," 20.
13. Gemünden, *A Foreign Affair*, 2.
14. *Billy Wilder Speaks* (Kino International, 2006).
15. Gemünden, 71.
16. Phillips, *Some Like It Wilder*, 248.
17. Warshow, "The Gangster as Tragic Hero," 97–103.
18. Fischer, "*Sunset Boulevard*," 100 and 103.
19. Sarah Street acknowledges this unreliable narration in "'Mad About the Boy,'" 223–33.
20. Swanson impersonated Chaplin in *Manhandled* (1924) and appeared in a number of early Mack Sennett comedies.
21. Mundy, "Wilder Reappraised," 17.

7. *Phenomenological Masking*

Complications of Identity
in *Double Indemnity*

PHILLIP SIPIORA

There will be time, there will be time
To prepare a face to meet the faces that you meet;
There will be time to murder and create.
— "The Love Song of J. Alfred Prufrock"

"I try to avoid used-up clichés, what's already been seen, and to shine a new light on them. There's a value in clichés, because you can elaborate on them."[1] Thus Billy Wilder's reflections offer a glimpse into the creative mind that makes him one of our most significant filmmakers, and provide an opening probe into his lifelong obsession with surface and depth, appearance and reality, mask and face. Wilder has always been concerned with the artistic challenges of dealing with artifice, yet he has also aggressively pursued inner kernels of truth hidden within his subject matter. Wilder incessantly searched for snippets of reality and, once discovered, he felt compelled to make the most of them. In his words:

> You could say that *Double Indemnity* was based on the principal of *M* [Fritz Lang, 1931] ... *M* was on my mind. I tried for a very realistic picture — a few little tricks, but not very tricky. *M* was the look of the picture. It was a picture that looked like a newsreel.... But like a newsreel, you look to grab a moment of truth, and exploit it.[2]

Wilder's reference to *M* has special resonance because Fritz Lang's seminal 1931 German film is considered by many to be the first feature-length noir film. Wilder, like Lang, was part of the contingent of German-speaking, filmmaking émigrés who so significantly shaped American cinema in the 1940s and beyond.

Double Indemnity (1944) is a groundbreaking cinematic masterpiece exemplifying Wilder's obsessive, probing intellectual curiosity, his insatiable inquiry into the impenetrable inscape of human consciousness, a strikingly aggressive and personalized descent into the subterranean world of noir. Wilder's labyrinthine noir journeys often begin with a mask—a form of cliché, a face "to meet the faces" in a desolated wasteland not unlike that of T. S. Eliot and his Modernist contemporaries in their aesthetic struggle to respond to the destruction of principal pillars of western civilization that was the residue of iconoclasts Darwin, Marx, Freud, and Einstein (and later Heisenberg). Wilder, too, examines a wasteland of ruthless ambition, avarice, egomania, and wanton disregard of ethical standards and moral propriety. Wilder, a Modernist himself in many ways, was intrigued by the challenges of telling stories that capture and convey rupture, disillusion, waste, and human wreckage. In speaking of the tenor and tone of *Indemnity*, Sylvia Harvey observes:

> It is at the additional and perhaps more important level of *mise en scène* or visual style that the physical environment of the lovers (whether created by landscape/set, or by camera angle, framing and lighting) is presented as threatening, disturbing, fragmented.[3]

Indeed, the writer-director's words and cameras are deeply immersed in the milieu of noir, terrain of sordid dreams, wreaked lives, and hopeless futures.

Wilder's major contributions to noir, *Indemnity* and *Sunset Boulevard* (1950), strike most viewers as innovative, rich in suspense, and intensely focused on the irresistible, darker impulses of life. Wilder was daring in confronting traditional modes of narrative exposition, such as employing one voiceover as a dying man (Walter Neff) and another voiceover as a dead man (Joe Gillis). The beginnings of both films are also the endings, but only in a tactical sense of plot segmentation. These narrative voiceovers take place at or near the temporal end of the narrative, yet describe events and evaluate characters as the scenes develop within the chronological pace of the film. Voiceover explanation imposed over a scene is, of course, after-the-fact reflection, in spite of the appearance of concurrent stream(s) of reflections. There is a critical difference between post-event analysis and contemporaneous commentary. Wilder is careful to remind us of the actual timeframe of narrative exposition by systematically interposing scenes of Neff speaking into his dictaphone machine.

Early scenes in *Indemnity* function as respective commencements of a face-making game in which central characters reveal shifting, mutating representations to other characters. *Indemnity* relies on a rolling series of flashbacks for its comprehensive narrative architectures. Yet in employing such a principle of organization, Wilder dismisses one issue, strategically and hermeneutically significant for many viewers, and a staple of noir cinema: *what* happens. Once we are told what has happened, narrator Neff is free to explain *how* things have happened. This crucial distinction between distinguishing the "how" from the "what" is an historic characteristic of Wilder's genius. This emphasis also calls attention to Wilder's lifelong fascination with meta-cinematic nuances of film-making. He well understood the seriousness of participating in an ongoing dialogue with his predecessors. The introduction and modification of inherited generic practices are but one avenue of such conversations. Wilder's aggressive deviations from the norm, shining new light on old clichés, reveal his knack for developing pioneering kinds of techniques: introducing paradigmatic voiceover leads, rethinking traditional noir points of closure, initiating critically innovative cinematography, and of course his idiosyncratic, ego-maniacal, depraved femme fatale, Phyllis Dietrichson.

What is infectiously engaging about Wilder's work is his introduction of complex exempla of masking or face-making (*prosopopeia*, the Greek trope of facial representation, disguise, voice). Character representation (including multi-representation and misrepresentation) is a driving motif in Wilder's vision and versions of noir. He creates individualized cinematic portraits that operate within reformative contexts and encounters with others. These engagements, situated in pivotally powerful scenes, encapsulate Wilder's concern for perception and character interconnections and intra-connections. Such confrontations in *Indemnity* are often churlish. Wilder's cinematic schema, reinforced by a sustained emphasis on masks and masking, is integrally related to fundamental principles of phenomenology, the philosophical home of perception and personal interrelationships for the last century (with antecedent roots much earlier). Interaction between and among characters is, of course, at the heart of cinema, but usually examined in configurations of plot complication, character exposition, and thematic currents, rather than analyzed systematically as a means of perception into a filmmaker's philosophy, sensibility, world view.

The Phenomenological Prism

Phenomenology, as a philosophical method, defies precise definition because there are so many variants within the century-old school of practitioners. However, there is a wealth of penetrating commentary on phenomenology, including its relevance to film studies. Vivian Sobchack, for example, provides a careful and useful description of certain objectives in phenomenological inquiry: "The goal of phenomenology is to describe experience. Experience comes to description in acts of reflection: consciousness turning reflexively on itself to become conscious of consciousness."[4] Sobchack sums up most articulately a dimension of phenomenology that is an explicit movement in Wilder's noir cinema. His unrelenting concern in depicting the evolving consciousness of characters, including the necessity of "dressing" consciousness with necessary artifice (faces to the world), is something that Wilder's creative calculus must engage because his sensibility insistently reveals there is no *essential* consciousness underlying consciousness. One of Wilder's paramount contributions is his exposition and interrogation of the complications and problematics of revealing consciousness. He does not pretend to understand essential human qualities, especially "sin," but he well understands the necessity, indeed the obligation, of articulating those gestures humans make in responding to their environments and the impulses of their lower (or higher) natures.

Fundamental principles of phenomenology, essential to my reading of Wilder, are drawn from the work of Maurice Merleau-Ponty and Emmanuel Levinas. Merleau-Ponty is concerned with philosophical and psychological modes of connections between humans: how and why we interact. Motivation is particularly important to his analysis, particularly as humans confront barriers that hinder communication and stifle humanistic rapport. An essential characteristic of being human, according to Merleau-Ponty, is the process of facilitating or rupturing communication — the phenomenological burden of obligation: "There is said to be a wall between us and others, but it is a wall we build together, each putting his stone in the niche left by the other."[5] There is an inextricable, undeniable bond between personae that is the inevitable residue of human interaction. Merleau-Ponty places a critical importance on the function of the face, literally and figuratively, as well as distortions of the face, what constitutes masks and masking:

> Along with time's secret linkages, I learn those of the perceived world, its incompatible and simultaneous "faces." I see it as it is before my eyes, but also as I would see it from another situation — and not as a possibility but as an actuality, for from this moment forth it gleams *elsewhere* from many fires which are *masked* from me [emphasis added].[6]

Phenomenology is not a series of steps to solutions, but rather the inception of a series of questions, as he suggests:

> Philosophy does not raise questions and does not provide answers that would little by little fill in the blanks. The questions are within our life, within our history: they are born there, they die there, if they have found a response, more often than not they are transformed there.[7]

The ethical, epistemological, and ontological convolutions and transformations that are represented in the character portraiture of *Indemnity* are, I would suggest, the emergence of questions about how and why characters appear as transfigured, unstable representations.

Emmanuel Levinas, a disciple of Martin Buber, draws upon modes of personal respect and understanding in formulating his theory of the "encounter," a linking borderland between individuals that serves as a birthing area for the determination of ethical positioning. Scenes of "facing" and "facing off" between and among humans determine moral stance(s). The act and fact of the encounter, for Levinas, necessarily calls into question self-definition. A collaborator or participant in a discourse exchange necessarily undergoes some level of ethical transaction precisely as a result of the encounter. In the words of Levinas, "For me, the term ethics always signifies the fact of the encounter, of the relation of myself with the Other: a scission of Being in the encounter — without coincidence!"[8] Ethics is always and already revealed and determined by our interactions with others.

The agitator in the ethical transaction, according to Levinas, is the manner in which the other sparks self-recognition in the self: "For the ethical relationship which subtends discourse is not a species of consciousness whose ray emanates from the I; it puts the I in question. This putting in question emanates from the other."[9] One dimension of the "putting in question" movement is the generation of positive resistance, a force that is necessary for productive dialogue. For Levinas, positive resistance is a discernibly ethical act: "The 'resistance' of the other does not do violence to me, does not act negatively; it has a positive structure: ethical."[10] According to John Wild's reading of Levinas, a response to the resistance of the other, to the "questioning glance," is necessary for effective, ethical discourse that translates into social action:

> If communication and community is to be achieved, a real response, a responsible answer must be given. This means that I must be ready to put my world into words, and to offer it to the other. There can be no free interchange without something to give. Responsible communication depends on an initial act of generosity, a giving of my world to him with all its dubious assumptions and arbitrary features.[11]

It is the phenomenological dimension of the discourse with the other that renders behavior, especially language acts, as ethical: a world into words. In the philosophy of Merleau-Ponty, one must practice the explication of perceptual relations, as they are revealed in the subject's opening to the world.[12] What are possible connections between these phenomenological perspectives and the reading of Wilder's powerful films?

Wilder's aggressive vision opens up alternative hermeneutic possibilities because his signature development of the genre raises calculated questions of ethical perspective and its expression through language and social interaction. The ethics of character are shaped by actions and words, always and necessarily a residue of dynamic engagement(s) with other characters. From this perspective, value systems can never be static or perceived as stable causes. On the contrary, these codes systematically become dynamic effects that, in turn, transform into causes, generating a progression of effects until closure of some form takes place — death, other dispatch, or cessation of narrative. Further, the ancient trope of mask (a specific "face" crafted in response to a particular time and place) and masking (the ability to create new faces, as a process of being, according to the circumstantial exigencies of the moment) come together in a series of performative gestures that constitute a major motif in Wilder's canon of noir.[13] My exploration of phenomenological encounters, in conjunction with the necessity of masking, attempts to suggest an interrelationship that offers an interpretive pathway into Wilder's genius. Encounters and facial identities are interwoven, but cannot be understood as functions of uncomplicated causation. Does the encounter determine the mask or does the mask shape the encounter? Both strands are highly energized components of human transactions, their synergism undeniable.

Boarding the Trolley Car

Double Indemnity opens with Walter Neff, mortally wounded, driving erratically back to his office, the film's point of departure and locus of settlement for his sins. He has returned to confess his crimes and balance his ethical books, or at least buy enough time to flee to Mexico after having murdered his co-murderer, Phyllis. Although moribund, he barks an order to the night elevator operator: "Let's ride." Indeed, Neff is riding to the climax of his life. His memorandum to Barton Keyes, Claims Manager, resolves the circumstances of an insurance murder and places *Indemnity* in the familiar noir tradition of chronicling the recollected events of a central character. As Claire Johnston observes, "The plot resolution is known from the outset, the film taking the form of a memory."[14] Neff tells Keyes that he became a criminal for usual noir motives— lucre and lust. It was all for naught, as Neff admits his wrongdoing to Keyes: "I killed him for money and a woman," adding sarcastically, "I didn't get the money and I didn't get the woman." Neff and Gillis are clearly motivated by greed, as Nora Henry points out: "In both cases the hero's guilt originates from material greed, and in Neff's case, also from a sexual motive."[15] Yet are Neff and Gillis "forgiven" by viewers for their transgressions as a result of their respective admissions? Henry believes so: "Both male characters who are shot by their female counterparts redeem themselves through a confession."[16] Neff's capital punishment by femme fatale gunfire is, it seems to me, quite appropriate (and typical) noir adjudication.

What follows Neff's declaration of financial and sexual failure is a series of flashbacks recounting the six weeks that encompasses the summer narrative set in 1938. The plot elements of *Indemnity* are simple and pure noir: greed, crime, sex, and money. The stakes are upped when the avarice is boundless, the crime is homicide, the sex is illicit, and the money is big. The narrative is relatively uncomplicated: Walter Neff, a rogue insurance salesman, schemes with Phyllis Dietrichson, a shrewish wife, to kill her husband for his accidental death policy, which is obtained without the husband's knowledge by the agent and the spouse. The policy pays double, $100,000 total, if the death is unlikely to happen, as in "death while traveling by train." Such an "accident" is exactly what transpires as the hapless husband is killed and his body dumped on the rail tracks. Simple, deadly, and possibly the perfect crime, except for Keyes, a tough, street-smart insurance manager, who happens to be Neff's boss at Pacific All Risk Insurance Company. Keyes is a stand-in for the usual police presence in noir culture, and the absence of law enforcement involvement is only one dimension that separates *Indemnity* from many noir films. Neff, like Dietrichson and Keyes, dons a number of masks—faces—in response to the ever-changing challenges of his crimes. His opening mask (also the closing mask, as the film begins at the end) depicts Neff in a truth-telling mode. Other masks of deceit, passion, and treachery are discarded at the film's opening and closing. Neff attempts to explain his motives and behavior, perhaps seeking atonement, possibly aware of the consequences of the bullet in his shoulder. Neff establishes his ethos in coming clean about what he has done. His admission reveals his self-knowledge of his immoral ways, and serves to clean up the messy entanglement of his lies to and deceit of his boss and friend. Or does it?

What motivates Neff to own up to his nefarious deeds? Does he suffer feelings of guilt over having misled his supervisor and mercantile father figure? The opening confessional scene serves at least two tactical purposes: (1) it clears the way for viewers to accept the accuracy of the unfolding narrative now that we probably have reason to trust our narrator; and (2) it foreshadows the impending exposition of hard hearts and dark crimes. As Claire Johnston notes, one might regard Neff's autobiographical tale with some healthy skepticism: "The first person narration presents itself as a 'confession' which reveals the truth of the narrative of events ... it purports to provide the knowledge of how things really happened."[17] Further, Andrew Dickos argues that Walter's confession is to show the intellectual and psychological processes by which he came to comprehend the meaning of his actions through his inevitable, final moments:

> His confession to Keyes is that privileged analysis that strikes the noir consciousness at the moment of hopeless resignation to doom, and Walter simply wants to speak of *how* he has come to understand where he finally finds himself.[18]

Neff's confession, to be sure, is a powerful synecdoche for the dark forces that preside over noir culture, a milieu rich in immorality and amorality. Jason Holt observes that by film's end "poetic justice fades, displaced, almost to the point of irrelevance."[19] The murky world of noir, by its nature, consistently emphasizes the how over the what. Thus the conspiracy between Neff and Phyllis requires their respective (sophisticated) abilities to invent themselves—that is, slip into masks as needed—in order to launch and sustain their crime spree. They must be ready to put their "world into words"—that is, translate thought and language into action. Such a transaction carries an ethical obligation, as Levinas insists, and it is the explicitly unethical imperative governing the motives and deeds of Phyllis and Neff that makes them such compelling, fascinating characters.

Masked Partners in Sex and Crime

Masking is but one component of the tapestry of revelation. Disguise is an integral part of a dynamic process that inevitably invokes "knowing" and "being," epistemology and ontology, and the requisite face-changes can only come into being by means of a series of encounters and their causal connections. Thus a very complex narrative or, more precisely, a series of narratives, is played out. As Johnston argues:

> The process of articulation between the narrating discourses at play is foregrounded by the "novelesque" aspect of the genre itself, providing a complex interplay of convergence/divergence — a conflict at the level of the knowledges which the film provides for the viewer, setting in motion its own enigma.[20]

Wilder's rife sense of irony is explicit in the opening encounter (Neff's confession in spite of his denial of confessing), which sets in motion subsequent encounters, except for the death scene. Thus first is last and last is first, yet not only in plot segmentation, but also in other ways. Is the "cleansed" Neff a figural prototype, a deathbed convert? What of his eleven-year exemplary work record? Is Neff an archetype, an everyman, capable of good or evil depending upon circumstances and strength of moral conscience and consciousness of conscience? These questions, it would seem, are never answered. They serve, strategically and tactically, as cultural and philosophical points of departure. Wilder's knack for posing difficult and disturbing questions signifies his probing instincts and extensive intellectual curiosity.

Wilder's calculus of masks and encounters unveils an atypical crime drama, one that challenges us to consider not only complicated ethical questions, but, more importantly, the means by which characters, through their "knowing," come to make ethical decisions and choose courses of action or being, inextricably intertwined. They become defined by their representations to the world (evolving guises) and engagements with others. Thus masking and evolving, through encounters, are inseparably interrelated.

Perhaps the most critical encounter of the film takes place early on at the Dietrichson home, where Neff makes his initial sales call to renew an auto insurance policy. Phyllis appears clad only in a towel, and the sight of her ignites Neff's lust. All noir, good or bad, capitalizes on the use of explicit metaphor, nuanced language that hides sexual content from the surface of dialogue, but not so submerged that adult audiences do not get the message.[21] Neff and Phyllis generate potent sexual banter as he stares at her bare legs, one wearing a gold anklet. As James Maxfield notes, this early symbol carries great import as Phyllis "could very well have the title 'Evil Woman' engraved on her anklet ... the label is apparent in nearly all of her behavior."[22] Neff is very curious about the sultry blond, but he has no inkling of "time's secret linkages" that lurk in her heart. Neff makes obvious his carnal interest, but Phyllis slows him down: "There's a speed limit in this state, Mr. Neff. Forty-five miles an hour." Neff does not miss a beat: "How fast was I going, officer?" She replies, "I'd say around ninety." He retorts: "Suppose you get down off your motorcycle and give me a ticket." At this point in their skirmish, the repartee is thick, saucy, acerbic. Kate Stables concludes that the repartee reveals Phyllis as a figural officer of the law:

The exchange is a consummate example of the male-female verbal tennis of classic noir, with the *femme fatale* putting the spin on the ball. Phyllis, as traffic cop, "regulates" the speed of Neff's approaches, proposes to punish his transgression, and ends their exchange with a reminder of her status and that of her husband/"master."[23]

Phyllis intensifies as a manipulating, controlling figure in subsequent scenes.

Neff is neither naïve nor unaggressive, but there is no indication that he is much different from a stereotypical salesman, on the prowl for lonely, attractive, and available women. His face glows with wit, confidence, chivalry, and innuendo. All of the temptations are propitious for Neff to evolve from businessman to criminal, according to Harvey: "It is no accident that Walter Neff ... seeks an escape from the dull routine of the insurance company he works for, in an affair with the deadly and exotic Phyllis Dietrichson."[24] Phyllis is sophisticated, seductive, sexy, yet there is no indication that murder lurks deep in her heart. Her face to Neff (and us) is that of a bored, mistreated, and misunderstood housewife. The first encounter, however, transforms both of them, putting them on the trolley car to the cemetery.

Neff soon departs the Dietrichson residence, and it is obvious that he is charged with passion. His confession recalls his mindset on that sultry May afternoon: "You were thinking about murder, and I was thinking about that anklet." We soon come to know that Phyllis is inspired by the thought that Neff is a possible accomplice in her murder scheme. Once Neff mentions insurance, Phyllis envisions the outline of a crime. Yet her suffering-wife posture is quickly perceived by Neff, whose instincts, seemingly, do not initially involve murder, at least until his sexual and financial desires overcome him. It is not clear which impulse takes precedence, although in his confession he identifies "money" as his primary motive. Neff later admits to Keyes that he was always looking for ways "to crook the house." John Irwin, drawing upon Cain's novella, offers an intriguing analysis of less obvious motives fueling the salesman-killer:

> There are two other, less-than-obvious motives, and in associating the first of these with an irresistible impulse that has him standing at the edge of a drop, drawing closer and closer to get a better look, Cain echoes two Poe tales that are the origin of this particular motive in American crime fiction ... a principle he names *perverseness*.[25]

Neff, however perverse, clearly leaves the Dietrichson home with sex on his mind, as Harvey observes: "The possession of Dietrichson, as any of the other film noir women who function as sexual commodities, is ... held up as a tempting means of escape from the boredom and frustration of a routinized and alienated existence."[26] Phyllis shows Neff the door with homicide on her mind.

This initial encounter is a catalyst for the next scene, the sexual consummation of their relationship, which now includes the plotting of a capital crime. Neither Phyllis nor Neff displays any sense of "consciousness of conscience" in their previous exchanges. Once Neff discards his law-abiding principles, he surrenders himself to absolute manipulation, including murder for hire. Phyllis holds heinous values: she has killed before, if we are to believe her stepdaughter, Lola. Indeed, Phyllis may be an exemplar of femme fatales, with no positive qualities to offset her insatiable greed. She is a "cold-hearted manipulative bitch," in the words of Maxfield.[27] Phyllis is one of Wilder's two stunning, daring noir women, both of whom murder their lover. (The other woman is, of course, Norma Desmond of *Sunset.*) Neff is unable to resist Phyllis' sexual charms: her face and body become the sum total of her identity. Phyllis perceives Neff as an ideal co-conspirator: an insider who knows what technical mistakes to avoid. Her motivation is money. His motivation is sex. Things change quickly, however, as their preliminary motives mutate.

The second encounter, once again at the Dietrichson home, reveals Phyllis' freshly reconstructed face to Neff. She is not reluctant to let him know the crime that is on her mind. Phyllis is a form of vampire, and in order to survive she must continually draw blood from new victims. Neff's face reveals outrage at Phyllis' hints of murder, but his sexual instinct is quietly and powerfully nullifying whatever moral principles he may have held (at least those involving more than crooking the house) before he encountered Phyllis. In Merleau-Ponty's perspective, they are together slowly building a wall of crime, brick by brick, each putting his or her stone in the niche left by the other. Neff becomes the strategist and Phyllis assumes the role of first engineer, carefully manipulating her husband and brainstorming with Neff the logistics and grisly steps of a perfect crime.

Keyes wears faces also, of course, but his persona is quite unlike that of Neff. We first see him as a crafty, punctilious claims manager, disposing of fraudulent claims the way a dog detects and devours fresh meat. Neff watches Keyes in awe as the manager berates a novice in fraud, Mr. Garlopis, who has set fire to his truck for the insurance. This encounter places the viewer in a role parallel to that of Neff, as observer of Keyes' considerable skills in detection. Nothing is lost on Neff, a pretty shrewd operator himself. His voiceover acknowledges not only his boss' expertise, but also Keyes' softer side: "You had a heart as big as a house." Neff is incapable of predicting Keyes' behavior at any particular time, principally because Keyes acts according to not only principles of insurance logic, but also by "hunches." He is a man of logic and intuition, a powerful combination. Further, Neff knows that Keyes is very fond of him, which gives Neff a sense of security.[28]

Neff and Phyllis recognize at this point that the principal barrier between them and their dark desires is the oddly eccentric Keyes and his "little man inside" instincts. Less than a quarter of an hour into the film, the forces in conflict are firmly established, along with the surface identities of the principal players. Indeed, Wilder has strategically introduced his clichés—seemingly simple noir characters—and prepares the way for their elaboration as poignant and penetrating characters in evolution.

As the narrative unfolds, Wilder's clichés become more aggressive in their respective pursuits. Neff revisits Phyllis and is pleased to discover that they are alone. His metaphors become highly charged, pulsating with insinuation: "As long as it's the maid's day off, maybe there's something I can do for you, like running the vacuum cleaner." "Fresh," says Phyllis, in a playful rebuke. The wife from hell has something far more important on her mind than sex: hatching homicide. Neff does not read the murderous face behind the flirtatious face. Phyllis reads his face as if it were a blank sheet of paper, which later proves to be fatal for both of them. Neff has no reason to don much of a mask when the stakes are as simple as adultery. Yet when Phyllis probes more deeply into accident insurance, Neff's visage quickly changes in response to her question, "See what I mean, Walter?" Neff sees all too clearly: "Sure, I got good eyesight.... You want him to have the policy without knowing it. That's the set-up, isn't it?" Neff admonishes her as he storms out: "Look baby, you can't get away with it. You want to knock him off, don't you?" Phyllis wears innocence on her face, yet her voice resonates with guile. Neff, however, has now begun to read the layers of faces behind the face, and his voiceover summarizes his newfound knowledge: "She didn't fool me for a minute, not this time." In his solitude, Neff realizes that the result of their re-encounter was not his rejection of baser impulses, but rather his acceptance: "The hook was too strong. This wasn't the end between her and me." The wheels of passion and greed now turn quickly as the plot is planned in Neff's apartment.

"It was the most natural thing in the world," drones Neff's voiceover as he recalls Phyllis' visit to his apartment for their third encounter. "It," of course, is murder for money. Copulation has taken second place for both schemers in the scheme of things. Phyllis and Neff both now wear faces of dedicated criminals as they create and refine their stratagem to dispatch Mr. Dietrichson. The potential killers become giddy with passion and greed. Phyllis claims to have come to return Neff's hat, and he tells her to put it on the chair. However, there is no hat and this shared joke shows how focused they are on their nefarious scheme, oblivious to much else. Their masks are now deadly serious. Neff ponders the murder deal, and we learn through his voiceover that he has been thinking about scamming the company for years, but only when a perfect opportunity presents itself. "I know how to do it," Neff brags to his now lover as they consummate their bargain with copulation, a reasonable inference given the couch interlude that we are given. Barbara Stanwyck, who gives a stunning performance as Phyllis, considers their throbbing passion as one of the focal points of the film: "It is not their inevitable demise we remember but rather their strong, dangerous, and above all, exciting sexuality."[29] Wilder's generic clichés have now transformed into criminal conspirators, highly individualized in their demeanor, intensity, and thinking. Phyllis, especially, is no longer merely a figural femme fatale, but has become a representation of the totality of evil in one package, a synecdoche for the *genus*.

Murder is committed, Keyes investigates, the vice tightens, conspirators squirm, and the narrative rushes toward its fatal conclusion. However, the systematic masking of Neff and Phyllis continues until they are dead. Only the cessation of life itself halts their performances, precisely because each successive encounter calls for yet another expedient masked performance. A critical scene reveals the depth of their respective duplicity when Neff and Phyllis agree to meet at her house, where each plans to kill the other, which in fact happens. "I guess I don't have to tell you what I intended to do," Neff later confesses to Keyes. Neither killer anticipates the potential homicidal intentions of the other, an indication of either how little they know one another or, more compelling, an acknowledgement of the impossibility of their respective abilities to project a stable profile of their conspirator. The characters' identities depend upon the complex dynamics of interactions, each of which necessitates a series of freshly modified faces to express evolving (devolving?) identities. Notions of evolution or devolution depend, of course, upon one's criteria in defining the capacity to adapt, or failure to adapt, to changing circumstances.

Reaching the Cemetery

The lovers' final scene is complex, but is it inevitable, given Wilder's predisposition to shine new light on old traditions? Harvey argues that the climactic double deaths are a necessary resolution to the ultimate crime of the annihilation of the family:

> The act of killing the husband serves as the supreme act of violence against family life, and has, in some sense, to be atoned for through the mutual destruction of the lovers in the macabre shootout, at the family house, which ends the film.[30]

Phyllis and Neff are both on the trolley car to the cemetery, although neither anticipates the other's plan to kill the partner. Once the killing has begun, it becomes easier for them, especially Neff. "We're both rotten," sighs Phyllis just before she shoots Neff in the shoulder. He approaches her and challenges Phyllis to finish the job. Neff now sees her objectively and insightfully — "from another situation" — in the sensibility of Merleau–Ponty. Phyllis has a failure of nerve, something that she has never before displayed. Her reluctance, we are told, is not because of any love for Neff. Indeed, she says to him: "I never loved you or anyone else ... I'm rotten to the heart." Her hesitation to kill Neff is inconsistent with her character and has confounded several commentators. What is consistent, however, is her donning of yet another mask as a result of her inability to act. What are we to make of Phyllis' possible transformation? There are ambiguities underlying Phyllis' motivations, as Dickos argues:

> Phyllis presumes to reveal that the mystery behind her motive to rid herself of her husband and have his money is much more than murderous and greedy, and

we are left with the image of a bullet-stricken blond falling into Walter Neff's arms, not quite sure whether she loved him unto death despite all that drove them apart out of mutual suspicion.[31]

A complex, enigmatic ending for Phyllis, to be sure, but this ending is the kind of character resolution that one comes to expect in Wilder's *oeuvre*. As Phyllis departs for the netherworld, she remains a mystery, an unbalanced killer lost in her world of delusions. Wilder is not willing to provide the traditional forms of closure one finds in other noir filmmakers.

There is little question about the psychological stability of Phyllis. For her character to have the most impact, she must be both evil and mentally ill, not unlike Norman Bates in *Psycho* (1960). Chris Straayer cautions against placing much trust in the debased siren:

> The words of the unrepentant *femme fatale*, however, should not have been trusted in the first place. It is her duplicity that precludes romantic coupling.... Typically, after sharing in murder, the female-male partners-in-crime are destroyed by mutual, although dissimilar, distrust and disgust.[32]

Maxfield, too, places little credibility in Phyllis' sudden change of heart: "Because sociopaths do exist, Phyllis is not an unconvincing character — until she undergoes a totally unmotivated character change just before the end of the film."[33] What is powerful is her lapse into a confessional mode in which she pleads with Neff to accept her description of herself as truth. Neff, however, resumes his role as an automatonic, cold-hearted killer, firing two bullets into Phyllis as she embraces him. "Goodbye, baby," he calmly intones. Dispatching Phyllis proves no more difficult or unsettling for Neff than his cold-blooded murder of her husband, except that the motive has changed from money and sex to self-preservation.

Neff's face in this final scene is counterpart to an earlier mask of Phyllis'. He now kills with cold logic and no emotion. Once the deed is done, he quickly dons another mask as he waits outside the house for Nino, Lola's former boyfriend and recent, frequent visitor to Phyllis. Neff seems to be in the process of adjusting his moral ledger, at least somewhat, as he arranges for the young man to reconcile with Phyllis' stepdaughter. Neff could have killed him inside the house with Phyllis' gun, and the police might well have concluded that the widow and boy lover killed each other. Does Neff have a conscience under his masks? Has the murder of Phyllis cleansed him to the point that he can now wear the face of a repentant killer? The balancing of books continues as he drives madly to confess his crimes to Keyes. In his final moments, Neff asks Keyes to "take care of" Lola and Nino. The penitent seems to seek some kind of absolution, but his crimes, like those of Phyllis, are far too dark for forgiveness, much less redemption. Has Neff been "transformed," in the lexicon of Merleau-Ponty? The question is unanswerable. Neff's next encounter will be otherworldly, requiring yet another mask.

Wilder's wild noir ride, I would suggest, calls attention to some strategic and tactical issues of subtle and explicit phenomenological movements in crime drama that extend the possibilities of analysis to a different kind of speculation. The complications of noir characters (and their motivations) always reside in a murky, subterranean world of desire, sin, crime, logic, and illogic. Their behavior derives, significantly, from subconscious terrain(s) that are inherently unknowable, thus complicating any analysis. If the preceding reading of *Indemnity* has interpretive usefulness, perhaps it might be as a point of departure in examining the encounters and the residues of those engagements, including self-recognition, of other noir figures who have so captivated us for so long by their seductive, illicit behavior.

Notes

1. Ciment, "Apropros *Avanti!*," 76.
2. Quoted in Crowe, *Conversations with Wilder*, 53.
3. Harvey, "Woman's Place: The Absent family of Film Noir," 39.
4. Sobchack, *The Address of the Eye*, xvii.
5. Merleau-Ponty, *Signs*, 19.
6. Ibid., 15.
7. Merleau-Ponty, *The Visible and the Invisible*, 105.
8. Quoted in Critchley, *The Ethics of Deconstruction*, 17.
9. Levinas, *Totality and Infinity*, 195.
10. Ibid., 195.
11. Wild, "Introduction," 14.
12. Kinneavy, *A Theory of Discourse*, 397.
13. The ancient Greeks referred to "special time" or "circumstantial time" as *kairos*, a dominant concept in Greek and Roman aesthetics, philosophy, and rhetoric. If one possesses an understanding of *kairos*, it means that he or she could create responses to situations that explicitly address the contextual imperatives of the moment. See Sipiora, "Introduction."
14. Johnston, "Double Indemnity," 89.
15. Henry, *Ethics and Social Criticism in the Hollywood Films of Erich von Stroheim, Ernst Lubitsch, and Billy Wilder*, 130.
16. Ibid., 130.
17. Johnston, 90.
18. Dikos, *Street With No Name*, 177.
19. Holt, "A Darker Shade," 39.
20. Johnston, 90.
21. I draw a distinction between explicit metaphor, the kind of language audiences immediately recognize as familiar, non-literal expressions, and implicit metaphor, those linguistic constructions that are no less figural than their recognizable relatives, but are less apparent and consequently rely upon a series of referential turns and displacements in generating momentary meaning. Noir writers and filmmakers are usually careful to employ explicit metaphors, often sexual, as long as they are not too explicit.
22. Maxfield, *The Fatal Woman*, 30.
23. Stables, "The Postmodern Always Rings Twice," 176.

24. Harvey, 37.

25. Irwin, *Unless the Threat of Death Is Behind Them*, 72.

26. Harvey, 39–40.

27. Maxfield, 12.

28. Much has been said about Keyes' possible homosexual attraction for Neff. Even Wilder, co-author of the film, wrote: "The idea was to write a love story between the two men and a sexual involvement with the woman." Allyn, *"Double Indemnity,"* 137. A "love" story can, of course, have many meanings, including a father-son type of relationship of love and respect, which clearly is part of the Keyes-Neff relationship.

29. Quoted in Place, "Women in Film Noir," 48.

30. Harvey, 42.

31. Dickos, 157.

32. Straayer, "*Femme Fatale* or Lesbian Femme," 153.

33. Maxfield, 177.

Part Three:
Production and Reception

8. *"A Small, Effective Organization"*
The Mirisch Company, the Package-Unit System, and the Production of *Some Like It Hot*

PAUL KERR

Some Like It Hot (1959) is almost certainly Billy Wilder's most popular film and in many senses it is *Wilder's* film — he is credited as producer, director and co-writer — making it an especially appropriate subject for this volume. In this essay, however, I want to discuss it not as a Billy Wilder film, but as an industrially authored, package-unit film, independently produced by the Mirisch Company.

The Mirisch Company was the most commercially and critically successful independent production company in Hollywood in the late 1950s and 1960s, winning the Best Picture Oscar three times between 1960 and 1967, and supplying United Artists with five of its ten most profitable films between 1957 and 1969. However, there is still no book length, academic analysis of the company. The best available study is an excellent chapter in Tino Balio's book on United Artists, which complements Walter Mirisch's recent autobiography.[1]

The Mirisch Company was founded in 1957 by three brothers, Harold, Marvin and Walter Mirisch. Harold and Walter had previously been executives at Allied Artists. In the wake of the Paramount decree of 1948, which led to the break-up of the vertically integrated Hollywood majors, the Mirisch Company was one of many independent production companies set up to supply the newly divorced distributors with product. The brothers swiftly signed a multi-picture deal with United Artists, with UA agreeing to finance a minimum of four pictures a year for three years beginning September 1, 1957. These films were to be cross-collateralized with profits split 50/50 between the two companies. UA paid the overhead for the brothers' small offices in Goldwyn Studios and a weekly producer fee, divided equally between them. The company was owned 96 percent by the brothers and 4 percent by key employees. Harold Mirisch was company president, Marvin vice-president and secretary-treasurer, and Walter executive in charge of production. The rest of the staff comprised a production manager, a lawyer, the head of their television production unit and an in-house editor, a publicist, and two secretaries.[2]

The trade papers were quick to detect differences between this new, slimmed-down operation and the old, vertically integrated studios, in a combination of what we might describe as downsizing, outsourcing and casualization. As *Variety* reported it, "the company will concentrate on low overhead while maintaining as high quality as possible.... Approximately 98% of all costs of a picture will be on the screen."[3] Similarly, *Business Week* noted that, "Unlike the majors, the Mirisches don't burden themselves with bricks and mortar. They rent office space by the week and sound stages by the day. The overheads stay low."[4] While some independents were co-founded by stars (Hecht-Hill-Lancaster is the best known example), the Mirisch Company was built on its relationships with directors. In an undated United Artists press release, the brothers announced their corporate ambition to:

> find the best filmmakers and provide them with the very best story material and most talented associates— enable the filmmaker to do the thing he most wants to do—concentrate completely on the films, on what appears on the screen and let a small, effective organization handle all the other complex matters that are part of making a movie, ranging from negotiating contracts and financing, to persuading actors to work under the Mirisch banner, to arranging pre-production logistics, and perhaps most important, taking the completed film and supervising its merchandising on a coordinated world-wide basis.[5]

The deals with these directors were for profit sharing "joint production ventures." Wilder's first contract with the company called for two features, for which he was to be paid a director's fee of $200,000 per film plus 17.5 percent of the gross after each film broke even (a figure which was set at about twice the negative cost). If a film grossed $1 million above that point, Wilder's share rose to 20 percent. Those first two films turned out to be *Some Like It Hot* and *The Apartment* (1960).

As Wilder put it: "All the Mirisch Company asks me is the name of the picture, a vague outline of the story and who's going to be in it. The rest is up to me. You can't get any more freedom than that."[6] The implication is that Wilder was *Some Like It Hot*'s signature author. But far from merely freeing the filmmaker-artist from industrial chores, companies like Mirisch played a crucial role in shaping and "packaging" the films they produced. Yannis Tzioumakis's *American Independent Cinema* points out that Mirisch also "represented the next step to another recent development, the rise of talent agencies into a central position in the American film industry."[7] Denise Mann's *Hollywood Independents: The Postwar Talent Takeover* describes the "paradigm shift" such agencies and independents represented in Hollywood business practices, and the impact on the aesthetic strategies of the films those new businesses produced. Mann's book charts "the paradoxical collusion between many of the new breed of talent-turned-independent producer and the newly empowered talent agencies, epitomized by MCA."[8]

MCA's extensive roster of stars after the war enabled Lew Wasserman, who succeeded Jules Stein as president of MCA in 1946, to negotiate new terms for his clients. Instead of asking for higher salaries, Wasserman began demanding a percentage of the profits. In a percentage deal, a star worked for a lower salary than usual, but received a share of the profits if the picture was a success. This arrangement lowered the (initial) cost of production for producers, and provided an opportunity for the star to earn more *and* save on income tax. In a landmark deal with Universal-International in 1950, Wasserman negotiated a 50 percent profit participation for James Stewart to star in *Winchester '73*. Stewart received over $600,000 from the film. In comparison, a top studio star such as Clark Gable never earned more than $300,000 for an entire year's work while at MGM. Stewart's deal with MCA changed the face of the business; profit participations for "packaged" talent became standard practice. Together MCA and Mirisch assembled the package that was *Some Like It Hot*.

The concept of the package-unit system was first analyzed in detail by Janet Staiger. A typical package usually comprised a story "property," director and/or star(s). Staiger defined an independent production company as "a film company which was not owned by nor owned a distribution organization."[9] The major studios were no longer the source of on and off-screen talent, equipment or materials. Now independent producers had the entire industry at their disposal when assembling their projects, securing financing, freelance staff, technical equipment, the literary "property" on which the film was to be based, the physical property (location, studio sets, facilities etc.) where it was to be shot and edited, and the props used to make the film. While the vertically integrated majors had owned their own studios, sets, cameras, lighting and recording equipment, costumes, special effects technology, editing suites etc, and had employed long-term staff to operate them, independents like Mirisch could rent or lease the physical equipment or props they needed and hire the staff to work with them on a daily or weekly basis. This, in turn, had consequences for the kinds of film that independents like the Mirisch Company were inclined to make: "Instead of the mass production of many films by a few manufacturing firms, now there was the specialized production of a few films by many independents.... This change encouraged the companies to load up each film with as much talent and spectacle as possible."[10]

Billy Wilder had first worked with Harold and Walter Mirisch at Allied Artists, where he had co-written (with I.A.L. Diamond) and directed *Love in the Afternoon* (1957) for them. At the Mirisch Company, he teamed up again with Diamond as co-writer and Associate Producer, and together they made

Some Like It Hot, The Apartment, One, Two, Three (1961), *Irma la Douce* (1963), *Kiss Me, Stupid* (1964), *The Fortune Cookie* (1966), *The Private Life of Sherlock Holmes* (1970) and *Avanti* (1972). But was the Mirisch Company's role in the relationship more than executives "freeing" a filmmaker to get on with the job of making movies as they happily took the administrative chores off his hands?

House Style

The idea of Hollywood studios each having their own "house style," and the role it played in the era of the vertically integrated companies, when the majors all had actors, writers, directors, designers, cameramen, editors and composers on contract, has been detailed elsewhere. In an essay on the director Raoul Walsh and his 1940s films for Warner Brothers, for instance, Edward Buscombe noted that, "What seems to be lacking is any conception of the relations between the economic structure of a studio, its particular organization and the kind of films it produced."[11] Thomas Schatz, in his book *The Genius of the System,* tried to develop this "conception," describing what he calls "a melding of institutional forces ... the studio's production operations and management structures, its resources and talent pool, its narrative traditions and market strategy."[12]

Can a comparable case be made for the Mirisch Company and their package-unit system of production? Did the Mirisches have a business policy or strategy that can help explain why *Some Like It Hot* is the way it is, despite their lack of a studio or contract talent? Without access to the Mirisch Company's internal documents (unavailable until the death of the last surviving brother, Walter), this essay attempts to answer Buscombe's question about "the relations between the economic structure of a company, its particular organization and the kind of films it produced," using *Some Like It Hot* as a test case.

In discussing the symbiotic relationship that existed in the vertically integrated companies between genre, contract stars and studio, Buscombe points out:

> In working for Warner Brothers, Walsh was obliged to use the stars which the studio had under contract.... One can't say exactly that Walsh was forced to make gangster pictures because he had to use these stars for they weren't the only ones available on the Warner lot. But stars and genre were, particularly at Warners, mutually reinforcing. Because the studio had Bogart, Cagney and the rest under contract they made a lot of gangster pictures; and because they made a lot of gangster pictures they had stars like this under contract.[13]

By the time Wilder cast *Some Like It Hot,* stars were no longer, as a rule, under studio contract. (Monroe was contracted to Fox, Lemmon to Columbia, but MCA easily freed them from their contractual commitments.) Instead, there were talent agencies, freelance contracts, and packages, and the attitude to traditional studio genres (and stars) was, accordingly, becoming nostalgic/self-conscious. Hence the casting of gangster film icons George Raft and Pat O'Brien in *Some Like It Hot.*

Wilder, like Walsh, was a veteran of Paramount. Unlike Walsh, who simply moved to another vertically integrated studio, Wilder was obliged, in the wake of divorcement, to sign up with an independent. Not having any actors under contract, the Mirisch Company had no built-in, star-based propensity for particular genres. Any such propensities were based on their own predilections, past experience and reading of the industry, together with the preferences of the directors they signed. Wilder, having spent seventeen years at Paramount where he made eight films, after a brief hiatus at various other companies, spent another seventeen years, making eight further films, at the Mirisch Company. But without a stock company of regularly collaborating talent on contract, could this corporate entity be said to have co-authored Wilder's films, rather than simply facilitated their production?

As with the Mirisch Company, there are no academic studies of MCA, although three recent journalistic accounts provide some useful context for *Some Like It Hot.*[14] Meanwhile, Denise Mann's study of agency-dominated Hollywood, barely mentions *Some Like It Hot*, referring to it only three times as the work of a writer-director, as a characteristic shop window of talent assembled by MCA, and as an example of cinematic self-referentiality, in its sending up of Cary Grant (by Curtis) and George Raft (through an exchange between Edward G. Robinson, Jr., and Raft himself). Grant and Raft were both, of course, studio era stars. According to Mann, "self-referential themes and self-reflexive strategies" were characteristic of independent films in postwar Hollywood in transition, a distinct cinematic style illustrating an aesthetic shift from the classical to post-classical.[15]

One such scene occurs early in *Some Like It Hot*, though Mann doesn't mention it. Tony Curtis and Jack Lemmon are in a corridor entering several offices looking for work. As the door of one office closes, the viewer can clearly read the nameplate:

MUSIC CORPORATION OF AMERICA
    JULES STEIN, *President*
Joe opens the door.
JOE: Anything today?
SECRETARY (drinking from a bottle): Nothing.
JOE: Thank you.[16]

This, right down to the illicit swig of prohibition liquor, is, of course, an in-joke, a bit of "self-referentiality," of the kind to which Mann refers. But it is more than that. It is also a denial of *corporate* agency and an implicit avowal of *human* agency. I trust that what follows will make this distinction clear.

The film begins in 1929 in Chicago and tells the story of two unemployed musicians in Prohibition America who witness the St. Valentine's Day Massacre.

This period and place was also the origin of MCA. Mann's chapter about MCA begins in the 1940s, so she omits to mention that the Music Corporation of America was founded in Chicago by Jules Stein in 1924, specifically as a band-booking agency. MCA helped pioneer the business of booking touring jazz bands for clubs, concert halls and speakeasies, many of them run by the Capone mob. It was in 1920s Chicago that Stein's MCA first deployed the art of block booking entertainers.[17] Block booking works essentially on the same principle as packaging, leveraging unwanted acts or products on a customer as obligatory parts of a deal involving one or two specifically required performers or films.

The connection between a story about two freelance musicians who need work and the history of the agency, MCA, that arranged the signing of the actors who played those roles is far from accidental. This is both the story of the pre-war beginnings of MCA itself and, by analogy, the story of all talent in the post–anti-trust era. In 1957 Hollywood was for the first time dominated by independent producers and the package unit system, with employment on a film-by-film (like the musicians hired for specific dates and locations) rather than firm-by-firm basis (with careers sometimes spent for years, if not decades, on staff at a single company). Indeed, Hollywood's own musicians were negotiating new contracts with the studios in 1958, just as *Some Like It Hot* was being made, and subsequently film work for studio musicians would be freelance. *Some Like It Hot* was shot between August 4, 1958 and November 6, 1958. The studio musicians had gone on strike in February 1958, and the dispute was settled on July 11, 1958.[18] The Screen Actors Guild was following the dispute closely, and began its own negotiations with the studios in late 1959. So this film about freelance musicians was made precisely as Hollywood's own musicians were being forcibly casualized by an industry in which many had previously enjoyed staff contracts, and was acted by performers whose own job security was being hit in the same way.

Of course, this brief agency-visiting scene could be explained as a quintessentially auteurist fingerprint, a trace of Wilder's reflexive, writer-directorial DNA. But in the mid–1950s, for the first time in his Hollywood career, Wilder, as a freelance talent for hire, was in the same position as his film's protagonists. That the premise of *Some Like It Hot* reflected the economics and employment practices of Hollywood, not at the time the film was set but precisely at the moment of its production, is intriguing. But it is also the case that much of the film's key talent — the human aspect of the "package" — Wilder himself, of course, but also Curtis and Monroe, the biggest box office names above the title, not to mention Persoff and O'Brien, were MCA clients. (Sources disagree about whether Lemmon, too, was on MCA's books.) Indeed, Wilder, Curtis and Monroe all enjoyed lucrative MCA-negotiated profit-sharing percentages on the film, from each of which the agency took its share. And Wilder, with his three credited roles, was a particularly valuable client. His first casting choices for the film, however — Frank Sinatra, Danny Kaye and Mitzi Gaynor — were all rejected.

Even the title, *Some Like It Hot*, previously the name of a Bob Hope comedy, was owned by MCA through its recent acquisition of Paramount's pre–1948 back catalogue, and could thus be re-charged to Mirisch/UA. The original title, *Fanfares of Love*, was changed during production to *Not Tonight, Josephine*, before that, too, was jettisoned; neither would have led to profits for MCA.

Since Buscombe and Schatz wrote about "house style," a number of other scholars have developed the concept of "studio autobiography" or "studio authorship."[19] Mark McGurl argues that at a critical moment in a studio's history, a film can function as "a confessional text, an entry, of sorts, in the spiritual diary of the corporation,"[20] or, as Jerome Christensen puts it: "Certain Hollywood films allegorically reflect on the motives and methods of the studio and its agents."[21] Christensen and others use the term "studio allegory" to describe such films. As Christensen describes it: "It is an allegorical characteristic of a certain privileged class of motion pictures that their extra-diegetic aims, such as an aspiration for Oscars, must be "invisible" to the studio and to the trade — not just in the promotion of the picture but in the picture itself."[22] Jared Gardner, meanwhile, has described Billy Wilder's *Sunset Boulevard* (1950) as a studio allegory for Paramount.[23] Similarly, it is my contention here that, consciously or not, the Mirisches entrusted Wilder with an allegory of, or subliminal marketing campaign for, their new company and the package-unit system. Both productions came at critical times for Hollywood — in the wake of the Paramount decision of 1948 which put an end to vertical integration in the industry, and, a decade later, the launch of a new independent to exploit precisely that situation — both moments facilitating, if not actively necessitating an exercise in corporate (re)legitimation.

Another extremely successful Mirisch film among the company's first productions was *The Magnificent Seven* (1960) which, even more centrally, dramatizes the putting together of a professional team of freelancers, literally "hired guns." Mirisch's later *The Great Escape* (1963) also focuses on the assembly of a team of skilled specialists to undertake a specific mission. Indeed, this was the era of narratives dramatizing the assembling of an ensemble of experts for a specific project, with caper or heist films like *The Asphalt Jungle* (1950), *The Killing* (1956) and *Ocean's Eleven* (1960) also centering on the putting together of a team for a one-off job. Why?

Understanding the industrial imperatives of the package-unit indies begins to answer that question. These might best be summarized as maximizing profits (and thus maximizing the attractions of each film) while minimizing risks and costs. As habitual cinemagoing decreased and industry ploys like double bills, block booking and blind selling were outlawed, each film became its own marketing, its own combination of unique selling points. It was no longer enough to produce a genre film or even a conventional star vehicle; successful films had to combine attractions, often deploying a number of simultaneous strategies— and scholars have identified several of them.[24]

- Casualizing employment
- Profit-sharing rather than/or in addition to weekly wages (for above-the-line talent)
- Location filming/runaway production
- Demographic targeting of young adult audiences
- Differentiation via innovations in stars, story, subject matter and style
- Employing hyphenates above the line
- Adapting pre-sold literary or theatrical properties, often exploring class, race and gender with sexually provocative themes
- Generic hybridity
- Challenging the censors
- Marketing the film/the film as marketing

For the Mirisch Company, these industrial imperatives led to two key cinematic strategies. The first was a propensity for pre-tested properties from Broadway (*West Side Story*, 1961) to best-sellers (*Hawaii*, 1966), from cinematic remakes (*The Magnificent Seven*) to recycling extra-cinematic stars (Elvis in *Kid Galahad* and *Follow that Dream*, both 1962). The second strategy was to look for a fertile franchise, amenable to sequels and spin-offs, rich in returnable characters and situations. Examples include *In the Heat of the Night* (1967) which spawned two sequels, *The Pink Panther* (1964) which also spun off two further films for the company, plus a TV series, *The Magnificent Seven* (which led to three sequels), while the success of *Hawaii* led to *The Hawaiians*, adapted from the second half of the same James Michener bestseller. Of fifty-four Mirisch films released between 1958 and 1973, fifteen were in such series.

This strategic combination of two risk-aversion techniques meant that Mirisch films were, in Staiger's sense, top heavy, combining as many "attractions" and as much on-screen insurance as possible. Of course, none of these strategies was unique to the Mirisch Company. On *The Young Lions* (1958), for instance (another MCA package, combining three of the agency's clients in one package — Marlon Brando, Montgomery Clift and Dean Martin), Tony Randall had originally been cast in Martin's role. But MCA insisted that Martin replace Randall so they would have what the agency considered "a quadruple threat" (an audience from four sectors): nightclubs, recordings, television and movies.[25] *Some Like It Hot* could be considered a triple threat, combining the audiences of recorded music (Monroe), cinema (Monroe, Curtis and pastiched genres), and magazines (Monroe), while it made nightclubs its subject and TV its implicit "other."

But whatever talent was packaged for it, a prior question remains. Where did the idea for *Some Like It Hot* itself come from? Why that story, at that time, and can the film's status as a package-unit independent production have had an impact on that choice? According to the opening credits, the screenplay is by Billy Wilder and I.A.L. Diamond "Suggested by a story by R. Thoeren and M. Logan." Wilder always claimed that it had its origins in an old German musical, which he saw before leaving for Hollywood:

> There was a German picture (*Fanfares of Love*) before the war, about two musicians who are looking for jobs, and they find jobs in various disguises: Bavarian music, mountain music, by doing music in black face — we could do that in Germany, in black face — but ultimately they have jobs in a girls' orchestra. We omitted everything but the girls' orchestra. From then on it becomes absolutely new, the screenplay.[26]

Wilder seems to have mixed up two films. *Some Like It Hot*'s plot actually derives from a 1935 French musical, *Fanfare d'amour*, directed by Richard Pottier and co-written by Robert Thoeren and Michael Logan. Logan and Thoeren wrote their original script in Weimar Germany, in German. Forced to emigrate to Paris to escape the Nazis, the film was first made in French instead. After the war, the film was finally made in German as *Fanfaren der Liebe* (1951). The opening credits of *Some Like It Hot* mention a story by Thoeren and Logan, but don't mention the original film title(s), or even that there was a previous film, let alone the French original.

Fanfaren der Liebe, based on Thoeren and Logan's original idea, tells the story of two unemployed musicians, Hans and Pete, who wear blackface to get one gig and don drag to get another. They make regular visits to a booking agency, but there are no jobs, so they dress up in women's clothes to get work in an all-woman band, The Alpine Violets. They pass a quick audition, and board the night train to Ingolstadt, a resort hotel in the Alps, where the band has been booked to play. They are introduced to the other girls, who are already in their pajamas in their sleeping berths. Next morning, Hans goes to the breakfast car in his male clothes. A romance develops with the singer, Gabi, while Hans (back in female costume) is pursued by a man. According to Walter Mirisch himself: "In his [sic] screenplay, Billy used little material from the original film, except the idea of two men who disguise themselves as women so they can get jobs in an all-girl band. Nearly everything else was original."[27] As the synopsis above reveals, this is untrue. In fact, virtually the whole of *Fanfaren der Liebe* deals with the two musicians who join an all-girl orchestra. There is a gruff, older band leader, à la Sweet Sue; a singer whom both men lust after, like Sugar Kane; an overnight train ride to a tourist resort; much changing in and out of drag to woo the band singer, and close escapes from being unmasked.

Some Like It Hot shares the characteristics of many other independent films in deploying the plot of an already successful film as a risk aversion strategy. It wasn't a remake or adaptation of an already known quantity, but it was a remake of a highly successful story (if not one well-known in America). Indeed, the film was so successful in Germany that a sequel was released two years later, *Fanfaren der Ehe* (1953), with the same stars. Thus, far from being an obscure, old film, this was a recent and very successful, albeit German, film. According to Mirisch, Wilder "proposed that we acquire the rights to *Fanfaren*. It became a real test for the attorneys to find the then-owners of the film and to acquire the rights to remake it."[28] Having gone to such lengths to acquire the rights, the filmmakers seemed equally keen to conceal the extent to which *Some Like It Hot* borrows from its predecessors. Nor was it the first project Wilder proposed to the Mirisch brothers. According to Walter Mirisch, soon after signing Wilder, the brothers "acquired an idea called *My Sister and I*" from Wilder, but it was never made.[29]

So why did *Some Like It Hot* (and *The Magnificent Seven*) seem like the right projects at the time? An initial answer, that both were adapting successful film formulae from one market to another (*The Magnificent Seven* was also a remake of a successful foreign film, *The Seven Samurai* (1954)), doesn't explain why *Fanfaren der Liebe* and *The Seven Samurai* were adapted when and how they were. One of the most promising attempts to theorize the relationship between the narrative structures of successful Hollywood films and the American society that produced and consumed them was proposed by Will Wright.[30] Wright argued that a structural study of the history of box office hits in the western genre reveals a shift from a classic plot to a "professional" plot. He then related those generic shifts to shifts in American capitalism, specifically from an individualist market economy to a corporate or managed one. Thus, among what he called "professional westerns," Wright identified films like *Rio Bravo* (1959), *The Professionals* (1966), *The Wild Bunch* (1969) and *Butch Cassidy and The Sundance Kid* (1969). Another western, which fits both Wright's narrative structure and his dates is *The Magnificent Seven*. But, rather than try to relate such films to America's capitalist mode of production, why not try to relate them to the industry in which such plots were deployed, and ask whether they might have made particular sense to their producers? This essay, adapting Wright's approach, attempts to relate *Some Like It Hot*'s plot (and style) to the employment and economic structures in which the film was produced.

The economic model of independent production at the Mirisch Company, the package-unit system, might illuminate some of these narrative choices. For instance, Wright dates the emergence of what he refers to as the professional plot to 1958, and it was precisely in 1958 that not only *The Magnificent Seven* but also *Some Like It Hot* began to be formulated. Indeed, *The Magnificent Seven* is not just one of the first of Wright's "professional westerns." The protagonists (a team of freelance gunfighters put together to do a job — protect the village) and the performers and crew (a team of freelance employees put together to do a job — produce the film) are mirror images of each other.

For purposes of brevity, let's recap the Mirisch Company's characteristic strategies—casualization, "runaway" production, employing above-the-line hyphenates, profit sharing with top agency-packaged talent, the big/quality picture (alternated with make-weight, low cost films, which helped fulfill the company's commitment to UA), the pre-sold property, the potential franchise, differentiating style, subject and story, courting controversy, reflexivity and demographic (adult) targeting. I want finally to discuss these strategies as they are deployed in and by *Some Like It Hot*.

Casualization: *Some Like It Hot* was crewed and cast by hiring freelance on-camera and behind-the-camera workers on short term, daily or weekly contracts. As Monroe's Sugar Kane puts it: "So you pull yourself together, you go on to the next job, the next saxophone player; it's the same thing all over again." This is very much the life of the freelance artist, going from film to film, gig to gig, rather than the staff contract player on salary at a studio. But the role of the successful independent producer was to ensure that each production was precisely not, or *not precisely*, "the same thing all over again." And casualization played a crucial role in this differentiation, ensuring that each new collaboration never quite reassembled the same team as before.

Property: The Mirisch Company based many of its films on "pre-texts," pre-existing, pre-tested stories and subjects that had already been tried out in other media. In particular, a number were adapted from literary and theatrical texts, pre-sold properties including *The Children's Hour* (1961), *West Side Story*, *Hawaii*, *Irma la Douce*, *Kiss Me, Stupid*, *In the Heat of the Night* and *Toys in the Attic* (1963). *Some Like It Hot* was adapted from a cinematic property, but that was concealed from most viewers at the time. Indeed, the contribution of *Fanfaren der Liebe* to the plot and characterization of *Some Like It Hot* was always downplayed, if not explicitly denied, by both the writer-director and Mirisch, so that the artistic "originality" of Wilder and his collaborators could be emphasized. This allowed the production company to maximize the risk aversion of a tried and (thrice) tested premise, but to minimize audience awareness of that strategy by ignoring the existence of those previous versions.

Generic Hybridity: *Some Like It Hot* is ambitious in its reversals and confusions of A and B film genre, as well as gender, formulae (gangster film meets farce, men wear frocks). Indeed, the Hollywood genre pastiche into which the film slides *Fanfaren*'s screwball premise is what differentiates *Some Like It Hot* from its original. Wilder, who himself described it as "*Scarface* meets *Charlie's Aunt*," liked repeating David O. Selznick's response to the film's premise: "You want machine guns and dead bodies and gags in the same picture? Forget about it Billy, you'll never make it work."[31] In fact, such hybridity is a strategy for differentiation. As the trailer puts it: "Boy never met girl like this before." Although, in a sense, of course, "boy" had — three times!

Franchise: The film successfully spun off two soundtrack albums, by Monroe and Lemmon, as well as the untransmitted TV pilot (1961), in which Lemmon and Curtis briefly resumed their roles, only to opt for facial cosmetic surgery to evade the mob and enable recasting of their parts. A series was never made, but at the time of writing a cinematic remake is imminent, to be directed by Ron Howard and to star Scarlett Johansson, Ashton Kutcher and Shia LaBoeuf.

Location: *Some Like It Hot* was, in part, a "runaway production." It was shot at rented Goldwyn Studios space (for interiors and the railway station sequence), but also on location at the Del Coronado Hotel in San Diego (standing in for Florida). Not being restricted to traditional Hollywood studio stages and contract employees encouraged the use of cheaper locations and, sometimes, cheaper, non–Hollywood crews. But the film also dramatized this very process by focusing on protagonists (Joe, Jerry, Sugar, not to mention Sweet Sue and the band) whose occupations involve them traveling from job to job. Thus the film not only required its "casualized" cast and crew to work away from the studio, it also made such freelance, "movable" employment part of its plot. The train journey to Florida stands in for the journey to San Diego undertaken by the below-the-line crew and extras. Tony Curtis, both literally and metaphorically, got on his bike to get into costume, character and role/job/gig.

Style: The film is in black and white, which differentiates it from mainstream contemporary Hollywood output. Of course, in 1958, this did not distinguish it from cinema's new rival, television, and the film did not deploy the newly available spectacle of widescreen. The usual explanation for *Some Like It Hot* being in black and white is that it suited the period and its conventional cinematic depiction. Wilder also felt that test shots of Lemmon and Curtis in costume and make-up were much camper and less credible in color than in monochrome. However, Monroe's contract stipulated that all her films had to be in color, so the decision to shoot in black and white was guaranteed to offer a "different" Monroe, and to earn press attention for this departure. Furthermore, Wilder was resistant to color, and this resistance to the new industrial standard defined his authorial defiance and Mirisch's corporate difference.

The opening four minutes of the film are dialogue-free and all-but silent, except for the sounds of police sirens, car wheels, gunshots and breaking glass. They are reminiscent of silent cinema, which of course was how cinema was when the film was set, on the cusp of the coming of sound, when films were also in black and white. There is a reprise of this silence towards the end of the film, when Little Bonaparte turns down his hearing aid to reduce the volume of the machine gun bullets being fired at Spats and his gang. This is also a "quotation" from/reference to a scene in *The Big Combo* (1955). The Head of Production at Allied Artists, which produced *The Big Combo* in 1955, was Walter Mirisch.

Demographics and Censorship: *Some Like It Hot* challenged the content restrictions of the Production Code Administration and received a "C" (Condemned) rating from the Catholic Legion of Decency. The Legion's Monsignor Little declared that "The subject matter of 'transvestism' naturally leads to complications ... in this film there seemed to us to be clear inferences of homosexuality and lesbianism. The dialogue was not only 'double entendre' but straight smut. The offense in costuming was obvious."[32] It was released without the MPAA logo in the credits or title sequence, since the film did not receive Production Code approval. It was banned in Kansas by the all-women Review Board, and in Memphis it received an "Adults Only" label. The Mirisch Company was to continue with this strategy. *Irma la Douce* was recut for one city censorship board; UA promised that it would "be sold and advertised as a strictly adult film." *Kiss Me, Stupid* was condemned by the Legion of Decency as "morally repulsive" and was given an "adults only" rating by several municipal censors; UA recut it for the censors and released it through a subsidiary, Lopert Films.[33] In 1961 *The Children's Hour* was one of several films which pressured the PCA into finally modifying its Code's restrictions against depicting homosexuality.

A 1957 survey revealed that 72 percent of American filmgoers were under thirty.[34] *Some Like It Hot* was aimed at this young, adult audience. This may help to explain the notorious walk-outs by families with children at the first preview in December 1958 at the suburban Bay Theatre in Pacific Palisades, where it was screened on a double-bill with *Suddenly, Last Summer* (1959), a melodrama about cannibalism and homosexuality. This disastrous preview contrasts dramatically with the huge success of the second, minimally recut version, a week later, in front of a younger UCLA audience in Westwood. (Francis Ford Coppola joined the University the following year.) The film is aimed at an adult, somewhat sophisticated audience, hence the suitability of students at that decisive second preview. Walter Mirisch was well aware of the market shift towards more "adult" fare.[35]

Marketing: Sex is a selling point of the film: the trailer has the caption "Marilyn Monroe and her bosom companions" over a picture of Monroe in a low cut dress, with Lemmon and Curtis, and later the voiceover lines "So much Marilyn" and "You've never laughed more at sex — or a movie about it." Monroe was the only top rank star in the cast, and she had not been seen on screen for two years since *The Prince and the Showgirl* (1957). At one point in the film, Lemmon remarks to Curtis of Monroe: "How about that talent, huh? Like falling into a tub of butter" — a remark neatly equating talent/stardom with spectacle/sexuality.

Saul Bass' celebrated career as a titles designer began with this new need to differentiate and sell films individually in the wake of the Paramount Decision. Bass designed both the poster and the credit sequence for *Some Like It Hot* and for several high profile Mirisch films, including *The Magnificent Seven* (unused), *West Side Story* and *The Fortune Cookie*. Bass' career took off at precisely the moment that saw the rise of independent production in the 1950s. Independent producers like the Mirisch Company could control the publicity for their films in ways unavailable to employees of the vertically integrated majors. Once films were sold as one-offs, and each film needed to establish its uniqueness, Bass' signature designs could help differentiate it from its competitors.

Release: The film premiered at the Loew's State Theater, New York on

March 29, 1959, and was released across the U.S. that month. By the end of 1959, it was the third most profitable film at the U.S. box office. According to *Variety*, it played in 18,000 of a total of 20,000 domestic cinemas.[36] By 1963, *Some Like It Hot* had earned $7.5 million in the U.S. alone and an additional $5.25 million abroad.

Conclusion

If Wilder's 1950 film, *Sunset Boulevard*, is, among other things, an allegory for the studio which produced it and the mode of production that studio deployed, the producer-unit system, in the wake of the Paramount anti-trust decision, then *Some Like It Hot* performs a comparable function a decade later for the Mirisch Company and its mode of production, the package-unit system. The film functions as an allegory for the business strategy deployed by the Mirisch Company, and a showcase for the adaptability, mobility and flexibility of independent producers like themselves and the package-unit system they adopted in the new industrial circumstances. In doing so, it foregrounds the skills of freelance performers (whose roles involve acting, singing, etc), and a corporate flexibility with costumes, locations, genres and generic hybridity. Thus we see Curtis as Josephine and Cary Grant, George Raft as both a gangster and a pastiche of his own gangster roles, and Edward G. Robinson, Jr., repeating Raft's coin-tossing riff from *Scarface* (1931) in an implicit reference to his father's iconic roles in that genre. (Robinson Sr. was another "unavailable" William Morris client.)

But the gangster setting and characters aren't there simply to provide opportunities for genre pastiche. The gangster board meeting also functions as a pastiche of a meeting of a big American corporation, like the vertically integrated studios themselves, with delegates from across the country. The same applies to Junior's (Curtis in his Cary Grant persona) assumed role in his family business, the Shell Corporation. In Wilder and the Mirisches' next collaboration, *The Apartment*, the office set was specifically designed as a pastiche of the anonymous workspaces of contemporary corporate bureaucracy, and, implicitly, of the vertically integrated majors that companies like Mirisch were challenging.

Writing of the allegorical function performed by *Mrs. Miniver* (1943) for Louis B. Mayer and MGM, Jerome Christensen concluded that "*Mrs. Miniver* was the chosen vehicle for Mayer to vindicate MGM's commitment to quality, both in the eyes of its public audience, whom the film endeavors to confirm in its choice, and in the hearts and minds of the Hollywood faithful, for whom the film attempts to devise its future and perform quality."[37] This essay has argued that the independent, package-unit production of *Some Like It Hot* was a vehicle for the Mirisches to vindicate their own and United Artists' commitment to quality, both in the eyes of the new, young, adult audience, and in the hearts and minds of the industry, for whom the film attempts to lay out a blueprint for its future business and aesthetic strategy. *Some Like It Hot* is thus both textual evidence of the company's on-screen differentiations from mainstream studio product (a one-off in every sense), and, at the same time, an allegory about the company's strategy — and ability — to undertake just such a differentiation.

Notes

1. Balio, *United Artists*; Mirisch, *I Thought We Were Making Movies, Not History*.
2. Mirisch, 89.
3. Balio, 165.
4. Ibid., 161–62.
5. Ibid., 161.
6. Wood, *The Bright Side of Billy Wilder, Primarily*, 179.
7. Tzioumakis, *American Independent Cinema*, 119.
8. Mann, *Hollywood Independents*, 2 and 8.
9. Bordwell, Staiger and Thompson, *The Classical Hollywood Cinema*, 330.
10. Ibid., 331–32.
11. Hardy, *Raoul Walsh*, 52.
12. Schatz, *The Genius of the System*, 6–7.
13. Hardy, 59.
14. Bruck, *When Hollywood Had a King*; McDougal, *The Last Mogul*; Sharp, *Mr. and Mrs. Hollywood*.
15. Mann, 117 and 87.
16. Castle, *Some Like It Hot*.
17. Bruck, 16.
18. Lev, *The Fifties*, 213–14.
19. Christensen, "Studio Identity and Studio Art"; Christensen, "The Time Warner Conspiracy"; Christensen, "Neo-Corporate Star-Making"; Gardner, "Covered Wagons and Decalogues"; McGurl, "Making It Big."
20. McGurl, 416–17.
21. Christensen, "Studio Authorship, Warner Bros. and *The Fountainhead*," 19.
22. Christensen, "Neo-Corporate Star-Making," 282.
23. Gardner, "Covered Wagons and Decalogues," 361–62.
24. Bordwell, Staiger and Thompson; Balio; Mann.
25. McDougal, interview with the author, 2000.
26. Castle, 244.
27. Mirisch, 100.
28. Ibid., 100.
29. Castle, 36.
30. Wright, *Sixguns & Society*.
31. Rolston, *Some Like It Hot*, 6.
32. Leff, *The Dame in the Kimono*, 259.
33. Ibid., 259.
34. Lev, 214.
35. Mirisch, 91.
36. Balio, 165.
37. Christensen, "Studio Identity and Studio Art," 271.

9. *"Esthetically As Well as Morally Repulsive"*

Kiss Me, Stupid, "Bilious Billy," and the Battle of Middlebrow Taste

KEN FEIL

The dramatic, noisy reception of Billy Wilder's sex comedy *Kiss Me, Stupid* in December 1964 yields a triumph for the traditional American middlebrow, a taste public whose hegemony is nevertheless in decline. Bourgeois moral and aesthetic assumptions inform the Legion of Decency's "Condemned" rating, United Artists' distribution and marketing strategies, the onslaught of negative reviews, the few positive ones, and the film's bitter demise at the box office. *Stupid* premieres "to some of the most resoundingly disapproving reviews in cinema history," Peter Bart recalls in a 1965 *New York Times* article, "and proceeded to play to nearly empty theatres."[1] Middlebrow commentators blame Wilder for the film's brazen tastelessness and accuse the Production Code Administration (PCA), which approves the film, of betraying its own petty-bourgeois standards of taste, morality, and decorum. Wilder's authorship also proves pivotal in the sparse middlebrow approval given *Kiss Me, Stupid.* Cult film sensibility guides these dissident middlebrow defenses, signs of an emergent generation directly challenging the old guard over the tenuous distinction between high and low.

Kiss Me, Stupid revolves around piano teacher and wannabe songwriter Orville J. Spooner (Ray Walston). Residing in Climax, Nevada, a desert town of puritans, swollen cacti, and a bar-brothel called the Belly Button, Orville composes ditties like "Gently Baby, It's Mother's Day" with gas station attendant Barney (Cliff Osmond). He also obsessively suspects his wife Zelda (Felicia Farr) of cuckolding him. Orville and Barney happen upon the opportunity to peddle a tune to Dino (Dean Martin), a lascivious superstar passing through Climax. To grease the deal without sparking Orville's jealousy, Barney hires the Belly Button's Polly "the pistol" (Kim Novak) to impersonate Zelda and sleep with Dino.

Over the course of a drunken dinner, Dino flirts relentlessly with Polly/ "Zelda." Orville finally explodes, evicts the "Rat Pack" playboy, and retires with Polly to the boudoir, both maintaining the marital charade. Undaunted, Dino ventures to the Belly Button for "cuisine" and mistakes Zelda for Polly. Initially resistant, Zelda/"Polly" recalls her teenage crush on Dino, makes love to him, and even hawks one of Orville's songs. The film closes with Dino singing Orville and Barney's "Italian number" on television, Zelda and Orville's reconciliation, and Polly's escape to a better life, funded by Zelda with Dino's payment.

In its story of unpunished mutual adultery abundant in dirty jokes, double entendres, and exaggerated gags, *Kiss Me, Stupid* transgresses the standardized rules of the romantic comedy genre that, for the prior three decades, fulfill the Code's regulations of "good taste."[2] Romantic comedies of the 1930s and 1940s translate erotic desire and spectacle into "playful" courtships concluding in marriage,[3] but 1960s sex comedies represent, according to Frank Krutnik, an "erosion of confidence, both in the application of generic formulas and in the status of marriage as the legitimizing framework for heterosexual relations...."[4] *Stupid* stands out for critics and commentators; its PCA-approved egregiousness portends the decline of the Code and the loss of cultural taste standards.

Critics utilize *Kiss Me, Stupid* to retrench the boundaries of a middlebrow precariously balancing oppositional sensibilities: "petty bourgeois" taste, which favors moralistic Hollywood kitsch; and an art-for-art's-sake rationale reserved for sexy European art films. American "adult" movies and sex comedies complicate the middlebrow's balancing act; inspired by the commercial success of art films, these movies feature sexually frank content and occasional nudity, but usually lack the philosophizing of art films as well as Hollywood pictures' stringent moralizing. Drawing the line between artistic foreign art movies and prurient, commercially exploitative American adult movies, middlebrow critics locate an ideal target in *Stupid*'s taste transgressions and "C" rating.

Wilder's authorship exacerbates *Stupid*'s perceived offenses. Boasting a slew of Code-approved, critically celebrated, Oscar winning commercial hits, Wilder remains an enduring figurehead for middlebrow Hollywood filmmaking. The jocular nickname "Bilious Billy" suggests how his latest films *Some Like It Hot* (1959), *The Apartment* (1960), and *Irma la Douce* (1963) pushed boundaries, but middlebrow reviewers praised Wilder for his urbane "satires" that nevertheless uphold bourgeois morality.[5] With the "vulgar," "immoral" *Stupid*, critics denounce Wilder for betraying his reputation and venally exploiting the salacious elements of art cinema.

Wilder's authorship also underscores a growing divide among middlebrows of the 1960s, the "cultists" versus the traditionalists.[6] Cult sensibility informs the few positive reviews of *Kiss Me, Stupid*, which reverse the terms of detractors by positioning the film among art movies and canonized literature, differentiating it from "vulgar" Hollywood- and Legion-approved kitsch, and praising Wilder's morality, satire, and social commentary. Cult approval of Wilder and *Stupid* reflects an emergent "good taste of bad taste" and foreshadows radical transformations of mainstream taste in the dawn of New Hollywood.

The Production Code, the Legion of Decency, Art Films and "Adult" Movies

Arbiters of middlebrow taste anxiously use *Kiss Me, Stupid* to stabilize their territory as record numbers of Hollywood films defy the Code by emulating the sexual freedom of foreign art films. Middlebrow taste defines itself in the cultural hierarchy between "high" art and "lower-middle" mass culture, to a certain degree merging its neighbors' priorities and styles.[7] High culture typically treasures aesthetic experimentation over moralizing, Pierre Bourdieu observes, in the aesthetic of "art for art's sake."[8] Lower-middle culture's "petty bourgeois aesthetic" rejects, however, "decadent art ... respecting neither God nor man," and prefers standardized works that "arouse the moral sense ... inspire feelings of dignity and delicacy ... idealize reality ... educate."[9] Middlebrow taste balances these interests by favoring mass culture formulas, maintaining bourgeois values, and espousing a degree of "art" and stylistic novelty.[10] Sociologist Herbert Gans describes the general purpose of middlebrow (or "upper-middle") cultural commentators: "to differentiate between high and upper-middle culture content — and also between lower-middle and upper-middle content ... disapproving of content which they perceive as too experimental or philosophical on the one hand, or too clichéd and 'vulgar' on the other hand."[11] When European "art" films threaten to complicate middlebrow taste hierarchies with their explicit sexual content and spectacle,[12] critics approach such experimental and daring subject matter with caution. They tolerate, sometimes celebrate these foreign films' "seamier" attributes as "artistic," as long as films also deliver morality tales about the tolls of debauchery, narcissism, moral and spiritual malaise.[13]

That vast urban audiences in the United States flock to "European works" in the 1960s, many unapproved by the PCA and scorned by the Legion for their "[moral] dangerousness,"[14] indicates changing popular tastes and motivates Hollywood to mine them. A 1966 *Film Quarterly* essay recalls the unprecedented appeal of "continental and experimental film-makers" beginning in 1963.[15] By 1965, Bart remarks in the *New York Times*, "the films that are creating the most talk and the biggest profits are generally being made abroad either by Europeans or by expatriate Americans.... It's the profits, to be sure, that most impress the studio brass." Bart attributes the popularity of foreign films to "creative initiative" that Hollywood films lack, crippled by a Production Code "steeped in hypocrisy and desperately out of date."[16]

Hollywood's doubts about the Code and inspiration from foreign films yield a crisis among middlebrow "custodians" about the fate of mainstream taste. Although Bosley Crowther of the *New York Times* confidently defended the bourgeois virtues of *The Moon Is Blue* in 1953, despite the PCA's refusing a seal and the Legion's "Condemned" rating,[17] this influential middlebrow voice wavers with anxiety in 1964 over the loosening of the Code motivated by popular European imports: "there was nothing they [the PCA] could do to control the taste and content of films that came from abroad"; as a result, "the patroling [sic] of taste by the custodians of the Code was considerably relaxed."[18] As for consequences, Crowther subsequently observes, "While some of the seamiest material has been shockingly but validly contained in films of a serious, artful nature that have been meant to give profound reports of life, too much of it has been jammed into pictures for sheer sensation sake, presumably to titillate the patrons and make them think they're being naughty as all get-out." Crowther can appreciate the "seamy" shocks of "serious, artful" foreign films— "Tony Richardson's ribald 'Tom Jones' and Ingmar Bergman's neurotic 'The Silence'"—and even some Hollywood ones (*The Americanization of Emily*, 1964).[19] Fears linger over "Bad Taste" in American movies: the "disgusting" *The Carpetbaggers* (1964), enticingly labeled "ADULT ENTERTAINMENT"; and the "distasteful" *A House Is Not a Home* (1964).[20] Historian Robert C. Allen characterizes Hollywood's enduring assumption "that the largest possible audience could be attained by appealing to middle-class interests and tastes,"[21] but the spectacles of immorality flaunted in *Carpetbaggers* and *House* raise a big question in 1964/5: how now to define "middle-class interests and tastes?"

Sustaining bourgeois taste without seeming provincial, American middlebrow critics of the mid–1960s engage high culture's *"ars gratia artis"* rationale to approve of open sex and exposed bodies in foreign art films, while sex and nudity in Hollywood movies most often amount to vulgar, commercially motivated exploitation. As director of the 1965 New York Film Festival, Amos Vogel validates the "eroticism" of "experimental," primarily European art movies "[u]nencumbered by the usual box office considerations," by contrast to the "[s]exual titillation" of profit-driven movies.[22] Crowther similarly acknowledges "valid" uses of sex and nudity in cinematic imports and rebukes American "adult" movies for "suggestive situations and themes," "nude exposures and cheap double-meaning gags."[23] This qualitative distinction allows middlebrows to have their profanity and chastise it too. They can "legitimate the cinema as art" (in Mark Betz's words)[24] through art-for-art's-sake, praising "valid" "eroticism" in art films, and defend petty bourgeois moral and educational precepts, condemning "cheap" "titillation" in commercial, "Adult" films.

The Stupid *Reception*

Reports begin to circulate in early December 1964 about the Legion's "condemned" rating of *Kiss Me, Stupid*, and numerous articles quote from Legion Secretary Reverend Thomas F. Little's public statement: "Crude and suggestive dialogue, a leering treatment of marital and extramarital sex, a prurient preoccupation with lechery compound the film's bald condonation of immorality."[25] United Artists removes its name from all of *Stupid*'s marketing, labels ads with "ADULTS ONLY" warnings, and distributes the film through its art film subsidiary, Lopert Pictures.[26] Movie exhibitors in the hinterlands and smaller cities cancel bookings.[27] And reviews from a range of publications corroborate the Legion's "C" rating.

Kiss Me, Stupid joins other Hollywood films enlisted by critics around the same time to contain the crisis of middlebrow taste. The "adult" drama *The Carpetbaggers* (released in July 1964) and the ribald comedy *John Goldfarb, Please Come Home* (initially meant for release in December 1964) provide comparable targets for the petty-bourgeois aesthetic, but *Stupid* proves exceptionally explosive because of the middlebrow authorship of Billy Wilder.

Joseph E. Levine's production of *The Carpetbaggers* paves the way for *Kiss Me, Stupid* in many regards: the PCA passes it, despite fornicating characters and feeble moralizing; the seductive warning "Adult Entertainment" decorates ads; and critics consider the film vulgar and tasteless.[28] *Time* predicts *Carpetbaggers'* wide appeal and booming box office based upon the exploitative, taboo-breaking, sexually titillating material: "The Carpetbaggers, based on the baldly sleazy bestseller by Harold Robbins, is the kind of movie you cannot put down ... it scores its cheap success as a swift, irresistibly vulgar compilation of all the racy stories anyone has ever heard about wicked old Hollywood of the '20s and '30s."[29] Such "irresistibly vulgar" material reflects troubling trends. Crowther's campaign against declining morals and aesthetics in American films repeatedly singles out both *Carpetbaggers* and *Stupid*.[30] One piece rebukes producer Levine's "compendia of smut" and approves of the Legion's "condemned rating" for *Stupid* as "a loud complaint against the evidences of deterioration or what it calls a slide of movies towards 'moral brinkmanship.'"[31] Crowther eventually blames both films for giving American movies the reputation of "deliberate and degenerate corruptors of public taste and morals."[32] Despite their semblance of moral awareness, Crowther posits, the films' sensationalistic emphasis on the "seamy" and the "sordid" negates any such redeeming features.[33]

In December 1964, another Hollywood sex comedy meets with sensational hullabaloo alongside *Stupid*: *John Goldfarb, Please Come Home*. A court-ordered injunction delays the "ugly, vulgar and tawdry" film's release amid a defamation lawsuit brought against 20th Century–Fox by Notre Dame University.[34] Of particular offense, *Goldfarb* shows the Notre Dame football team "under the influence of harem girls," "depicted as undisciplined gluttons and drunks," and worse, they lose.[35] Middlebrow reviewers concur with both Notre Dame and the injunction ruling upon the film's release in March 1965: "a breathtaking display of tastelessness," a "puny Hollywood farce" stuffed with "offenses against taste."[36] *Goldfarb*'s low profits and vulgarity compare closely to *Stupid*'s, and amid the eruptions about both films, the *Times*' Bart brands them as "Two of Hollywood's most blatant sex comedies," ones that "confused crudity with comedy."[37] Crowther charges *Goldfarb* for humiliating the dignified image of Notre Dame "in a familiar low-comedy way" and, expressing the kind of moral outrage he vents at *Stupid*, "it also demeans the prestige of movie humor and, indeed, of the human race."[38]

If all three films have in common charges of vulgarity and PCA seals, *Kiss Me, Stupid*'s combination of "Adult" sexuality, moral ambivalence, and carnivalesque humor prove volatile enough to earn the Legion's "condemned" rating. Just as prominently, *Stupid* boasts Billy Wilder, renowned in middlebrow terms for his "proven skill in handling sensitive material."[39]

Wilder's late 1950s and early 1960s films present critics with many opportunities for indicting immorality and tastelessness, such as cross-dressing, slapstick, and homosexual hints (noted by the Legion) in *Some Like It Hot*,[40] the dirty-joke premise and playboy libertines of *The Apartment*, and unrepentant prostitutes in *Irma la Douce*. Although these pictures never entirely escape accusations of vulgarity,[41] numerous commentators celebrate them, with considerable credit given to Wilder. The director-writer delights middlebrows with his combination of high and low, "exuberant vulgarity," "sophistication" and "satire."[42] *The Apartment* proves the pinnacle of such celebration, as encapsulated in *Time*: "Director Wilder in this picture establishes himself as one of the cinema's most skillful creators of comedy, low, medium, or high."[43] *Time* soon devotes a feature article on Wilder that compares him to Bertolt Brecht but, with the best middlebrow intentions, stresses his mission as commercial "entertainer."[44] Crowther questions if the premise of *The Apartment* is "particularly funny or morally presentable," then assures readers of Wilder's "clever supervision," "ingenious" direction, "brilliant little touches," and "dialogue tumbling with wit."[45] *Irma la Douce* provokes fewer artistic plaudits and earns no Best Picture, Director, or Screenplay Oscars, but reviewers approve of its treatment of harlotry. Crowther affirms, "as light and satiric entertainment, it is certainly acceptable to me," despite the "obvious needle of 'bourgeois morality.'"[46] *Time* calls it "a raffishly sophisticated screen comedy that makes streetwalking seem almost as wholesome as the 50-mile hike."[47]

For the same critics, Wilder transgresses the limits of tastefulness that his prior "classics" respect with *Kiss Me, Stupid*. Creative authority is surely an issue in reviews of *Carpetbaggers* and *Goldfarb*, but neither of these movies boasts anyone comparable to Wilder. *Carpetbaggers* director Edward Dmytryk remains all but forgotten in light of producer Levine and novelist Robbins, fountainheads of vulgarity who capture audiences by tastelessly violating bourgeois taboos. Wilder's name suggests middlebrow sophistication and restraint; consequently, *Stupid* strikes critics as both an artistic failure and an act of crass, commercial betrayal. Its reception becomes an exercise in middlebrow boundary maintenance by demoting Wilder.

Review after review accuses Wilder and his film of "vulgarity" or something akin. Where A.H. Weiler of the *New York Times* describes *Kiss Me, Stupid* as "short on laughs ... long on vulgarity," *Life*'s Thomas Thompson complains that the film violates at least two of the Code's prohibitions: "Vulgar expressions and double meanings" and positive depictions of adultery.[48] Thompson extends his censure with many related terms: "*Kiss Me, Stupid* is a titanic dirty joke.... One woman sitting near me said, 'This is filthy,' and she pushed through to the aisle."[49] Although *Time* grants the film "a kind of vulgar integrity," similar to its review of *The Apartment*, it also likens *Stupid* to "dirty jokes" and accuses Wilder of "exploiting [sex] as a commodity."[50] Philip T. Hartung of *Commonweal* finds the film "tasteless and insulting," with performances that "accentuate the vulgarity," and *The New Yorker*'s Brendan Gill calls it a "squalid," "repellent, oversized trifle."[51] The *Chicago Tribune* review reads as a compendium of all the other reviews: "vulgarity," "a prolonged, dirty and unfunny joke," "heavy with crude innuendo."[52] "vulgar," "dirty," "crude," "filthy," and "repellant," Wilder's film threatens to contaminate audiences with its sleazy, commercial exploitation of sex.[53]

The Legion, as well as many film reviewers, condemn *Kiss Me, Stupid*, morally and aesthetically, by distinguishing between high satirical comedy in Wilder's earlier works and low, vulgar, physical comedy in *Stupid*.[54] High comedy appeals to middlebrow predilections in its emphasis upon constructing a narrative with moral implications, while physical comedy appears to exist solely for inspiring pleasure.[55] Legion Secretary Reverend Little esteems *The Apartment* as an "effective comic satire" that uses humor to expose moral weakness. "Crude and suggestive dialogue" personify *Stupid*, however, as do "a leering treatment of marital and extramarital sex, a prurient preoccupation with lechery," rendering the film "a thoroughly sordid piece of realism which is esthetically as well as morally repulsive."[56] *Time* encapsulates such divisions, claiming that Wilder "wears a lascivious grin where his satirical smile ought to be."[57] *Life*'s Thompson similarly contrasts Wilder's "classic comedy" *Some Like It Hot* and Academy Award–winning *The Apartment*, "adult" films, "made with taste and discretion," to *Stupid*'s "vulgar script and a highly questionable premise."[58] Weiler likewise discerns the "artistry and imagination" of *Some Like It Hot* from the "pungent" and "heavy-handed sex fable" *Stupid*.[59]

Wilder's recent Hollywood comedies earn him middlebrow critical respect and vast audiences through their vaunted taste, originality, and commercial acumen,[60] but the director also ascends to the position of artist comparable to European art film directors.[61] A 1963 *Playboy* interview poses the director questions about his artistic influences (Brecht? Lubitsch?), his "mastering ... the American comic idiom," his "uncompromising standards," and the "levels of social and satirical comment in your films, even in the comedies."[62] The year 1964 heralds Wilder's ascension into high art when, just days before *Kiss Me, Stupid*'s premiere, New York's Museum of Modern Art launches a special retrospective of sixteen of Wilder's films.[63] MOMA's film curator reconstructs Wilder's mainstream Hollywood films as meaningful art films deserving focused, deep speculation into their "sharp-edged bite of truth" and "long observation of and involvement with the American ethos on all its levels."[64]With *Kiss Me, Stupid*, middlebrow critics reject Wilder's proximity to art film directors, and some emblematize his film as the kind that cynically exploits the "adult" content of art films. Wilder actually observes critics' double-standard over sexual content, the "art for art's sake" permission for foreign films and petty-bourgeois rebukes of Hollywood movies: "What the critics call dirty in our pictures, they call lusty in foreign films.... This is not a French film or an Italian film.... It is a Hollywood film. Automatically it goes under the microscope as very suspect."[65] Thompson and Crowther personify Wilder's example.[66] Like Crowther, Thompson discerns "vulgar" Hollywood "adult" films motivated by commerce versus European films (and a few American ones) inspired by art:

> The growing audience interest in imports cannot be blamed entirely on the occasional shots of nudity or the preoccupation with explicit sex. One of the reasons ... is the skill and imagination with which the films are made. In an effort to fight back, Hollywood has gone in for bolder movies.... This new tack has brought this year such excellent "adult" films as *The Night of the Iguana*, *Dr. Strangelove* and *The Americanization of Emily*.... But the trend also has brought such trash as *The Carpetbaggers*, which has had a fantastic success at the box office.[67]

As for *Stupid*, Thompson attributes purely financial motives to the PCA's seal of approval: Hollywood's "desperate fight to stay alive," "competition from foreign films" with "nudity" and "explicit sex," and the fabulously lucrative *Irma la Douce*.[68]

Although reviews and commentary on *Kiss Me, Stupid* in 1964 and 1965 construct middlebrow taste as unilateral and invincible, disagreements rage. Generated by the "middlebrow's disgruntled fringes," Greg Taylor explains, the cult appreciation for Hollywood movies and directors in the 1960s emerges, its "oppositional fandom" openly hostile to "middlebrow pretense in popular culture."[69] Support for *Stupid* indeed emerges through cultist appreciation for Wilder in light of the arrogant jeremiads leveled against the director and his film. Cultists of the 1960s might disagree about Wilder's standing in the new "pantheon" of Hollywood "auteurs," but even Andrew Sarris, the figurehead of this new trend and no advocate for Wilder, validates the director's "satiric savagery" and aesthetic honesty in *Stupid*.[70] Wilder's *Playboy* interview and MOMA retrospective provide two suggestions of the Wilder cult, but the testimonies for Wilder that emerge amid the *Stupid* scandal prove especially "oppositional" since they appear in two middlebrow publications, *Vogue* and *Newsweek*.[71]

Vogue critic Joan Didion subtitles her admiration for *Kiss Me, Stupid* "minority report," signaling her resistant cult perspective.[72] In his 1950 study of taste publics, sociologist David Riesman distinguishes "minority" taste as one "in which certain socially rebellious themes are encapsulated."[73] Cult sensibility remains "socially rebellious" toward middlebrow elitism, especially the dismissal of mass cultural works as art, and revises the typical terms of "good taste": seriousness, morality, decorum, and the maintenance of a high/low hierarchy. As Taylor observes, "The movies could be rescued from middlebrow tyranny ... only through a vigorous reassertion of oppositional snobbism."[74] Cultists of the 1960s delight in evaluating Hollywood movies, genres and directors in the terms of high art "connoisseurs."[75] They read interviews with Hollywood directors, flock to theaters playing Hollywood classics (for example, the New Yorker Theater in Manhattan, the Brattle Theater in Cambridge, Massachusetts),[76] and devote as much esoteric analysis to this mass culture as expected of "art" movies.[77] Wilder's fall from middlebrow grace and cultism's fondness for especially "low," suggestive mass culture render *Stupid* an ideal attraction.[78]

Both Didion and the *Newsweek* critic engage in "oppositional snobbism" to resist the "middlebrow tyranny" of *Kiss Me, Stupid*'s detractors, to begin with, by seizing on key terms of petty-bourgeois sensibility: morality, seriousness, and tastefulness. The *Newsweek* writer declares, "Billy Wilder is a moralist," then playfully puns on the Legion's censure of *Stupid* as a "bald *condonation* of immorality," calling it "a cleverly charming *condemnation* of immorality."[79] *Vogue*'s Didion strikes a proximate pose and defines Wilder's "own special genius" as "a moralist, a recorder of human venality." If *Newsweek* examines *Stupid*'s serious moral critique of "jealousy and greed," so Didion explores Wilder's "compelling and moving" commentary on American "venality," "the true country of despair ... an America that many of us prefer not to know."[80]

The *Vogue* and *Newsweek* writers practice "oppositional snobbism" in their assertion of *Kiss Me, Stupid* as art and Wilder as artist. *Newsweek* traces *Stupid*'s lineage as moralistic sex comedy back to canonized literature (Chaucer, Boccaccio, Restoration theatre) and through the Hollywood comedies of Ernst Lubitsch. *Stupid* ranks with the best in Wilder's oeuvre, on display at MOMA, and well above other box office hits and Legion-approved family fare truly deserving the label "vulgar": *The Carpetbaggers*, *Goliath and the Sins of Babylon* and *Godzilla vs. the Thing*. *Stupid* also joins a prestigious family of foreign art films "condemned" by the Legion: *Breathless, Jules and Jim, My Life to Live*, among others.[81] Likewise, Didion defends *Stupid* precisely *because* it repulses mainstream audiences, by contrast to "the real tastelessness, the true venality of pictures like *The Pink Panther* or *Bedtime Story*," two Hollywood crowd-pleasers of 1964.[82]

As cultist testimonies, the *Newsweek* and *Vogue* reviews reveal signs of a "third stream of taste, entirely apart from good taste or bad taste," as one *New York Times* writer ponders in 1965, one that questions and redefines the conventional meanings of high and low.[83] Didion characterizes Wilder as a "moralist" with "a relentless eye for the sleazy": "a world of cheap double entendre," "the desolate glare of Vegas," and

> the ugliness of a town on that desert ... where time is told by television schedules, where no one is beautiful or gifted ... a place where the flesh is urgent because nothing else is. In its feeling for such a world, such a condition of the heart, *Kiss Me, Stupid* is quite a compelling and moving picture.[84]

If at first Didion's observations sound like typical, modernist swipes at the mass culture "wasteland," the last line stresses sympathy and identification.[85] Such sentiments evoke two of Susan Sontag's comments in "Notes On 'Camp,'" published contemporaneously in the highbrow *Partisan Review*: "the lover of Camp appreciates vulgarity ... the connoisseur of Camp sniffs the stink and prides himself on his strong nerves"; and, "Camp taste is a kind of love, love for human nature ... Camp taste identifies with what it is enjoying ... Camp is a tender feeling."[86] Didion and the *Newsweek* critic do not deliver camp testimonies, but they share with Sontag one key concept: the "good taste of bad taste," the idea that high and low are not fixed categories, and that "bad" or "low" taste could exemplify a kind of good taste. Wilder's "relentless eye for the sleazy" renders *Kiss Me, Stupid* a high expression of vulgarity.

The commercial and cultural ignominy of *Kiss Me, Stupid*, bolstered by a wall of bad press and moralistic jeremiads, disguises the fact that the Code and the Legion are on the fast track toward obsolescence, the birth of the ratings system and "New Hollywood" on the horizon. When UA releases the "Adults Only" sex comedy *What's New, Pussycat?* in June 1965, middlebrow vitriol persists against this "vulgar," "decadent" farce, but this time in direct contrast to booming popularity, the fifth highest grossing film of 1965.[87] In 1966, the "black comedy" *Who's Afraid of Virginia Woolf?* is greeted with astronomical box office, positive reviews, and the declaration: "The Code Is Dead."[88] The reception of *Kiss Me, Stupid* offers something of a last ditch effort to defend middlebrow taste. If the traditionalists win this battle, they clearly lose the war.

Amid the debris stands "Bilious Billy," whose reputation and popularity never manage to recover. In the explosion of film cultism during the late 1960s and 1970s, acclaim for Wilder never reaches the fervor accorded to his colleagues Howard Hawks and Alfred Hitchcock.[89] Among mainstream audiences, Wilder's "adult" sensibility remains eclipsed by auteurs of vulgarity such as Mel Brooks and the rise of R-rated "gross out" comedies.[90] Wilder summarizes matters best in 1976 — and provides another of his gem-like closing lines — recalling the *Kiss Me, Stupid* debacle:

> The question of bad taste has followed me for years. Mel Brooks is a very talented director, but I wonder what would have been said if Wilder had filmed something like the bean supper around the campfire in *Blazing Saddles*. When I made *Kiss Me, Stupid* (1964) the film ... caused a big scandal and they were going to tear up my citizen papers! Today *Kiss Me, Stupid* would seem like Disney fare, and I wonder what all the screaming was about.[91]

Notes

My sincerest thanks go to folks who richly contributed to this essay at various stages over the years: Michael Bronski, Richard Cante, Michael S. Keane, Karen McNally, Walter Metz, Carl Perry, Thomas Schatz, and Janet Staiger.

1. Bart, "When the Cookie Crumbled," X11.
2. Miller, *Censored Hollywood*, 296.
3. Neale and Krutnik, *Popular Film and Television Comedy*, 149–66; Krutnik, "The Faint Aroma of Performing Seals," 57–58.
4. Krutnik, 61.
5. Bart mentions Wilder's nickname in "When the Cookie Crumbled."
6. Taylor, *Artists in the Audience*, 52, 77.
7. MacDonald, "A Theory of Mass Culture" 62–63, 63–65; Bourdieu, "The Aristocracy of Culture," 168.
8. Bourdieu, 187.
9. Bourdieu, 187; Gans, *Popular Culture and High Culture*, 112–13.
10. Bourdieu, 168, 186–88; Gans, 108–109; MacDonald, 63–65.
11. Gans, 109. For a sample of American publications addressed to the middlebrow taste public see Gans, 108–109.
12. Betz, 204.
13. For instance, see Crowther's reviews of *Breathless*, 8½, and *The Silence*.
14. *New York Times*, "Vatican Movie Unit," 27. The *Times* brackets the word "moral."
15. Polt, "Notes on the New Stylization," 26.
16. Bart, "Europe's Successes Worry Hollywood," 5.
17. Crowther, "The Screen in Review," 18; "Outside the Code," X1.
18. Crowther, "Bad Taste in Films," X1.
19. Crowther, "Moral Brinkmanship," X3. See also: Crowther, "Screen: 'Tom Jones,'" 48; "Cinematic 'Tom Jones,'" 119; Balio, *United Artists*, 243–44; Miller, 185; Walsh, *Sin and Censorship*, 315. On Ingmar Bergman's middlebrow significance, see Gans, 108, 143.
20. Crowther, "Bad Taste in Films" X1.
21. Allen, "The Movies in Vaudeville," 81. See also: Neale, *Genre and Hollywood*, 86, 201; Sklar, *Movie-Made America*, 174; Staiger, *Interpreting Films*, 102.
22. Vogel, "Films: Fashion of the Fashionable," X7.
23. Crowther, "Moral Brinkmanship," X3.
24. Betz, 204.
25. *New York Times*, "Legion of Decency Condemns a Movie," 57; *Variety*, "A Kick Instead for 'Kiss Me, Stupid,'" 5; Thompson, "Wilder's Dirty-Joke Film Stirs a Furor," 56A–56B.
26. *Variety*, "Shurlock's Legion Slants Recalled," 4; *Variety*, "A Kick Instead for 'Kiss Me, Stupid,'" 5; *Variety*, "'Kiss Me, Stupid' Ads Toned Down for Lopert Sell," 5. See also: Balio, 183; Miller, 195; Sikov, *On Sunset Boulevard*, 493.
27. Crowther, "The Heat Is on Films"; Sikov, 495; Miller, 195.
28. For ads of *The Carpetbaggers*, see *New York Times*: June 28, 1964: X8; August 5, 1964: 24. For examples of ads for *Kiss Me, Stupid* stamped with "Adults Only," see *New York Times*, December 21, 1964: 43; December 22, 1964: 34, and June 28, 1964: X8.
29. *Time*, "Low and Inside," 86.
30. See Crowther's "Bad Taste in Films," X1; "Moral Brinkmanship," X3; "Time to Face Facts," X1, "Great Grief!" X1; "Goodbye, Summer," X 1and "The Heat Is on Films," X1.
31. Crowther, "Moral Brinkmanship," X1.

32. Crowther, "A Time to Face Facts," X1.

33. Crowther, "Screen: 'The Carpetbaggers' Opens," 24; "Bad Taste in Films," X1; "The Heat Is on Films," X1.

34. Crowell, "Notre Dame Wins Suit," 1; *Newsweek*, "'Goldfarb' vs. Notre Dame," 53; Bart, "Lots of Comedies but Few Laughs," 79.

35. Tomasson, "Notre Dame Seeks To Block New Film," 55.

36. *Time*, "The Importance of an Image," 69; Crowther, "The Screen: 'John Goldfarb' Arrives," 42. See also Hartung, "The Screen," 422.

37. Bart, "Lots of Comedies but Few Laughs," 79.

38. Crowther, "The Screen: 'John Goldfarb' Arrives," 42. See also *Time*, "Goldfarb v. The People," 101.

39. Crowther, "The Heat Is on Films," X1. See also Thompson, 51, 56B; *Time*, "Hipster's Harlot," 69; *Variety*, review of *Kiss Me, Stupid*.

40. Miller, 181; Walsh, 291.

41. McCarten, "The Current Cinema," 71; Gill, "The Current Cinema," 54; Tinnee, "Film 'Irma la Douce' Is Short of Hilarious," B9.

42. Tinnee, "'Apartment' Is a Skillful Film Satire," B18; *Time*, "Just Lucky, I Guess," 92; Crowther. "Screen: Busy 'Apartment,'" 37; "Playboy Interview: Billy Wilder." *Playboy*, (June, 1963): 57–66; *Time*, "The New Pictures," 47; *Time*, "Policeman, Midwife, Bastard," 75–76; Taylor, 77.

43. *Time*, "The New Pictures," 47.

44. *Time*, "Policeman, Midwife, Bastard," 75–76.

45. Crowther, "Screen: Busy 'Apartment,'" 37.

46. Crowther, "The Screen: "Wilder's 'Irma la Douce,'" 37.

47. *Time*, "Just Lucky, I Guess," 92.

48. Weiler, "'Kiss Me, Stupid,'" 22; Thompson, 53.

49. Thompson, 51.

50. *Time*, "Hipster's Harlot," 69.

51. Gill, "The Current Cinema" (1964), 74; Hartung, 421–22.

52. Tinnee, "New Wilder Film Crude and Clumsy," A2.

53. For a historical analysis of the vocabulary of taste, hygiene and disease, see Stallybrass and White, *The Politics and Poetics of Transgression*, 125–48.

54. Sikov (495) and Walsh (316) emphasize the Legion's distinction between satire in *The Apartment* and vulgar, low humor in *Kiss Me, Stupid*.

55. Neale and Krutnik, 14–15. On the bourgeois bias against low comedy, see: Neale and Krutnik, 96–131; Jenkins, *What Made Pistachio Nuts?*, 28–58; Paul, *Laughing Screaming*, 49–52, 85–137, 147–55.

56. *Variety*, "A Kick Instead for 'Kiss Me, Stupid,'" 5; Thompson, 56A–56B. In 1963, the Legion describes *Tom Jones* as an adult, "earthy satire," even after the PCA initially denies it a seal. See Walsh, 315.

57. *Time*, "Hipster's Harlot," 69.

58. Thompson, 51, 56B.

59. Weiler, 22.

60. Thompson, 51, 56B; Miller, 181, 194; Sikov, 426–27, 442–45, 476–77.

61. Taylor, 77; *Playboy*, 57–66.

62. *Playboy*, 57, 60, 61, 62.

63. *New York Times*, "Wilder's Work to Be Shown at Museum of Modern Art," 45.

64. *New York Times*, "Wilder's Work," 45; MOMA's film curator, Richard Griffith, is quoted in *Newsweek*, "Moral or Immoral?" 54.

65. Thompson, 56B.

66. Crowther, "Moral Brinkmanship," X3, and "A Time to Face Facts," X1.

67. Thompson, 56A.
68. Thompson, 56A.
69. Taylor, 87, 91, 95.
70. Sarris, *The American Cinema*, 166–67; Taylor, 77, 92.
71. Gans, 108, 109.
72. Didion, "*Kiss Me, Stupid*, 'Minority Report,'" 97; *Newsweek*, "Moral or Immoral?" 53.
73. Riesman, "Listening to Popular Music," 6.
74. Taylor, 91.
75. Taylor, 87–94.
76. *Time*, "'Camp,'" 24; *Time*, "Letters to the Editor," 2; *New York Times*, "Old Bogart Films Packing Them In," 19; Meehan, "Not Good Taste, Not Bad Taste — It's 'Camp,'" 30–31, 113–15; Gommery, *Shared Pleasures*, 194.
77. For one example, see Sarris, "The Auteur Theory and the Perils of Pauline."
78. Taylor, 33–48, 76–85.
79. *Newsweek*, "Moral or Immoral?" 53–54. Italics are mine in both quotations.
80. Didion, 97.
81. "Moral or Immoral?" 54.
82. Didion, 97.
83. Meehan, 30.
84. Didion, 97.
85. For a discussion of the mass-culture-as-wasteland trope, see Ross, *No Respect*, 151.
86. Sontag, "Notes on Camp," 289, 291–92.
87. See Feil, "'Talk About Bad Taste'" and "Sex, Comedy, and Controversy: *Kiss Me, Stupid*, *What's New, Pussycat?*, New Hollywood, and Metropolitan Taste."
88. Canby, "Public Not Afraid of Big Bad 'Woolf,'" 20.
89. Hoberman and Rosenbaum, *Midnight Movies*, 37. The authors do refer to a six-week run of *Some Like It Hot* in 1973, amid the craze for "transvestite midnight films": 264–65.
90. See Paul, 49–52, 85–137, 147–51, 155–252.
91. Phillips, "Billy Wilder," 108.

10. Censorship, Negotiation and Transgressive Cinema

Double Indemnity, Some Like It Hot and Other Controversial Movies in the United States and Europe

DANIEL BILTEREYST

Billy Wilder holds a significant place in the history of Hollywood censorship. Though he was not interested in being canonized in a Walhalla of cultist filmmakers with a full record of forbidden movies, many of Wilder's movies intensively challenged the majors' internal censorship. Working within the studio system and communicating with a mass audience, Wilder's work remains special in the ways in which it succeeded in defying the moral standards which the Hollywood studios had adopted in the inter-war years and which they continued to apply until the 1960s. The Production Code Administration (PCA, 1934–1968), often referred to as the Hays (or Breen) Office, was the MPPDA's central organization headed by Will Hays, which required filmmakers to submit their films for approval, often including the supervision of treatments, detailed screenplays with dialogue, and the final film, eventually leading to the PCA's seal.

Looking back at his American movies, it is astonishing the extent to which Wilder helped change the ways in which the motion pictures dealt with sexual taboos (*The Major and the Minor*, 1942, *Double Indemnity*, 1944), alcoholism (*The Lost Weekend*, 1945, *A Foreign Affair*, 1948), murder (*Double Indemnity*, *Sunset Boulevard*, 1950), collective murder (*Stalag 17*, 1953), adultery (*Double Indemnity*, *The Seven Year Itch*, 1955, *The Apartment*, 1960, *Avanti!*, 1972), exploitative sex affairs (*Sunset Boulevard*), homosexuality and gender bending (*Some Like It Hot*, 1959), and prostitution (*Irma la Douce*, 1962). Although he

145

was often associated with light-hearted, commercial comedies, Wilder produced movies within a broad variety of genres, by-passing Hollywood's self-regulation. His popular, often farcical fare also misled many critics who blamed Wilder for his cynicism, bad taste and "vulgarity," often overlooking the subversive power behind movies full of anarchy, excess and gross caricatures.

In several interviews — the other art form he continued to cultivate — Wilder openly expressed his resistance to any kind of censorship, and talked about the censors' role in his work. He often referred to the cat-and-mouse game he played with the "lord high executioner of industry censorship"[1] Joseph I. Breen, his successor Geoffrey Shurlock, and other PCA representatives. One of his strategies was refusing to send in complete screenplays, while changing scenes or dialogue afterwards. Wilder frequently expressed his admiration for Ernst Lubitsch, the other master of indirect narration, sharp dialogue, and suggestive action with whom he had collaborated in the second half of the 1930s. Lubitsch had taught Wilder not only how to by-pass censors without violating the internal codes, but also how to use censorship restrictions as a productive force, and to stir up the audience's imagination. By omitting specific information (for example, an explicit love scene) Lubitsch had demonstrated how to ensure "the audience has to add it up for themselves."[2] Wilder admitted that he "learned from Lubitsch that the scene between the two lovers the next morning tells you much more about their sexual behavior than actually showing them having sex, and pushes the story forward."[3] Commenting that "censorship is always stupid," Wilder conceded that it had an unintentionally positive effect: "It naturally stimulates us to fool it. One could probably say that this is also the reason why Lubitsch's films are so full of wit. Because he had to find strategies against censorship."[4] In later years, when internal censorship was more relaxed, while still critical of censors' narrow-minded, conservative and paternalist stance, Wilder commented with nostalgic irony, "there are times when I wish we had censorship, because the fun has gone out of it, the game you play with them."[5]

Despite this somewhat amiable picture, it is important to acknowledge the huge impact on filmmaking of the PCA, the American Legion of Decency and its overseas counterparts, as well as the role of self-censorship. Concentrating on the U.S. and Europe, this article examines the various ways in which some of Billy Wilder's most canonical movies were censored. Besides PCA files, I will rely upon original film censorship records, censors' internal correspondence, and religious (Catholic) classification files, with a special focus upon the UK, France, Germany and a number of other European countries. Focusing in particular on *Double Indemnity* and *Some Like It Hot*, I will argue that Wilder did not only challenge the PCA, but that his subtle attempts to transgress the accepted boundaries of screen representations also resulted in a severe response from European censors.

The Road to Double Indemnity

Wilder's first experiences with Hollywood's internal censorship occurred one year after he left Europe for Hollywood. In the summer of 1935, Gaumont British Picture Corporation asked the PCA for its opinion about a possible remake of *Mauvaise Graine* (*Bad Blood*, 1933), Wilder's debut as a director (with Alexandre Esway). The subject matter of this movie about a Paris playboy associated with a gang of car thieves was unacceptable to the Administration, unless it was completely rewritten. The PCA argued that the movie was in violation of the Production Code for various reasons, including its illustration of the methods of the characters' crime.[6] Through his screenwriting collaboration with Charles Brackett, Wilder further refined his art of working around the Hays Office sensitivities. Particularly important movies in this respect were Lubitsch's *Ninotchka* (1939), and Mitchell Leisen's *Midnight* (1939) and *Arise, My Love* (1940). The latter picture about an adventurous love affair between a pilot (Ray Milland) and a news reporter (Claudette Colbert) in the Spanish Civil War and World War II raised several controversial issues around international politics and diplomacy. (Paramount feared the release of the picture about this war topic in some of its foreign markets.) Some of Wilder and Brackett's vibrant dialogue was vetoed by the PCA, especially in the highly problematic scene in which Milland is seen in a private bathroom with two other male characters. At one moment, one of the men looks at Milland in the bathtub, commenting "I didn't know you were Jewish." This line had to be removed, and for Breen, who wrote about the scene in a letter to Hays, this was "a new low in purported screen entertainment" and the "most shocking exhibition of consummate bad taste which we have ever seen on the motion picture screen."[7] Breen's rage was inspired by a view of "one of the men [...] *seated on a toilet*" [italic in original], followed by "several scenes of Ray Milland in the bathtub *shaving himself*" whereby "the camera angles on these several scenes are pitched in such a way as to come as near as possible to the exposure of Mr. Milland's sex organs." While the scene was re-edited, a number of critical references to the war situation were retained without comment.[8] Putting some openly offensive material in the script in order to prevent other cuts being made became one of Wilder's strategies in his often teeth-grating negotiations with the PCA.

With a growing reputation as a talented screenwriting team, Wilder and Brackett became "executive writers" at Paramount, resulting in more autonomy and responsibility and Wilder's first movies as a director. Although Wilder's first Hollywood pictures were still made under Breen's supervision, problems with the PCA were minimal. *The Major and the Minor*, a comedy about a woman (Ginger Rogers) who disguises herself as a twelve-year-old girl in order to save money for the train fare home from New York to Iowa, had some Code troubles, mainly due to what were thought to be the film's suggestions of paedophilia. Breen also objected to particular lines in the script of Wilder's war espionage thriller *Five Graves to Cairo* (1943), including the idea of a dead body in a woman's bed, but the movie was a success and Wilder was now ready for more serious work.

The PCA and *Double Indemnity*

By 1943 James M. Cain's controversial short crime story *Double Indemnity*, first published in *Liberty* magazine in 1935, had gained a reputation in Hollywood for being "unfilmable." The history of the film adaptation and its censorship problems goes back to the PCA's initial refusal of Cain's story when approached by several studios about the possibility of a film version.[9] In a two-page letter to MGM's L. B. Mayer dated October 10, 1935, Breen outlined the novella's violations of the provisions of the Code. According to Breen, *Double Indemnity* dealt with "an illicit and adulterous sex relationship," described the "details of the vicious and cold-blooded murder," and the leading characters were "murderers who cheat the law and die at their own hands." According to the letter, the first part of the novella was "replete with explicit details of the planning of the murder and the effective commission of the crime," while the second had to do with the "successful efforts of the criminals to avoid arrest and punishment, and culminates in the decision of the man to kill his accomplice." In the original short story the crime is finally confessed to officers of the insurance company, who decide to withhold the information from legal authorities, thereby enabling the murderous couple to escape. At the conclusion, the couple desperately commits suicide. Breen concluded that, given the "general low tone and sordid flavor ... the story under discussion is most objectionable and, unless it can be materially changed, both in structure and in detail, all consideration of it for screen purposes should be dismissed."[10]

Eight years later, when the novella was to be published in book form, Paramount reconsidered the possibility of an adaptation of *Double Indemnity*, sending a new request to the PCA. Breen's reaction in March 1943 was identical to his 1935 veto.[11] However, the studio decided to proceed, and in September 1943 Paramount's liaison to the PCA, Luigi Luraschi, submitted a partial script and outline. Surprisingly, Breen's reaction was that apart from some "minor items ... the basic story seems to meet the requirements of the Production code." [12] Sheri Chinen Biesen has convincingly argued that this sudden change of attitude was due to the fact that "Hollywood's industrial self-censorship by the PCA certainly eased during (and after) World War II."[13] However, the fact that this initial outline, later versions of the script, and the finished picture were no longer in violation of the Code was mainly due to major changes in the adaptation. Following Brackett's expression of his thorough disapproval of the story, Wilder completed the script with hard-boiled fiction writer Raymond Chandler. The screenplay developed from the short story featured several changes, which can be interpreted as signs of goodwill towards the PCA. One of these changes was the elimination of the criminal protagonists' suicide, an act to which religious groups usually strongly objected. In their approach, Walter Neff kills his accomplice, followed by his confession into a dictaphone at his office. By that time, Neff's boss and insurance investigator Barton Keyes (played by Edward G. Robinson) is closing in on him, and hears his last words. Wilder and Chandler decided to build up the character of Keyes, who is, as Ed Sikov indicates, "not only a moral force in the film, but also becomes ... a paternal, fraternal, and avuncular character, all in one."[14] In contrast to the original story, the insurance investigator has not assisted the murderers' escape. These interventions, as well as the strength of the confession, which brings the film its ultimate sense of morality and is a driving narrative force in the movie (told in flashback), were key factors in the script obtaining Breen's approval. Most important was the decision that the protagonists mortally wound each other and therefore comply with the Code's requirement that criminals pay for their transgressions. Finally, the PCA objected to the inclusion of the scene of Neff's trial and execution in the death chamber. Breen, who had already referred to this scene in his first letter on the script in September 1943, repeated that "as we advised you before ... the details of the execution ... seem unduly gruesome from the standpoint of the Code, and also will certainly be deleted by censor boards."[15] This controversial ending, which was filmed by Wilder for inclusion in the film, was ultimately removed.[16]

Power, Negotiation, Productivity

Between September and December 1943 more than twenty letters were exchanged between Paramount and the PCA, all indicating that there were no major obstacles, strange for a movie which is often considered important in the history of American movie censorship.[17] Returning to the question of power, it could be argued that Wilder (and Chandler) changed the overall structure of the story (no suicide), modified or included actions (confession) and remodeled characters (Keyes) in order to comply with the morality behind the Code. It is true that they left out details (for instance, the murder or the disposition of the body), and even followed Breen's explicit demand to leave out key scenes (gas chamber). On the other hand, *Double Indemnity* was still a bold, daring picture in which two protagonists and lovers conspire to murder, and where adultery was examined with an unusual degree of openness and candor. Wilder's cat-and-mouse game and clever negotiation strategy enabled him to by-pass specific provisions and explicit demands from the PCA (for example, the bath-towel did *not* fully cover Phyllis' knees in the movie), while he also mastered the art of not showing specific acts and letting the audience fill in what went against the Code (for example, sex and murder). Wilder and Chandler's dialogue, for instance, became famous for its sexual innuendo. "In *Double Indemnity* we had to be very careful with sex," Wilder later relayed in an interview, but "the fact that they sleep together was the whole motivation behind the movie."[18] In a key scene in Walter's apartment, we see him smoking a "postcoitus" cigarette on a living room sofa, while Phyllis uses a lipstick and paints her lips red. The same kind of "offstage" subtlety was applied in the murder scene, where Wilder kept his close-up on Phyllis' face while her lover choked her husband to death: "We were on her face as she was driving and we knew that offstage it was happening."[19] The fact that Phyllis' facial reaction shows a mixture of pleasure, excitement and satisfaction gives the picture a gruesome dimension of sadism and sexual perversion which went straight against the spirit of the Code. Seen from this perspective, *Double Indemnity* was subtle in by-passing Breen's 1935 original judgment of the story which he rejected because of the "vicious and cold-blooded murder," the "illicit and adulterous sex relationship," and the film's "general low tone and sordid flavor." [20]

When James M. Cain saw *Double Indemnity*, he commented: "it is one of the finest pictures ever made," which "violates practically all the rules imposed by the Hays office — it is about a married woman who falls in love with another man, kills her husband, fraudulently attempts to collect insurance.... It presents these people sympathetically, with compassion and understanding."[21] In a later interview, Wilder suggested, "we had no problem with the Production Code."[22] However, Wilder was certainly forced to take into account the Code, making compromises and looking for other creative solutions. It was clearly a process of negotiation on both sides, where the "adaptation of *Double Indemnity* was influenced by the Production Code," as Biesen underlines, but where the movie also "pushed the envelope of the Motion Picture Production Code of 1930 to its limit, and paved the way for dark, controversial films to be produced in the future."[23]

European Censors and the Church

Although *Double Indemnity* was not an immediate box-office hit, it was a critical success and gained several Oscar nominations. The PCA, whose mission it was to prevent studio pictures from running into problems with local and foreign censorship boards, was successful in enabling the film to pass through local American censorship boards without being cut.[24] The picture did not seem to have problems with the often more severe Legion of Decency, which did not accept depictions of adultery or any other kind of illicit sex, but which gave *Double Indemnity* a very mild "A-II" rating (adults and adolescents).

The picture was received less favorably when it crossed the ocean. In Europe, where a myriad of censorship and classification boards were active, *Double Indemnity* received more severe ratings than in the United States, often being reserved for adults only. The picture first came to the United Kingdom, where it was released during war time. The British Board of Film Censors (BBFC) examined Wilder's movie in July 1944 and passed it uncut, giving the movie an "A" certificate, meaning that children had to be accompanied by an adult.[25] Two months later, the Irish censors rejected *Double Indemnity*, but passed it later after Paramount's appeal.[26] One of the first censorship boards to examine the movie after the war, was the French *Commission de Classification*, an official state film control board with a reputation for being relatively tolerant towards violence and sex, although less so in relation to politics and the image of France. The *Commission de Classification* had no problems with *Double Indemnity*, which was released in France for "all audiences."

In the following months and years *Double Indemnity* was released in other European countries under a variety of titles. While in the Netherlands the picture was presented to the censors as *Bloedgeld* or *Blood Money*, the German distributor launched the movie as *Frau ohne Gewissen* (*Woman without a Conscience*). In Italy, *Double Indemnity* had a clear connotation of sin and faith (*La Fiamma del Peccato*, or *The Flame of Sin*). These provocative titles did not help *Double Indemnity*'s career. In most European countries, children and young adolescents were not allowed to see Wilder's movie. In Belgium, Denmark, Finland, Norway and Sweden, for instance, the censors prohibited youngsters under sixteen or eighteen respectively from seeing *Double Indemnity*, a decision which hindered the picture's commercial success as family entertainment. The censors' verdicts expressed their aversion to or anxiety over the murder scene, the female protagonist's immorality, and the picture's general gruesomeness.[27] A case in point is the Netherlands, where the Centrale Commissie voor de Filmkeuring decided in April 1947 that the movie could not be screened to people under eighteen years of age. Although the national control board argued that it was an "honest picture," Wilder's *Bloedgeld* showed an "accumulation of abjectness, murder, deceit and adultery." Some board members objected to the film being granted any classification and went to appeal, resulting in a total ban (in June 1947). It is interesting to note how Breen's original arguments about the novel seemed to reappear in the Dutch report. Although the board praised *Double Indemnity* from a technical standpoint, it argued that this "cynical film" shows "the technique of crime in such a manner that it can be used in university classes on criminal law or during crime gang meetings." The Dutch ban lasted for eight years. A slightly shortened version of the movie was presented in March 1955 under a less provocative title, *De Volmaakte Moord* (*The Perfect Murder*), and awarded an age limit of eighteen.[28] In Germany, finally, where the film industry had installed a self-regulatory body, the Freiwillige Selbstkontrolle (FSK), the movie was not released until 1950. The FSK turned out to be quite severe, especially to this kind of film noir or "Sensationsfilme," where, it was suggested, one could learn "the tricks [of] how to prepare and carry out a murder." *Frau ohne Gewissen* received an age restriction of sixteen and could not be shown on holydays.[29]

In European countries with a Catholic majority, religious groups were active in various fields of cinema. Inspired by the American Legion of Decency, these groups aimed at influencing the press in their film coverage, as well as trying to put pressure upon official censorship boards and commercial cinemas where "unhealthy" pictures were screened. These national Catholic film organizations, which were coordinated on an international scale via OCIC (*Organisation Catholique Internationale du Cinéma*), had also installed censorship or classification boards. The files and internal reports of these often quite powerful pressure groups turn out to be a very interesting read: while *Double Indemnity* was mostly praised on aesthetic grounds, the picture was severely attacked in terms of morality. The French Catholic organization, for instance, was less enthusiastic than the official censors: in January 1946 they awarded the movie a very negative 5 or "forbidden" rating (6 was the highest code). French Catholic censors (and film critics) criticized *Double Indemnity* for the central theme of adultery and murder, and for its portrayal of an "ignoble woman."[30]

On Hotter Ground

Following *Double Indemnity,* Wilder's reputation as a Code challenger only grew with movies such as *The Lost Weekend*, a picture dealing with alcoholism, *A Foreign Affair*, a comedy about a U.S. congressional committee investigating the morals of American troops in Berlin, and the now classic *Sunset Boulevard*. These three pictures were a critical and commercial success, but the productions proved to be as difficult as *Double Indemnity* had been. Wilder and Brackett continued to submit small portions of their scripts to the Breen Office, which urged the scriptwriters of *The Lost Weekend* to downplay any suggestions of homosexuality and prostitution and the realistic depiction of alcoholism.[31] In the case of *A Foreign Affair*, the PCA objected to the ridiculing of U.S. members of Congress and argued that some lines had to be eliminated.[32] "*Sunset Boulevard* was a more daring picture than *Double Indemnity*," Wilder argued, causing him to use his "piecemeal" strategy again. Wilder and Brackett passed their entire script to the PCA only after principal photography had been completed. Prior to this, Breen had regularly complained that the material was "still incomplete," and repeatedly asked questions about the affair between the two protagonists, but finally accepted the script.[33]

The PCA's role of protecting the MPPDA's members' pictures against further censorship proved to be relatively successful again, at least in the U.S. *The Lost Weekend*, for instance, was passed almost everywhere without deletions, except in Pennsylvania and Ohio where cuts were demanded. In the United Kingdom the BBFC demanded two cuts, including a key scene showing the reason for Ray Milland's dipsomania, and gave it an "A" certificate.[34] The movie was also given a subtitle (*Diary of a Dipsomaniac*), and special trailers warned British audiences about the "grim and realistic sequences contained in this unique diary carrying such a powerful moral."[35] *Sunset Boulevard*'s censorship was, again, more problematic in Europe than in the United States, where it passed all local censorship boards, except in Ohio, where one scene had to be deleted (a scene between silent movie star Norma and "gigolo" Gillis, after he finds Norma lying on a bed).[36] In Europe most censors gave the picture an "adults only" certificate, but in some countries censors were even more severe. In Ireland *Sunset Boulevard* was at first banned because it was centered around "the infatuation of a wealthy middle-aged ex-film star" for a young man, but the film was later passed with one cut following the distributor's appeal.[37] In the United Kingdom the BBFC also cut a crucial line revealing Norma's previous marriage to her butler.[38] In most other European countries *Sunset* was banned for children and as family entertainment. The censors mostly outlined some vague criticism towards the "unhealthy affair" between the two protagonists and the "detailed description of the murder."[39]

New Challenges, Gradual Relaxation, Pragmatism

During the early 1950s, the PCA's self-imposed morality gradually came into conflict with audience interests and new industry conditions. Besides the threat of television and increasing competition from more *risqué* foreign movies, the censorship system was challenged by independent and studio film productions exploring more sensational and adult subjects. Even before foreign movies began to make inroads at the box office, the Code was challenged by adult pictures like Elia Kazan's *A Streetcar Named Desire* (1951) and *Baby Doll* (1956), and Otto Preminger's *The Moon Is Blue* (1953). The latter picture did not receive a seal of approval, but was released and proved to be commercially successful. Preminger's victory over the PCA inspired him to tackle more daring topics in ground-breaking movies such as drug addiction in *The Man with the Golden Arm* (1955), rape in *Anatomy of a Murder* (1959), and homosexuality in *Advise and Consent* (1962). In 1954 Breen was replaced by the more pragmatic and less dogmatic Geoffrey Shurlock, a Protestant who was less engaged with the Legion of Decency, and who dared to make decisions against the Legion's advice.

In the 1950s Wilder continued to make more controversial movies, including *Ace in the Hole* (1951) with its attack on sensationalist journalism, *Stalag 17*, a war drama centered around prisoners in a German prisoner of war camp, and *The Seven Year Itch* and *Some Like It Hot*, both starring Marilyn Monroe. Most of these movies still went through the regular PCA control system, where Wilder was fully engaged in a negotiation process.[40] The PCA files on *The Seven Year Itch*, for instance, contain correspondence between Breen, Shurlock and the Fox representative to the Office, as well as internal memos and summaries of meetings. In a memo dated November 17, 1953, Shurlock wrote that the play upon which *The Seven Year Itch* would be based was "flatly in violation of the Code clause which states that adultery must never be the subject of comedy or laughter."[41] Wilder again started the game of sending pieces of the script to the

Office, and waiting for approvals, finally leading to the PCA Certificate. The Certificate clearly came as a result of a meeting dated March 1, 1955 between Shurlock and his staff on the one hand, and 20th Century–Fox representatives on the other. In an internal note to Wilder and producer Charles Feldman, Fox's liaison to the PCA, Frank McCarthy, summarized the agreement between the studio and the PCA, wherein he referred to the changes to be made in the finished picture. These included sections of dialogue, references to glands, and the agreement that "of the three cuts showing the girl's skirt being blown up by the air from the subway, one should be eliminated." The letter concluded that the "Shurlock office will issue the Seal to us on the condition of making these changes."[42] Wilder, who wanted to be more frank about the idea that the girl (Monroe) and the tempted married man (Tom Ewell) slept together, felt he had lost a new battle. In order to please the Legion of Decency, Fox removed some footage, but this failed to prevent the picture from receiving a "B" rating ("morally objectionable in part for all") due to the judgment that the "film treats in a flippant and farcical manner marital fidelity and is suggestive in costuming, dialogue and situations."[43] The picture was banned in Ireland because it was considered to be "indecent and unfit for general exhibition," [44] while other European censors gave it an adult restriction.

Some Like It Hot and the Censors

In the mid–1950s Wilder decided to no longer submit scripts to the PCA, leading to more troublesome films like *Some Like It Hot, The Apartment* and *Irma la Douce*. Concentrating on the first, now mythical movie, produced by the Mirisch Company, it is clear that there is little to tell about Wilder's confrontation and negotiation with the PCA. The finished picture did not go through the PCA's "protective" guidance, was presented to the Office, and received Shurlock's approval in February 1959.[45]

Before turning to problems with and complaints from pressure groups and foreign censorship boards, it is interesting to look at the movie from a "censorial" point of view. *Some Like It Hot* is now regarded as a classic comedy, where Wilder used a wide variety of means to transgress the hegemonic representation of gender and sexuality. The movie is notorious, for instance, for its risqué dialogue and sexual innuendo with clear references to heterosexual intercourse (Curtis suggesting "I gave her three transfusions"), oral sex (Monroe talking about "getting the fuzzy end of the lollipop") and masturbation (Curtis giving Lemmon the advice to "pull the emergency brake"). The movie shows men and women kissing, women undressing, and goes rather far in representing Marilyn Monroe's bosom, but Wilder's picture is also revolutionary within 1950s mainstream cinema in crossing accepted gender boundaries in terms of dressing and sexual preferences. We see Jack Lemmon (as Jerry or "Daphne") and Tony Curtis (as Joe or "Josephine") dressed in women's clothing and behaving as women, and there are many more clear references to homosexuality, lesbianism and bisexualism. The clearest example is the final scene in which Lemmon reveals to the millionaire Osgood who fell in love with "Daphne" (Jerry's female alter ego), that he is a man. Osgood's reaction ("Well, nobody's perfect") is now regarded a classic scene which crosses sexual boundaries and represents the act of coming out.

Although *Some Like It Hot* is an anthology of transvestism, gender-bending and lines full of *double entendres*, the movie contains many more items to upset the censors. Wilder's picture, for instance, shows a broad spectrum of violence with massive use of gunfire, as well as all sorts of crime and corruption like gambling and the illegal alcohol trade. *Some Like It Hot* contains a rather morbid game with corpses, for instance, at the very start of the movie when gangsters are disguised as funeral undertakers using a coffin to hide liquor. The theme continues throughout with the final giant cake submachine gun massacre, dead gangsters, and the two male protagonists hiding under a trolley with a dead body on it as they try to escape. The picture also cynically deals with a mixture of serious issues including the power of the mafia, unemployment, and alcoholism. (Monroe explains: "Don't think I'm a drinker. I can stop anytime I want to. Only, I don't want to.")

Some Like It Hot, which was released with the tagline "The movie too HOT for words," received a PCA certificate in February 1959, but soon encountered a long series of complaints and protests from other censors and pressure groups. The first in line, of course, was the Legion of Decency. In a letter to Shurlock, Mgr. Thomas Little announced in March 1959 that *Some Like It Hot* was rated as a "B" movie, or "morally objectionable," because the picture was "offensive to Christian and traditional standards of morality and decency." Arguing that the Legion should have given it a "C" or "condemned" rating, and that "this film has given the Legion the greatest cause for concern in its evaluation of code seal pictures," Little complained that the picture was full of "inferences to homosexuality and lesbianism."[46] In the same month Bishop McNulty, chairman of the Episcopal Committee for Motion Pictures, Radio and Television, wrote an angry letter to Eric Johnston, Hays' successor at the MPAA, complaining that this picture about "transvestism ... homosexuality and lesbianism" was in flagrant violation of the spirit and the letter of the Code.[47] In his reply, Shurlock now had to defend the PCA's decision, indicating that "there is simply no adverse reaction at all; nothing but praise for it as a hilariously funny picture," while transvestism "has been standard theatrical fare."[48]

Now that Wilder had not negotiated with the PCA, but still received a seal, it was unclear how state censorship boards would react. The Kansas Board, at least, decided to cut one scene (the love-making scene on the yacht), while the Board in Memphis restricted the picture to adults.[49] All over Europe, *Some Like It Hot* was unavailable as family entertainment, except in France where the censors gave it an "all audiences" certificate (May 26, 1959). In all other countries, the most severe age restriction was awarded — "adults" in the UK (March 3, 1959), eighteen in Germany (May 12, 1959) and the Netherlands (June 30, 1959), and sixteen in Denmark (August 1959), Sweden (June 26, 1959) and Finland (July 3, 1959). In other countries censors decided to cut the picture. This was the case in Norway, where the picture received an age sixteen restriction with a cut (July 17, 1959), while in Italy (September 1959) two scenes were mutilated (the long kiss on the yacht, and Monroe in a short dressing gown).[50] In Francoist Spain a local company tried to tone down the deviant sexuality in the dubbed version of the picture in order to get *Some Like It Hot* past the censors. In the Spanish version, possibly subversive references to homosexuality were flattened out in translation, but even then *Some Like It Hot* was banned until 1973.[51] In the 1960s and 1970s the picture was re-released in several countries, at which time distributors tried to get more favorable age categories. Even then, *Some Like It Hot* continued to be controversial fare. In Germany, for instance, the age restriction went from eighteen to sixteen years in 1971, and the FSK still argued that this "mix of a love and a crime story might still be confusing for youngsters."[52] Given the Legion's reaction, it was clear that the European Catholic film boards would be no less critical. Catholic audiences were dissuaded from seeing the picture by all means — mainly through negative film reviews and discouraging ratings in religious newspapers and magazines. The Italian Catholic film organization, for instance, gave Wilder's *A qualcuno piace calvo* the most severe rating ("E," or "forbidden"), while their Belgian, Dutch, French, German and Spanish counterparts had similar reservations, mostly denouncing the picture's violence, sexuality and vulgarity.[53]

Conclusions

In the 1960s the Hollywood internal censorship system slowly came to an end, leading to the MPAA ratings system which came into effect in November 1968. Wilder had been a prime contributor to this process, not least with *Some Like It Hot*, a picture which appeared at a moment when the social mood was changing and the censorship structures in place since the 1930s were breaking down. *Some Like It Hot* at least contributed to a more tolerant attitude toward sexuality in American films and to the PCA's decision, in October 1961, to weaken its position on the representation of homosexuality. Later pictures like *Irma la Douce* and *Kiss Me, Stupid* (1964) helped equally in this process because they were, at the same time, successful, controversial, and condemned by pressure groups.

Given his ability to by-pass censors and his willingness to avoid bans, Wilder is often not, or only marginally represented in scholarly overviews of film censorship history, at least those concentrating on big censorship battles.[54] In other, more specialized fields within film studies, though, Wilder's pioneering work in challenging the censors and transgressing boundaries of representation is now widely recognized. This is, for instance, the case with work on film noir,[55] on the representation of the Holocaust,[56] and within queer studies,[57] where movies such as *Double Indemnity, Stalag 17,* and *Some Like It Hot* have received a near classic status. In retrospect, it is recognized that Wilder's career stimulated changes in the Hollywood self-regulatory system. In fact, Wilder's position as an *auteur,* a questionable concept establishing canons and hierarchy, might well be defined around the idea that he was provocative, sometimes subversive, and often transgressive in the ways in which his movies searched for the boundaries in representing contemporary societal and moral issues. Wilder produced a cinema of transgression, less in a formal or stylistic sense associated with underground cinema, but rather on the level of content and attitude.

This article concentrated upon the role censorship and classification boards played in Wilder's work, whereby the "cynical master with Vienna roots" learned the art of negotiating with, by-passing, and productively using censorship.[58] Whether these censorship restraints were forms of social responsibility or reactionary resistance, is not important — a cinema of transgression lives by a refusal to accept certainties stipulated by a dominant order. In this sense, censorship was a vital part of Wilder's art of transgression. Some of Wilder's most canonical pictures benefited from an internal moral guidance, while they ran into problems once they crossed the ocean. In understanding the historical reception and the different forms of censorship in the U.S. and Europe, it turned out that European censors were mostly no more progressive or tolerant than their American counterparts. State censorship was not the sole, undisputed disciplining force in the field of cinema. Both in the United States and Europe, there was a competition among different forces trying to discipline controversial, transgressive material. As this essay indicates, censorship was an interplay of various institutions, ranging from industrial self-regulation and state censors to ideologically inspired pressure groups, which were engaged in a negotiation with filmmakers, the film industry and public morality.

Notes

1. Staggs, *Close Up on Sunset Boulevard,* 33.
2. Lally, *Wilder Times,* 73.
3. Prelutsky, "An Interview with Billy Wilder," 186.
4. Vandaele, "Funny Fictions," 270.
5. Staggs, 34.
6. Sikov, *On Sunset Boulevard,* 111.
7. Ibid., 147.
8. Lally, 95.
9. Biesen, *Blackout,* 96–123; Lally, 125–39; Sikov, 194–217.
10. Letter from J.I. Breen to L.B. Mayer, October 10, 1935, *Double Indemnity* File, Production Code Administration Files, Margaret Herrick Library, Academy of Motion Picture Arts and Sciences, Los Angeles (hereafter: PCA).

11. Letter from J.I. Breen to L. Luraschi, March 15, 1943, *Double Indemnity* File, PCA.

12. The latter referred to the unacceptable exposure of the female body ("this bath-towel must ... go below her knees"), and details about the exposition of the murder of the husband. Letter from J.I. Breen to L. Luraschi, September 24, 1943, *Double Indemnity* File, PCA.

13. Biesen, 97.

14. Sikov, 204.

15. Letter from J.I. Breen to L. Luraschi, December 1, 1943, *Double Indemnity* File, PCA.

16. Naremore, *More than Night*, 81–95.

17. Biesen, 98; Schumach, *The Face on the Cutting Room Floor*, 63.

18. Hesling, *Billy Wilder*, 30.

19. Allyn, "*Double Indemnity*," 136.

20. Letter from J.I. Breen to L. Luraschi, March 15, 1943, *Double Indemnity* File, PCA.

21. Hanna, "Hays Censors Rile Jim Cain," 13.

22. Allyn, 136.

23. Biesen, 97, 98.

24. For censorship in New York, Maryland, Kansas, Ohio and by other boards between February and July 1944, see *Double Indemnity* File, PCA.

25. The picture still has a PG rating. See www.bbfc.co.uk. The original BBFC files were destroyed.

26. Rockett, *Irish Film Censorship*, 125, 403.

27. *Double Indemnity* file, Archive of the Belgian Board of Film Control, Brussels; *Double Indemnity* file (with information on Denmark, Finland, Norway, Sweden), Archive of the Danish Media Council for Children and Young People, Copenhagen.

28. *Bloedgeld* file no. N0666 (1 April 1947; 12 June 1947); *De Volmaakte Moord* file no. X0333 (2 March, 1955), Archive of the Centrale Commissie voor de Filmkeuring (CCF), Nationaal Archief, Den Haag.

29. *Frau ohne Gewissen* file, Protokoll no. 1097, 28 March 1950, FSK, Wiesbaden.

30. In other countries like Austria, Belgium, Germany and the Netherlands, Catholics turned out to be more severe on the movie than the official censors, labeling it a dangerous movie. *Assurance sur la mort* file, 1946–48, DOCIP/OCIC Archive, Brussels.

31. Lally, 144. Sikov, 217–28.

32. Lally, 182. Sikov, 276–77.

33. Letter from J.I. Breen to L. Luraschi, May 24, 1949, *Sunset Boulevard* File, PCA.

34. Mathews, *Censored*, 125.

35. Lally, 160.

36. Certificate Ohio, May 27, 1950, *Sunset Boulevard* File, PCA.

37. Rockett, 127.

38. Mathews, 125.

39. *Sunset Boulevard* file no. T0011 (8 January 1951), Archive CCF, Nationaal Archief, Den Haag.

40. For more details on the PCA interventions on these and other Wilder film projects see Lally, 224–26; Sikov, 318–19, 338–39, 369–71.

41. Memo G. Shurlock, November 17, 1953, *The Seven Year Itch* File, PCA.

42. Letter from F. McCarthy to B. Wilder and C. Feldman, March 1, 1955, *The Seven Year Itch* File, PCA.

43. Legion of Decency memo, June 30, 1955, *The Seven Year Itch* File, PCA.

44. Ireland censorship file, November 1, 1955, *The Seven Year Itch* File, PCA.

45. Letter from G. Shurlock to W. Mirisch, February 10, 1959, *Some Like It Hot* File, PCA.

46. Letter from T. Little to G. Shurlock, March 5, 1959, *Some Like It Hot* File, PCA.

47. Letter from Bishop McNulty to E. Johnston, March 1959, *Some Like It Hot* File, PCA.

48. Letter from G. Shurlock to T. Little, March 18, 1959, *Some Like It Hot* File, PCA.

49. Various censorship records, March 1959, *Some Like It Hot* File, PCA.

50. Baldi, *Schermi Proibiti*, 48.

51. Vandaele, 294, 299.

52. *Manche mögen's heiss* file, Protokoll no. 19682, April 4, 1971, FSK, Wiesbaden.

53. *Certains l'aiment chaud* file, 1959, DOCIP/OCIC Archive, Brussels.

54. Wilder is not mentioned, for instance, in general overviews such as Dawn B. Sova's encyclopedic *Forbidden Films*, or Jean-Luc Douin's *Dictionnaire de la Censure*, while other scholarly works contain only small references to a handful of his movies (e.g., Leff and Simmons' *The Dame in the Kimono* and Mathews' *Censored*).

55. Biesen; Naremore.

56. Haggith and Newman, *Holocaust and the Moving Image*.

57. Russo, *The Celluloid Closet*; Barrios, *Screened Out*.

58. Ciment, "Sept Réflexions sur Billy Wilder," 9.

Part Four:
Europe, America and Beyond

11. "I Don't Have a Home!"
Paris Interregnum in *Mauvaise graine*

LEILA WIMMER

Mauvaise graine (1934) is a largely forgotten, unseen and neglected film. Even Gerd Gemünden in *A Foreign Affair*, his fine study of the experience of exile and the outsider/insider perspective that inform Billy Wilder's films, has little to say about it. While a great deal has been written about Wilder's contribution to the Hollywood studio system, in contrast, his passage in Paris has tended to be ignored. And although the sense is given that his American work is often concerned with confronting the Old world with the New, scholarly accounts of his career are usually dominated by the critical centrality of his Hollywood films, while his formative years in Europe have not received the detailed attention that they deserve. *Mauvaise graine* is nevertheless an important film in Wilder's filmography for two main reasons. On the one hand, it was Wilder's debut feature and the only one he directed in Europe, an instance of French émigré productions of the interwar years that have long been unjustly neglected. On the other hand, it is also a film about exile and migration, suggesting that the émigré legacy dynamic that characterizes Wilder's Hollywood period was already there in his earlier work.

The French title, *Mauvaise graine*, refers to a bad lot, someone unlikely to produce anything good. Scripted by Wilder himself with Berliner émigrés Hans G. Lustig and Max Kolpé, the film tells the story of Henri Pasquier (Pierre Mingand), the playboy son of a wealthy doctor (Paul Escoffier) who joins an organized ring of thieves after his father, who is fed up with his son's idleness, sells his automobile. Henri refuses to work, loves mobility, and has a date with a young woman, so he steals a car. The gang observes the theft, and they chase Henri across Paris. Henri does not want to go home, so he joins the gang and is adopted by Jean-la-cravate (Jean of the ties), one of its younger members, played by Raymond Galle. Jean has a compulsion to steal neckties. He has accumulated three hundred and fifteen in his closet, and even boasts of having

161

stolen one from Marcel Pagnol, the author of regional dramas, who adapted his plays for the cinema in his film studio outside Marseilles. Meanwhile, in a typical "meet-cute" situation, Henri falls in love with Jean's sister Jeannette, played by Danielle Darrieux, who works as decoy for the gang by luring rich Parisian gentlemen away from their luxury automobiles. Henri rebels against the gang's boss (Michel Duran) by demanding higher wages for everyone. The boss grudgingly gives in and, to calm the gang, invites everyone to the country. He then sends Henri on a mission to Marseilles in a stolen racing car with a damaged front axle, expecting it to crack, and hoping Henri will be killed. Jeannette accompanies Henri, but they are stopped by the police. Henri punches a policeman, and the police chase them. The car crashes, but without injuring the pair. They start to walk back to Paris and decide to leave the country. While Jeannette waits in Marseilles, Henri goes back to fetch Jean who is then killed by the police. After having confessed to his father that he was a thief, Henri leaves for Marseille to join Jeannette. Henri and Jeannette board a ship to start a new life together, crossing the Mediterranean to Casablanca.

Most of Wilder's work has resulted from migration and exile, drawing from a specific central European background mixed with American cultural influences, and eventually synthesized in a cinematic practice assumed to be a classical Hollywood style. In his book on Wilder, Gerd Gemünden notes that "there is a decidedly transcultural dimension to Billy Wilder's work, a status of being in-between nations, and drawing on very distinct cultural sensibilities."[1] Some of the key features of Wilder's cinema pertain to the way in which all of Wilder's cinema is "a cinema of in-between," a form of cinematic expression which "highlights the dialectics of outsider and insider, of the liminal, fluid, and temporary, of upward and downward mobility, of high brow and low brow."[2]

Though the notion of Wilder as an author has been greatly contested, most famously by American critic Andrew Sarris, Gemünden's conceptualization of the thematics that have inflected his work can already be traced in his directorial debut, a transit film par excellence. This essay will concentrate on *Mauvaise graine*, and will seek to identify how different traditions and influences collide within this film. More particularly, I will consider the way in which the Wilderian trope of mobility and the dialectic of insider and outsider are articulated within the film, and how the narrative of the journey works as a metaphor for self-transformation, new identity and new beginnings. I will begin by briefly documenting the place of the émigrés in French film culture of the period, before looking at *Mauvaise graine* in its specific context.

On the Road

Billy Wilder's early life was characterized by geographical movement and border crossing as he moved across the European landscape, from one culture to another, from the Western metropolitan centres of Poland and Vienna, to Germany and France, eventually settling in the United States. Leaving Austria for Germany in 1926, Wilder arrived in Berlin, working as a freelance reporter for the leading newspapers of the day. Just as Berlin saw itself as the most "American of modern cities,"[3] Wilder's professional interests were nurtured by a heavy dose of Americanization. Wilder wrote widely on popular culture, and he spoke of jazz as "the exigent rejuvenation of fossilized Europe."[4] Making the transition to scriptwriter from 1929 onwards, he forged himself a successful career in the German film industry. After collaborating on the screenplay for the critically acclaimed avant-garde, non-commercial city documentary *Menschen am Sonntag* (*People on Sunday*, 1929), a team work between Wilder, Robert and Curt Siodmak, Moritz Seeler, Eugen Schüfftan (later Shuftan), Edgar G. Ulmer and Fred Zinnemann, Wilder was offered a contract at the prestigious UFA (Universum Film Aktiengesellshaft) German film studios. By the time the Nazis came to power in 1933, Wilder had received writing credit on around thirteen films, including the screen adaptation of Erich Kästner's novel for children set in Berlin, *Emil und die Detektive* (*Emil and the Detectives*, Gerhard Lamprecht, 1931). After the Nazi takeover of the German film industry in 1933, most of the team of *Menschen am Sonntag* would become Hitler refugees, some stopping in Paris before taking the path of exile, mostly to London or the United States.

Like many of his peers fleeing Berlin after the Reichstag fire of February 1933, Wilder was in transit in Paris for almost a year. Fluent in French, in the City of Light, he co-directed his first film, the French émigré feature *Mauvaise graine*. Wilder's stay in France coincided with a massive influx of political exiles from the German film industry, who came to Paris fleeing racial persecution after Hitler's rise to power. Paris in the 1930s had the third largest Jewish community in the world after Warsaw and New York and, between 1918 and 1939, 150,000 Jewish emigrants arrived in the city.[5] For a short period, the French capital thus became a "waiting room"[6] for the enforced exile to France of a large cohort of émigré filmmakers, set designers, cameramen and composers such as Fritz Lang, Max Ophüls, G. W. Pabst, Robert Siodmak, Anatole Litvak, Peter Lorre and countless others. Paris became a temporary refuge for a large number of European film personnel, mostly Jews from Germany and Austria. Some remained there until 1939; others soon left for Britain or America. Film history has tended to ignore the Paris episode as "a thin slice sandwiched between the glories of a German career and its Hollywood apotheosis."[7] In his work on émigré filmmakers in Paris between 1929 and 1939, Alistair Phillips suggests that the French films by German émigrés are often neglected: "Because of the glamour of this final destination, and despite the fact that émigrés made a significant contribution to French cinema, there is still little written in English about this unique and fascinating phenomenon."[8]

Hollywood/Europe

Discussing *Mauvaise graine* involves discussing the inter-relationship between European cinema and Hollywood on a textual level. Work on émigré filmmaking has highlighted the complexity of the conjunction of a diverse range of directors, modes of production and genres. *Mauvaise graine* is an archetype of such complexity, though it is a film that has elicited surprisingly few analyzes. *Mauvaise graine* is inscribed within a dual problematic, the relationship between German émigrés and French cinema in the 1930s, on the one hand, and the relationship between Hollywood and Europe on the other. Émigré films have often been described as a "hybrid" mode of filmmaking. However, if there is a definitive heterogeneity in French émigré films, I would agree with Ginette Vincendeau that this phenomenon is more revealing of the problematic of the Hollywood/Europe axis, rather than a Franco–German dichotomy.[9] One feature common to all European cinemas is the cultural mythology of Hollywood, "not the real city but the capital of the imaginary," that since the beginnings of cinema and of its global ramifications, Hollywood has created a web of transatlantic exchanges "made of fantasies and celluloid, a never ending chain of links consisting of successive migrations, reciprocal influences, and nourishing oppositions."[10] In many ways, *Mauvaise graine* reveals the traces of these flows, and shows "how these encounters can be creative, hybridising processes in which the combination of two or more different elements creates something entirely new and different."[11] This also highlights how permeable the borders between Hollywood and Europe have been, and how, in the study of European film cultures and national cinema, it is impossible to treat Hollywood as extrinsic. In his study of Hollywood in Berlin, Thomas J. Saunders has suggested that, "be it French, German, British, Italian or even Soviet, the culture of interwar cinema was first and foremost American."[12]

Recent scholarship on European cinema has challenged the idea that the national cinemas of Europe should be seen as discrete, self-contained entities, shifting from the idea of the national to the notion of the transnational. Tim Bergfelder, for instance has argued that border crossing and transcultural exchange are neither recent phenomena nor marginal or alternative practices, but, on the contrary, should be seen as having characterized film history from its very beginning.[13] Furthermore, the identity of Europe and its cinema, according to Wendy Everett, is "multiple, unstable and perpetually changing."[14] From its early beginnings, then, European film culture has been characterized "not so much as a stable cultural identity or category, but rather as an ongoing process marked by indeterminacy or 'in-between-ness.'"[15] In this context, the narrative of exile and the work of émigré filmmakers such as Billy Wilder, and *Mauvaise graine* in particular, can be understood as emblematic examples of transnational filmmaking: "I don't have a home!' exclaims Henri when he joins the gang of car thieves. Finally, transnationalism, suggests Tim Bergfelder, "always needs to encompass a dialogue between transitoriness and location, and between émigrés and hosts, and involve a process that blurs and ultimately dissolves the boundaries between these oppositions."[16]

Film Europe

The period leading up to the arrival in Paris of the émigrés from the German film industry was marked by the advent of sound cinema, an era of great change for French cinema since, like the film industry all over Europe, it had to reorganize itself. According to Thomas Elsaesser, the years 1930 to 1936 are a contradictory period for European cinema. On the one hand, "it was the time of the conversion to sound, of multiple-language versions of films and the trade-off of stars across national boundaries." On the other hand, "the political changes had created a situation, where economic, technological and geo-political factors were so tightly meshed together that they generated the kind of ideological incoherence that could itself serve as one of the definitions of modernity."[17] The industry in the 1930s was an international business. That there was a considerable movement and flow among the film industries of France, Germany and Hollywood in the 1920s and 1930s is evidenced by the production of films in multiple language versions (MLVs), and not only the movement of personnel, directors, stars and producers, but also patents and facilities. After the advent of the sound film, Berlin and Paris had developed close cinematic relations through MLVs, Franco–German co-productions, the leasing of stars, directors and production facilities, and patent and distribution rights deals.

Produced between 1929 and 1932, and part of the Film Europe movement instigated by German producer Erich Pommer, MLVs aimed to overcome the linguistic and cultural barriers brought to a head with the conversion to sound. MLVs were shot simultaneously in different languages, using the same screenplay, sets, and often the same director. Thus, on the one hand they were made with the aim of providing a new answer to the marketing of films within Europe, while on the other they presented a united front against the international dominance of Hollywood. At the same time, Hollywood companies themselves had to adopt certain strategies in order to meet the need to produce films adapted to national markets, importing directors, scriptwriters and actors to studios such as MGM, or investing in production centres in Europe such as the Paramount studio in Joinville near Paris.[18] In 1931 dubbing and subtitling were standardized, which meant that MLVs were no longer needed to overcome language barriers.

However, France during the 1930s was marked by an economic and financial crisis, the rise of the extreme-right and anti–Semitism, and a period of economic instability within French cinema. While the German film industry was thriving, French cinema was floundering, plunged into a deep financial crisis. In 1929 German films represented thirty per cent of the film market, against twelve per cent for French films. With the return of producer Erich Pommer from America, the methods of Hollywood had entered into UFA, which allowed it to be relatively successful in Europe and other markets during the 1930s, producing fast-paced and witty films that projected a youthful, sporty image of Germany to the world.[19] UFA was perhaps the only European film industry able to compete with the Hollywood studios; it had one of the most modern and efficient production facilities outside of Hollywood. During the interwar period, there was an ongoing interchange of personnel between the French and German film industries in a process of "competition by co-operation between the two film industries."[20] In many ways, then, the Paris stopover also "points to the dominance of the German industry over that of France and Europe from the late 1920s throughout the 1930s."[21] This highly developed industrial and modern managerial model was in stark contrast to the precarious conditions experienced by the French film industry during the early years of sound cinema. In contrast to the vertically-integrated patterns of countries such as Germany, the U.S., Japan and Great Britain, France's film industry was characteristically artisanal, marked by the fragmentation of production among a myriad of small, privately owned production companies. This lack of economic and industrial stability, along the lines of the model of the American studios in Hollywood, nevertheless had both positive and negative outcomes for German directors since, as Colin Crisp has suggested, this instability resulted in great diversification in terms of access to capital and distribution.[22]

Émigré activity in the French film industry of the 1930s is often seen as having had a beneficial influence on French filmmaking. During their brief residence, not only did the émigrés expand French sound cinema's range of expressive possibility, but they also invested in film production. According to Dudley Andrew, by 1936 UFA had "moved in to become the most consistent force in the French industry."[23] Moreover, besides directors, scriptwriters, actors, cinematographers and set designers, the work of the émigrés made its mark on French cinema, bringing to Paris "a visual sensibility different from the theatrical one that was then dominant ... from wherever they came, as a group the émigrés entering the French film industry raised standards and expectations."[24] During the 1920s many Russian émigrés had come to Paris and had lasting effects in several areas of French cinema, particularly in set design and production. That foreign personnel played such a pivotal role in the making of French films clearly underlines the cosmopolitan character of cinema in the 1920s and 1930s.

However, it is important to recognize that the phenomenon of German emigration to France was also marked by a certain ambivalence and reluctance.[25] In a climate of growing xenophobia stirred up by the far-right, more overt anti–Semitic manifestations in the right-wing press concerning the alleged stranglehold of Jewish personnel over the French film industry, the émigrés became the subject of increased hostility, and quotas on the numbers of foreigners working in the French film industry were eventually enacted. As the 1930s wore on, the atmosphere became increasingly sinister towards émigré filmmakers among some sections of the French film industry: "The perception of special job opportunities opening up for the refugees led to intense hostility among the French film personnel, aggravated by traditional chauvinism on both sides and the wounded pride of France's film industry no longer occupying its number one position."[26] The right-wing *Action Française*, as well as eminent French directors such as Jacques Feyder and René Clair, talked of France and the film industry being "swamped" by foreigners, and in 1935 Maurice Bardèche and Robert Brasillach published their monumental, right-wing, even fascistic, *Histoire du cinéma*. These tensions, and the fact that the French trade unions were susceptible to this kind of propaganda, meant that "the émigrés could only effectively find work in either B-productions, undertaken by one of the many small companies that had sprung up in Paris, or in 'international' productions."[27] In the context of a worsening political and economic crisis from 1934–1935, the situation of German refugees in France was to worsen considerably as "France's Jewish population became a particular part of the way that definitions of the French nation state were fought over by both sides of the political spectrum in the 1930s."[28] Although some left later than others, this would explain why German émigrés were only in transit in France.

Mauvaise graine

Wilder directed *Mauvaise graine* in collaboration with Hungarian émigré Alexander Esway, who had had experience of directing films both in France and London since the mid–1920s, though it is important to note that Danielle Darrieux has recalled that Wilder was the principal director of the film, always on the set, coaching the actors during rehearsals.[29] The production of the film was overseen by a small company called Compagnie Nouvelle Commerciale, which was headed by Édouard Corniglion-Molinier, a French flying hero who had invested in the Victorine Studios in Nice in 1927. This was an independent production firm, and, on the one hand, this allowed Wilder and Esway greater artistic freedom, but, on the other, the shoot was marred by economic difficulties and had to take place outside of the studios. The film was hard to finance, and Wilder had no experience of directing. However, perhaps because of his previous experience in the realist tradition with *Menschen am Sonntag* and *Emil und die Detektive*, both filmed in real location settings in Berlin, Wilder was able to adapt successfully to this particular set of industrial imperatives, especially shooting documentary style and using direct-sound methods. As Wilder recalled, "we did *Mauvaise graine* [*Bad Seed*] on a shoestring ... we didn't use a soundstage. Most of the interiors were shot in a converted auto shop, even the living-room set, and we did the automobile chases without transparencies, live, on the street. It was exhausting. The camera was mounted on the back of a truck or in a car. We were constantly improvising."[30] The cast and crew shot the film on location in Paris, at the riverside beach of l'Isle d'Adam, a popular 1930s weekend destination for Parisians located twenty-five miles south of Paris, and in the port city of Marseilles. Marseilles was at the time a centre of film production and, with the studios of Marcel Pagnol and La Victorine studios in Nice, the South was a significant film center outside Paris.

Mauvaise graine's description of a cross-social relationship though the formation of the couple is reminiscent of two romantic comedies which are related to a Parisian location, *Sabrina* (1954) and *Love in the Afternoon* (1957), while the role-playing enacted by both characters announces Wilder's future style with its realism tinged with light comedy, and the theme of impersonation and deception that informs several of his later films, for instance *Some Like It Hot* (1959) and *Irma la Douce* (1963). The actual urban settings, as well as the main character's predicament, also look to *Double Indemnity* (1944) with its real location settings and its couple on the run from the police.[31] The opposition between Paris and Marseilles works in similar ways to that of Chicago and Miami in *Some Like It Hot*. Paris is associated with gangsters and cars, predominantly the domain of the male. Marseilles, on the other hand, is immediately associated with sun, life and new beginnings: a female world.[32]

The Sound of Modernity

Patrice Petro has suggested that the specificity of Weimar culture resided in "an exploration of modernity defined by states and conditions of immanence, not just the loss of fixed values in the wake of industrial expansion, but also gendered categories and sexual identities in the face of an increasing visibility and mobility of classes, races, sexes and nations within an urban context."[33] This state of immanence she finds in Wilder's later work such as *Some Like It Hot*, based on a Weimar script and made in France in 1935 as *Fanfare d'amour*, then remade in Germany in 1951 by Kurt Hoffman as *Fanfaren der Liebe*. A trace of this Weimar legacy is also present in *Mauvaise graine* where, according to Gene D. Phillips, Wilder "slyly introduced a homosexual subplot into the film. Baby-faced Jean has a crush on Henri, whom he invites to share his flat and sleep on his couch."[34] This sense of change is also expressed through the representation of a black man as one of the gang, who masquerades as a fake taxi driver and creates a diversion with his fake customer while Henri and Jean are stealing a car.

In *Mauvaise graine*, as in *Sabrina*, *Love in the Afternoon* and *Irma la Douce*, Paris is a place of transit that eventually allows its characters to find themselves.[35]

Like so many Wilder films, *Mauvaise graine* is in many ways a film about performance, disguise and finding oneself. The key to this is the recurrent Wilderian motif of "the binary opposition of being and appearance (between "Sein" and "Schein") that provides the central structuring device of [*Some Like It Hot*],"[36] and is dramatized in *Mauvaise graine* through the two central characters, Henri and Jeannette. Acting as bait, Jeannette, a young ingénue, disguises herself to lure gentlemen away from their cars, while Henri, the bourgeois playboy and son of a rich doctor, masquerades as a gangster.

As Gene D. Phillips has noted, *Mauvaise graine* is significant because "it fills a gap in Wilder's filmography" and, like some of his later Hollywood films, "it is a pot-boiler that mixes comedy with crime melodrama."[37] Moreover, it is simultaneously "typically French and a typical émigré production."[38] Although, because of their specific individual trajectories and personal biographies German émigrés did not constitute a uniform grouping, what unites their films stylistically, according to Thomas Elsaesser, is a refusal to privilege the actor and a fetishistic attachment to technique, almost to the point of abstraction. In contrast with an actor's cinema, such as the one that prevailed in France, the German cinema of the 1920s and 1930s was generally a cinema "of mise-en-scène and space [which] may well have been the biggest obstacle to critical success for émigrés films."[39] Indeed, French cinema of the 1930s was based on foregrounding the actors' performance as spectacle and psychology, often beyond the demands of narrative, an emphasis which was directly inherited from the live stage and had a particular appeal for French audiences. Weimar cinema, in contrast, seemed to have been permeated by stylized abstraction and design. According to Patrice Petro, "it is both the last grasp of modernist experimentation in the popular cinema and an early example of classical narrative style."[40]

Although Wilder's shooting style has been criticized for being essentially functional, *Mauvaise graine* uses a mixture of camera movements consisting of pans and tilts and intricate visual compositions, and a change of focus through editing, recalling the constructivist tendency and the detached mode of Weimar, *Neue Sachlichkeit*. *Neue Sachlichkeit*, or New Objectivity, in German cinema meant a "move toward realism, contemporary settings, combined with a technical virtuosity in camera work, optical printing and editing, that was not completely subordinated to the story."[41] Wilder was at home with this tradition, as he had written the scripts for *Menschen am Sonntag* and *Emil und die Detektive*. Dominique Païni has also pointed out that the film is reminiscent of the Constructivist interest in the image, for instance the photomontage of Moholy-Nagy or Herbert Bayer.[42] At times, one is also reminded of the Constructivist work of Dziga Vertov through editing techniques and an almost abstract lingering on objects with a camera that seems intent on "conveying an essential sense of leave-taking, an awareness that, once noticed, these things will cease to be."[43]

Described by Wilder as "a kind of avant-garde film"[44] and a "cinéma-vérité experiment,"[45] *Mauvaise Graine* mixes several styles and introduces motifs from different genres. In terms of stylistics, *Mauvaise graine* marries some of the avant-garde and documentary techniques of Weimar New Objectivity within the fictional narrative of the "meet-cute" and the road movie, a light comedy tinged with dramatic overtone, with a stylized realism in the documentary setting of Paris in the 1930s. Though marked by hybridity, the films of the German émigrés, according to Ginette Vincendeau, also inscribed themselves fully within French cinema of the 1930s. The "mixing of genres, for instance, is a characteristic feature of French cinema of the time, in contrast with German and Hollywood cinemas' much more structured genre production."[46] The first striking thing about *Mauvaise graine* is how its sense of movement and mobility is underlined by the kinetic energy of the mise-en-scène in a film that is mostly silent, and thus extremely reliant on visual effects and music and sound for its impact. *Mauvaise graine's* fast-paced rhythm and sense of mobility is matched by a syncopated, jazz-influenced score filled with foxtrot tunes co-written by two of Wilder's fellow émigrés from UFA, Allan Gray (originally Josef Zmigrod) and Franz Waxman (Franz Wachsmann). Gray would go to England to write music for the Emeric Pressburger and Michael Powell team, while Waxman, who would later provide the music for *Sunset Boulevard* (1950) and *The Spirit of St. Louis* (1957), became a major composer, writing the score for over a hundred and fifty films during Hollywood's classical period. During his short stay in Paris, Waxman would also score the émigré features of Fritz Lang (*Liliom*, 1934) and Robert Siodmak (*La crise est finie*, 1934).

In *Mauvaise graine*, the syncopated jazz music underscores speed, movement and the urban modernity of Paris, as well as underlining several references to silent cinema, with "chase sequences between police and criminals and the use of sight gags" that allude to "the American tradition of fast-paced urban visual comedy exemplified by Mack Sennett and Harold Lloyd."[47] Henri Pasquier's imitation of Maurice Chevalier to impress a young woman is also a reference to *Monkey Business* (Marx Brothers, 1931), where the brothers are trying to get to the United States without passports by pretending they are Chevalier. Henri starts to sing and then adds, "as for Josephine Baker — well!" Although mainly associated with Paris in the twenties, Josephine Baker was also a major star in Berlin.[48] In the interwar period, jazz was part of the "polyglot cosmopolitanism of Europe's capitals."[49] Universal and cosmopolitan, its appropriation by intellectuals expressed an ambivalent relationship towards past traditions and culture. Heard in Europe as specifically American, jazz functioned as the sound of modernity, "confounding hierarchies of cultural values" as well as signifying "a loss of confidence in European culture and the desire for a new cultural authenticity."[50] *Mauvaise graine* is infused with "Wilder's fascination with things considered typically American — fast cars and jazz — and thus functions as a bridge between his Weimar self–Americanization and a more critical stance towards the American dream that he developed in Los Angeles."[51] As Patrice Petro has noted, "Berlin during the Weimar years was a node within a network of global cities that included London and Paris, Moscow, Mexico City, Los Angeles and New York. Via this network, images, performers and personnel travelled across temporal and cultural boundaries to emerge as part of a new ensemble."[52] In Weimar Germany, *Amerikanismus* meant embracing the American spirit, progress, the marvels of technology and invention, the urban environment: "sport, jazz, film — in a word mass culture, with its commercial, social, and supranational ramifications, gained acceptance as progressive, democratic and dynamic."[53]

The sense of movement and mobility that contributes to the dynamics of the narrative is especially channelled through the character of Jeannette and the energy and vivaciousness of Danielle Darrieux's performance, which anchors the film's sense of dynamism, and matches the speed of the fast-moving automobiles. Introduced to us through her compact mirror (an early use of the compact repeated in *The Apartment*, 1960), Jeannette appears to be one of the emancipated young women of the 1920s who expected mobility, self-reliance and economic independence. Through the character of Jeannette, the film thus presents an image of the new woman on the streets of Paris. Darrieux has had one of the longest film careers of all French actresses. Aged seventeen, she was relatively new to the film industry and was not yet a major star when she made *Mauvaise graine.* She was already establishing for herself a distinctive star image, eventually becoming one of the most popular French actresses towards the end of the 1930s. Darrieux left for Hollywood in 1937 with a five-year contract with Universal.

Frequently cast as the rebellious, modern young woman, her first part, aged fourteen, was as the unruly daughter in Wilhelm Thiele's *Le Bal* (1931). This set the foundations of her early star persona of the 1930s. In *Mauvaise graine* she is often in motion, a walking figure in the city, and like many of Wilder's heroines (Susan Applegate in *The Major and the Minor*, 1942; Ariane Chavasse in *Love in the Afternoon*) she is an active young woman, an impetuous and mobile Parisian young woman, a heroine who seems much more liberated than the emasculated hero. Darrieux's kinetic performance is in stark contrast to the stage-trained actors who defined French cinema of the 1930s. She is a figure on the move that strides along space. Just like a car, she moves fast. Thus, just like the figure of the emancipated modern young woman in interwar Berlin and Paris, mediated through the image of the *Neue Fraue* or *La femme moderne*, she is literally "going places ... a figure in transit and in transition."[54] Wearing fashionable clothes, hats and jewellery, she is on display, visible and mobile on the streets of Paris, and if we never see her drive, she is nevertheless an active participant in the homosocial world of the gang.

As its only female member, she is thus in many ways a typical Wilder character, an outsider, belonging yet not belonging to this tough underworld, a male domain. A typical Wilder heroine, through Jeannette Wilder also alludes to the French social context. When asked by Pasquier why she has joined the gang, she responds that she "used to work as a secretary. But it is because of the crisis, there are no jobs." Henri, another outsider due to his class, is also a typical Wilder character, a playboy in the mould of Frank Flanagan (Gary Cooper) in *Love in the Afternoon*, who will come to reject his lifestyle. Whereas French cinema was marked by daughter-father relationships within a master narrative of paternal seduction,[55] in contrast, Weimar cinema's Oedipal master-narrative was characterized by the father-son axis.[56] Behind the light comedy tone of the film, Wilder offers a portrait of French society where relations of power dominate.[57] The belated tension between social classes and between the generations is exemplified by the relationship between father and son, and the power relations within the gang itself. The gang leader is another oppressive "father" figure who is challenged by Henri. In its dramatization of the conflict between classes and generations, however, and in particular the rejection of the Law of the Father, which is enacted in the film with the conflict between Henri and his authoritarian father, we might also see a certain dismantling of the links with the Fatherland and, with the departure to foreign lands, the entering of the realm of a new country, a severance with the past that in *Mauvaise graine* nevertheless still relies on the father's approval. Thus, Henri will never fully lose all traces of his former cultural self.

Paris as Transit City

As Hamid Naficy in his study of accented cinema has suggested, films by deterritorialized filmmakers share certain features such as the motif of the journey: "journeys, real or imagined, form a major thematic thread in the accented films."[58] This motif is signalled at the beginning of *Mauvaise graine* with a credit sequence showing a rapidly spinning wheel. This is followed by onscreen intertitles telling us that "Happy people don't have troubles. It is perhaps not so. Henri Pasquier is very happy. The only thing he is missing is a new horn." As soon as the credit sequence ends, the film opens on a freewheeling view of fast-moving cars in Paris, in a constant spectacle of movement and action and rapid transitions, emphasizing the link between urban modernity and transportation, geographic circulation and the city. We then cut to yet another fast-moving car that enters a garage at great speed, and we are introduced to Henri in his American Buick with five young male friends.

These opening shots foreshadow some of the film's major preoccupations: mobility and space. *Mauvaise graine*'s sense of urban flow and modernity is underscored by an extremely energetic and kinetic mise-en-scène where the camera is positioned on moving vehicles. This sense of mobility is also foregrounded by the centrality of the car as a mechanical object that facilitates movement. In *Mauvaise graine* Paris is turned "into a spectacle by integrating a sense of the space and freedom of the city with the modern sensations of speed and mobility."[59] Some of the action, made of high-speed, frantic nighttime car chases, races, pursuits and long walks, shows a preoccupation with "disjuncture, space and light"[60] that plays with mirrors and reflections, mobilising the nexus between "film, migration and the urban experience," identified by Anton Kaes in his reading of Walter Ruttman's 1927 semi-documentary, *Berlin: Symphony of a City*.[61] The camerawork and the jazz music are accompanied by superimpositions, wipes, dissolves and jump cuts that show Wilder's interest in the intellectual avant-garde developed during his time at the Romanisches Café in Berlin. The few moments of stasis that contrast with the hectic movement of inner-city traffic take place within the claustrophobic confines of the gang's garage, but overall in the film "there is an inherent instability that is suggested most forcefully by the constant framing in motion of the city passing by from the vantage point of the motor car."[62]

Montage editing is abandoned in the final ride into Marseilles. After a night-time, high-speed car chase by the police, Henri and Jeannette have a car crash, though they escape unharmed. Like the chase, the long walk that follows is a key sequence. Lasting just over six minutes and shot in direct-sound, the camera is planted on the bonnet of a car as we face the couple on foot, on the road, with the heavy sound of their feet pounding as they reflect on their situation. The pace of the film is slowed down as they decide to walk back to Paris. We then see them on the back of a truck, riding south. Henri declares that he does not want to go back, yet he is not sure why. This utterly romantic sequence abandons montage for traveling shots; the mise-en-scène encompasses a vast expanse of sky and sun-lit Mediterranean Sea, while a train slowly crosses a roman-aqueduct-type bridge (which seems to be the famous Roman Pont du Gard in Provence). And just as we are shown this idyllic view of Marseilles from the back of a truck, Jeannette declares that she knows why they have to leave: it is because they belong together. A transitional space of border crossing that invokes belonging and self-transformation, the bridge seems to act as a signifier of hope and change; they decide to leave France for far-away places together.

On the Road to Marseilles

Significantly, however, the film can also be seen as a journey narrative when, during its second half, the film adopts a road movie structure as Jeannette and Henri drive to Marseilles, eventually deciding to emigrate. As Naficy has observed, in accented films "once initiated, journeys often change character: begun as escape, for example, a journey may become one of exile, emigration, exploration, or return."[63] The road movie is "obsessed with home,"[64] argues

Pamela Robertson, while Wendy Everett has suggested that within the narrative structure of the European road movie, home itself is problematic, "functioning as a utopian concept; a no-place that has been replaced by the mobile car."[65] In the traditional road movie, suggests Everett, "the car functions as a key signifier, not least in its representation of the protagonist's male identity, through its status as an object that combines technology, speed and modernity."[66] As a "phallic machine which prefaces seduction," according to John Orr, "underlying the loss of automotive possession is the fear of lost masculinity."[67] Furthermore, in the European road movie, the car tends to be "disposable, transient, and temporary."[68] The car is also "generally old and unreliable, repeatedly breaking down, acquiring punctures, or even being stolen."[69] The confiscation of Henri's car, and his subsequent theft of a vehicle to go on a date, are what triggers the narrative of *Mauvaise graine*. In the second part of the film, after Henri and Jeannette's car crash, the ride to Marseilles on a truck offers a moment of reflection. The mise-en-scène replaces montage editing with traveling shots and a fluid moving camera that seems to convey a new found sense of freedom and self-knowledge, as Henri and Jeannette come to the understanding that to change their life they have to move on and take leave. The sense of movement and change had been underlined by their fast-paced drive to the South of France, on the run from the police. This temporal and spatial journey of change and transformation is a typical road movie trope with "bodies at rest, bodies in motion." The road film could be likened to "an entire physics," a genre that "belongs ... to a social and historical mode of being with difference. On the road there are, inevitably, encounters, which have to do with precisely how men, women, things, and places will be with one another."[70]

Arrivals and Departures

The critical reception of *Mauvaise graine* is inscribed within the context of the advent of sound that generated considerable debate in France. Some critics and directors were hostile to sound, seeing it as a regression undermining cinematic specificity, and thus a threat to cinema as an art form. Marcel Pagnol, on the contrary, promoted sound in the cinema as an extension of theatre. In the context of debates around "filmed theatre," Pagnol's films were often critically dismissed. Although contemporary reviews of the film are scarce, which seems to indicate that it was in the cinemas for only a very short time, *Mauvaise graine* seems nonetheless to have been rather well received by the press at the time of its release, and to have been seen as indicating a fresh new direction in French cinematic expression. Pointing to its formal attributes, one critic inserted the film within the debates around "filmed theatre," and argued that "the public will be exposed to a style of direction which represents a true renewal, a reaction against the 'Pagnolisation' of cinema,"[71] while a critic in *La*

Comédia of 8 October 1934 praised the film for its "combination of the charming music of Allan Gray and Franz Wachsmann which we have already tasted in *Emil and the Detectives*, a completely innovative use of sound, which promises us passionately created rhythms." With "the work of these young actors and technicians," added the critic, "we'll see new kinds of images unfurl in a sharp and vivacious style."[72]

Marseilles, the principal port city of France and a city of transit par excellence offers the couple a gateway to new beginnings. Henri goes back to Paris to fetch Jean and convince him to change. Jean refuses to change his life and to join them. He refuses to move on, not wanting to admit that moving on will save his life, and is killed by the police. Henri admits to his father that he has been a thief, and then leaves to join Jeannette in Marseilles. On a thematic level, this sense of saying farewell to the past, of leave-taking, is a major trope of French cinema of the 1930s and its "myth of departure" to foreign lands.[73] Yet this going elsewhere and the association of movement with life also brings us back to Wilder's own trajectory as a displaced person, in transit, in Paris. By the time of *Mauvaise graine*'s French release in the summer of 1934, Wilder had already crossed the Atlantic, having sold a script to fellow émigré from UFA, Joe May, now a producer at Columbia Pictures in Hollywood. But Wilder would have to move again and stay in Mexico for a while before being able to settle permanently in America, and it would be nine years before Wilder directed his next film, *The Major and the Minor*, yet another story of role-playing and disguise, escape and change. The exile perspective that informs *Mauvaise graine* will be dramatized again in most of Wilder's American films, fusing the Old World with the New World, and the notion of being in-between into a permanent dialectic of insider and outsider within the classical Hollywood studio system.

Notes

1. Gemünden, *A Foreign Affair*, 2.
2. Ibid., 25.
3. Nenno, "Femininity, the Primitive and Modern Urban Space," 155.
4. Gemünden, 104.
5. Phillips, *City of Darkness, City of Light*, 52.
6. Elsaesser, "The German Émigrés in Paris During the 1930s," 278.
7. Ibid., 279.
8. A. Phillips, 9.
9. Vincendeau, "Des portes ouvertes seulement à contrecoeur," 49.
10. Michel Boujut, "Transatlantique," 6.
11. Mills, *Loving and Hating Hollywood*, 27.
12. Saunders, *Hollywood in Berlin*, 2.
13. Bergfelder, "National, Transnational or Supranational Cinema?," 1–23.
14. Everett, *European Identity in Cinema*, 6.

15. Bergfelder, "National, Transnational or Supranational Cinema?," 323.
16. Bergfelder, *Destination London*, 16.
17. Elsaesser, *Weimar Cinema and After*, 398.
18. Vincendeau, "Hollywood Babel," 207–24.
19. Elsaesser, *Weimar Cinema and After*, 387.
20. Ibid., 406.
21. Elsaesser, "Ethnicity, Authenticity, and Exile," 104.
22. Crisp, *The Classic French Cinema*, 266–323.
23. Andrew, *Mists of Regret*, 99.
24. Ibid., 176.
25. Vincendeau, "Des portes ouvertes seulement à contrecoeur."
26. Elsaesser, *Weimar Cinema and After*, 406.
27. Ibid., 406–7.
28. A. Phillips, 60.
29. Chandler, *Nobody's Perfect*, 63.
30. Ibid., 62.
31. Gemünden, 41.
32. Sinyard and Turner, *Journey Down Sunset Boulevard*, 115.
33. Petro, "Legacies of Weimar Cinema," 235.
34. G. Phillips, *Some Like It Wilder*, 11.
35. Jacobs, *Billy Wilder*, 44.
36. Gemünden, 102.
37. G. Phillips, 10.
38. A. Phillips, 104.
39. Elsaesser, "The German Émigrés in Paris during the 1930s," 283.
40. Petro, 237.
41. McCormick, *Gender and Sexuality in Weimar Modernity*, 53.
42. Païni, "Le passage en France," 61.
43. Elsaesser, "The German Émigrés in Paris During the 1930s," 282.
44. Jacobs, 61.
45. Colpart, *Billy Wilder*, 46.
46. Vincendeau, "Des portes ouvertes seulement à contrecoeur," 49.
47. A. Phillips, 103.
48. Nenno, 146.
49. Donald, "A Complex Kind of Training," 28.
50. Ibid., 30.
51. Gemünden, 41.
52. Petro, 240.
53. Saunders, 243.
54. Chadwick and Latimer, "Becoming Modern," 3.
55. Vincendeau, "Family Plots," 14–17.
56. Elsaesser, "The German Émigrés in Paris During the 1930s," 282.
57. Jacobs, 62.
58. Naficy, 222.
59. A. Phillips, 77.
60. Elsaesser, "The German Émigrés in Paris During the 1930s," 278.
61. Kaes, "Leaving Home," 179.
62. A. Phillips, 104.
63. Naficy, 222.
64. Robertson, "Home and Away," 271.
65. Everett, "Lost in Translation?" 170.

66. Ibid., 172.
67. Orr, *Cinema and Modernity*, 131.
68. Ibid., 132.
69. Everett, 172.
70. Schaber, "'Hitler can't keep 'em that long,'" 22.
71. Unknown source quoted in A. Phillips, 204.
72. *La Comédia*, 8 October 1934, quoted in Ibid., 204.
73. Vincendeau, "Des portes ouvertes seulement à contre-coeur," 49.

12. *Palimpsest*
The Double Vision of Exile
NANCY STEFFEN-FLUHR

"Whoever has two countries has none."[1]

In May 1945, Billy Wilder, who was in London to edit the first footage of the Nazi death camps, had a conversation with Hungarian screenwriter Emeric Pressburger, an old friend from Berlin: "We [émigrés] wondered where we should go now that the war was over.... Should we go home? *Where was home?*"[2]

The question of home and homelessness haunted Wilder throughout his life. It haunts his films as well, generating a deceptive double vision in which past/present, Europe/America, living/dead coexist in the same highly metaphoric space, as in the layers of a palimpsest. The fundamental paradox of exile — to be two places at once and therefore no place — is the fundamental condition of Wilder's style, especially during the crucial period 1941–1951. Thus, *The Lost Weekend* (1945) is set in New York and in *Die Todt Stadt* simultaneously. And the Sinai of Exodus masquerades as the New Mexican desert in *Ace in the Hole* (1951).

Wilder's earliest work, *Mauvaise graine* (1934), is full of palimpsests: for example, a man chains his car to a no parking sign, then peels off the sign, revealing another sign beneath. This semiotic playfulness goes underground once Wilder reaches Hollywood, prompting critics to misread his films as normative products of studio realism. This is a mistake. Wilder's realism is *trompe l'oeil*, designed to conceal the sign under the sign, undermining verisimilitude in the very act of establishing it. None of this duplicity is obvious. Indeed, at first glance, Wilder seems to have assimilated easily to the Hollywood system.

Inside Outsider

Wilder fled Nazi Germany in 1933, arriving in Hollywood a year later. Only twenty-eight, he had already achieved success as a screenwriter in Berlin, but exile stripped him of everything, his money, his status, his language. Six years later, he was collecting an Oscar nomination, for writing *Ninotchka* (1939). Over the next two decades, he would amass twenty-one Oscar nominations, more than half of them for writing ... in a language that he did not begin to learn until he was nearly thirty. In interviews, Wilder presented himself as *mishpokhe* ("one of us"), speaking as an established Hollywood industry man, not an exiled *auteur*. Like his rapid success, this posture is deceptive, however. In subtle ways, Wilder remained an outsider even when he became an insider. His aggressive, no-nonsense public persona was a carefully crafted directorial legend, distinct from the directorial sensibility immanent in the films themselves. It served Wilder as a trademark and a protective screen, directing our eye away from the authorial spoor in the *mise en scène*: the artistry, the vulnerability, the immense personal pain.

That pain was inseparable from his Otherness. Wilder was never really *mishpokhe*. Not in Poland where he was born into a family of itinerant German-speaking Jews. And not in anti–Semitic Vienna where he was baited as a "dirty Polack" throughout his schooling. "The Wilders may have spoken German, but they would never *be* German, nor would they be Austrian."[3] Wilder was *Ausländisch* even in his home. He described himself as growing up alone, on the streets.[4] He learned early to take care of himself; but his proud spirit put him in conflict with his equally spirited mother, Eugenia. As a girl, Genia had lived briefly in Manhattan, where she saw Buffalo Bill's Wild West Show, a tale she often recounted to her family. Wilder ("Buffalo Billie") remembered his mother as a "Scheherazade," a term he used later to describe himself as a filmmaker. Genia was a "hard audience," however. Billie got her attention by playing hooky and stealing cars. She reacted by trying to break him. She "beat the hell out of me!" Wilder remembers. Then one day, the beatings stopped: "I don't know what kind of stick she had there, but I grabbed her hand and looked at her, and she knew she could never beat me again."[5] In this paradigmatic story, Wilder takes control of his life by taking his mother's stick into his own hand. But there is a downside to his survival strategy. Wilder's status as a non-victim is contingent upon the stick remaining in his hand. He can never let go.

Wilder left Vienna for Berlin in 1926, hitching a ride with Paul Whiteman's band, the Jazz Age equivalent of running away with the circus. After Whiteman left, Wilder survived by becoming a Scheherazade for the film industry, bonding with fellow writers at the Romanisches Café. By 1933 he had made a name as a UFA screenwriter. Berlin was his *Stammtisch*, his home. Then, on January 30, Adolf Hitler became Reich's Chancellor. Wilder was *Ausländisch* again. He told various stories about what happened next. In one version, he hears the news while skiing in Davos. He turns to his girlfriend, Hella Hartwig, and says, "I think it's time to leave." A month later, they are in Paris. In another version, however, Wilder's decision to flee is more traumatic: in February Wilder is "on the Zinnstrasse," watching a gang of Nazis beat an old Jew: "They battered him mercilessly. And I was just standing there, completely helpless, with tears in my eyes and my fists clenched in my pockets."[6] The next day the Nazis burn the Reichstag. The day after that Wilder is gone. Both stories may be true, but they frame Wilder rather differently in relationship to the Holocaust. In the Davos story, Wilder is cool and decisive, a quintessential survivor. The stick is in his hand. In the Zinnstrasse story, the stick is *not* in his hand, nor is he emotionally removed. He is in pain. And he is helpless.

Helplessness— the fear of it and the illicit desire for it — is the emotional pivot point around which Wilder's cinematic world turns. The issue at stake is the paradoxical relationship between *surviving* and *living*. The first rule of survival is "take care of yourself," something Wilder had been doing since he was a little boy. The desire to be "taken care of" was not only unmanly, in Nazi Germany it was deadly, especially for a Jew. And yet, as Wilder's films consistently demonstrate, the walls we build to protect ourselves can entomb us, blocking intimacy; and survival without intimacy is a living death. All Wilder protagonists struggle with this conundrum, especially in the films he made from 1943 to 1951, when his success as a director was contingent on his ability to mask his identity, keeping his fists in his pockets.

Despite his macho public persona, Wilder was attracted to images of male vulnerability. Late in life, he described how he wept uncontrollably at the sight of Homer, the amputee in *The Best Years of Our Lives* (1946).[7] Homer is at the center of the film's infantalization fantasy, a fear/desire that culminates in his naked disclosure: "This is when I know I'm helpless. My hands are down there on the bed." In artful disguise, Homer's moment "when I know I'm helpless" is the moment for which all of Wilder's films exist, from straitjacketed Gary Cooper in *Bluebeard's Eighth Wife* (1938) to the trussed up Jack Lemon in *Buddy, Buddy* (1981). His protagonists are Rube Goldberg devices, engineered to break. Typically, Wilder's scenarios end in a male swoon, of which Joe Gillis' belly flop is the most spectacular. This *mise en scène* of desire is one of the authorial spoors that I will track in the remainder of this essay. Another spoor is absent tears.

Long before *The Sopranos*, Wilder liked to tell interviewers about a great idea he had for a screenplay: a tough Mafia *capo* suddenly starts to weep uncontrollably at inopportune moments, so he sees a shrink. This troubles his fellow gangsters, but the *capo* reassures them: "Do not worry, boys," he says, "as soon as I am cured, I will *kill* him."[8] Like the weeping *capo*, Wilder's films delete the emotion they exist to express. Revealing and concealing occupy the same semiotic space. Although Wilder defined himself as a writer, his style is rooted in silent cinema, in which "material objects ... often take on a life of their own."

As Anton Kaes reminds us, "Where nobody speaks, everything speaks."[9] The snappy dialogue for which Wilder is known is not really the text; it points *to* the text, which consists of arcane bits of business, strung together diachronically like a rebus. This prop-driven "Indian Sign Language" is the hallmark of Wilder's style, allowing him to create complex, often contradictory double visions of reality.

Wilder's alienated double vision is already apparent in the first film he directed, which was also the first film of his exile: *Mauvaise graine.* Shot on the streets of Paris, *graine* is often described as proto-*cinema vérité*, but the film's documentary look is deceptive. Beneath the surface, *graine* is full of metaphorical props. The plot involves a young playboy, Henri, who ends up working in a chop shop. There is a nominal boy-girl romance, but the central couple is an Odd Couple: Henri and a young man named Jean, a kleptomaniac with an obsession for other men's neckties. Henri's tie to Jean is a proxy for the infantilizing tie that binds Henri to his patriarchal father. That tie breaks at the beginning of the film, triggering Henri's journey to the underworld, a structure that marks the French *Graine* as a German *Strassenfilm.*

At the beginning of the film, Jean and Henri swap cravats, like blood brothers touching fingers, a ritual that anticipates *Double Indemnity* (1944). However, the tie exchange is also quotation that silently relocates *graine* from Paris to Berlin: *Zwei Krawatten* was the title of the 1929 Berlin musical that gave Wilder's blood brother Marlene Dietrich her big break. The "two neckties" motif is part of a transnational semiotic system structured around the double meaning of the English word *tie*: necktie and connection.[10] Jean's dangerous desire for *les cravates* acts out a desire for *Die Krawatten* which, in turn, functions as a synecdoche for the lost world of Berlin, a dangerous "tie" to the past. Near the end of the film, as Henri prepares to sail away to a new life, he is approached by a man selling neckties. The sight of the *krawatten* reminds him of his tie to Jean, and he returns to Paris in a futile effort to save the boy, nearly trapping himself.

The dangerous nature of emotional ties—a core issue in all of Wilder's films—surfaces in a surreal swimming pool scene during which Jean's illicit *Krawatten* are transformed into a scourge. The whip belongs to The Chief, the leader of the gang. His signature prop, a wooden ruler, never leaves his hand. (The ruler comes out of Wilder's personal prop chest, an enormous collection of canes and umbrellas he clutched as he dictated his scripts, pacing compulsively.)[11] In *graine*, the stick and the tie come together when the Chief corners Jean in a closet-like cabana and, temporarily ruler-less, uses the stolen ties to whip the helpless boy. ("A child is being beaten.") Henri intervenes, striking The Chief. The next time we see The Chief, his arm is in a sling; he can no longer hold anything in his hand. Now *he* is completely helpless. That is, helplessness has not been vanquished; it has simply been displaced.

Nosferatu

Graine is the first of Wilder's many Prodigal Son stories. "Ah, I get it," Jean observes. "You're the prodigal son. Maybe you'd rather go home." "Home?" Henri replies. "Go screw yourself! I don't have a home." By 1934, neither did Wilder. On January 22, leaving Hella Hartwig in Paris, he crossed the Atlantic, on a one-way ticket to Hollywood. Like Henri, Wilder had unfinished business, however. In September 1935, he returned briefly to Vienna to see his mother.[12] Perhaps he tried to persuade her to flee, or perhaps not. (Like Jean-La-Cravate, she had ties.) Wilder left several days later, alone. When he returned to Europe in 1945, the Berlin he had known had disappeared. So had his mother. The Red Cross conjectured that Genia had been deported to Krakow after the Anschluss, along with her mother and second husband, and that they had all ended up in Auschwitz.[13] There was no record of their fate.

It was under these circumstances that Wilder began the harrowing work of editing the first footage of the Nazi death camps. One image in particular mesmerized him: "There was a field of corpses, a field, and one corpse was not quite dead. And he looked and he saw the camera ... and stared at us."[14] This liminal figure — the living deadman — haunts the entire body of work Wilder produced during the 1940s, not only after the war but before it as well, uniting such apparently disparate films as *Five Graves to Cairo* (1943), *Double Indemnity*, *The Lost Weekend*, *The Emperor Waltz* (1948), *A Foreign Affair* (1948), *Sunset Boulevard* (1950), and *Ace in the Hole*. In one way or another, all the protagonists in these films are *nosferatu*, in whom the land of the living is sutured to the land of the dead. They express not merely a survivor's guilt but a survivor's desire, a yearning for a *Liebestod*. Like the secret caches that Rommel digs into the Egyptian desert in *Graves*, Wilder has buried a series of personal images below the commercial surface of these films: images of the death he chose not to die, of the escape that was forever fettered to abandonment. Over and over, he does the moral calculus: "I think I could have ... saved my mother — but I didn't dare because then there would have been one more [dead Jew]."[15]

Like *graine*, Wilder's World War II–era films are palimpsests, located in the present and in the past — America and Europe — simultaneously. Wilder always denied the existence of such "underwriting," of course, but he was wrong, as I will demonstrate. First, a brief word about artistic agency, however — in particular, the crucial distinction between intention-as-desire ("I want to do this rather than that") and intention-as-analysis ("I want to do this *because*"). The former drives all great filmmakers, including Wilder, who intuitively manipulates his industry collaborators in ways that fulfill his obsessional needs. The latter (analysis) powers Stanley Kramer to make *Guess Who's Coming to Dinner* (1967), the kind of Message Picture that Wilder stayed clear of throughout his career. That is, Wilder's "serious" work takes place in cinematic venues that don't seem to be very serious at all.

Five Graves to Cairo is a case in point. Cameron Crowe compliments Wilder by comparing *Graves* to *Indiana Jones* (1981), but he has mistaken Wilder's patter for his legerdemain.[16] Unlike Lucas' *joujou*, *Graves* is a work of deceptive complexity in which a visible palimpsest (Rommel's map) mirrors the structure of the film as a whole. Below the genre text, Wilder has underwritten a Passover fable, wrapped up in a red, white and blue disguise. Unlike the Haggadah, *Graves* is not an unqualified celebration of escape, however; in Wilder's Egyptian fable, to survive is to be buried alive inside the deaths one did not die.

The film begins inside a "five passenger hearse," a driverless British tank weaving out of control through the Egyptian desert. The only survivor, J.J. Bramble, is buried alive under a pile of corpses. By chance, he is thrown free and makes his way to an oasis hotel, the Empress of Britain.[17] When General Rommel commandeers the hotel as his headquarters, Bramble survives by playing dead, disguising himself as Paul Davos, the hotel's limping waiter, whose body lies buried in the cellar. The first of Wilder's *noir* Zombies, Bramble is an existential immigrant, inhabiting multiple worlds: a living Englishman passing as a dead German in the Land of the Pharaohs. His masquerade saves his life, but he is trapped in his disguise: Davos was a German agent. Unwittingly, Bramble has become his own worst enemy.

Just as *Egypt* signals the Diaspora (Exodus), *Davos* marks the beginning of Wilder's own flight. Mouche, the female lead, is part of the fight/flight game as well. Her nickname ("housefly") sets up a "child is being beaten" moment in which Rommel flogs her with his "flyswisher." For Rommel, Mouche is a pest to be exterminated — i.e., a synecdoche for the "vermin" Jews. Ironically, it is Bramble who flies away, however, abandoning Mouche to be murdered. The script justifies Bramble's flight in patriotic terms, but the *mise en scène* undermines the rhetoric. The white parasol Bramble brings Mouche at the end is stained not only by bad timing (she is already dead), but by the fact that he transports the umbrella in the gun rack of his tank, a placement that makes it metaphorically equivalent to Rommel's flyswisher.

Moral equivalence goes both ways in *Graves*, however. In Hollywood films, bad guys wear black hats and good guys wear white ones. In 1943 the Black Hats had German accents, a conjunction that put Wilder at odds with the German-in-himself. Like German-Jewish refugees who survived in Hollywood by playing Nazis, Wilder's Rommel is an "impersoNation."[18] Doing Rommel, Stroheim is "doing" himself as "Von," an American caricature of Teutonicity. And he is doing Wilder. Like The Chief's ruler, Rommel's flyswisher comes out of Wilder's prop chest. The flogging of Mouche replicates the excised opening of *Hold Back the Dawn* (1941), in which self-loathing refugee Georges Iscovescu smashes a cockroach with his cane as it hides behind his mirror.[19] In *Graves*, Iscovescu's angst is built into the prop: the Nazi flyswisher is shaped like a penitent's scourge. That is, *Rommel* is an act of authorial self-flagellation.

And a buried act of mourning. In a crucial scene, Rommel uses salt shakers to represent Egyptian cities, daring his audience to guess where he has hidden five supply depots. "[They say] that I am a magician," Rommel says, knocking over a saltcellar. He picks up a pinch of salt and throws it over his shoulder. This ritual gesture points to the ritual nature of the *mise en scène*, for Rommel's dinner party is far more kosher than it has any right to be. As he struggles to understand the meaning of the objects on Rommel's table, Bramble becomes the son whose questions initiate the Haggadah, a story at whose semiotic center is a bowl of salt water, representing the tears of the Jews. That is what Rommel holds in his hand when he picks up the spilled salt, dry tears that cannot be shed until death has a local habitation and a name.

Dead Man Talking

In Wilder's next film, *Double Indemnity*, the dry sands of Egypt morph into the wet streets of Los Angeles, and thirsty J.J. Bramble becomes flowing Walter Neff. The widening circle of blood on Neff's jacket is a body-clock to which the film has been calibrated. As he enters the Bradley Building, a Prodigal Son returning, Neff is already a dead man walking. ("I couldn't hear my own steps.") And a dead man *talking*: his self-accusing voiceover frames the film, creating a palimpsest in which past and present exist simultaneously, a German *Strassenfilm* shimmering beneath the hardboiled American plot. Wilder's femme fatale is "Dietrichson," a name that personifies Weimar Berlin, a tie that binds. By analogy, *noir* LA becomes *Die Tote Stadt*. Plotting murder, Dietrichson meets Neff in Jerry's Market, a location shoot often praised for its realism. The store is a doppelganger, however: "Jerry" is derogatory 40s slang for "German." Like many other spaces within the film, Jerry's is a House of Death. Standing behind rows of columbarium-like boxes, Dietrichson is a mourner at her own funeral.

In *Strassenfilms*, the anti-hero begins his journey by breaking with his wife or father (cf. *Graine*). In *Indemnity* that role is played by Barton Keyes, the mother-hen/papa to whom Neff dictates his confession. Keyes is defined by the chain that runs across his vest, like a fence barring entry to his heart. It is equivalent to the chain that cuts into the flesh of Dietrichson's ankle. Ironically, Neff's effort to cut his ties to the domineering Keyes tethers him to the dominatrix Dietrichson. Ultimately, Dietrichson, Neff, and Keyes are caught in the same net, trapped by their emotional untouchability. Of the three, only Keyes— the most untouchable of all — lives to the end of the script. And his survival is his tragedy. The Sherlock Holmes of Pacific All-Risk, Keyes is an inveterate bachelor, suspicious of irrational emotion. He machine-guns Neff with words, pacing restlessly, waving his unlit cigar. (Like Rommel, Keyes is "doing" Wilder.) Periodically, Keyes prompts Neff to light his cigar. (The self-protective Keyes doesn't carry matches, afraid they will "explode.") Keeping his left hand in his pocket, Neff uses his right hand to strike a matchstick on his thumbnail. He gives the stick to Keyes, who lights his stogie. (The stick is in *his* hand.) It is an awkward gesture, signaling the emotionally awkward touch-at-a-distance between the two men. It also signals Neff's fate: although he says he has "no visible scars," the one-armed Neff of the match-lighting ritual is already walking wounded.

At the end of the film, Wilder returns to the wounded Neff, pulling back to reveal Keyes in the doorframe, hearing Neff's confession. Neff expects to be whipped by Keyes' "two-dollar words." Instead, like the Prodigal Son, he is forgiven. "You're all washed up, Walter," says Keyes, a line that means two things at once. As an idiom, it means Walter's life is over. Literally, however, "washed up" means "no longer contaminated," i.e., a couple of murders notwithstanding, this film has a happy ending. That was not the ending Wilder originally shot, however. The *Indemnity* script ends in the San Quentin death house, a structure that contains two separate chambers, one for the living and one for the dead man walking. Neff is walled in; Keyes is walled-out. Like Wilder on the Zinnstrasse, the untouchable Keyes can only stand by helplessly and watch. After Neff's execution, Keyes stands stunned in an open doorway, an unlit cigar in his mouth. He fumbles for matches, and then suddenly stops, "a look of horror on his face."[20] *This* is how *Indemnity* really ends. The open door merely leads from one prison space into another. Neff will be buried; Keyes will be buried alive, in solitary confinement for the rest of his life. Like Neff at the beginning, Keyes at the end is a dead man walking, *nosferatu*.

Dead Man Walking

Alcoholic Don Birnam in *The Lost Weekend* is another dead man walking, traversing an urban desert emptied of its Jews (*Die Todt Stadt*). That absence is the hole around which the film's semiotic system revolves, a system in which missing objects stand in for missing persons. Missing bottles drive the plot; but other things are missing as well. Consider the opera sequence. Don checks his wet raincoat, stashing a pint in the pocket. As the chorus sings "Libiamo," he becomes uneasy. Wilder cuts to a grotesque, low-angle view of the swaying singers, then to an expressionist shot of identical raincoats swaying on their hangers. The coats are notable for what they do *not* contain: living bodies. They connote absence, multiplied to infinity. The singers have disappeared, replaced by synecdochic "hanged men."

Don repeatedly describes himself to Nat the Bartender as a dead man. ("If it's dawn, you're dead.") Nat seems to agree, reproving Don for abandoning the women in his life and for his suicidal self-pity: "[You can kill yourself] for a nickel, in a subway under a train." As he speaks, Nat makes a crisscross gesture, a cryptic sign of the cross that simultaneously marks Don as *nosferatu* and transforms him into the walking dead man of the Via Dolorosa. As he moves painfully up Third Avenue, Don struggles to understand the inexplicable disappearance of the city's pawnbrokers (implicitly, its Jews). At each closed gate, he asks "why?" (the Haggadah question). Over and over, the answer is death. ("Somebody passed away, most likely.") Finally, two Jews in black hats appear and explain that it is Yom Kippur, the Day of Atonement. Don's own atonement begins as he wanders past a wooden Indian and a striped barber's pole. Earlier, b-girl Gloria told Don about a wooden Indian near her door. ("They've got the Indian sign on me, I always say.") Tipsy, Don promised to take her out but then abandoned her. Come full circle, he climbs the stairs to Gloria's flat and gives her a Judas Kiss. She gives him $5. As he leaves, he passes a little girl hitting a stick repeatedly against the banister. Suddenly dizzy, Don plunges headlong down the stairs, the beginning of a journey to the underworld.

Here and throughout the film, Wilder's realism serves a private semiotic system. Gloria's "Indian sign" is a proxy for a tale that Genia Wilder used to tell about a wooden Indian that helped her find her way home when she was lost in Manhattan.[21] In *Weekend* the Indian thus serves as a double place marker — a metonymy for home and homelessness (for loss and being lost). So does the other object outside Gloria's door: a "Pole" is a person as well as a thing. The "stick" is a marker, too, fusing two kinds of brutality. Arranged in the frame, these talismanic objects — the Indian, the pole, the stick — form a rebus we can read. Or not read. These are dreamwork puns, in a film that Wilder is making behind his back. They are liminal and invisible at once, like the stripes on the pole that become the striped bathrobes of the Bellevue inmates, trapped in a vicious circle that looks a lot like Dante's hell. Or a Nazi concentration camp.

The Ninth Circle

Five months after he shot the Bellevue scenes, Wilder was back in Europe for the first time in a decade. He was haunted by what he found — and by what he did not find: his mother and grandmother had simply disappeared. He responded by re-making the Holocaust as a Bing Crosby musical — *The Emperor Waltz* — set in jolly Austria in the palace of the "Duke of Auschwitz."[22] Crosby plays an American named Virgil Smith who comes to Vienna, circa 1906, to persuade Emperor Franz Josef to buy a Victrola. He falls in love with an icy aristocrat (The Countess), then abandons her. The film begins near the end of the story when Smith returns to Vienna to make things right. "Making things right" is what *Waltz* is all about. Crosby's Swing-era presence in *fin de siècle* Vienna creates an inverted palimpsest, overwriting Hapsburg snobbery before it becomes Nazi eugenics. The poignancy of this fantasy is inextricable from its impossibility, an impossibility that film acknowledges at every point, deliberately calling attention to the surreal phoniness of its Ruritanian *mise en scène*.

Waltz begins with an *Ausländer* (Crosby) shattering the Emperor's window, a gesture that metaphorically reverses the *Kristallnacht* ... but only for a moment. When Wilder returned to Europe in 1945, he found a graveyard where his home used to be. Smith's return to the imperial palace silently replicates that journey; like Dante's *Inferno* guide, Virgil is a dead man walking through the frozen Ninth Circle. Franz Josef is *nosferatu*, too, an Emperor of "I(s)cream." ("You're full of cracked ice!") Throughout the film, he suffers from a cold, a visual sign of Austrian *froideur* — and of something else as well. By 1906, the Emperor's brother, son, and wife were all dead. In *Waltz*, these crushing losses are concentrated in a single prop: the handkerchief that services Franz Joseph's "cold." It is a synecdoche for frozen tears.

In *Weekend*, Third Avenue ultimately flows to Don: "I found this floating around on the Nile," says Nat, returning his Prodigal Son's lost typewriter. In *Waltz* the river has frozen up, blocked by anger. That anger is displaced onto the film's canine subplot in which Smith's mongrel *schtupps* the Countess' black poodle, creating "impure" puppies slated for extermination, a bitter riff on the Nazi view of Jews as dirty dogs. Wilder personalizes the shtick by naming the black bitch Scheherazade. The fictional Scheherazade was an archetypal survivor. She could have talked her way out of Auschwitz. Genia Wilder — the Scheherazade of Krakow — could not. That is the difference between stories and histories. Scheherazade in *Waltz* can howl, but she can't talk. Neither could Wilder, when it counted. He stood silent on the Zinnstrasse. Virgil speaks up, wrapping the pups in his arms. "I'm not going to let you [kill them]!" It doesn't take a semiotician to read this text, a fantasy whose poignancy flows from its reduced scope. Genocide has become a shaggy dog story, reality being literally unspeakable.

The Sewer

In *Waltz*, the Emperor's *froideur* is synonymous with disease (his cold) which, in turn, is part of a contamination metaphor that runs like a sewer under the surface of Wilder's *noir* films. *Foreign Affair*, *Sunset*, and *Ace* are especially obsessed with pollution, guilt and desire commingling in a dirty touch. In *Affair*, the chief hygienist is hyper-controlled Iowa congresswoman Phoebe Frost who comes to Berlin ("that pest-hole") to prevent American GIs from being contaminated by European decadence. Like the mysophobic Wilder,[23] Frost has an eye for dirt, particularly a "sewer" called the Lorelei Club and its star, Erika von Schluetow, a Nazi collaborator who is being protected by someone in the U.S. military. Determined to find the culprit, Frost enlists the help of Capt. John Pringle, a fellow Iowan whom she assumes shares her values. We already know, as Frost does not, that Pringle is von Schluetow's lover.

Von Schluetow is the film's Lorelei — a soiled "lady of the night," a Siren, and a rock. Frost only seems to be hard; she is really an ice crystal that melts at the first hint of flame. Von Schluetow *is* hard: untouchable, *nosferatu*. Like Murnau's Dracula, she is a creature of the night, associated with contamination. When we first see her, she spits a mouthful of foamy white toothpaste at Pringle, polluting him. The contamination flows both ways, however. In the opening scene, Frost brings Pringle a chocolate birthday cake. He promptly barters the cake at the black market for a used mattress, a gift for von Schluetow. "*Heil,* Johnny!" she says, caressing his face. The gooey brown cake moves through the ruined city like fecal matter through the body politic, ending up in the Lorelei "sewer." The cake-as-mattress fuses Pringle to von Schluetow, a phantom of the past who threatens to pull him down into the grave. Wilder signals Pringle's contamination in a characteristically odd bit of business: his finger becomes stuck in an inkwell, fouling his hands. Thus stained, he is forced to watch a Nazi newsreel of Hitler kissing von Schluetow's hand, the same hand that had caressed his face a few hours earlier. Von Schluetow's corruption is implicit in her surname, an allusion to UFA actor Hans Schlettow, a Nazi who died defending Hitler.[24] It is "Schlettow's" putrid corpse that lies in Pringle's arms on the black market mattress ... and lies hidden in the file room below U.S. Army Headquarters, a metaphorical space whose sliding drawers create a double *double entendre*, fusing sex and decay. Frost's hysterical "Midnight Ride" is a seduction in a morgue.

All Washed Up

Sunset Boulevard is a seduction in a morgue as well, literally so in Wilder's original cut, which opened on a row of numbered corpses.[25] He later deleted the morgue scene, erasing the faint Auschwitz aura that the numbered bodies conveyed. In the new opening, Joe Gillis' corpse floats face down in Norma's pool, a metaphorical conjunction that points to *Gatsby* outside the film and to a large image set associated with flow within the film. Most of all, it is a metaphysical conceit: *Gillis* has gills. His unreliable narration of his own desires notwithstanding, the fluid world of Norma's pool is his natural element. He is at peace there, going with the flow. A Prodigal Son, returned to his amniotic home, he is "all washed up."

Like Gillis, Dom Mom Norma Desmond is a liminal being, undead. A silent screen Scheherazade who needs no words to tell her tale, she lives in the past in the present. The script signals her limbo-like condition by comparing her to Dickens' rotting Miss Havisham. "Dead in this town," the abandoned Norma waits in her sepulchral mansion for her time to return, putting the vamp in vampire. Raising her claw-like hands, she is "doing" Max Schreck doing *Nosferatu*. (In the script, her shadow appears in the frame before she does.) The rats in her pool suggest a vulvar sewer (like the Lorelei), but they are also a metonymy for the plague-bearing Orlok, whose coffin is filled with dirt and vermin. Wilder's allusions to *Nosferatu* are not the film's subtext, however. They are a vehicle that takes us to the subtext the way Gillis' limping car takes him to the 10,000 block. Dracula is the quintessential *Ausländer*, an exile condemned to carry a coffin full of home wherever he goes. Murnau locates Orlok's home in the Carpathian Mountains, amid the *shtetls* (home of the swarming rats in *Der Ewige Jude*). Wilder's grandmother owned a hotel in those mountains. He played there as a child.[26] When Gillis wanders into Norma Desmond's garden, he is thus walking on home soil, the dirt from which the Wilders came and into which some of them returned.

At the end of the film, Betty asks, "[Can't we] get out of here?" Gillis' answer is a flat "no." That is, in abandoning Betty, he refuses to abandon Norma. He is faithful unto death. In the script, Norma screams "You're not leaving me!" as Gillis walks through the French doors. It is not a question; it is a command. (The stick is in her hand.) It is also simply a statement of fact. Metaphorically, Gillis is *not* leaving Norma; he is joining her in a *liebestod*. In 1935 Wilder left his mother to be killed by the Nazis in order to avoid being killed himself. Gillis' walk toward the pool reverses the film of Wilder's life, canceling death even in the act of embracing it.

Indian Signs

Ace in the Hole is the final transformation of an image set that Wilder had been working with since 1943, a seven-picture fugue on the theme of living death. A catalog of the film's motifs reads like an index to Wilder's entire World War II oeuvre. The desert sands in *Graves*; the spreading stain of blood in *Indemnity*; the thirsty crucifixion in *Weekend*; the underworld journey in *Waltz*; the contaminated cake in *Foreign Affair*; the live burial in *Sunset* — all reappear in *Ace*, woven into a textual fabric of guilt and grief. The most elaborate of Wilder's geo-temporal palimpsests, the American desert in *Ace* is full of Indian Signs. Buried alive under a sacred Indian mountain, Leo is haunted by the spirits of the dead. A throwaway line about King Tut relocates Leo's burial site metaphorically to the land of the Egyptian Captivity. The film's Christian iconography has an analogous function: as in *Weekend*, it connects the pain within the frame to an archetypal "Suffering Jew." In this guise, Leo is a synecdoche for all the Jews of Europe who did not get out in time. Leo's need to escape is also a proxy for the emotional imperative at stake in the film: desire for release. His physical status (buried alive) mirrors the psychic status of Wilder's protagonist, Chuck Tatum, a hard-drinking reporter exiled to the New Mexico desert. "Dead" in New York, Tatum is the most poignant of Wilder's *nosferati*, a liminal status telegraphed in the original script which opened with Tatum narrating from his coffin.[27] Wilder later excised the voiceover, prompting critics to misread *Ace* as an exercise in gritty realism. In fact, it is the most metaphorical of all his films, and the most emotional.

The first of Wilder's Indian signs *is* an Indian Sign: "How," says Tatum sarcastically, raising his palm as he passes a silent Native-American copyboy in the *Sun–Bulletin* newsroom. The hand up is a heads up: if we pay attention to the business, the *mise en scène* will unfold like a rebus. Consider the matchstick ship that Tatum builds inside an empty bottle of booze. A proxy for all the live burials in the film, it suggests not only entrapment but also intestinal-as-emotional blockage. Like Leo in the tunnel, the boat is impacted, lacking the fluid necessary for movement. The empty bottle thus defines the film's central issue: is Tatum empty (*nosferatu*) or can he be made to flow? The answer is hidden in the apparently innocuous surname of the *Sun* editor, Mr. Boot. For Americans, there is nothing unusual about finding a boot in the desert. In German, however, *boot* means *boat*. An anomaly in a waterless land, editor Boat embodies the unanticipated flow that will move Tatum. The boat in the bottle is a sign that points to the onomastic doppelganger, a hinge that fastens together the two halves of Wilder's fractured cultural identity.

The editor's first name is a hinge as well: Jacob, the progenitor of the twelve tribes of Israel. Boot is thus a special kind of boat: the Ark of the Covenant. It is in this crypto–Hebraic guise that he appears suddenly in Tatum's room just as Tatum opens a bottle. On the wall is an iconic image of a Suffering Jew (a crucifix) and an altar to Mother Mary, holding two "candle jiggers": *Yartzeits* in Christian disguise. The altar belongs to Leo's mother. A ghostly figure, she has no dialogue at all; but, like Scheherazade, she tells the story. Tatum is part of that story, his identity marked on his body. In the beginning, he adopts Patriarch Boot's cautious practice of wearing a belt and suspenders. (He covers his ass.) In the altar scene, however, Tatum has undone his suspenders, which hang from under his shirt like the fringe on a *tallis katan*. And he has added an accessory: a star on his chest. The star marks him as the evil Sheriff's deputy. Even more obviously, however, it marks him as a member of Jacob's tribe, a persecuted Jew.

The film's Judaic imagery is concentrated in its strangest prop, the snake. Wilder had wanted *Ace* to open with a shot of a rattlesnake crawling onto a Paramount logo.[28] Paramount killed that snake, but Wilder planted others: for example, the rattlesnake Tatum fantasizes about hiding in order to create a hot news story, an anal-retentive image that presages how he will hold back Leo's release. Or Sheriff Kretzer's pet snake, coiled inside a cake box that probably once contained a *Torte Schokolade*. (The juxtaposition of the caged snake and the impacted acehole, Leo, establishes a fecal equation that makes Tatum a "shit.") The snake metaphor points toward release as well as blockage, however. In Exodus, Moses has a water-producing rod that morphs into a snake. The fur boa that Tatum uses to choke Lorraine is another kind of snake, a tie that binds. Lorraine cuts the tie by stabbing Tatum, forcing him to release her—a move that releases him as well. Bleeding, weeping, he watches as the priest touches a rod to Leo's head, anointing him. At the end, Tatum speaks from the mountaintop, like Moses on Sinai, the most overt of the film's Biblical allusions. The most poignant moment is much smaller, however: as Tatum staggers through the crowd, he passes a little boy wearing an Indian headdress. Like Don Birnam passing the wooden Indian as he goes up the stairs into the dark, and Norma Desmond as she comes down the stairs into the camera, Chuck Tatum is ready for his final dissolve.

"Listen to me!" says Tatum from the mountain. The film says "listen," too. But nobody did. *Ace* was Wilder's first big bomb, a failure that profoundly altered the artistic decisions he made in subsequent years. From Wilder's hyper-protected point of view, the film was nakedly emotional. He was stunned that nobody "got it." But, of course, most moviegoers are not fluent in Indian Sign Language. In Chuck Tatum's big carnival, everything important takes place below the surface. The crowd watching above ground sees nothing and knows only what it is told. *Ace* is structured the same way, as are all of Wilder's films of this period. The emotional engineering is buried underground. Too far underground. Psychologically protected to a fault, Wilder has unwittingly put a mountain of textual bedrock between himself and his audience. Ironically, the most personal and passionate of Wilder's films thus seems to be the most impersonal.

Much the same can be said of the other films I have discussed in this essay. Immensely entertaining and satisfying as movie movies, they leave us with a vague feeling of disquiet, sensing that we have "seen" but have not "observed." Wilder wanted it that way, insisting ferociously to his dying day that "There's no 'Wilderesque.' It's just ... stuff."[29] Like the Mafia capo that kills his shrink, Wilder used both ends of the pencil simultaneously, erasing his subtexts in the act of creating them. Working intuitively, largely behind his own back, he was probably genuinely unaware of any obsessional patterns in his films: "[My characters] have secrets they keep, even from me."[30] In this essay, I have tried to Sherlock out a few of those secrets, with help from the late Dr. Cronstaetter, close-reading the semiotic underwriting that remains visible on the film stock, despite Wilder's careful erasures. The films that I have been describing are not the films that first run audiences and critics saw in real time in the 1940s or 1950s. That is, I have assembled the artifacts I have been analyzing, choosing attractive *objets trouvées* from among the vast array in the textual field. Other choices are possible. The critical imperative is simply to continue to play with the goods, recognizing that *everything* in Wilder's frame is a semiotic "good to think with." (Realism was the patter, not the legerdemain.) In this manner, ignoring Wilder's defensive "Don't touch!" signs, we can begin to capture the distinctive patterns that constitute this extraordinary, and extraordinarily deceptive, body of art.

Notes

1. Siodmak, *Wolf Man's Maker,* 206.
2. Sikov, *On Sunset Boulevard,* 236.
3. Ibid., 15; Gemünden, *A Foreign Affair,* 2–5, 25–28. Gemünden shares my view that Wilder's exile — his sense of "being in-between" cultures— is central to his sensibility. However, Gemünden persists in the Armstrong tradition of reading Wilder as a realist/social critic, ignoring what, I argue, is a hallmark of Wilder's style: the highly metaphorical/semiotic nature of his *mise en scène.*
4. Crowe, *Conversations with Wilder,* 183, 227–31; Sikov, 12–14; Chandler, *Nobody's Perfect,* 19–21; Zolotow, *Billy Wilder in Hollywood,* 21–24; Brown, "Broadcast to Kuala Lumpur," 68.
5. Crowe, 183.
6. Sikov, 86; Lally, *Wilder Times,* 53–54.
7. Crowe, 280.
8. Zolotow, 174.
9. Kaes, "Urban Vision and Surveillance," 82, 86.
10. In 1934, Wilder was already learning English in anticipation of the next phase of his exile.
11. Gehman "Charming Billy," 31, 33. Virtually every Wilder interviewer mentions his pacing and his collection of canes.
12. Crowe, 21, 183; Sikov, 111–12. Hella Hartwig ended up in a concentration camp but survived.
13. Sikov, 243; Lally, 153; Crowe, 21,184. Testimony from Genia's brother Mikhael in the Yad Vashem database asserts that she and her mother died in Krakow during the 1943 "liquidation" of the ghetto. See http://www.yadvashem.org.
14. Crowe, 71. *Todesmullen* (1946) is not Wilder's cut, but it contains a shot similar to the one Wilder described.
15. Sikov, 243.
16. Crowe, 267.
17. The Empress is a proxy for the "Hotel City" in Poland where Wilder spent his childhood. Sikov, 4, 6.
18. Elsaesser, *Weimar Cinema and After,* 13.
19. Sikov, 100, 155–57.
20. Wilder, *Double Indemnity: The Complete Screenplay,* 123.
21. Zolotow, 22.
22. Franz Josef's hereditary titles included "King of Galicia" and "Duke of Auschwitz."
23. Wilder suffered from many phobias. See Zolotow, 285–86; Barnett, "The Happiest Couple," 12; Crowe, 202.
24. See "Hans Adalbert Schlettow" at http://www.cineartistes.com.
25. Sikov, 283. Zolotow, 167.
26. Sikov, 4.
27. Ibid., 314.
28. Sikov, 325.
29. Crowe, 39.
30. Chandler, 82; Crowe, 71.

13. Sabrina, *Hollywood and Postwar Internationalism*

DINA SMITH

Cultural Anxiety and a New Era of Internationalism

In the years immediately following World War II, under such measures as the European Recovery Program, better known as the Marshall Plan, the United States doled out some $23 billion to Western European nations with the return promise of increased capital investments as well as unlimited free trade. This assistance, combined with military and cultural expansion, promised America an "empire by invitation," to use historian Geir Lundestad's phrase. This so-called historical seduction invites a critique of the ways in which U.S. foreign policy has continually used gendered metaphors to describe its foreign relations. In other words, gender structures, such as the metaphor "empire by invitation," inform not only international relations but the era's various social relations as well.

This essay poses a series of "love matchings" between various levels of discourse, focusing on the way these structures enter the social imaginary, particularly in Billy Wilder's popular 1950s Cinderella films, which continually cast women/country as part of a profitable exchange. These films, specifically *Sabrina* (1954), provide a way into the intersecting cultural/economic discourses of the period. *Sabrina* most richly dramatizes the dominant foreign policy narrative of the time: a culturally savvy orphan girl (Europe) is in need of a strong rich male (American assistance). Wilder seems self-consciously to foreground economic and cultural exchanges between postwar Europe and the United States. Indeed, that an Austrian immigrant had clout in Hollywood (he is alleged to have told Louis B. Mayer to "fuck off" after a screening of the 1950 *Sunset Boulevard* and got away with it, career unscathed) bespeaks the era's and Hollywood's new internationalism.

Cast as the orphan girl in desperate need of American assistance, Europe, more specifically Paris, no longer operated only as the "other woman," as Geoffrey S. Smith describes America's long-standing prewar vision of Europe as temptress.[1] More to the point, postwar Paris became the international gamin. Sophisticated yet displaced, Paris as Cinderella desired a commodity makeover (a new gown and glass slippers). She eagerly awaited her wedding to the prince, American capitalism. The United States, then, privileged its Western European economic and military support for a reason: America continued to rely on and to usurp Western European culture, while it secured European markets and forestalled the growth of communism in this pivotal geopolitical arena. Indeed, after the war, the USSR was not very important to the United States except that its "very existence complicated the overarching American task of reconstructing Western Europe and integrating it into a global free market."[2]

The battle against communism began over reconstruction and the rebuilding of Europe's decimated national economics. In a poll taken after the war, the French chose the U.S. (47 percent) over the Soviet Union (23 percent) as the preferred leader of wartime reconversion and reconstruction[3]; U.S. control over reconstruction assured its economic and military hegemony. As Lundestad notes, "U.S. economic assistance was normally given with several strings attached. The French had to agree to promote trade with the rest of the world and to discourage the setting up of regional trading blocs." This aid "represented an instrument with great potential for intervention, since the various countries could draw upon these funds with the consent of the United States."[4] After the war, not only did the U.S. influence Western Europe militarily, politically, economically, and culturally, but it also secured once-inaccessible, provincial European markets for Americans. Goods such as German machinery and French fashions flooded the American market during the 1950s. In this context, Western Europe operated as a sort of postwar trophy wife for aspiring American capital and culture. According to this logic, Paris and, by extension, Western Europe needed America's protection both economically and culturally.

This "Americanization" of Western Europe had its price, however, most notably renewed anxiety among American critics over the inferior quality of mass-produced U.S. culture. New York critics, such as Clement Greenberg and William Philips, bemoaned this lack of "quality" culture, given the powerful leadership role of the U.S. in the world's political economy. In "The Portrait of an Artist as an American," Philips bespeaks this anxiety:

> In the past, our own creative energy has been nourished by new literary movements in Europe. Today, however, an impoverished and politically tottering Europe is not only dependent on the economic resources of the United States but is also, apparently, more *receptive* than ever before to its cultural advances. The historical irony in this dual role of the United States is merely an extension of the contradiction at the heart of our civilization. For, on the one hand, our eco-

nomic power and democratic myths behind our institutions are all that stand in the path of Stalinist enslavement in Europe. On the other hand, the United States might well become the greatest exporter of *kitsch* the world has ever seen.[5]

In the years following this pronouncement, Greenberg, Philips, and others created a "new" American avant-garde, seemingly independent of its more "feminine," orphaned Parisian counterpart. Indeed, according to Serge Guilbaut, American critics argued that "success had spoiled Parisian art," which was "effeminate and altogether unsuited to confront the violent dangers in store for Western Culture."[6] Jackson Pollock's "action" paintings, then, were the bold reply to Paul Cézanne's soft apples and pears. As Aldous Huxley described early-modern French art, those still life paintings had become equated with passivity and contemplation, an attitude, we are supposed to believe, that led to occupation.[7] French culture, like France itself, had become vulnerable. According to this logic, the Cold War required a more insurgent art form that abandoned the complacency offered by old Europe.

What is fascinating about this argument is the way in which it affirms larger international discourses concerning Europe's economic future. For, if Paris needed America, America also needed Paris. The expansion of U.S. markets and the selling of American culture were ultimately tempered or balanced by America's anxieties over its cultural vacuity. The U.S.' altruistic impulses, as well as concern among critics regarding its exportable kitsch, thus became a projection of U.S. cultural anxieties, an expression of its continuing reliance on (and consumption of) European culture. In other words, critics had to rebuild and dismiss a Cézanne to create a Pollock.

Hollywood and Billy Wilder

To understand these cultural and economic anxieties, we might begin with Hollywood, which had historically employed Western European immigrant talent, bridging the European and American cultural divide. Many European artists left Nazi Europe for the lucrative promises of Hollywood. These writers, actors, and directors found themselves under contract at Hollywood studios, where their cultural capital was incorporated into Hollywood's classic aesthetic. Thus, National Socialist Europe was good for Hollywood, which became a haven for the continuous supply of pre- and postwar émigrés. European "aura" then infected even "reproducible" Hollywood, adding art value to this aesthetic enterprise.

Billy Wilder's postwar films, including *A Foreign Affair* (1948), *Sabrina*, and *Love in the Afternoon* (1957), all wrestle with issues of internationalism, linking American cultural production to Cold War foreign relations. Emily Rosenberg has documented how *A Foreign Affair* and other foreign correspondent films, such as *The Man in the Gray Flannel Suit* (Nunnally Johnson, 1956), engage America's new diplomatic role after World War II. She argues that these films revolve around the prolonged pun of "foreign affairs," a pun situated within a history of U.S. sexualization of its foreign policy. *A Foreign Affair* espouses an isolationist position by figuring Europe within the Marlene Dietrich role as an evil, conniving seductress. (The film's production and release coincided with the formation of NATO as well as preliminary negotiations over the General Agreement on Tariffs and Trade [GATT].) These films often narrativize the need for American ("male") responsibility, leadership, and protection at home and abroad, an ideology that helped inform U.S. economic intervention in Western Europe.[8] They responded to a liberal postwar internationalism that "venerated those gender and sexual values and roles that World War II enshrined: male bonding, leadership, and domestic security."[9]

Yet, as we will see, Wilder's films during this period do not offer easy answers regarding the United States' emerging economic and cultural internationalism or firmly established gender roles. (Wilder was, after all, the director of the gender-bending *Some Like It Hot* [1959].) Rather, Wilder's Cinderella films question the romance and potential "marriage" of U.S. and Western European markets. Even the films made after the mid–1950s, which illustrated the European embrace of American protection, are bittersweet romances, tinged by the losses inherent in such forced relations.

Part of this ambiguity may stem from Wilder's own vexed history as an Austrian Jewish immigrant who fled fascist Germany. After writing and directing in Hollywood for a decade, Wilder covered World War II as an American war correspondent. While safe in Europe in an American uniform, he discovered that his entire extended family had been killed at Auschwitz. The America-Europe divide thus resonated more profoundly for Wilder. His films reflect the Jewish émigré's cynical evaluation of the blinding imperialist tendencies of postwar America. Like Douglas Sirk, Wilder seemed to luxuriate in Hollywood narrative practices while simultaneously critiquing American myths of upward mobility, rabid postwar consumerism and industrial imperialism. His films marvel at the booming American economy while foregrounding the losses within such a boom.

Wilder also demonstrated that Europe was at times complicit in its World War II and postwar takeover. After the war, treaty and trade negotiations between Western European nations and the United States often compromised various national cinemas, particularly in France, whose integrity was subordinated to economic interests favoring U.S. commerce. As if to illustrate Europe's pliant position, his films proliferate with European orphan girls who too readily give in to American wooing. And, for all their crass, brusque economic imperialism, Wilder's American moguls often have a naive vulnerability; they seem charmingly immune to European cultural splendors. Wilder's other Cinderella films of this period, such as *Love in the Afternoon*, linger on these ambiguities that resist being easily wrapped up by the romance narrative, and that bring us back to larger political and cultural ambiguities. They question the very workings of romance, but more specifically political romance: "How could Europe fall for America, and what are the consequences?"

In his repeated casting of Europeans, some of them with dubious backgrounds such as Maurice Chevalier (who had entertained Nazis during the war) in *Love in the Afternoon,* Wilder is also suspicious of a Hollywood that fetishized Europe and its émigrés. Postwar Hollywood (circa 1947–1962) had a number of foreign starlets— Hepburn, Sophia Loren, Gina Lollobrigida, Leslie Caron, Brigitte Bardot — who helped translate a soft, desirous exportable culture. Yet, and perhaps not so coincidentally, Hollywood during this period was seemingly devoid of virile, foreign leading men, save perhaps for the less-than-tough Louis Jourdan. Those foreign actors (Charles Boyer, Cary Grant, David Niven) who still circulated in 1950s Hollywood were conceived in a different era. Postwar Hollywood presented a different, homegrown image of masculinity inspired by such new talent as James Dean, Marlon Brando, Robert Mitchum, and Montgomery Clift. Hollywood, like New York, favored the tough American who saved the "feminine" European. A Brando or Dean became Hollywood's version of Pollock, and waning stars such as Peter Lawford signified a "soft" Europe, one eventually wedded, in Lawford's case, to a Kennedy (and in 1954, the year *Sabrina* was released).

Sabrina *and the Postwar Hollywood Cinderella Film*

Sabrina fixates on its title character as a European émigré (literally, since its star, Audrey Hepburn, was a Belgian World War II refugee), and on her ability to export and teach the lessons offered by Europe. Thus, French cooking, poetry, fashion, romance, and style become the film's antidote to America's buy-and-sell culture. Postwar France is a glamorous ingénue waiting to be consumed, her cultural capital vital to postwar America's emerging cultural hegemony.

Sabrina is the story of the daughter of a British chauffeur who drives for wealthy industrialists, the Larrabees. As a teenager, Sabrina goes to the Paris Cordon Bleu and later returns to the Long Island estate of her father's employer as a "displaced" person. She is a Cinderella in search of a ball to attend. In the film's terms, she exists outside the economy of the Larrabee estate; too adult to be a chauffeur's daughter yet definitely not a servant, she adopts the role of the culturally desirable European other. She constantly circulates within the film as an object of desire, someone to be gazed upon, purchased, traded, and ultimately bedded/wedded to industrialist Linus Larrabee, the stiff and aging heir played by Humphrey Bogart.

Bogart was an interesting casting choice since he was immediately associated with a tradition of rugged American cowboy individualism forced in

Casablanca (Michael Curtiz, 1941) into a liaison with foreign diplomats. As Rick Blaine, Bogart begins that film as an isolationist American. Yet, when imposed upon by his former foreign lover, Ilsa (Ingrid Bergman), who is both temptress and girl in need, Rick becomes the man of action and enters into foreign relations.[10] A reluctant but heroic internationalist, Bogart's Rick comes to signify an America that grudgingly entered into the war.

As Linus Larrabee, Bogart is still the internationalist, but Wilder illustrates the ironic underside of the heroic image of American intervention shown in *Casablanca*. Linus sees other countries in merely transactional terms; he travels to Iraq for oil deals, and although he occasionally stops in Paris, he never leaves the airport. Linus' unmarried status— his resistance to romantic involvement— recalls Rick's isolationism. By film's end, however, Linus sails off with Sabrina to Europe, engaged to both the girl and the Continent.

Foreign relations here no longer signify an honorable fight, a romance with Europe in order to dispel Nazi totalitarianism and imperialism. In *Sabrina*'s terms, American foreign relations are inextricably linked to cultural and economic imperialism. The era's global logic centered on productionism "producing the largest volume of specialized goods for sale in the widest possible world market."[11] Local, national economies thus take second place to the greater good of the world economy.

The film's narrative makes clear that the wooing of Sabrina is merely the means to the end of a merger. However, as part of Larrabee's "domestic" economy, she stands in the way of that larger merger. Desired by both Larrabee brothers, David and later Linus, Sabrina is complicating Larrabee Industries' plans for David to marry the daughter of Linus' merger partner. Initially, Linus woos Sabrina in order to get her out of the way, to secure David's marriage and the merger. Sabrina must be bought out by romance, her cultural capital subsumed, if Larrabee Industries is to expand. The means of postwar production and expansion thus consume/subsume all other social relations.

David Larrabee eventually questions Linus' desire for more capital: Why more money? Why secure a new multi-million dollar plastics merger. Why must he marry to ensure such an acquisition? Linus responds: "So a new industry goes up in an underdeveloped area and once barefooted kids have shoes, washed faces, and their teeth fixed." Linus' pat, pedantic reply evokes a scene from Charles Dickens or an Italian neorealist film, say from *Paisan* (Roberto Rossellini, 1946): a black-and-white image of dirty foreign children begging American soldiers for help, the same soldiers who helped bomb the children's cities. And let us not forget that industrial and market expansion, aiming for higher levels of international exchange and "welfare," was intended to "benefit American producers who could compete vigorously in any market where the 'open door' and the free convertibility of currencies into dollars facilitated equal access."[12] So teeth and American dollars point to the site of international consumption: fix their teeth and they will surely consume.

Dental hygiene jokes proliferate in *Sabrina*, exposing the hubris of an American stereotype that reduces Europeans (and its recent émigrés) to "those with bad teeth." Such jokes mock an America obsessed with white teeth and hygiene and perhaps refer to the slave status of tottering Europe, chained to American commodities. As Kristin Ross has suggested, in France images of the clean household filled with shiny new appliances and sparkling housewives worked to reconstruct the national identity — one devoid of "dirty" occupation and colonization policies.[13] This hygienically sealed, decolonized identity was indelibly tied to American consumer durables. One need only remember Richard Nixon's famed kitchen debate with Nikita Khrushchev to be reminded of the virtues of a hygienic American Cold War capitalism that, as Elaine Tyler May has argued, marketed the spotless American home and housewife as signifiers of the affluence of American/democratic capitalism.[14] If American hygiene proved capitalism was superior, then it also helped reintegrate postwar Europe. French and American exchanges thus dominated not only economic but also cultural transactions during the postwar period. The clean American home and woman promised modernization and mobility, luring foreign markets and Communist governments to a commodity-rich American lifestyle.

According to Ross, French mass culture highlighted state-led modernization/Americanization, shifting the focus from decolonization to the new, modern domestic space. According to Alan S. Milard, Marshall Plan aid maintained the flow of imported capital goods.[15] The ultimate purpose was to develop a "bloc of states which would share similar political, social, economic and cultural values to those which the United States itself publicly valued and claimed to uphold."[16] Domestic hygiene for both countries became a means of restructuring foreign relations: the United States colonized through commodity relations (through shiny refrigerators), whereas France decolonized after occupation and refocused its energies on filling the home front with consumer durables, ushering in a new era of isolationism. For both countries, the woman as housewife, signifier of cultural stability, marked these dramatic shifts in diplomacy. Kristin Ross describes these shifts in France:

> In the roughly ten-year period of the mid–1950s to the mid–1960s in France — the decade that saw both the end of the empire and the surge in French consumption and modernization — the colonies are in some sense "replaced," and the effort that once went into maintaining and disciplining a colonial people and situation becomes instead concentrated on a particular "level" of metropolitan existence: everyday life.... And women, of course, as the primary victims and arbiters of social reproduction, as the subjects of everydayness and as those most subjected to it, as the class of people most responsible for consumption, and those responsible for the complex movement whereby the social existence of human beings is produced and reproduced, are the everyday: its managers, its embodiment.[17]

Women as mothers, wives, pliant consumers, and country were then re-"vamped"; these women recast relations between the U.S. and France.

Linus' quip about foreigners needing dental hygiene, combined with Sabrina's fetishized status and the references to her own perfect (dental) hygiene, is telling given the desire for post-occupation France to be hygienically sealed in American exports.[18] His comment reminds us that Sabrina represents both old and new France: the older, distinct French culture (we see her cooking soufflés) as well as the new, Americanized, sparkling-toothed promise of postwar France. Sabrina negotiates these conflicting images as she eventually finds herself "sealed" within or "consumed" by the Larrabees' estate.

Sabrina is a completely enigmatic figure. As father Larrabee comments, how can a chauffeur's daughter be named Sabrina? The father articulates a single instance of several paradoxical threads in Sabrina's character. She is "just a girl" (a meager chauffeur's daughter) and thus coded as nonthreatening, a far cry from the image of Europe as a beguiling seductress. Yet she creates chaos in her wake once she has been recoded as European. Such mayhem seems overdetermined, given her vulnerable, girlish persona. She stands as the wrench in the Larrabee system — the excess component in this efficient production — and perhaps the still pervasive aura surrounding Europe: its ability to captivate and hold Americans captive. This aura is inherently inefficient, as is Sabrina's narrative position, in that Sabrina holds up to Linus the talisman of "unproductive" living: the desire for long walks along the Seine and for long suppers at chic restaurants—for pure leisure. She is a reminder of an "older" nationalism that stands outside the logic of globalization, as well as the desire for a leisure culture (consumerism) "married" to American corporate capitalism.

Sabrina ultimately acknowledges her own conscription into the new world order, into the Larrabees' economy. Sabrina's opening voiceover ironically introduces, in stage-direction fashion, the ways in which 1950s affluence had an underside, an unmentionable labor class. Audrey Hepburn's voice adjoins a series of establishing shots that narrate and make visible the vacant affluence permeating the Larrabees' Long Island estate. This sequence also suggests the opening tableaux of the decaying Xanadu in *Citizen Kane* (Orson Welles, 1941) and the devastated Mandalay in *Rebecca* (Alfred Hitchcock, 1940). Both films begin with a series of interior shots that never fully penetrate the wealth or the logic behind excessive accumulation. Much like the gloomy voiceover opening of *Rebecca*, another May–September romance, Sabrina's voiceover is unmistakably jaded, suggesting not fascination but boredom with ostentatious luxury. Her disembodied voice permeates the Larrabees' wealth and belies her potential as both laborer and object to be consumed; she has tended to and participated in this luxury. In this fairy-tale world, Sabrina describes a space filled with unused luxuries: "an outdoor tennis court, an indoor tennis court, an outdoor swimming pool, an indoor swimming pool." This linguistic volley suggests that commodities cover every possible Larrabee space. The family's estate revolves around control, or, as Sabrina reminds us, "It never rained on the night of the Larrabee party. The Larrabees wouldn't have stood for it." Such control bespeaks their desire to reproduce their wealth in spectacular fashion, both to show and to tell. Yet within this land of named luxuries exist unnamed individuals who attend the Larrabees: those who "rub the bottom of the sailboats" and the "man with no particular title who tends a goldfish named 'George.'"

Sabrina continually mocks Linus' authority and thus the logic of postwar conversion (and its intricately drawn divisions). For instance, while visiting Linus' office, Sabrina proceeds to spin in a boardroom chair, the head chair, Linus' chair. Like an out-of-control top, she turns around and around, destroying all sense of control. Her spinning reflects her own vacillations between the Larrabee brothers and the estate's divided space (family/servants' quarters). The boardroom's space represents the larger economy, where there always appear to be distinct winners and losers sitting on opposite sides of the table. By turning, Sabrina also calls attention to the complex machinations and manipulations that occur at this table.

Producing and Reproducing
Audrey Hepburn as Sabrina

Sabrina is a displaced person (DP) not unlike Audrey Hepburn, who was herself a DP lured to the United States by Hollywood. However, Sabrina's status as displaced person — "She doesn't belong in a mansion, but then she doesn't belong above a garage either" — refers not only to the numerous dislocated and out-of-work nationals who jostled in and out of the U.S., but to the European economies that were subjected to foreign currency controls during the postwar conversion (when the American dollar became the standard). Sabrina bemoans these cultural (and concomitant economic) exchanges, suggesting that inevitably cultural uniqueness would be lost. For instance, desiring a distinctly French education, Sabrina enrolls at the Paris Cordon Bleu to gain culinary/cultural authenticity. However, Sabrina finds the cooking school has come to resemble an American automobile plant where cooks are produced on an assembly line and then sent abroad. The film thus serves up an acerbic portrait of French culture as irrevocably influenced by fascism and Fordism; the scene suggests that France's most sacred cultural artifact — its cuisine — is now constructed in the American way and sold to an eager international (American) market.

This scene draws on the rationality of National Socialism, giving way to an eerie reading of Nazi death camps as having mimicked efficient kitchens, as a logical extension of American-style Fordism ("home economics" was, after all, an application of Taylorism). Indeed, since much of Wilder's family died at Auschwitz, he had first-hand knowledge of its rationalized atrocities. From this perspective, the chef at Cordon Bleu, who gives exacting orders regarding the size, shape, and feel of a soufflé, reminds us of the Nazi fixation with methodical control over "beauty." The Cordon Bleu's efficient space, filled with rows of ovens, suggests other World War II "ovens," as well as the effects of the American-style Fordism that informed not only the Nazi extermination projects but also the efficient Hollywood studio system in which Wilder flourished.

Given the film's complicated international exchanges and consolidations, Linus' altruistic desire to "help" foreign countries seems absurd, especially when we consider his complete detachment from the labor that surrounds him, from his chauffeur to his secretary to Sabrina. The film's mise-en-scène shores up this irony by presenting Linus as removed from the world in his high-rise office building, as absorbed by capital and its clichés. In Linus' office, an Alexander Calder mobile hangs from the ceiling and a Joan Miróesque painting sits on his salon wall staring at numerous gadgets: a speaker phone, electric doors, and lights; a row of secretaries lines the outer wall to his office. The office space suggests the sterility and efficiency of an invasive Fordist modernism.

Linus collects paintings, secretaries, and foreign markets, yet he never seems to know or experience these things. Crunching orders to an obedient secretary, Linus is part of the sterile and mechanized terrain of his office. Intrigued by nonrepresentational art, produced by the French (Miró) or expatriate Americans (Calder), he neglects the people around him. His secretary and chauffeur speak to him of their worries, but he ignores them as he interrupts or distractedly reads a paper. And, although he speaks of underprivileged children, he never encounters these children. He thus represents postwar fears of systemization, the fear of huge corporations and the Cold War meta-narratives that hang over him like the cold Calder mobile. Although by film's end Linus is softened by his relationship with Sabrina, it is the portrait of him as the paradigmatic American industrialist/imperialist that sticks. Bogart, from Rick Blaine to Linus Larrabee, suggests the shifting ethos of an American multinational. Linus is to be feared, for without a Sabrina he might very well consume the world without ever looking up from his desk.

As depicted in the film, American capitalism is a bully sorely in need of Europe's "feminization" and seems to foreshadow later images of American capital, namely men like Bill Gates who never have to leave their homes, never mind their offices, to control vast global empires. Accordingly, postwar Fordism is shown to be about the appropriation of labor and cultural capital, which, in the figure of Sabrina, become blurred. The film reminds us that limousines require chauffeurs. Indeed, the limousine is a recurring class metaphor; for Americans, it is just as easy to import a British chauffeur to drive the Rolls-Royce. Sabrina's father, Fairchild, equates the limousine with society: there is "a front seat, a back seat, and a window in-between." His is a European vision of a clearly autonomous and stratified class structure; for him, the limousine's space represents a distance firmly separated that constitutes one's social position. Yet the back and front seats often converge within the film's narrative, and even though Linus sits in the back seat, he needs a Fairchild to control and drive the car.

Class itself seems dislocated in the film. For instance, once Sabrina has the proper dress and accent, she figuratively and literally moves into the back seat. After her return from Europe, Sabrina attends a Larrabee party where she is unrecognized by the Larrabee elders. She dances comfortably with David Larrabee; as one observer notes, her dress and dancing indicate that "she belongs up there" as "the most sophisticated woman at the ball." And if these cultural codes indicate class, then Sabrina does indeed belong up there, and the barrier between servant and Larrabee momentarily dissolves. In this same scene, while serving at the party, one of the Larrabee stewards sees Sabrina dancing and runs away to tell the other servants of her apparent rise. As he does so, he shoves an hors d'oeuvres tray into a guest's hands. The surprised guest finds himself in the position of server, for both guest and server wear the same outfit, a tuxedo. Only the tray of hors d'oeuvres (labor's marker) separates the server from the guest, the server from the served. To punctuate this joke, each guest in a row of guests takes a drink and hors d'oeuvre from the bewildered guest-as-server.

In these switches, the film's narrative exposes the ways in which High-Fordist class categories, newly lodged in consuming practices and the acquisition of cultural capital, destabilize once-entrenched boundaries. A waiter and a guest look the same; Sabrina dresses, dances, and speaks as well as, if not better than, a Larrabee. Can a servant purchase the signifiers of prestige and "pass" as a Larrabee? What are the effects of postwar legislation, such as the G.I. Bill, which expand educational opportunities, thereby lowering class barriers or the limousine's window? Guest becomes waiter as European becomes American. Can an American export European markers of taste and style to succeed as an economic, military, and cultural power? Is French cultural insularity and uniqueness forever made vulnerable by postwar economic treaties and the reorganization of nation and capital dependent on U.S. aid?

Reminiscent of Henry James' *The American*, in which an American capitalist goes to France and purchases copies of French paintings as well as a dispossessed French girl for his cultural repertoire, Wilder's Cinderella films wrestle with a newly emerging gendered internationalist ideology tied to cultural transactions. Just as Henry James responded to the Industrial Revolution and an American cultural identity tied to foreign cultural capital/purchases, these films respond to America's emerging geopolitical postwar presence amid the fractious Cold War. Both pivot on the image of the dispossessed girl as a national abstraction for foreign relations between two countries. James and Wilder point to the U.S.' persistent and anxious desire to please Europe — a desire that reached its summit in the mobile postwar years. Yet this desire is ultimately cast in terms of sexual relations between the economic aggressor and the vulnerable, culturally desirable other. Moreover, these patterns find their expression in a new economy in which taste, habits, and purchasable cultural knowledge designate class, the means by which postwar Americans may achieve mobility. While James' American can only hope to secure status through European purchases, Linus Larrabee has indeed achieved an international position (he simulates the very rapacious appetites of American capital), given a shattered and dependent world economy. He has achieved this status through economic and cultural expansion, while potentially obliterating cultural/national boundaries. For Linus, France is merely another airport; Sabrina, however, reminds him of the particularity of French nationhood.

Focusing on the losses and gains within such expansion and consumption, *Sabrina* also narrativizes postwar France's fascination with America vis-à-vis Hollywood movies. The Larrabee parties become a flickering film screen, a moving shop window for Sabrina's many fantasies of upward mobility. As a child, Sabrina watches and consumes these parties from high in a tree, a scene that prefigures her eventual status as the primary watched and consumed object in the film.

Like other European spectators, Sabrina buys into the Larrabee narrative. Their parties act out a Hollywood-style fantasy for the rapt, hungry spectator. Yet, amid the display and consumption, Sabrina writes in a letter of her desire to escape from the hold of the Cinderella narrative. She admits to her father that Paris taught her not only how to cook soufflés but also how to "be in the world and of the world and not just stand aside and watch." Her letter expresses a utopian illusion of self-determination (especially when we consider her eventual absorption into the Larrabee estate), while nevertheless calling attention to the spectator-participant divide. Sabrina wants to be a part of the cultural grammar of Europe — "in and of" a social and cultural repertoire — but, ironically, she wants to move from spectator to object (here, the object of a preposition), not a subject.

The film notes these changes as part of the metamorphosis of its Cinderella figure. The inevitable Cinderella makeover finds the "useful" girl turning into an "exchangeable" woman. She does so by "putting on" the right clothes. Wilder's and the 1950s' fascination with the Cinderella narrative (from *Gigi* [1958] to *Gidget* [1959]) bespeaks the era's own desire for a makeover. As we watch Sabrina evolve from being an awkward, barefoot émigré's daughter to being a foreign-inspired "American" beauty, the U.S.' own recent history finds expression — from Depression, war, and reconversion to "boom," or, diplomatically, from provincial isolationist to global world power.

Sabrina channels this export/import globalization logic. Of European descent yet raised in America, she moves back and forth and finally "remakes" herself during her last trip to the Continent. The film begs us to wonder exactly what her cultural origins are. Sabrina is a blank page, an open script, as she falls or shuttles between cultural/national domains, suggesting the collapsing boundaries after the war. She becomes a buffer figure in the film's terms, the perfect marriage between French Continental and American mythologies. Sabrina is simultaneously exotic and banal (as is Hepburn), suggesting a new American persona: homespun/international, simple/savvy, and hard-working

(working-class)/leisure-oriented. Her "conversion" into an either/or figure reminds us of, or brings us back to, Jackson Pollock's paintings, which can be read either as "just" paint drips on a canvas or as America's ecstatic painting id finally unleashed.

Sabrina also suggests the makeover of the Hollywood aesthetic. Much has been made of the film's use of French couture (Givenchy) fashions to create the quintessential Hepburn look. *Sabrina* represents the first full-scale use of European fashions, documenting the decline of studio control over costumes and the eclipse of the costume designer's role. In this case, Hollywood purchased French fashions to make over the Hollywood look, enunciating its long-term relationship to the European market. These new fashions respond to their larger political context. Thus, Hollywood, like the U.S., moves from a provincial (in-studio) aesthetic to being an international player/figure.

Audrey Hepburn's look is central to this new aesthetic. Where Marilyn Monroe and Jane Russell are grain-fed, "booming" beauties, Hepburn's body and "face," to recall Roland Barthes's famous musing, suggests something entirely different.[19] Hepburn's body is so thin, so "hungry" looking, as to recall the then-popular image of a ravaged Europe. It also suggests the mannequin's body, the perfect figure for costuming. Hepburn literalizes the department store mannequin look, an apt figuration for postwar consumer logic.[20] Hepburn's body becomes the clothes she wears. Yet her face is unique, alive in its movements (the sideways glances, the tilt of her head, the flirtatious smile), reminding us of the distinctiveness of old Europe itself.

As Pierre Bourdieu summarizes this logic, "Nothing more rigorously distinguishes the different classes than ... the principles of a 'pure' aesthetic in the most everyday choices of everyday life, in cooking, dress, or decoration."[21] Hepburn as Sabrina performs such a pure aesthetic: the Givenchy fashions, the simple, cropped hairstyle, and the tasteful gold earrings. Aesthetically, Sabrina comes "closer to heaven" than the garish Larrabees, whose parties display more than anything an awkward Long Island demimonde, with its clumsy, giggling society girls and its ostentatious display of diamonds (including tiaras and other affectations of royalty). If, as Sabrina confesses in ironic voiceover, the Larrabees' world was "as close to heaven as one could get on Long Island," then Wilder's mise-en-scène reminds us that Long Island is far from heaven. The Larrabee household reminds us that 1950s national culture is partly a glossy reproduction of prewar Europe.

The film enjoys this "reproduction" pun when the camera introduces the Larrabees as they sit for a family photograph, thus posing for two cameras. To compound this visual layering, on the background wall hangs an earlier family portrait, a painting. This series of portraitures—from painting to photograph to film — produces a mise-en-abyme that alludes to the space of reproduction. After all, the photo does not necessarily replace the painting but merely updates it. The Larrabees represent themselves in the older "auratic" work of art as well as in the mass-culture currency of the photograph. In other words, they may be able to afford the "original" painting, which recalls European ancestral halls, but in a modern postwar world, devoted to flexible, easily produced products such as plastic, they prefer the photograph.

Original paintings and the Sabrinas of the world authenticate the Larrabees' enterprise, namely plastics, a commodity that more than anything replaced (reproduced) glass in a lighter, more flexible, and less expensive product. After sitting on a pair of champagne glasses, David Larrabee reminds Linus of the mass appeal of plastic when he suggests that the family factory begin work on the construction of unbreakable, plastic champagne glasses. It is the mass-produced, good plastic or the Hollywood Cinderella romance that secures and maintains America's economic and political hegemony.

The film here comments on the symbiotic, if not mirroring, relationship between America's disposable mass culture and its consumer durables. Fredric Jameson describes the incredible influence and power American mass reproducible culture has had on world economies since World War II:

> The GATT talks are there to remind us that American film and television fall under base and superstructure alike, as it were; they are economics fully as much as they are culture, and are, indeed, along with agribusinesses and weapons, the principal economic export of the United States—an enormous source of sheer profit and income.[22]

This mise-en-abyme structure predicts and illustrates the logic of America's increasing emphasis on the exportation of its mass culture as a double-sided, mirroring relation or, as Jameson phrases it, "the becoming economic of the cultural" and vice-versa. In a word, the Larrabees reinvent themselves, from painting to reproduction, as their empire moves from work in New York real estate to global plastics mergers. The Linus Larrabee in the family photo helps sell the plastic (as Bogart sells the image of rugged American capital within the film). The photograph is as exportable as Linus' plastic; Linus can sell the Larrabee name and family image alongside his resilient new product.

Capital's Overcooked Soufflé

The Larrabees, much like the postwar United States, base their new global order on a manufactured good that Linus pitches in cinematic terms. And it is the cinema, along with Linus' bazooka-proof plastic, that is today "the principal economic export of the United States." The cinema and the cult of the photograph help produce global desire for American products; Sabrina narrates these collaborative, late-capital cultural and economic exigencies. Sabrina both attends to this Larrabee/post-reconversion luxury and, as the voiceover suggests, exposes it (she is also ultimately consumed by it). Barefoot, as her father's assistant in America, she washes the Larrabees' numerous automobiles and later changes their spark plugs. These opening sequences call attention to the rear-guard servants who support the Larrabee lifestyle, thus foregrounding those spaces inhabited by labor. Yet later, while in Paris, Sabrina is befriended by a wealthy, elderly baron who teaches her about opera, fashion, and European culture. Sabrina then becomes immersed within a Parisian elite, reborn in a postwar Europe seemingly devoid of Wall Street's influence. The film conjures up a utopian Paris opposed to American materialism, yet one that must inevitably be wedded to U.S. capital.

Sabrina thus returns to the Long Island estate, made over into a European Cinderella. David Larrabee chases her; Linus then steals her away. Linus gives her back to David; David gives her back to Linus. At the end of the film, David Larrabee appears at a board meeting and tells an unsuspecting Linus that, after being passed around, Sabrina is now traveling alone, back to Europe. David thus wrests control of Larrabee Industries, allowing the befuddled Linus to meet his unsuspecting Sabrina. Linus ultimately loses control of both himself and Larrabee Industries. In essence, he gets conned by his own con. This shift links Linus' happiness to a loss of control. Linus thus finds himself (like David) susceptible to the lure of the European. These last two exchanges happen without Sabrina's knowledge; she is passed around without even being around.

Like all Cinderellas, Sabrina becomes a gift to her prince, a passive participant in a larger economic transaction. And if she is the gift, the complicit David, Linus, old man Larrabee, and even her father are the givers. Linus "deals with" her father in the limousine, with David and old man Larrabee in the Larrabee boardroom. After all is said and done, David finally arranges for Linus' "takeover" or "merger" with Sabrina at the end of the film. She is a gift to Linus for his accomplishments. *Sabrina* suggests that the exchange of women occurs when they take part in maintaining historically situated economic and social relations. Gayle Rubin has described such "traffic" in women:

> If women are the gifts, then it is men who are the exchange partners. And it is the partners, not the presents, upon whom reciprocal exchange confers its quasi-mystical power of social linkage.... As long as the relations specify that men exchange women, it is men who are the beneficiaries of the product of such exchanges— social organization.[23]

The social bond between men, between capital, supersedes Sabrina's needs. She is a body, a woman, given up in a circuit of exchange. She assures Linus' status in a postwar America still awed by European cultural capital. Paris stands in for Sabrina as Sabrina stands in for Paris. She is a "feminine" Europe, a gift to a United States that somehow needs this orphaned elite to bolster its new political, cultural, and economic ascendancy. And postwar America had learned to exchange, to make gifts of, and to receive various pieces of Western Europe for the purpose of "social organization." According to the logic of Cold War U.S. diplomacy, "the rest of the world would win more than it would lose by acquiescing in American hegemony; greater security and material rewards in exchange for diminished autonomy."[24] At the film's end, Linus sails with Sabrina on the ship Liberté back to France. Both presumably are "free," wedded to a future in which European and American economies and culture are united. The softer and kinder Linus needs his Sabrina, the feminine underside to the mighty hand of capital, the soft soufflé cooked in a plastics merger.

Notes

1. Smith, "Commentary," 88.
2. McCormick, "America's Half Century," 38.
3. Lundestad, "Empire by Invitation?," 158.
4. Ibid., 151.
5. Philips, "Portrait of the Artist as an American," 18–19 (emphasis added).
6. Guilbaut, *How New York Stole the Idea of Modern Art*, 203.
7. Huxley, *The Doors of Perception*, 41–42.
8. Rosenberg, "Foreign Affairs after World War II," 66.
9. Smith, 84.
10. Ray, *A Certain Tendency of the Hollywood Cinema*, 89–112.
11. McCormick, 29.
12. Maier, "The Politics of Productivity," 171.
13. Ross, *Fast Cars, Clean Bodies*, 71–105.
14. May, *Homeward Bound*, 16–36.
15. Milard, "The Reconstruction of Western Europe," 254.
16. Ibid., 265.
17. Ross, 77.
18. Ibid., 79.
19. Barthes, *Mythologies*, 56–57.
20. Studlar, "Chi-Chi Cinderella," 164–67.
21. Bourdieu, *Language and Symbolic Power*, 40.
22. Jameson, "Globalization as Philosophical Issue," 60.
23. Rubin, "The Traffic in Women," 37.
24. McCormick, 33.

14. Evolving Modernities
Formation of the Urban Imagination in Hindi Cinema

SUNNY SINGH

"I consider Billy Wilder my god," Manmohan Desai, Mumbai's greatest peddler of lavish celluloid dreams, declared in the 1980s.[1] It was a strange statement, especially as Desai was known for his convoluted, fast-paced scripts that piled on characters, motivations, events with mind-boggling extravagance with little discernible evidence of any influence of Wilder's tightly controlled, stark scripting.

At the first instance, looking for Wilder's influence in the kaleidoscopic world of Hindi commercial cinema seems a lost cause. Indeed, the very idea of the "all-inclusive" Bollywood filmic narrative runs counter to the classical Hollywood model of the linear plot with a limited number of highly individuated characters. However, over the years, various directors—albeit not Desai—have turned to Wilder for his scripts, embellishing the spare, clean narratives with trademarks of commercial Hindi cinema: songs, emotional complications, tangential narratives, and the replacement of the individual at the heart of the narrative with a community-driven identity. Initially, these adaptations of Wilder's scripts seem travesties of the original screenplays, with little by way of links to the original films, except in patches.

Prior to beginning the discussion on Wilder's influence on specific films, it is necessary to note some crucial points on remakes and adaptations in India. While Hollywood has long served as a resource for plots for Hindi films, these are neither straight translations of the script nor remakes of the original film. Filmmakers will routinely "Indianize" plots, which in most cases means providing complex backstories and a web of relationships for the characters, adding "emotions" and inserting song sequences. This reworking of the plot also leads to greater narrative and thematic complexity. Moreover, it must be noted that this form of adaptation or, more precisely, "homage" is in accordance with the Copyright Act in India which "protects the original expression of an idea but not the idea itself."[2]

In fact, one reason Wilder's sparse scripts may appear nearly unrecognizable when seen in their Hindi guise is because of the complex web of relationships that his highly individuated protagonists acquire in translation. Hindi filmmakers often speak of "Indianization" of a Hollywood script. Scriptwriter Anjum Rajabali explains the crucial criteria for this process: "Relationships! That seems to be the primary criteria when Indianising a subject. Lots of close, strong, intense relationships that will have interesting, moving stories/graphs of their own."[3] Indian filmmakers often qualify Hollywood cinema as "dry" and "Indianize" scripts from Hollywood by "adding emotions," and placing characters in a complex social and familial web of relationships. Indeed, "Hollywood films are frequently described as 'single-track' and Hindi filmmakers express their amazement and envy at how films can be made on 'one line'—a phrase denoting a story's simplicity as it can be relayed in a sentence."[4] Not surprisingly, as the discussion below shall demonstrate, none of the three films are straightforward remakes of Wilder's scripts.

Moreover, situating these adaptations of Wilder's cinema within the larger trajectory of global media flows over the past century is relevant and useful to understanding how modernities are formulated across the globe, not only as theorized by some as imitations of the western modernity, but also as reformulations, resistances and appropriations of the same. Post-1947 and throughout the "nation-building" project of the past six decades, Hindi commercial cinema has repeatedly turned to classical Hollywood cinema, primarily from the 1930s to 1950s, and specifically to romantic comedies, to find vehicles for articulating the changes brought forth by rapid post-colonial modernization, with its corollary urbanization, as well as the resultant social changes. Thus, the scripts are translated to address the stylistic, narrative or philosophical confines of Hindi filmic representation. Moreover, the scripts have been clearly altered to address the specific political, social and cultural ethos of the primary audiences.

This "borrowing" of scripts from Hollywood becomes crucial to understanding representations of modernity in Hindi cinema, given the growth of the industry since independence in 1947, the significance of cinema to the national politico-social discourses, as well as the concurrent industrialization and urbanization of the country. Indeed, the films have "not only portrayed the process of urbanization as a struggle towards coming to terms with and formulating agendas for modernity" but also "have in themselves been central rallying points, symbols and institutions of modernization, and battlefields for the understanding of, for formulations and appropriations of, the conditions of the new life as against 'what used to be.'"[5]

A closer look at just three Hindi films, all adapted from Wilder's scripts, and made between 1975 and 2007, reveals the complex and myriad ways in which American films are re-inscribed culturally not only to create an "alterity to Hollywood domination but offer their own aggressive commercialism in its stead that is at the same time traditional and modern."[6] It is crucial to note that although the three Hindi adaptations are spread over a span of three decades, they all draw on Wilder's film scripts produced during the latter half of the 1950s. Yet the choices driving the Hindi remakes of the three films—*Sabrina* (1954), *Some Like It Hot* (1959) and *The Apartment* (1960)—are not only indicative of the zeitgeist of the nation, but also provide a valuable insight into the trajectory of the nation's dual project of modernization/urbanization.

Although a comprehensive debate on issues of imagining modernities in non-western societies is beyond the scope of this discussion, it is necessary to note — before beginning to consider the films themselves or the ways in which they represent and (re-)imagine cityscapes— that theories of urbanization/modernization as well as ideas of modernity have long been considered from a Eurocentric perspective. Hence, while much has been written about the role and representation of western cityscapes and their link to modernity, it is necessary to note that neither experiences nor theories of modernity or urbanization are universal or, in the case of post-colonial societies, free from political and ideological agendas. Instead, the experience of colonialism has meant that ideas of "progress" have long been politically charged and have often identified "modernization" with "westernization":

> In this way, a dualism was established and consolidated between "modernity" and "tradition" which disregarded internal struggles, debates and contradictory dynamics in the life worlds of non-western colonies, and reduced them to homelands of custom into which European progress and modernity could only gradually be introduced.[7]

However, the debates in India regarding urbanization/modernization as well as its representations have been complex and long-standing. Recognizing that the colonial enterprise identified itself with a programme of modernization and progress, colonized societies like India developed counter-strategies that "relied on the elaboration of alternative notions and programmes of modernity that might not simply reject Europeanness as modernity per se, but situated Indian experiences and agendas against it."[8]

Indeed, in India as in other parts of the globe, Hindi commercial cinema has long offered post-colonial models of modernity that negotiate the liminal spaces between "tradition" and "modernity" without relying on expressly western models. Nowhere is this sense of alterity to Hollywood more overtly articulated than in the ways Hindi cinema imagines the city as its narrative-scape. Drawing on long-standing traditions of imagining modernity in dichotomous ideals of city vs. village, Hindi cinema — like Hollywood and other film industries—has constantly and consistently imagined and re-imagined the urban cityscape in symbolic, psychological and narrative terms.

A great part of this re-imagining is due to the intrinsic nature of the city itself, as well as the narrative possibilities it offers. "The city, by nature, is capable of containing, without loss of credibility, an infinity of fictional characters and events. This is because a city is experienced as a space inhabited by a *population* whose numbers can be counted more or less accurately, but whose mutual relationships cannot be easily specified."[9] Indeed, this conceptualization of the urban space as the stage for infinite numbers of credible stories may be considered key to Wilder's oeuvre, where there is a possibility for the "individuals to encounter each other as strangers, reified entities, whose position in a social network cannot be known immediately."[10] It is this possibility of encounter amongst strangers, with the corollary of the potential for discovery, betrayal and/or intimacy, that provides crucial plot trajectories in urban films: the accidental witnessing of the mob murder in *Some Like It Hot/Rafoo Chakkar* (1975) or the complex web of office affairs in *The Apartment/Life in a Metro* (2007).

The following discussion does not focus so much on Wilder's *oeuvre*, but rather on the ways his scripts are transformed for the Indian audiences and the ways in which they intersect with issues of change brought on by the urbanization/modernization process. The films are discussed chronologically, based on the Hindi adaptations, primarily because these reference key moments of social and political change in the country. Indeed, as the discussion below will demonstrate, the choice of Wilder's scripts is specific to the zeitgeist of each decade, especially in evolving national debates on gender, class and social mobility, ensuring that the films would probably have been less successful or even impossible to produce at other points in time.

Poverty, Crime and Restitution

Rafoo Chakkar, directed by Narendra Bedi, is a 1970s reworking of Wilder's *Some Like It Hot*, with familiar elements: two musicians on the run from gangsters after watching an accidental killing; the gender-bending masquerade with an all-girl band; the escape to the holiday resort apparently rife with millionaires. The film also translates some of Wilder's snappy dialogue to Hindi, including "nobody's perfect" as the riposte to Salim's declaration of being a man to his infatuated suitor.

Yet the film is not simply a remake of Wilder's script, as it attempts, like many films of the era, to symbolically refer to and address issues of post-coloniality and dilemmas of modernity. As in Wilder's film, much of the action takes place in the non-urban holiday resort — Florida here is replaced by Kashmir as the ideal playground in the national imaginery. However, conceptualizations of urbanity and modernity play a crucial and often sinister part in the development of the narrative. In doing so, both the comedy and the romantic storyline are thematically reduced to a secondary level, while issues of morality, specifically framed in terms of economic deprivation, crime and restitution, are foregrounded.

In structural terms, the film is thus framed by initial scenes that establish the consequences of crime and its impact on the criminal's family, especially the protagonist, Dev (Rishi Kapoor), based on the character Joe played by Tony Curtis in Wilder's original. The narrative device requires a circular structure, culminating in the recognition and reconciliation of the father and son, with the remorse and confession forming the moral core of the plot.

The film opens, like Wilder's original, with an encounter between criminals and police. However, unlike the Prohibition era den, with its glamorous secret club, the crime here is at first sight a seemingly minor one: two petty criminals Prakash (Madan Puri) and Ranjit (Anwar Hussain) are involved in adulterating food stuffs. Unlike the Prohibition era gangster violence referenced by Wilder, the crime here is calculated to create utmost revulsion amongst the audiences who had not only struggled with the food shortages and chronic famines of the previous decades, but also would have relatively fresh memories of contaminated or poor quality grains sold by western nations, primarily the U.S., during those famines. The scene thus signals the current dilemmas of the nation, of grinding poverty and food shortages, while also reminding the knowing audience of the colonial legacy driving those dilemmas. The initial crime is further compounded by the decision of the two criminals to lock their accomplice in the burning warehouse in order to escape the police.

However, Bedi chooses a device familiar to Hindi film audiences to compound the moral universe established by the opening sequence by following it up with a scene in Ranjit's home, which establishes the fact that he has a young son, Dev (Rishi Kapoor). Although Ranjit remains a thoroughly unpleasant character, the sequence does articulate his desire for procuring material wealth for his son, leavening the horror of the preceding sequence. His motivation for his crimes is not only greed or depravity, but also a keen desire for economic mobility for his offspring. This scene with the argument between Ranjit and his wife Shanti (Sulochana) provides the historicity and symbolic reference — a device used often by 1970s filmmakers — to reference a past which in this case can only be a colonial one. Ranjit's crimes thus become part of a greater malaise caused by an unjust state as well as a desire for economic betterment, a signal to the audience that he will be redeemed before the end, unlike his partner, Prakash.[11] Following Ranjit's arrest, Shanti flees with Dev to the "city." Although the city remains unnamed at this juncture, the popular imagination establishes it as Bombay/Mumbai.[12] This fact is further highlighted by Shanti and Dev finding refuge with a Muslim friend (Mumtaz Begum) whose son, Salim (Paintal), is of the same age, as Mumbai as *the* city has long been imagined as the space where caste, creed and regional boundaries were blurred to form a national whole.

After the initial establishment, the film unfolds quite similarly to Wilder's original, with plot complications involving gender identities, misplaced romantic interests, and Dev and Salim trying to escape the criminals. However, a few differences must be noted, especially as they signal specific differences in narrative conventions and ideological contexts.

Using changing dates on a wall calendar, Bedi cuts from the prologue set in the past to the present with a grown-up Dev and Salim (Wilder's Joe and Jerry [Jack Lemmon]) who ply their trade as musicians playing in wedding bands. He also adds another twist intended to highlight viewing pleasure for the audiences familiar with conventions of commercial Hindi cinema, which emphasize that the audience is interested not in what happens next but rather how the foreseeable events unfold.[13] In the sequence that introduces Dev and Salim as grown-ups, they have been hired to play at Prakash's wedding. Even though Dev interacts with his father Ranjit, the father and son are unable to recognize each other. This eventual mutual recognition and reconciliation forms the crux of the narrative.

The passage of time, as well as the circular narrative structure, is emphasized towards the end of the film by Dev's discovery of Prakash and Ranjit's now escalated criminal activities, which include the sale of national patrimony and currency fraud. A curious link connects the two to the beginning of the film and their initial offence: they continue to be involved in, albeit on a far grander scale than ever before, food adulteration. The discovery also leads to a re-encounter between father and son, as well as the emotional climax which focuses on Ranjit's remorse for having abandoned his family. Bedi again chooses to complicate the moral standpoints by expressly letting Ranjit explain to Dev that it was poverty and circumstances that drove him to crime. His remorse is not for the wrong he has done, but for the fact that he lacked the strength required to remain law-abiding.

It is interesting to note, unlike other filmmakers of the time, Bedi spends little time establishing boundaries of urbanity, focussing on neither monuments nor the iconic urban spaces of Mumbai. Instead, he chooses to focus on nondescript streets, internal spaces in homes that contrast the prosperity Prakash and Ranjit have achieved through their life of crime with the stark poverty Dev and Salim must endure. Unlike Joe and Jerry, whose lack of funds appears to have little consequences, Dev and Salim cannot easily escape the poverty that surrounds them: when Prakash refuses to pay them for their services, the consequence is hunger for them and their families. In a deft association, Bedi also establishes prosperous spaces as morally, and legally, problematic ones. The film moves quickly between opulent homes occupied by Prakash/Ranjit to Shanti's bare impoverished one, establishing the contrasts. A quick intercut introduces Dev and Salim, now adult and playing in Prakash's wedding procession, before switching to another opulent space, this time occupied by Reetu (Neetu Singh) who is being forced by her aunt to marry Prakash.

Opulent domestic spaces thus become signifiers of moral corruption and oppression, a visual trope used frequently by post-colonial filmmakers. Not surprisingly, domestic spaces are barely seen in the film after this initial establishing set of sequences. After this point, the film occupies primarily public spaces: hotel lobbies and rooms, stage spaces, train interiors, and a surfeit of external spaces.

As the film moves into the main narrative, the post-colonialist identification of urban spaces as potentially corrupting and sinister is highlighted. While gardens of Kashmir serve as safe havens for romance and emotions, even apparently natural spaces in the city such as parks are tinged with danger: it is an ill-planned short cut through an immaculately maintained cemetery that leads Dev and Salim to witness the mob murder which turns them fugitive.

Here it is important to note the crucial role played by natural spaces, especially gardens, mountains and water-bodies, as sites of romantic love, not only in Hindi cinema but in the long tradition of Indian art and literature.[14] As such, Dev and Reetu's love can only mature in the non-urban spaces, a fact emphasized by their explicitly urban and modern upbringing and identities. However, the insertion of urban characters into the non-urban space not only provides the space for romance, but also references a range of interstices of power. Nowhere are the dilemmas of urban life more explicit than in the context of modernity and gender, especially in the adaptation of Sugar Kane (Marilyn Monroe) to the expectations of the Indian audience as Reetu.

Reetu's character is far less sexualized than Sugar, in part because of Indian sensibilities, but also of the difficulties in recreating the combination of the hyper-sexuality and innocence embodied by Monroe. However, Reetu is also hemmed in by the socio-economic realities of the 1970s, where jobs were acutely limited by gender considerations. Moreover, cultural sensibilities ensure that Reetu is no footloose party girl looking for love, but rather escaping a forced marriage. While her ultimate goal, like Sugar, is to find a husband — preferably a rich and handsome one — her situation is more precarious as the option of making a career of her singing talents is not available to her. Instead, the job in the girl's band has been arranged for her as a stop-gap measure by a friend, in order to help her escape the city and the forced marriage. This cultural framing has extensive impact on the adaptation, as Reetu is far more vulnerable, and thus less sexually explicit: for example, the bunk scene in the train with Salim is rewritten to highlight her vulnerability.

At the same time, there are some unintentional corollaries of this unsexing of the central female character. Instead, Dev's female impersonation becomes the locus of sexual desire, highlighting the ways in which Hindi film employs gender and sexuality codes in overtly "camp" ways.[15] Indeed, the first song in the film references Sugar's hip-wiggling "Running Wild" number in Wilder's film, with the exception that it is centered on the masquerading Dev. Dressed in an outfit that echoes Marilyn's fringed dress, and parodying the hip-

wiggle, the song centers the actor Rishi Kapoor — known for his "pretty" looks—
as a gender-fluid locus of both straight and queer desires. Although a comprehensive discussion of the conventions of queering desires in Hindi cinema is
beyond the scope of this article, it is crucial to note that "the aesthetic and traditional conventions of Bollywood need to be considered further as hybrid,
'queer' and 'camp' from their outset."[16] Indeed, the gender fluidity that marked
early Indian cinema, as well as pre-cinematic theatre traditions, has not been
entirely replaced by hetero-normative conceptualizations of gender and sexuality and requires further enquiry.

Finally, it is crucial to note that Bedi's remake at no point officially credits
Wilder's film or acknowledges it in the credits. This may in part be a result of
what Prasad terms "the heterogenous mode of production" [17] in the industry,
where members of the crew are/were often involved in fluid ways across the
production and at the end randomly assigned title credits. At the same time,
the "borrowing" of the script is acknowledged tongue-in-cheek within the die-
gesis. When Dev — still in his female finery — is propositioned after a stage
show, he rejects the suitor by airily declaring that he "doesn't watch Hindi films"
which are "copies of foreign films." Bedi employs an oft-employed technique
of direct address to the audience to make Dev's admission function as a cheeky
reminder and acknowledgment to the knowledgeable viewer that the film is a
remake of a foreign script.

Urban Potential — Modernity as Opportunity

Yeh Dillagi (1994), directed by Naresh Malhotra and a remake of Sabrina,
reflects a transitional moment in the process of growing modernization and its
consequent social changes.[18] The film was released soon after the country had
embarked on the economic liberalization policy in 1992, and reflects not only
the enormous optimism for economic growth, but also shifting attitudes
towards social mobility, placing economic aspirations at the heart of the narrative.

The film follows the general plotline of Sabrina, with Sapna (Kajol) as the
chauffeur's daughter brought up on the estate grounds. The two brothers Vijay
(Akshay Kumar) and Vicky (Saif Ali Khan) also follow the general characterization of Linus (Humphrey Bogart) and David (William Holden) Larrabee,
with the older one being in charge of the business while the younger one parties
to his heart's content. However, that is where the similarities in characterization
end.

Although the film replicates the sequence with Sabrina watching the
Larrabee party, there is a clear difference: Sapna is fascinated by the lifestyle,
one she aspires to, but she is not in love with Vicky, whom she holds in contempt. Moreover, Vicky, unlike David Larrabee, is a spoilt rich kid with an

enormous sense of his own consequence. He is also devious in his ways of seduction, relying for example on drugged coffee, which makes him far more reprehensible than the bumbling, oft-married playboy David. Similarly, Vijay, who manages the family businesses, is the entrepreneur, like Linus. However, he is also one aware of the social and economic changes sweeping the land, and willing to adapt as necessary. Moreover, unlike Linus, his business acumen does not extend to arranging marital alliances for his brother. Instead, he is represented as the only one capable of traversing the class boundaries while also forming the moral centre of the family: he protects and tries to guide Vicky, treats Sapna and her friends as equals, and, despite his serious demeanor, is caring and warm.

While retaining the general plotline of romance, *Yeh Dillagi* foregrounds dilemmas raised by liberalization. As in Wilder's script, Sapna's father has long been employed by the Saigal family, and is grateful for the employment he holds. He is subservient to the Saigals, explaining to Sapna that the "poor" must depend on the generosity of the rich. In contrast, Sapna refuses to tow the line, believing herself to be a social equal of the Saigals, as well as morally superior to Vicky. As she explains to Vicky, she can gain his status by earning money, but he can't gain integrity. Not surprisingly, unlike Sabrina, she doesn't see life through "rose-tinted glasses," is not sent off to the city for further training, but rather decides to pursue her dreams of material success in Mumbai. Her goal is not sophistication and glamor that will make her attractive to Vicky, but rather an attempt at "trying to change her destiny." Not surprisingly, Sapna is no ingénue; she is feisty, convinced of her own abilities, and far more street smart. This also ensures that she is capable of resisting Vicky's seduction schemes by simply turning the tables on him.

Prasad points out that the city in much of early post-independence cinema is "a city of pleasure and danger, of a thrilling anonymity as well as distressing inequality, both joyous and fearsome ... a space where class conflict is a dominant thematic concern."[19] Yet by the 1990s, and in the first flush of economic liberalization, the city is also the place where class divides can be bridged and social mobility achieved, regardless of birth and, more importantly, gender. Not surprisingly, the film reflects the vast social changes that had taken place in the years since *Rafoo Chakkar,* where not only are jobs available for women, but where a young woman could aspire to not only economic independence, but also prosperity.

The aspirational values driving the narrative also provide the first clear inversion of the postcolonial conceptualization of the city as a modern, corrupting, westernized space vs. the purity and safety of non-urban spaces. In earlier films, "the metropolis is, by turns, a site of decadence and extravagance, luring 'innocent' people into its web; a progressive influence upon 'backward' intellect, and the promise of a contractual civil society which would undermine the atavism of kin and caste affiliations, ostensibly typified by the cinematic village."[20] With the backdrop of economic growth, the city's extravagance no longer appears corrupting or decadent, but rather a promise of material prosperity. At the same time, the "backwardness" of small towns and villages is emphasized and critiqued by the spatial order employed by the film.

In the film, Simla, the pristine colonial hill town where Sapna and the Saigals live, is instead a confining space, hemmed in by misplaced ideas of tradition and a stifling hierarchical society that inhibits social mobility. Sapna can only be the chauffeur's daughter in Simla, while Mumbai offers her the possibility of being a successful, wealthy professional. Not surprisingly, the film also inverts the traditional conceptualization of romantic spaces. The hills around Simla are beautiful and pristine, but they can only offer a false love, as symbolized by Vicky's attempts to woo a sceptical Sapna. In contrast, Vijay fantasizes about declaring his love for Sapna in entirely urban spaces: with dark city streets lit by bright shop windows and neon signs and full of people. The urban space thus not only provides a chance at social mobility for Sapna, but also provides Vijay and her with the opportunity for "real" love, one that is based on social equality, as well as endowed with material wealth. It is only after Vijay decides to use the site planned for his factory as a home for Sapna that the hills become a site for romance. The insertion of urban values, embodied by Vijay and Sapna, into rural spaces destabilizes earlier representations and notions of a threatening modernity, and privileges urban social mobility, marking a shift towards an ease with both modernity and urbanity that will reflect in the cinema of the new millennium.

A final point must be noted: the film again obliquely credits Wilder as the source of its plot. Sapna is aided in Mumbai by a friend's uncle who is also a film director. The dialogues between Sapna and the film director (Deven Verma) become cheeky commentaries on filmmaking, adaptations, as well as cinematic "quality."

At Ease with Modernity's Discontents

Life in a Metro, directed by Anurag Basu, is a complex reworking of *The Apartment* and, not surprisingly given its 2007 production date, the most urban of all three films. In fact, the film is not only shot in its entirety in Mumbai, with characters who are primarily urban, but also steadfastly refuses to escape to non-urban spaces as settings for love and romance. This last visual choice is a key indicator of socio-economic changes of the past thirty years which allow the cityscape to provide spaces for all human interaction without recourse to traditional romance sites, such as gardens and mountains.

Although the film uses the flat-swapping at the workplace at its core, it develops a net of inter-connected characters whose lives intersect with both positive and negative results. With Wilder's plotline as a foundation, C.C. Baxter

(Jack Lemmon) takes on a contemporary avatar of Rahul (Sharman Joshi) who is—not surprisingly for the globalized economy—the enterprising call center executive on the fast track to success by trading his flat to various managers. However, the shift in gender roles and opportunities, not only from the 1950s U.S. but also in post-globalization India, is clearly indicated as his love interest, Neha (Kangana Ranaut) is not the elevator girl, but rather another ambitious colleague trading sexual favors for the career fast track. Indeed, Neha's character is far more ethically ambiguous than Fran Kubelik's (Shirley MacLaine), as her boss Ranjeet (Kay Kay Menon) makes explicit: their affair has resulted in Neha receiving bonuses, promotions and overseas assignments, all of which have been denied to others in the office place.

The workplace triangle between Rahul, Neha and Ranjeet is scripted to play out nearly identically to Wilder's original script, with the key elements of the altruistic doctor next door, the suicide attempt by Neha, as well as the final replacement of the office key by Rahul. An interesting modernizing twist is provided by the replacement of Fran's cracked compact case by Neha's customized cellphone. However, *Life in a Metro* uses Wilder's script as a starting point to ruminate on the web of relationships that are affected by the central love triangle. The film focuses a great deal on Ranjeet's wife, Shikha (Shilpa Shetty), a character that is left relatively on the sidelines in Wilder's original. Shikha is not simply the ignored housewife, but an intelligent woman who has given up her career to raise her child. She clearly articulates that it is the power imbalance in the relationship caused by her lack of employment that allows Ranjeet to be unfaithful. The marital discord between Shikha and Ranjeet, and the choices they make, form a greater part of the film, articulating the complications of a marriage far more explicitly. For example, Shikha finds herself attracted to Akash (Shiney Ahuja) and is tempted to adultery, partly in response to Ranjeet's straying. She also takes back Ranjeet after Neha chooses Rahul, choosing stability for her daughter over her desire for Akash, articulating a possible resolution that Wilder's script ignores almost entirely.

Two other parallel plot threads reinforce the social changes in post-independence India and the evolving moral codes. Shikha's sister, Shruti (Konkana Sen), is not only Neha's flatmate and thus the first to find out about Ranjit's infidelity, she is also the most successful amalgamation of traditional and modern values. Unlike the glamorous and very westernized Neha, she wears traditional clothes even in the workplace, even though she is mocked for being old-fashioned by her colleagues. At the same time, she uses the internet to identify and interview potential husbands, taking a proactive and individual stance on the traditional arranged marriage: indeed, she is quite explicit that she is not dating, but rather arranging her own marriage. When she does fall for Monty (Irfan Khan), a man she had initially interviewed and rejected, the difference between her choice and Shikha's is indicated subtly: her sister's loveless marriage may well be a result of the traditional arrangement, a fate that obviously, the film suggests, will not befall Shruti's far more assertive character.

At the same time, the renewed romance between Amol (Dharmendra) and Shivani (Nafisa Ali) indicates the changes that have occurred since the 1970s. The script suggests that their initial relationship as young lovers in the 1970s had been thwarted by social mores, and that age as well as the new social values can provide them with a second chance. In a curious twist, it is Shivani's grown-up children who oppose the relationship, shocked that their widowed aging mother could even want a lover. Shivani's deliberate choice to live with Amol both contrasts with and reinforces Shikha's choice of remaining in her loveless marriage, indicating that perhaps children require a fettering, or at least delaying, of female desire.

However, it is necessary to note Basu's use of urban spaces to indicate both sorrow and partings in relationships as well as the possibilities of romance. Shikha and Akash carry out their tentative romance in crowded buses and commuter trains as they travel through the city. Amol and Shivani set up their first date on the same train platform where they used to meet as students. Shruti uses crowded cafes to interview the potential matches thrown up by the internet. Rahul lies in wait for Neha in crowded city streets, pretending that each meeting is accidental. Similarly, it was the train platform where Shivani and Amol had parted decades ago, a fact emphasized by Shikha and Akash's parting at the same place: public transport thus becomes central to not only meetings and potential intimacies but also to partings and heartbreaks.

In contrast to the potential for human interaction provided by public urban spaces, the film constructs interior spaces as claustrophobic and alienating. Shikha and Ranjeet's flat is always dimly lit, and the emotional distance between them consistently highlighted by the physical separation between them. Similarly, Neha and Ranjeet appear to inhabit separate worlds in Rahul's flat, despite the detritus of their lovemaking. When Akash takes Shikha to his friend's flat, hoping to make love to her, the space is dark and sinister, contrasting with his obvious affection for Shikha.

The visual spaces delineated by the film appear to suggest that human contact can only happen in public spaces, even if they are liminal, such as balconies, window frames, and doorways that overlook and have instant contact with the city. Indeed, the only safe interior space in the film is the flat that Amol and Shivani share, and even that is eventually rendered unsafe and tragic by Shivani's death.

Curiously, given its essential modernity, the film is also the only one of the three under consideration that does not contain any diegetic reference to the script's inspiration. It may be partly due to an implicit recognition that an audience accustomed to satellite television is likely to be aware of the Hollywood original, as well as due to such an extensive reworking of the script that the film resembles Wilder's in only one of its multiple narrative strands.

In his discussion of Hindi cinema, Larkin points out that "Indian films betray a love/hate relation with both the West and a mythic India and in doing so open up interstices in which heterogeneity and ambivalence flourish, allowing the films to be both Westernized and traditional; corrupter of local values and a defender of them."[21] However, this dichotomy appears to be increasingly unsustainable as Indian society has undergone rapid changes in the past decades brought on by a confluence of economic growth, social mobility and political franchise. As *Life in a Metro* reveals, Indian cinema is moving towards a far more complex relationship with both the West and India itself, reformulating ideas of modernity and modern, urban identities, that are neither de-linked entirely from the West nor afraid of it. Furthermore, neither do these conceptualizations retreat to post-colonial mythologies of indigeneity and rejection of urbanity as sites of anti-colonial resistance.

Life in a Metro marks the coming of age of the urban society in India as well as its films, the key reason why Wilder's *The Apartment* becomes the script of choice for the articulation of the phenomenon. Here, the city is neither sinister nor joyous, and the characters need not choose between escaping it for romance nor embracing it for economic betterment. Finally, with this film, as in Wilder's cinematic universe, the city becomes the amalgamation of the entire range of human experience, as well as an inhabitable narrative space for the now completely urban characters.

Conclusion

As the three films discussed demonstrate, Wilder's modern, urban sensibilities lend themselves easily to global media transfers, changing forms and languages in order to address dilemmas of modernities in societies undergoing the modernization process. One may wonder why and how an exquisitely urban and modern sensibility such as that of Wilder is able to address issues of a society in transition.

This paper can offer no solution to this question, but would postulate that perhaps it is the vulnerability and precarious social position of Wilder's characters in their urban, modern milieu that allows the possibility of transcultural transfer and communication. Whether it is the outsider Sabrina, or the threatened Joe and Jerry, or an acutely ambitious C.C. Baxter, these characters inhabit a precarious, liminal space where the slightest destabilization can jeopardize their social, economic and personal lives. Perhaps it is this fine balance of risk and ambition that allows the characters and their narratives to be transformed into profitable cinematic products across time, space, language and culture.

However, prior to concluding, it is also necessary to consider why more of Wilder's oeuvre has not been adapted by the Indian commercial film industry. While some of the political context of Wilder's comedies, such as *Ninotchka*

(1939), does not resonate with the concerns of a colonial and post-colonial nation, his more dramatic *noir* films such as *Double Indemnity* (1944) have also failed to find fans, despite the profusion of *noir*-styled Hindi films of the early 1950s.

Indeed, it is curious that much of Wilder's earlier work from the 1930s also finds few takers in India, even though the 1930s mark the highpoint in collaboration between Indian filmmakers (especially Himanshu Rai and Devika Rani of Bombay Talkies) and the German film industry. Although the interaction does throw up an interest in social concerns as a central point for cinema (*Achyut Kanya*, 1936), these are so different and culturally specific that they find little common ground, with German technicians and directors like Franz Osten working on Indian productions that are primarily aimed at an Indian audience.

Perhaps the key factor to consider here is the over-arching politics of post-coloniality, which indicates that the political and social issues as well as representations are quite different from those that serve as Wilder's creative context in both Europe and the U.S. Thus issues of morality and ideology in popular Hindi cinema are inextricably linked to the post-colonial politics of both the producers and primary audiences of this cinema.

More importantly, the issues of modernity and urbanity in development are quite different from those required by Wilder's urban narratives. For much of the twentieth century, commercial Hindi cinema has addressed itself to a primarily non-urban viewer, attempting to represent both the advantages and dangers of the modernities developing in the country. As such, it has trod a fine line between the pedagogic, ideological and entertainment incentives, thus managing a socio-cultural reality that is quite distinct from that of Wilder.

It is in this context that the twenty-first century homage to *The Apartment* discussed earlier throws up interesting potentialities for future adaptations of Wilder's work for an Indian audience. As the Indian spectators and filmmakers grow at ease with the concerns of urban modernity, perhaps more of Wilder's scripts will find themselves transformed into new cinematic products, intended for a time and space most likely unimaginable for Wilder himself.

Notes

1. Haham, *Enchantment of the Mind*, 26.
2. Ganti, *Bollywood*, 76.
3. Ibid., 182.
4. Ibid., 77
5. Kaarsholm, *Unreal City*, 1.
6. Larkin, "Itinerarires of Indian Cinema," 218.
7. Kaarsholm, 4–5.
8. Ibid., 7.

9. Prasad, "Realism and Fantasy," 84.

10. Ibid., 84.

11. The issue of an unjust state further resonated with the audiences as the country was undergoing "Emergency," or a suspension of civil rights, proclaimed by the Prime Minister Indira Gandhi in a bid to retain power.

12. Bombay changed its name to the more "indigenous" Mumbai in the 1990s. It was still known as Bombay at the time the film was released.

13. Vasudevan, "The Melodramatic Mode," 29–32.

14. Lutgendorf, "Love in the Snow," 2–6.

15. Rao, "Memories Piece the Heart," 304–5.

16. Dudrah, "Queer as *Desis*," 256.

17. Prasad, *Ideology of the Hindi Film*, 42–45.

18. Curiously enough, *Yeh Dillagi* catches the zeitgeist better than Sydney Pollack's 1995 remake of *Sabrina*, a fact perhaps obvious from its box office success.

19. Prasad, "Realism and Fantasy," 86.

20. Srivastava, "The Voice of the Nation," 142.

21. Larkin, 218.

Bibliography

Aldgate, Anthony, James Chapman, and Arthur Marwick, eds. *Windows on the Sixties: Exploring Key Texts of Media and Culture.* London: I.B. Tauris, 2000.

Allen, Robert C. "The Movies in Vaudeville: Historical Context of the Movies as Popular Entertainment." In Tino Balio, ed., *The American Film Industry,* 57–82. Madison: University of Wisconsin Press, 1985.

Allyn, John. "Billy Wilder: Interview." In Elsie M. Walker and David T. Johnson, eds., *Conversations with Directors: An Anthology of Interview from Literature/Film Quarterly,* 90–95. London: Scarecrow, 2008.

_____. "*Double Indemnity*: A Policy that Paid Off." In Robert Horton, ed., *Billy Wilder Interviews,* 132–39. Jackson: University Press of Mississippi, 2001.

Alton, John. *Painting With Light.* Berkeley: University of California Press, 1995.

Andrew, Dudley. *Mists of Regret: Culture and Sensibility in Classic French Film.* Princeton, NJ: Princeton University Press, 1995.

Armstrong, Richard. *Billy Wilder, American Film Realist.* Jefferson, NC: McFarland, 2000.

Baldi, Alfredo. *Schermi Proibiti: La Censura in Italia 1947–1988.* Venice: B&N, 2002.

Balio, Tino. *United Artists: The Company That Changed the Film Industry.* Madison: University of Wisconsin Press, 1987.

_____, ed. *The American Film Industry.* Madison: University of Wisconsin Press, 1985.

Barnes, Howard. "Double Indemnity." *New York Herald Tribune* (September 7, 1944) republished in *New York Motion Picture Critics' Reviews, 1944.* New York: New York Theatre Critics' Reviews, 1944: 253.

_____. "'Lost Weekend'—Rivoli." *New York Herald Tribune* (December 3, 1945) reprinted in *New York Motion Picture Critics' Reviews 1945.* New York: Critics' Theatre Reviews, 1945: 90.

Barnett, Lincoln. "The Happiest Couple in Hollywood" (1944). In Robert Horton, ed., *Billy Wilder Interviews,* 3–14. Jackson: University Press of Mississippi, 2001.

Barrios, Richard. *Screened Out.* London: Routledge, 2003.

Bart, Peter. "Europe's Successes Worry Hollywood." *New York Times,* September 20, 1965: 5.

_____. "Lots of Comedies but Few Laughs." *New York Times,* December 27, 1964: 79.

_____. "When the Cookie Crumbled." *New York Times,* November 7, 1965: X11.

Barthes, Roland. *Mythologies.* New York: Hill and Wang, 1972.

Bazin, André. *What Is Cinema?* Berkeley: University of California Press, 1972.

Bentley, Eric. *The Pirandello Commentaries.* Evanston, IL: Northwestern University Press, 1986.

Bergfelder, Tim. "Introduction." In Tim Bergfelder and Christian Cargnelli, eds., *Destination London: German-Speaking Emigrés and British Cinema, 1925–1950,* 1–23. London: Berghahn, 2008.

_____. "National, Transnational or Supranational Cinema? Rethinking European Film

Studies." *Media, Culture & Society* 27: 3 (Spring 2005): 315–31.

Betz, Mark. "Art, Exploitation, Underground." In Mark Jancovich, Antonio Lázaro Reboll, et al., eds., *Defining Cult Movies: The Cultural Politics of Oppositional Taste*, 202–22. Manchester: Manchester University Press, 2003.

Biesen, Sheri Chinen. *Blackout: World War II and the Origins of Film Noir*. Baltimore, MD: John Hopkins University Press, 2005.

Borde, Raymond, and Étienne Chaumeton. "Towards a Definition of *Film Noir*." In Alain Silver and James Ursini, eds., *Film Noir Reader*, 17–26. New York: Limelight, 1996.

Bordwell, David, Janet Staiger, and Kristin Thompson. *The Classical Hollywood Cinema: Film Style and Mode of Production to 1960*. London: Routledge and Kegan Paul, 1985.

Boujut, Michel. "Transatlantique." *Autrement* 79 (April 1986): 6–7.

Bourdieu, Pierre. "The Aristocracy of Culture." In Richard Collins, James Curran, et al., eds., *Media, Culture and Society: A Critical Reader*, 164–193. London: Sage, 1986.

_____. *Language and Symbolic Power*. Cambridge: Harvard University Press, 1991.

Bouson, J. Brooks. *Quiet as It's Kept*. Albany: State University of New York Press, 2000.

Breffort, Alexandre. *Les harengs terribles: Faits-divers tragi-comique et du milieu en trios déchéances et une rédemption*. Paris: Librairie théâtrale, 1950.

Breines, Wini. *Young, White, and Miserable: Growing Up Female in the Fifties*. Boston: Beacon, 1992.

Brown, Vanessa. "Broadcast to Kuala Lumpur" (1970). In Robert Horton, ed., *Billy Wilder Interviews* 64–69. Jackson: University Press of Mississippi, 2001.

Brownstein, Ronald. *The Power and the Glitter: The Hollywood-Washington Connection*. New York: Pantheon, 1990.

Bruck, Connie. *When Hollywood Had a King: The Reign of Lew Wasserman, Who Leveraged Talent into Power and Influence*. New York: Random House, 2003.

Caïra, Olivier. *Hollywood face à le censure*. Paris: CNRS, 2005.

Cameron, Kate. "'Double Indemnity' A Ten-sion Melodrama." *New York Daily News* (September 7, 1944) republished in *New York Motion Picture Critics' Reviews, 1944*. New York: New York Critics' Theatre Reviews, 1945: 253.

_____. "'Lost Weekend' Daring Film of Drunk's Orgy." *New York Daily News* (December 2, 1945) republished in *New York Motion Picture Critics' Reviews 1945*. New York: New York Critics' Theatre Reviews, 1945: 90.

"'Camp.'" *Time* (December 11, 1964). http://www.time.com.

Canby, Vincent. "Public Not Afraid of Big Bad 'Woolf.'" June 25, 1966: 20.

The Carpetbaggers. Advertisements. *New York Times*, June 28, 1964: X8; August 5, 1964: 24.

Castle, Alison, ed. *Some Like It Hot*. Cologne: Taschen, 2001.

Chadwick, Whitney, and Tirza True Latimer. "Becoming Modern: Gender and Sexual Identity after World War I." In Whitney Chadwick and Tirza True Latimer, eds., *The Modern Woman Revisited: Paris between the Wars*, 3–20. New Brunswick, NJ: Rutgers University Press, 2003.

Chandler, Charlotte. *Nobody's Perfect: Billy Wilder, a Personal Biography*. New York: Simon and Schuster, 2002.

Christensen, Jerome. "Neo-Corporate Star-Making: The Bandwagon and the Charismatic Margin." *Law and Literature* 20:2 (Spring 2008): 213–27 and 87.

_____. "Studio Authorship, Warner Bros., and *The Fountainhead*." *The Velvet Light Trap* 57 (Spring 2006): 17–31.

_____. "Studio Identity and Studio Art: MGM, Mrs. Miniver, and Planning the Postwar Era." *English Literary History* 67: 1 (Spring 2000): 257–92.

_____. "The Time Warner Conspiracy: *JFK*, *Batman*, and the Manager Theory of Hollywood Film." *Critical Inquiry* 28 (Spring 2002): 591–617.

Ciment, Michael. "Apropros *Avanti!*" In Robert Horton, ed., *Billy Wilder Interviews*, 70–80. Translated by Bridgett Chandler. Jackson, MS: University Press of Mississippi, 2001.

Cixous, Hélène. "The Laugh of the Medusa." In Elaine Marks and Isabelle de Courtivron, eds., *New French Feminisms*, 245–64. New York: Shocken, 1981.

Clurman, Harold. "Movies: Very Clever." *New Republic*, September 4, 1950: 22.

Cohan, Steven, and Ina Rae Hark, eds. *The Road Movie Book*. London and New York: Routledge, 1997.

Collins, Richard, James Curran et al, eds. *Media, Culture and Society: A Critical Reader*. London: Sage, 1986.

Colpart, Gilles. *Billy Wilder*. Paris: Édilig, 1983.

Conrad, Mark T., ed. *The Philosophy of Noir*. Lexington: University Press of Kentucky, 2007.

Cook, Alton. "Double Indemnity Excels as the Perfect Movie." *New York World-Telegram* (September 6, 1944) republished in *New York Motion Picture Critics' Reviews, 1944*. New York: New York Critics' Theatre Reviews, 1944: 253.

_____. "'Lost Weekend' Is Award Material — Saga of the Sodden Souse a Masterpiece of Film Technique." *New York World-Telegram* (December 1, 1945) reprinted in *New York Motion Picture Critics' Reviews 1945*. New York: New York Critics' Theatre Reviews, 1945: 91.

Cook, Pam. "Duplicity in Mildred Pierce." In E. Ann Kaplan, ed., *Women in Film Noir*, 68–82. London: BFI, 1978.

"Correspondence and Controversy." *Film Quarterly* 17 (Autumn 1963): 57–63.

Coursodon, Jean-Pierre, and Pierre Sauvage, eds. *American Directors I*. New York: McGraw-Hill, 1982.

Creelman, Eileen. "'Double Indemnity,' Billy Wilder's Exciting Version of the James M. Cain Novel." *New York Sun* (September 7, 1944) republished in *New York Motion Picture Critics' Reviews, 1944*. New York: New York Critics' Theatre Reviews, 1944: 254.

_____. "'Lost Weekend,' One of Hollywood's Most Important and Unusual Films." *New York Sun* (December 3, 1945) reprinted in *New York Motion Picture Critics' Reviews 1945*. New York: New York Critics' Theatre Reviews, 1945: 93.

Crisp, Colin. *The Classic French Cinema, 1930–1960*. Bloomington: Indiana University Press, 1997.

Critchley, Simon. *The Ethics of Deconstruction*. Oxford: Blackwell, 1992.

Crowe, Cameron. *Conversations with Wilder*. New York: Alfred A. Knopf/Random House, 1999.

Crowell, Paul. "Notre Dame Wins Suit to Block 'Goldfarb' Film." *New York Times*, December 18, 1964: 1.

Crowther, Bosley. "Bad Taste in Films." *New York Times*, September 6, 1964: X1.

_____. "Bing Crosby Rambles Through 'Emperor Waltz,' with Joan Fontaine, at Music Hall." *New York Times*, June 18, 1948): 19.

_____. "Cinematic 'Tom Jones.'" *New York Times*, October 13, 1963: 119.

_____. "'Double Indemnity,' a Tough Melodrama, With Stanwyck and MacMurray as Killers Opens at the Paramount." *New York Times*, September 7, 1944: 21.

_____. "'Five Graves to Cairo,' Drama of World Conflict, With von Stroheim and Franchot Tone, at the Paramount Theatre." *New York Times*, May 27, 1943: 21.

_____. "Goodbye, Summer." *New York Times*, September 13, 1964: X1.

_____. "Great Grief!" *New York Times*, July 5, 1964: X1.

_____. "The Heat Is On Films." *New York Times* , January 17, 1965: X1.

_____. "Jean Arthur, Marlene Dietrich and John Land a Triangle in 'A Foreign Affair.'" *New York Times*, July 1, 1948: 19.

_____. "'The Lost Week-End,' in Which Ray Milland Presents a Study in Dipsomania, Makes its Appearance at the Rivoli." *New York Times*, December 3, 1945: 28.

_____. "Moral Brinkmanship." *New York Times*, December 13, 1964: X3.

_____. "Outside the Code." *New York Times*, July 12, 1953: X1.

_____. "'Phantom Lady,' a Melodrama of Weird Effects, With Ella Raines and Franchot Tone, Has Premiere at Loew's State." *New York Times*, February 18, 1944: 15.

_____. "Screen: Busy 'Apartment.'" *New York Times*, June 16, 1960: 37.

_____. "The Screen in Review." *New York Times*, July 9, 1953: 18.

_____. "The Screen: 'John Goldfarb' Arrives." *New York Times*, March 25, 1965: 42.

_____. "Screen: 'The Carpetbaggers' Opens." *New York Times*, July 2, 1964: 24.

_____. "The Screen: 'The Major and the Minor,' a Charming Comedy-Romance, With Ginger Rogers and Ray Milland, at the Paramount." *New York Times*, September 17, 1942: 21.

_____. "The Screen: 'Tom Jones,' a Lusty Comedy." *New York Times*, October 8, 1963: 48.

_____. "The Screen: Wilder's 'Irma la Douce.'" *New York Times*, June 6, 1963: 37.

_____. "A Time To Face Facts." *New York Times*, March 14, 1965: X1, 5.

Debord, Guy. *The Society of the Spectacle*. New York: MIT Press, 1998.

Desser, David, and Garth S. Jowett, eds. *Hollywood Goes Shopping*. Minneapolis: University of Minnesota Press, 2000.

Dick, Bernard F. *Billy Wilder*. Boston: Twayne, 1980. Updated edition, New York: Da Capo, 1996.

_____. *The Star Spangled Screen: The American World War II Film*. Lexington: University of Kentucky Press, 1985.

Dickos, Andrew. *Street With No Name: A History of the Classic American Film Noir*. Lexington: University Press of Kentucky, 2002.

Didion, Joan. "*Kiss Me, Stupid*, 'Minority Report.'" *Vogue*, March 1, 1965: 97.

Doherty, Thomas. *Projections of War: Hollywood, American Culture and World War II*. New York: Columbia University Press, 1993.

Donald, James. "A Complex Kind of Training: Cities, Technologies and Sound in Jazz-age Europe." In Desley Deacon, ed., *Talking and Listening in the Age of Modernity: Essays on the History of Sound*, 19–34. Canberra: ANU E Press, 2007.

Douin, Jean-Luc. *Dictionnaire de la Censure au Cinéma*. Paris: PUF, 1998.

Dudrah, Rajinder. "Queer as *Desis*: Secret Politics of Gender and Sexuality in Bollywood Films in Diasporic Urban Ethnoscapes." In Rajinder Dudrah and Jigna Desai, eds., *The Bollywood Reader*, 243–63. New York: Open University Press/McGraw-Hill, 2008.

Elsaesser, Thomas. "Ethnicity, Authenticity, and Exile: a Counterfeit Trade?" In Hamid Naficy, ed., *Home, Exile, Homeland: Film, Media and the Politics of Place*, 97–124. London and New York: Routledge, 1999.

_____. "The German Émigrés in Paris during the 1930s: Pathos and Leave-Taking." *Sight and Sound* 53:4 (Autumn 1984): 278–83.

_____. *Weimar Cinema and After: Germany's Historical Imaginary*. London and New York: Routledge, 2000.

Everett, Wendy. *European Identity in Cinema*. Bristol: Intellect, 2005.

_____. "Lost in Translation? The European Road Movie, or a Genre 'Adrift in the Cosmos.'" *Literature/Film Quarterly* 37: 3 (2009): 165–75.

Farber, Stephen. "Billy Wilder." In Jean-Pierre Coursodon and Pierre Sauvage, eds., *American Directors I*, 367–381. New York: McGraw-Hill, 1982.

_____. "The Films of Billy Wilder." *Film Comment* 7: 4 (Winter 1971/72): 8–22.

Feil, Ken. "Sex, Comedy, and Controversy: *Kiss Me, Stupid*, *What's New, Pussycat?*, New Hollywood, and Metropolitan Taste." *Mediascape* (Fall 2009). http://www.tft.ucla.edu/mediascape/Fall09_1960sSexComedy.html.

_____. "'Talk About Bad Taste': Camp, Cult and the Reception of *What's New, Pussycat?*" In Janet Staiger and Sabine Hake, eds., *Convergence Media History*, 139–150. New York: Routledge, 2009.

Fischer, Lucy. "*Sunset Boulevard*: Fading Stars." In Janet Todd, ed., *Women and Film*, 97–113. New York and London: Holmes and Meier, 1988.

Frith, Simon, and Andrew Goodwin, eds. *On Record: Rock, Pop, and the Written Word*. New York: Routledge, 1990.

Fuller, Graham. "An Undervalued American Classic." *New York Times*, June 18, 2000: 26.

Gans, Herbert. *Popular Culture and High Culture*. New York: Basic, 1999.

Ganti, Tejaswini. *Bollywood: A Guidebook to Popular Hindi Cinema*. London: Routledge, 2004.

Gardner, Jared. "Covered Wagons and Decalogues: Paramount's Myths of Origins." *The Yale Journal of Criticism* 13: 2 (2000): 361–89.

Gehman, Richard. "Charming Billy" (1960). In Robert Horton, ed., *Billy Wilder Interviews*, 21–34. Jackson: University Press of Mississippi, 2001.

Gemünden, Gerd. *A Foreign Affair: Billy Wilder's American Films*. New York: Berghahn, 2008.

Giffney, Noreen. "After Shame." In Sally Munt, *Queer Attachments: The Cultural Politics of Shame*, x–xi. Aldershot, Hampshire, UK: Ashgate, 2008.

Gill, Brendan. "The Current Cinema." *The New Yorker*, June 15, 1963: 54.

_____. "The Current Cinema." *The New Yorker*, December 26, 1964: 74.

Goffman, Erving. *The Presentation of Self in Everyday Life*. New York: Anchor, 1959.

"'Goldfarb' vs. Notre Dame." *Newsweek*, December 28, 1964: 53.

"Goldfarb vs. The People." *Time*, April 9, 1965. http://www.time.com.

Gommery, Douglas. *Shared Pleasures: A History of Movie Presentation in the United States*. Madison: University of Wisconsin Press, 1992.

Greco, Joseph. *The File on Robert Siodmak in Hollywood: 1941–1951*. Dissertation.com, 1999.

Guattari, Felix. "Becoming a Woman." *Molecular Revolution: Psychiatry and Politics*. Trans. Rosemary Sheed. New York: Penguin, 1984.

Guilbaut, Serge. *How New York Stole the Idea of Modern Art*. Chicago: University of Chicago Press, 1983.

Habel, Franz. *Zerschnittene Filme: Zensur im Kino*. Leipzig: Kiepenheuer, 2003.

Haggith, Toby, and Joanna Newman, eds. *Holocaust and the Moving Image*. London: Wallflower, 2005.

Haham, Connie. *Enchantment of the Mind: Manmohan Desai's Films*. New Delhi: Lotus Collection/ Roli, 2006.

Hanna, David. "Hays Censors rile Jim Cane." *Los Angeles Daily News*, February 14, 1944: 13.

Hanson, Helen. *Hollywood Heroines: Women in Film Noir and the Female Gothic Film*. London: I.B. Tauris, 2007.

Hardy, Phil, ed. *Raoul Walsh*. Edinburgh: Edinburgh Film Festival, 1974.

Hartung, Philip T. "The Screen." *Commonweal*, December 18, 1964: 421–22.

Harvey, Sylvia. "Woman's Place: The Absent Family of Film Noir." In E. Ann Kaplan, ed., *Women in Film Noir*, 1978, 35–46. New edition. London: British Film Institute, 1998.

Head, Edith, and Jane Kesner Ardmore. *The Dress Doctor*. Boston: Little, Brown, 1959.

Head, Edith, and Paddy Calistro. *Edith Head's Hollywood*. New York: E.P. Dutton, 1983.

Heisner, Beverly. *Hollywood Art: Art Direction in the Days of the Great Studios*. Jefferson, NC: McFarland, 1990.

Henry, Nora. *Ethics and Social Criticism in the Hollywood Films of Erich von Stroheim, Ernst Lubitsch, and Billy Wilder*. Westport, CT: Praeger, 2001.

Hesling, Willem, ed. *Billy Wilder: Tussen Weimar en Hollywood*. Leuven: Garant, 1991.

Higham, Charles, and Joel Greenberg. *The Celluloid Muse: Hollywood Directors Speak*. Chicago: Henry Regnery, 1969.

Higson, Andrew, and Richard Maltby, eds. *"Film Europe" and "Film America": Cinema, Commerce and Cultural Exchange, 1920–1939*. Exeter: Exeter University Press, 1999.

"Hipster's Harlot." *Time*, January 1, 1965: 69.

Hoberman, J., and Jonathan Rosenbaum. *Midnight Movies*. New York: Da Capo, 1983.

Hodgens, R.M. "Review of *Kiss Me, Stupid*." *Film Quarterly* 18 (Spring 1965): 60.

Hogan, Patrick Colm. *Understanding Indian Movies: Culture, Cognition and Cinematic Imagination*. Austin: University of Texas Press, 2008.

Holt, Jason. "A Darker Shade." In Mark T. Conrad, ed., *The Philosophy of Noir*, 23–40. Lexington: University Press of Kentucky, 2007.

Hopp, Glenn. *Billy Wilder: The Complete Films*. Köln: Taschen, 2003.

Horton, Robert, ed. *Billy Wilder: Interviews*. Jackson: University Press of Mississippi, 2001.

Houston, Penelope. "Ace in the Hole." *Sight and Sound* (June 1951): 45.

Hunter, Lew. "A Dialogue with Mr. Wilder." *Creative Screenwriting* 13: 4 (July/August 2006): 72–75.

Hutter, Andreas, and Klaus Kamolz. *Billie Wilder: Eine europäische Karriere*. Wien: Böhlau Verlag, 1998.

"The Importance of an Image." *Time*, December 18, 1964. http://www.time.com.

Irwin, John T. *Unless the Threat of Death Is Behind Them: Hard-Boiled Fiction and Film Noir*. Baltimore, MD: Johns Hopkins University Press, 2006.

Jacobs, Jérôme. *Billy Wilder*. Paris: Rivage, 1988.

Jameson, Fredric. "Globalization as Philosophical Issue." In Fredric Jameson and Masao Miyoshi, eds., *The Cultures of Globalization*, 54–80. Durham, NC: Duke University Press, 1999.

_____, and Masao Miyoshi, eds. *The Cultures of Globalization*. Durham, NC: Duke University Press, 1999.

Jancovich, Mark. "Crack-Up: Psychological Realism, Generic Transformation and the Demise of the Paranoid Woman's Film." *Irish Journal of Gothic and Horror Studies* (October 3, 2007). http://www.irishgothic horrorjournal.homestead.com.

_____. "'Female Monsters': Horror, the 'Femme Fatale' and World War II." *Journal of American Culture* 27 (2008): 133–49.

_____. "Phantom Ladies: the War Worker, the Slacker and the 'Femme Fatale.'" *New Review of Film and Television Studies* 8:2 (2010): 164–78.

_____. "'Two Ways of Looking': Affection and Aversion in the Critical Reception of 1940s Horror." *Cinema Journal* 49: 3 (2010): 45–82.

_____. "Thrills and Chills: Horror, the Woman's Film and the Origins of Film Noir." *New Review of Film and Television Studies* 7: 2 (June 2009): 157–71.

_____, Antonio Lázaro Reboll, et al., eds. *Defining Cult Movies: The Cultural Politics of Oppositional Taste*. Manchester: Manchester University Press, 2003.

Jenkins, Henry. *What Made Pistachio Nuts? Early Sound Comedy and the Vaudeville Aesthetic*. New York: Columbia University Press, 1992.

Johnson, Liza. "Perverse Angle: Feminist Film, Queer Film, Shame." *Signs* (Autumn 2004): 1361–84.

Johnston, Claire. "Double Indemnity." In E. Ann Kaplan, ed., *Women in Film Noir*, 1978, 89–98. New edition. London: British Film Institute, 1998.

"Just Lucky, I Guess." *Time*, June 21, 1963. http://www.time.com.

Kaarsholm, Preben. "Unreal City: Cinematic Representation, Globalization and the Ambiguities of Metropolitan Life." In Preben Kaarsholm, ed., *City Flicks: Indian Cinema and the Urban Experience*, 1–25. London and Calcutta: Seagull, 2007.

_____, ed. *City Flicks: Indian Cinema and the Urban Experience*. London and Calcutta: Seagull, 2007.

Kael, Pauline. "Review of *One, Two, Three*." *Film Quarterly* 15: 3 (Spring 1962): 62–65.

Kaes, Anton. "Leaving Home: Film, Migration and the Urban Experience." *New German Critique* 74 (Spring 1998): 179–92.

_____. "Urban Vision and Surveillance: Notes on a Moment in Karl Grune's *Die Strasse*." *German Politics and Society* 74: 23 (1) (Spring 2005): 80–87.

Kaplan, E. Ann, ed. *Women in Film Noir*, 1978. New edition. London: British Film Institute, 1998.

Karasek, Hellmuth. *Billy Wilder: Eine Nahaufnahme*. Hamburg: Hoffmann und Campe, 1992.

Kibby, Marjorie, and Brigid Costello. "Displaying the Phallus." In Peter F. Murphy, ed., *Feminism and Masculinities*, 214–27. Oxford: Oxford University Press, 2004.

"A Kick Instead for 'Kiss Me, Stupid.'" *Variety*, December 9, 1964: 5.

Kinneavy, James L. *A Theory of Discourse*. New York: W.W. Norton, 1980.

Kirkham, Pat. "Saul Bass and Billy Wilder in Conversation." In Robert Horton, ed., *Billy Wilder Interviews*, 171–181. Jackson: University Press of Mississippi, 2001.

_____, and Janet Thumim, eds. *Me Jane: Masculinity, Movies and Women*. London: Lawrence and Wishart, 1995.

"'Kiss Me, Stupid' Ads Toned Down for Lopert Sell." *Variety*, December 9, 1964: 5.

Kiss Me, Stupid Advertisements. *New York Times*, December 21, 1964: 43; December 22, 1964: 34; June 28, 1964: X8.

Klinger, Barbara. *Melodrama and Meaning: History, Culture, and the Films of Douglas Sirk*. Bloomington: Indiana University Press, 1994.

Koepnick, Lutz. *The Dark Mirror: German Cinema Between Hitler and Hollywood*. Berkeley: University of California Press, 2002.

_____. "Doubling the Double: Robert Siodmak in Hollywood." *New German Critique* 89 (2003): 81–104.

Kracauer, Siegfried. "Hollywood's Terror Films: Do They Reflect an American State of Mind?" *New German Critique* 89 (2003): 105–111. First published in *Commentary* 2 (1946): 132–36.

Krutnik, Frank. "The Faint Aroma of Performing Seals: The 'Nervous' Romance and the Comedy of the Sexes." *Velvet Light Trap* 26 (Fall 1990): 57–72.

Kuleshov, Lev. "The Origins of Montage." In

Jean Schnitzer and Marcel Martin, eds., *Cinema in Revolution*, 66–76. New York: Hill and Wang, 1973.

Lally, Kevin. *Wilder Times: The Life of Billy Wilder*. New York: Henry Holt, 1996.

Larkin, Brian. "Itineraries of Indian Cinema: African Videos, Bollywood, and Global Media." In Rajinder Dudrah and Jigna Desai, eds., *The Bollywood Reader*, 216–28. New York: Open University Press/McGraw-Hill, 2008.

Leab, Daniel J. "A Walk on the Wilder Side: *The Apartment* as Social Commentary." In Anthony Aldgate, James Chapman, and Arthur Marwick, eds., *Windows on the Sixties: Exploring Key Texts of Media and Culture*, 1–18. London: I.B. Tauris, 2000.

Leff, Leonard J., and Jerold Simmons. *The Dame in the Kimono: Hollywood, Censorship and the Production Code*. Kentucky: University Press of Kentucky, 2001.

Legare, Robert. "Meeting at the Summit: Sinatra and His Buddies Bust 'Em Up in Vegas." *Playboy* (June 1960): 34–37, 48, 97–100.

"Legion of Decency Condemns a Movie." *New York Times*, December 3, 1964: 57.

"Letters to the Editor." *Time*, December 25, 1964: 2.

Lev, Peter. *The Fifties: Transforming the Screen, 1950–59*. Berkeley: University of California Press, 2006.

Levinas, Emmanuel. *Totality and Infinity: An Essay on Exteriority*. Trans. Alphonso Lingis. Pittsburgh: Duquesne University Press, 1969.

Lewis, Helen Block. *The Role of Shame in Symptom Formation*. Hillsdale, NJ: Lawrence Erlbaum, 1987.

"Low and Inside." *Time*, July 3, 1964. http://www.time.com.

Lundestad, Geir. "Empire by Invitation? The United States in Western Europe, 1945–1952." In Charles Maier, ed., *The Cold War in Europe*, 153–168. New York: M. Wiener, 1991.

Lutgendorf, Philip. "Love in the Snow: The Himalayas as Erotic Topos in Popular Hindi Cinema." Author's manuscript, 2005.

MacDonald, Dwight. "A Theory of Mass Culture" (1953). In Bernard Rosenberg and David Manning White, eds., *Mass Culture:*

The Popular Arts in America, 59–73. New York: Free Press, 1957.

MacLaine, Shirley. *My Lucky Stars*. New York: Bantam, 1996.

Madsen, Axel. *Billy Wilder*. Bloomington and London: Indiana University Press, 1969.

Maier, Charles S. "The Politics of Productivity: Foundations of American International Economic Policy after World War II." In Charles Maier, ed., *The Cold War in Europe*, 169–202. New York: M. Wiener, 1991.

Mann, Denise. *Hollywood Independents: The Postwar Talent Takeover*. Minneapolis: University of Minnesota Press, 2008.

Marks, Elaine, and Isabelle de Courtivron, eds. *New French Feminisms*. New York: Shocken, 1981.

Mathews, Tom Dewe. *Censored: The Story of Film Censorship in Britain*. London: Chatto Windus, 1994.

Maxfield, James F. *The Fatal Woman*. Cranbury, NJ: Associated University Presses, 1996.

May, Elaine Tyler. *Homeward Bound: American Families in the Cold War Era*. New York: Basic, 1988.

McBride, Joseph, and Michael Wilmington. "The Private Life of Billy Wilder." *Film Quarterly* 23: 4 (Summer 1970): 2–9.

McCarten, John "The Current Cinema." *The New Yorker*, June 25, 1960: 71.

McCormick, Richard W. *Gender and Sexuality in Weimar Modernity: Film, Literature and "New Objectivity."* New York: Palgrave, 2001.

McCormick, Thomas J. "America's Half Century: United States Foreign Policy in the Cold War." In Charles Maier, ed., *The Cold War in Europe*, 21–52. New York: M. Wiener, 1991.

McDougal, Dennis. *The Last Mogul: Lew Wasserman, MCA and the Hidden History of Hollywood*. New York: Da Capo, 2001.

McGurl, Mark. "Making It Big: Picturing the Radio Age in *King Kong*." *Critical Inquiry* 22 (Spring 1996): 415–45.

McManus, John. "Ray Milland KO's Kid Booze." *New York Newspaper PM*, December 3, 1945: 92.

McNally, Karen. *When Frankie Went to Hollywood: Frank Sinatra and American Male Identity*. Urbana and Chicago: University of Illinois Press, 2008.

McWhirter, David, ed. *Henry James's New York Edition: The Construction of Authorship*. Stanford: Stanford University Press, 1995.

Meehan, Thomas. "Not Good Taste, Not Bad Taste — It's 'Camp.'" *New York Times Sunday Magazine*, March 21, 1965: 30–31, 113–15.

Merleau-Ponty, Maurice. *Signs*. Translated by Richard McCleary. Evanston: Northwestern University Press, 1964.

_____. *The Visible and the Invisible*. Claude Lefort, ed. Translated by Alphonso Lingis. Evanston, IL: Northwestern University Press, 1968.

Miller, Frank. *Censored Hollywood: Sex, Sin, and Violence on Screen*. Atlanta: Turner, 1994.

Mills, Jane. *Loving and Hating Hollywood: Reframing Local and Global Cinemas*. Allen and Unwin: Crows Nest, 2009.

Milward, Alan S. "The Reconstruction of Western Europe." In Charles Maier, ed., *The Cold War in Europe*, 241–270. New York: M. Wiener, 1991.

Mirisch, Walter. *I Thought We Were Making Movies, Not History*. Madison: University of Wisconsin Press, 2008.

Monsey, Derek. "Talent-Wise, Seductive-Wise, Funny-Wise, and Touching-Wise — Shirley She's The Tops." *The Sunday Express London*, July 1960. Margaret Herrick Library clippings file for *The Apartment*. Los Angeles, CA.

"Moral or Immoral?" *Newsweek*, December 28, 1964: 53–54.

Mundy, Robert. "Wilder Reappraised." *Cinema* 4 (October 1969): 14–18.

Munt, Sally. *Queer Attachments: The Cultural Politics of Shame*. Aldershot, Hampshire: Ashgate, 2008.

Murphy, Peter F., ed. *Feminism and Masculinities*. Oxford: Oxford University Press, 2004.

Naficy, Hamid. *An Accented Cinema: Exilic and Diasporic Filmmaking*. Princeton and Oxford: Princeton University Press, 2001.

_____, ed. *Home, Exile, Homeland: Film, Media and the Politics of Place*. London and New York: Routledge, 1999.

Naremore, James. *More than Night: Film Noir in its Contexts*. Berkeley: University of California Press, 1998.

Nathanson, Donald. *Shame and Pride: Affect, Sex, and the Birth of the Self*. New York: W.W. Norton, 1992.

Neale, Steve. *Genre and Hollywood*. New York: Routledge, 2000.

_____, and Frank Krutnik. *Popular Film and Television Comedy*. New York: Routledge, 1990.

Nenno, Nancy. "Femininity, the Primitive and Modern Urban Space: Josephine Baker in Berlin." In Katharina von Ankum, ed., *Women in the Metropolis: Gender and Modernity in Weimar Culture*, 145–161. Berkeley and Los Angeles: University of California Press, 1989.

"The New Pictures." *Time*, December 3, 1945. www.time.com.

"The New Pictures." *Time*, August 14, 1950. www.time.com.

"The New Pictures." *Time*, June 6, 1960. www.time.com.

Nicholson, Linda, ed. *The Second Wave*. New York: Routledge, 1997.

"Old Bogart Films Packing Them In." *New York Times*, January 28, 1965: 19.

Orr, John. *Cinema and Modernity*. Cambridge: Polity, 1993.

Païni, Dominique. "Le passage en France: Lang, Siodmak, Trivas, Wilder." In Jacques Aumont and Dominique Païni, eds., *Les Cinéastes en exil*, 53–66. Paris: La Cinémathèque Française, 1992.

Paul, William. *Laughing Screaming: Modern Hollywood Horror and Comedy*. New York: Columbia University Press, 1994.

Pelswick, Rose. "'Weekend' at Rivoli." *New York Journal American* (December 3, 1945) reprinted in *New York Motion Picture Critics' Reviews 1945*. New York: New York Critics' Theatre Reviews, 1945: 92.

Petro, Patrice. "Legacies of Weimar Cinema." In Murray Pomerance, ed., *Cinema and Modernity*, 235–53. New Brunswick, NJ: Rutgers University Press, 2006.

Phillips, Alastair. *City of Darkness, City of Light: Émigré Filmmakers in Paris, 1929–1939*. Amsterdam: Amsterdam University Press, 2004.

Phillips, Gene D. "Billy Wilder." *Literature/Film Quarterly* (Winter 1976). In Robert Horton, ed., *Billy Wilder Interviews*, 99–109. Jackson: University Press of Mississippi, 2001.

_____. *Exiles in Hollywood: Major European Film Directors in America.* Bethlehem PA: Lehigh University Press; London: Associated University Presses, 1998.

_____. *Some Like It Wilder: The Life and Controversial Films of Billy Wilder.* Lexington: University Press of Kentucky, 2010.

Philips, William. "Portrait of the Artist as an American." *Horizon* 16: 2 (October 1947): 12–19.

Place, Janey. "Women in Film Noir." In E. Ann Kaplan, ed., *Women in Film Noir*, 1978, 47–68. New edition. London: British Film Institute, 1998.

"Playboy Interview: Billy Wilder." *Playboy* (June 1963): 57–66.

Poague, Leland. *The Hollywood Professionals, Vol. 7: Wilder and McCarey.* San Diego: A.S. Barnes; London: Tantivy, 1980.

"Policeman, Midwife, Bastard." *Time*, June 27, 1960. http://www.time.com.

Polt, Harriet R. "Notes on the New Stylization." *Film Quarterly* 19 (Spring 1966): 26.

Porfirio, Robert. "Interview with Billy Wilder." In Robert Porfirio, Alain Silver, James Ursini, eds., *Film Noir Reader 3*, 101–119. New York: Limelight, 2002.

_____, Alain Silver, James Ursini, eds. *Film Noir Reader 3.* New York: Limelight, 2002.

Powers, James. "The Apartment." *The Hollywood Reporter* (May 1960). Margaret Herrick Library clippings file for *The Apartment.* Los Angeles, CA.

Prasad, M. Madhava. *Ideology of the Hindi Film: A Historical Construction.* Delhi: Oxford University Press, 1998.

_____. "Realism and Fantasy in Representations of Metropolitan Life in Indian Cinema." In Preben Kaarsholm, ed., *City Flicks: Indian Cinema and the Urban Experience*, 88–92. London and Calcutta: Seagull, 2007.

Prelutsky, Burt. "An Interview with Billy Wilder." In Robert Horton, ed., *Billy Wilder: Interviews*, 182–93. Jackson: University Press of Mississippi, 2001.

Radner, Hilary. "Queering the Girl." In Hilary Radner and Moya Luckett, eds., *Swinging Single*, 1–38. Minneapolis: University of Minnesota Press, 1999.

_____, and Moya Luckett, eds. *Swinging Single.* Minneapolis: University of Minnesota Press, 1999.

Rajadhyaksha, Ashish. "India: Filming the Nation." In Geoffrey Nowell-Smith, ed., *The Oxford History of World Cinema*, 398–409. New York: Oxford University Press, 1996.

Rao, R. Raj. "Memories Pierce the Heart: Homoeroticism, Bollywood-style." In Andrew Grossman, ed., "Queer Asian Cinema: Shadows in the Shade." Special Issue of *Journal of Homosexuality* 39: 3/4 (2000): 299–306.

Ray, Robert. *A Certain Tendency of the Hollywood Cinema, 1930–1980.* Princeton: Princeton University Press, 1985.

"Review of *Kiss Me, Stupid*." *Variety* (December 16, 1964). In *Variety Film Reviews.* New York: Garland, 1983.

Riesman, David. "Listening to Popular Music." In Simon Frith and Andrew Goodwin, eds., *On Record: Rock, Pop, and the Written Word*, 5–13. New York: Routledge, 1990.

Robertson, Pamela. "Home and Away: Friends of Dorothy on the Road in Oz." In Steven Cohan and Ina Rae Hark, eds., *The Road Movie Book*, 271–286. London and New York: Routledge, 1997.

Rockett, Kevin. *Irish Film Censorship.* Dublin: Four Courts, 2004.

Rolston, Lorraine. *York Film Notes: Some Like It Hot.* London: York, 2000.

Rosen, Marjorie. *Popcorn Venus.* New York: Coward, McCann and Geoghegan, 1973.

Rosenberg, Bernard, and David Manning White, eds. *Mass Culture: The Popular Arts in America.* New York: Free Press, 1957.

Rosenberg, Emily. "Foreign Affairs after World War II: Connecting Sexual and International Politics." *Diplomatic History* 18: 1 (Winter 1994): 59–70.

Ross, Andrew. *No Respect: Intellectuals and Popular Culture.* New York: Routledge, 1989.

Ross, Kristin. *Fast Cars, Clean Bodies: Decolonization and the Reordering of French Culture.* Cambridge: Harvard University Press, 1995.

Rothman, William. "Nobody's Perfect: Billy Wilder and the Postwar American Cinema." In William Rothman, ed., *The "I" of the Camera*, 177–205. Cambridge: Cambridge University Press, 2003.

Rubin, Gayle. "The Traffic in Women: Notes on the 'Political Economy' of Sex." In

Linda Nicholson, ed., *The Second Wave*, 27–62. New York: Routledge, 1997.

Ruhle, Otto. *Karl Marx: His Life and Work*. Translated by Eden and Cedar Paul. Whitefish, MT: Kessinger, 2005.

Russo, Vito. *The Celluloid Closet: Homosexuality in the Movies*. New York: Harper and Row, 1981.

Sarris, Andrew. *The American Cinema: Directors and Directions 1929–1968*. New York: E.P. Dutton, 1968. New York: Da Capo, 1996.

_____. "The Auteur Theory and the Perils of Pauline." *Film Quarterly* 16 (Summer 1963): 26–33.

_____. "Notes on the *Auteur* Theory in 1962." *Film Culture* 27 (1962/62): 1–8.

_____. "Why Billy Wilder Belongs in the Pantheon." *Film Comment* 27: 4 (July 1991): 9–14.

Saunders, Thomas J. *Hollywood in Berlin: American Cinema and Weimar Germany*. Berkeley, Los Angeles and London: University Of California Press, 1994.

Schaber, Bennet. "'Hitler Can't Keep 'em That Long': The Road, the People." In Steven Cohan and Ina Rae Hark, eds., *The Road Movie Book*, 17–44. London and New York: Routledge, 1997.

Schatz, Thomas. *The Genius of the System: Hollywood Filmmaking in the Studio Era*. New York: Pantheon, 1988.

Scheur, Philip K. "Wilder Touch Brightens Sly Sex at High Altitude." *Los Angeles Times* (May 1960): H11.

Schickel, Richard. *Double Indemnity*. London: BFI, 1992.

Schnitzer, Jean, and Marcel Martin, eds. *Cinema in Revolution*. New York: Hill and Wang, 1973.

Schoell, William. *Martini Man: The Life of Dean Martin*. Dallas: Taylor, 1999.

Schumach, Murray. *The Face on the Cutting Room Floor: The Story of Movie and Television Censorship*. New York: William Morrow, 1964.

Sedgwick, Eve Kosofsky. "Shame and Performativity." In David McWhirter, ed., *Henry James's New York Edition: The Construction of Authorship*, 206–39. Stanford, CA: Stanford University Press, 1995.

Seidman, Steve. *The Film Career of Billy Wilder*. Boston: G. K. Hall, 1977.

Sharp, Kathleen. *Mr. and Mrs. Hollywood: Edie and Lew Wasserman and their Entertainment Empire*. New York: Da Capo, 2004.

Shaw, Arnold. *Sinatra*. London: Hodder, 1970.

Shearer, Lloyd. "Crime Certainly Pays on the Screen." *New York Times*, August 5, 1945: 77.

"Shurlock's Legion Slants Recalled." *Variety*, December 9, 1964: 4.

Sikov, Ed. "Billy Wilder's World War II." *War, Literature and the Arts: An International Journal of the Humanities* (Fall/Winter 1999): 180–90.

_____. *On Sunset Boulevard: The Life and Times of Billy Wilder*. New York: Hyperion, 1998.

Silver, Alain, and James Ursini, eds. *Film Noir Reader*. New York: Limelight, 1996.

Silverman, Kaja. *Male Subjectivity at the Margins*. New York: Routledge, 1992.

Simon, John. "Belt and Suspenders: The Art of Billy Wilder." *Theatre Arts* (July 1962): 20–21, 70–73.

Sinyard, Neil, and Adrian Turner. *Journey Down Sunset Boulevard: The Films of Billy Wilder*. Ryde, Isle of Wright: BCW, 1979.

Siodmak, Curt. *Wolf Man's Maker: Memoir of a Hollywood Writer*. Revised edition. Landham, MD: Scarecrow, 1997.

Sipiora, Phillip. "Introduction: The Ancient Concept of *Kairos*." In Phillip Sipiora and James S. Baumlin, eds., *Kairos and Rhetoric: Essays in History, Theory, and Praxis*, 1–22. Albany: SUNY University Press, 2002.

Sklar, Robert. *Movie-Made America: A Cultural History of American Movies*. New York: Vintage, 1975.

Smith, Geoffrey S. "Commentary: Security, Gender and the Historical Process." *Diplomatic History* 18: 1 (Winter 1994): 79–90.

Sobchack, Vivian. *The Address of the Eye: A Phenomenology of Film Experience*. Princeton, NJ: Princeton University Press, 1992.

Sontag, Susan. *Against Interpretation and Other Essays*. New York: Farrar, Straus and Giroux, 1966.

Sova, Dawn B. *Forbidden Films*. New York: Checkmark, 2001.

Srivastava, Sanjay. "The Voice of the Nation and the Five-Year Plan Hero: Speculation on Gender, Space, and Popular Culture." In Vinay Lal and Ashis Nandi, eds., *Fingerprinting Popular Culture: The Mythic and the Iconic in Indian Culture*, 122–55. New Delhi: Oxford University Press, 2006.

Stables, Kate. "The Postmodern Always Rings Twice: Constructing the *Femme Fatale* in '90s Cinema." In E. Ann Kaplan, ed., *Women in Film Noir*, 1978, 164–82. New edition. London: British Film Institute, 1998.

Staggs, Sam. *Close-Up on Sunset Boulevard: Billy Wilder, Norma Desmond, and the Dark Hollywood Dream*. New York: St. Martin's, 2002.

Staiger, Janet. *Interpreting Films: Studies in the Historical Reception of American Cinema*. Princeton, NJ: Princeton University Press, 1992.

_____, and Sabine Hake, eds. *Convergence Media History*. New York: Routledge, 2009.

Stallybrass, Peter, and Allon White. *The Politics and Poetics of Transgression*. Ithaca, NY: Cornell University Press, 1986.

Stanley, Fred. "Hollywood Crime and Romance." *New York Times*, November 19, 1944: X1.

Stevens, George, Jr., ed. *Conversations with the Great Moviemakers of Hollywood's Golden Age at the American Film Institute*. New York: Alfred A. Knopf, 2006.

Straayer, Chris. *Deviant Eyes, Deviant Bodies*. New York: Columbia University Press, 1996.

_____. "*Femme Fatale* or Lesbian Femme: Bound in Sexual *Différance*." In E. Ann Kaplan, ed., *Women in Film Noir*, 1978, 151–63. New edition. London: British Film Institute, 1998.

Street, Sarah. "'Mad About the Boy': Masculinity and Career in *Sunset Boulevard*." In Pat Kirkham and Janet Thumim, eds., *Me Jane: Masculinity, Movies and Women*, 223–233. London: Lawrence and Wishart, 1995.

Studlar, Gaylyn. "Chi-Chi Cinderella: Audrey Hepburn as Couture Countermodel." In David Desser and Garth S. Jowett, eds., *Hollywood Goes Shopping*, 159–178. Minneapolis: University of Minnesota Press, 2000.

Taylor, Greg. *Artists in the Audience: Cults, Camp, and American Film Criticism*.

Princeton, NJ: Princeton University Press, 1999.

Thompson, Thomas. "Wilder's Dirty-Joke Film Stirs a Furor." *Life*, January 15, 1965: 51–56B.

Tinnee, Mae. "'Apartment' Is a Skillful Film Satire. *Chicago Tribune*, June 16, 1960: B18.

_____. "Film 'Irma la Douce' Is Short of Hilarious." *Chicago Tribune*, June 17, 1963: B9.

_____. "New Wilder Film Crude and Clumsy." *Chicago Tribune*, December 21, 1964: A2.

T.M.P. "Gloria Swanson Returns to the Movies in 'Sunset Boulevard' Feature at Music Hall." *New York Times*, August 11, 1950: 15.

Todd, Janet, ed. *Women and Film*. New York and London: Holmes and Meier, 1988.

Tomasson, Robert E. "Notre Dame Seeks To Block New Film." *New York Times*, December 8, 1964: 55.

Tzioumakis, Yannis. *American Independent Cinema: An Introduction*. Edinburgh: Edinburgh University Press, 2006.

Vandaele, Jeroen. "Funny Fictions." *The Translator* 8: 2 (2002): 267–302.

Vasudevan, Ravi. "The Melodramatic Mode and the Commercial Hindi Cinema: Notes on Film History, Narrative and Performance." *Screen* 30: 3 (1989): 29–50.

"Vatican Movie Unit Rates U.S. Films Over Europeans." *New York Times*, February 19, 1965: 27.

Vincendeau, Ginette. "Family Plots: The Fathers and Daughters of French Cinema." *Sight and Sound* 11: 1 (1992): 14–17.

_____. "Hollywood Babel: The Coming of Sound and the Multiple-Language Version." In Andrew Higson and Richard Maltby, eds., *"Film Europe" and "Film America": Cinema, Commerce and Cultural Exchange, 1920–1939*, 207–24. Exeter: Exeter University Press, 1999.

_____. "'Des portes ouvertes seulement à contrecoeur.' Les cineastes allemands en France pendant les années trentes." *Positif* 323 (January 1988): 45–50.

Vogel, Amos. "Films: Fashion of the Fashionable." *New York Times*, September 5, 1965: X7.

Walker, Elsie M., and David T. Johnson, eds. *Conversations with Directors: An Anthology* of Interviews from Literature/Film Quarterly. London: Scarecrow, 2008.

Wallace, David. Exiles in Hollywood. Pompton Plains, NJ: Limelight, 2006.

Walsh, Frank. Sin and Censorship: The Catholic Church and the Motion Picture Industry. New Haven, CT: Yale University Press, 1996.

Warshow, Robert. "The Gangster as Tragic Hero" (1948). In The Immediate Experience, 97–103. London: Harvard University Press, 2001.

Weiler, A.H. "'Kiss Me, Stupid.'" New York Times, December 23, 1964: 22.

Wild, John. "Introduction." In Emmanuel Levinas, Totality and Infinity: An Essay on Exteriority, 11–20. Pittsburgh, PA: Duquesne University Press, 1969.

Wilder, Billy. Double Indemnity: The Complete Screenplay, with an Introduction by Jeffrey Meyers. Berkeley: University of California Press, 2000.

_____, and I.A.L Diamond. Irma La Douce. New York: Midwood-Tower, 1963.

"Wilder's Work to Be Shown at Museum of Modern Art." New York Times, November 25, 1964: 45.

Winsten, Archer. "Calling All Drunks, 'The Lost Weekend.'" New York Post (December 3, 1945) reprinted in New York Motion Picture Critics' Reviews 1945. New York: New York Critics' Theatre Reviews, 1945: 91.

_____. "Warning to Insurance Fakers: Check with 'Double Indemnity.'" New York Post (September 7, 1944) republished in New York Motion Picture Critics' Reviews, 1944. New York: New York Critics' Theatre Reviews, 1944: 253.

Wood, Tom. The Bright Side of Billy Wilder, Primarily. Garden City, NY: Doubleday, 1970.

Wright, Will. Sixguns and Society: A Structural Study of the Western. Berkeley: University of California Press, 1975.

Wurmser, Leon. The Mask of Shame. Northvale, NJ: Jason Aronson, 1994.

Young, Peter. History of the Second World War, Vol. 3. Glasgow: Purnell and Sons, 1965.

Youngkin, Stephen D. The Lost One: A Life of Peter Lorre. Lexington: University Press of Kentucky, 2005.

Zolotow, Maurice. Billy Wilder in Hollywood. New York: Putnam, 1977.

Documentaries and Interviews

American Film Institute Interview, 1986. Ace in the Hole Special Edition. The Criterion Collection, 2007.

Billy Wilder: The Human Comedy. American Masters Series. Directed by Mel Stuart. Originally Aired: February 4, 1998.

Billy Wilder Speaks. Directed by Volker Schlöndorff and Gisela Grischow. Bioskip, 2006 (TV). Kino International, 2006 (DVD).

Nobody's Perfect. A TV Documentary about the Making of Some Like It Hot. Produced and directed by Paul Kerr. Originally Aired: BBC, 16 April 2001.

Portrait of a "60% Perfect Man": Billy Wilder. A 1980 documentary featuring in-depth interviews with Wilder by film critic Michel Ciment. Ace in the Hole Special Edition. The Criterion Collection, 2007.

About the Contributors

Katherine Arens is a professor in the Department of Germanic Studies at the University of Texas at Austin, affiliated with the Program in Comparative Literature and the Center for Women's and Gender Studies. She has published widely on the intellectual and cultural histories of Germany and Austria from 1740 on.

Daniel Biltereyst is a professor in film and cultural media studies at the Department of Communication Studies, Ghent University, Belgium, where he leads the Centre for Cinema and Media Studies. His research on film and screen culture as sites of controversy and censorship has been published in various journals and edited collections, most recently Maltby et al., eds., *Going to the Movies* (2008).

Lance Duerfahrd is an assistant professor of film and visual culture in the English Department at Purdue University. His published work includes "Extras to the Extraordinary: The 'Other' Actors in the Marx Brothers' Films" in *A Century of the Marx Brothers* (2007) and essays on actor Klaus Kinski in *The Cambridge Companion to Werner Herzog* (forthcoming).

Ken Feil is a scholar-in-residence at Emerson College, Boston, Massachusetts. He is the author of *Dying for a Laugh: Disaster Movies and the Camp Imagination* (2006).

Alison R. Hoffman's research focuses on feminist media histories, alternative cinema practices, and minoritarian (self-) representations in U.S. visual culture. She also works as an independent film and video curator.

Mark Jancovich is a professor of film and television studies at the University of East Anglia. He is the author of several books, including *Rational Fears: American Horror in the 1950s* (1996) and *The Place of the Audience: Cultural Geographies of Film Consumption* (with Lucy Faire and Sarah Stubbings, 2003) and is also the editor of several collections.

Paul Kerr is a senior lecturer in broadcast media at London Metropolitan University and the author and editor of a number of books and articles on television and film. He worked on a variety of major series about the media including *Open The Box* (Channel 4, 1986), *The Media Show* (Channel 4, 1987–90), and the award-winning cinema series *Moving Pictures* (BBC2, 1990–96).

237

Karen McNally is a senior lecturer and course leader for the BA and MA degree programs in film studies at London Metropolitan University. She is the author of *When Frankie Went to Hollywood: Frank Sinatra and American Male Identity* (2008), and has contributed to various journals and edited collections with publications on Hollywood cinema.

Dale M. Pollock has produced thirteen feature films, including *A Midnight Clear, Set It Off, Mrs. Winterbourne* and *Blaze*. His films have been nominated for four Academy Awards, and starred actors such as Paul Newman, Shirley MacLaine, Denzel Washington, Queen Latifah, Tommy Lee Jones and Kathleen Turner. Pollock has been chief film critic and box office analyst for *Daily Variety* and chief film reporter for the *Los Angeles Times*.

Sunny Singh teaches creative writing and film studies at London Metropolitan University. Her essays and stories have appeared in publications around the world.

Phillip Sipiora is a professor of English and film studies at the University of South Florida. He is the author or editor of three books, has lectured on twentieth-century literature and film, and is the editor of *The Mailer Review*.

Dina Smith is an associate professor of English at Drake University, Des Moines, Iowa, where she teaches courses in film studies, American studies and Cold War culture, and has published in a variety of journals, including *Utopian Studies, Mississippi Quarterly* and *Mosaic*.

Nancy Steffen-Fluhr is an associate professor in the Humanities Department at the New Jersey Institute of Technology and a playwright (*Heartbreaker*, 2007). In addition to her work on Billy Wilder, she has written critical essays on a range of subjects, including actor Raymond Burr, science fiction writers H. G. Wells and Alice Sheldon ("James Tiptree"), and filmmakers Alfred Hitchcock, Don Siegel, Terry Gilliam and Ernst Lubitsch.

Leila Wimmer is a senior lecturer in film studies at London Metropolitan University and the author of *Cross-Channel Perspectives: The French Reception of British Cinema* (2009).

Index

239